MW00459430

EROS, AGAPE, AND PHILIA

ALSO BY ALAN SOBLE

Pornography: Marxism, Feminism & the Future of Sexuality

Philosophy of Sex: Contemporary Readings

The Structure of Love

Sexual Investigations

Sex, Love, and Friendship

The Philosophy of Sex and Love: An Introduction

EROS, AGAPE, AND PHILIA

Readings in the Philosophy of Love

EDITED BY

Alan Soble

UNIVERSITY OF
NEW ORLEANS

PARAGON HOUSE
St. Paul, Minnesota

Published in the United States by

Paragon House
2700 University Avenue West
St. Paul, MN 55114

Copyright © 1989 by Paragon House

Library of Congress Cataloging-in-Publication Data

Eros, agape, and philia : readings in the philosophy of Love / editor,
    Alan Soble. — 1st ed.
        p.   cm.
    Bibliography: p.
    ISBN 1-55778-278-4
    1. Love.   I. Soble, Alan.
    BD436.E76   1989
    128'.4—dc20   89-34674
                                                            CIP

Manufactured in the United States of America
The paper used in this publication meets the minimum requirements of
American National Standard for Information Sciences—Permanence of Paper
for Printed Library Materials, ANSI Z39.48-1984.

10 9 8 7 6 5 4 3

For Sara and Rachel

EROS, AGAPE, AND PHILIA:
Readings in the Philosophy of Love

CONTENTS

PREFACE

SOON AFTER editing *The Philosophy of Sex: Contemporary Readings*, I planned a companion volume of essays, of similar quality and philosophical sophistication, on love. My intention was to show that, behind our ordinary beliefs about and our everyday practice of love, there are intellectual puzzles that demand careful thought. I found that my undergraduate courses in the philosophy of sex were missing something, at least in the assigned readings (even in the *Symposium*), but not in the minds and questions of students, and hence not in my attempts to lecture, *sans* supporting texts, in response to these questions. How does this philosophical inquiry into the logical structure, psychological nature, and social morality of sexual desire and activity feed into a broader perspective that includes love? At the same time, however, the independent importance of love, or of the concept "love," had become more pressing to me. I was in the frame of mind (not totally unwarranted) that love was a phenomenon or concept that could, and perhaps should, be studied in its own right, for it is not obviously true that love and sex are "really" the same thing or that love and sex, logically, psychologically, or morally presuppose each other. Love is such a rich phenomenon, provoking questions in ontology, epistemology, the philosophy of mind, theology and philosophy of religion, that to restrict the investigation of its many forms and dimensions to the ties between love and sexuality is to commit a painful conceptual truncation.

For reasons that might be altogether transparent to some people, but which I still find elusive, stores in this country today stock and sell books on love by the millions: fictional, psychological and sociological, upliftingly practical, sentimental, and, with only a few exceptions, mildly to utterly conceptually confused. Students, like their elders, do more than a bit of reading, thinking and talking about love and sexual relationships. These preanalytic reflections are often worthwhile and provide a substantial touchstone for theorizing about love or for merely getting a handle on "our" conception of love. But their thinking, like that of their elders, is also influenced and infected by popular treatises on love, which is unfortunate. These items reinforce confusions and encourage the mechanical rehearsal of tautologous or fuzzily pseudoempirical platitudes. The purpose of a course in the philosophy of love should be to assist the attainment of precise and conceptually unambiguous discourse on love, and to do this in part by exhibiting exactly what meritorious discourse about love is and can be. Hence this new anthology.

Between 1980 and 1989 many people energetically discussed love with me and thereby nourished my continued scholarly interest in the philosophy of love, and others told me about events in their own lives that (often unintentionally or without their knowing it) provided me with material about which to think philosophically. I wish to thank Alison Jaggar, Mark Fisher, Carol Caraway, Russell Vannoy, my sisters Janet and Phyllis, Rebecca Carrasco, Elizabeth Peterson, Richard C. Richards, Stef Jones, Norton and Sue Nelkin, James and Hilde Lindemann Nelson, Richard and Elaine Hull, Veronica Thomas, Sylvia Walsh, Eva Joachim Haukness, and a good number of students in my philosophy of sex and love courses (especially those sharp and thick-skinned enough to realize that the goal of the course was a deeper understanding of conceptual matters and an appreciation of the complexity of love, rather than guidance about how to overcome the pain of busted romance or instructions for defining, once and for all, "love"). I am grateful for the essential tasks carried out by Marie Richelle, Debbie Anderson, and Huey Henoumont, who coaxed the copying machine and the interlibrary loan mechanism into performing dutifully. A special word of thanks is due to Edward Johnson, who removed a heavy burden from my editorial shoulders by transliterating and translating the Greek that appears in the essays by Gregory Vlastos and Aryeh Kosman. And to all my colleagues in the Philosophy Department, who worked on the galleys.

New Orleans
April 1989

AN INTRODUCTION TO THE PHILOSOPHY OF LOVE

Alan Soble

> To the lover the loved one is always the most beautiful thing imagin-
> able, even though to a stranger she may be indistinguishable from an
> order of smelts. . . . Actually, the prettiest [women] are almost always
> the most boring, and that is why some people feel there is no God.
>
> WOODY ALLEN, *Without Feathers*

I.

Not far beneath our laughter at Allen's cute and mildly sexist joke lurks a
haunting sense of the tragic irrationality of love: a person x, head over heels in
love with another person y, sees only beauty and goodness in y, ignoring all the
plain evidence that y is a selfish, unfaithful manipulator; x, under the spell of
his passion for y, sells his treasured thoroughbred horse in order to keep y's book
and record collection up to date; x, wanting to bind the two of them together
forever, shamelessly spills his guts to y, revealing all his secret hopes and fears,
about which y could not care less. No, there is no God. Or if there is, it is the
god Love, who (as Hesiod wrote long ago) damages the mind.

In a cool moment we should question this picture of the lover as an essentially irrational and possessed monomaniac. We should wonder, as philosophers are prone to do: if it is x's love for y that explains why x believes that y is
beautiful and good, then what is it that explains x's love itself? We cannot
answer, as much as we would ordinarily like to, that x loves y because x believes

The author of this Introduction, and of the introductory essays to Sections I through IV, is Associate
Professor of Philosophy at The University of New Orleans. In 1977 he founded The Society for the
Philosophy of Sex and Love. © 1989, Alan Soble.

that y is beautiful and good. For if that were also true of x, x would be not merely irrational but a logical impossibility. Perhaps x perceives y to be beautiful and good because x loves y, and x's love for y is reinforced by x's perception that y has the beauty and goodness that x has attributed to y—this just compounds x's irrationality without canceling x's existence. What cannot be true at the same time is that x perceives y to be beautiful and good because x's love for y is already in place, and that x's love for y gets into place because x perceives y to be beautiful and good. Indeed, the latter possibility taken alone is a central part of a comprehensible picture of rational love.

If x loves y because x perceives y to be beautiful and good, x's love for y is transparently explained as an everyday emotional phenomenon. It would be no different from x's hating y because x believes that y has done something nasty to x, or from x's fearing a bear because x believes that the bear's claws pose a threat to x's life and limb. The only question that would remain is why x perceives y to be beautiful and good in the first place (or believes that the bear's claws are dangerous). But that question, we think, admits of a fairly straightforward answer. By contrast, if x perceives y to be beautiful and good because x loves y, we have an answer to the question about the source of x's perception of y—not, however, a straightforward answer. Further, we are left with x's love for y dangling, unexplained. Since x perceives y to be beautiful and good just because x loves y, despite the fact that all the evidence indicates that y is a liar and a cheat, the answer to our first question, why x loves y, also cannot be straightforward. The cause of or reason for x's loving y cannot be something familiar, but will have to be something esoteric, if x's love is to have such a profound effect on x's cognitive, deliberative, and prudential faculties.

Were x to believe that y has done something nasty to x *because* x already hates y, or were x to believe that the bear's claws are a threat to x's limbs *because* x already fears the bear, we would immediately reach for a familiar sort of explanation: x already hates y because y earlier did do something nasty to y, and x already fears the bear because it is huge and strong. Thus, if x believes y to be beautiful and good because x loves y, our natural impulse is to say that x's love is already in place in virtue of x's perception that y is charming and inventive. But if that appealing and commonsensical move is blocked—x believes y to be beautiful and good because x loves y, and there are no other merits in y that explain x's love; x believes that y has done something nasty to x because x hates y, and x does *not* believe that y has already done something else nasty to x that warrants the hate—then explaining x's emotion, be it love, hate, fear, or whatever, is going to take a lot of dancing.

Clearly, it is true that in some actual cases x perceives y to be beautiful and good precisely because x loves y, and we have to search for an unfamiliar explanation for x's love itself. In still other actual cases x loves y simply because x perceives y to be beautiful and good; here the mystery of love is dispelled and x preserves his or her rationality. Thus we have two pictures of love, which correspond to these two scenarios, each of which can be advanced as being the more accurate picture of what love really is. We will return to the dispute between these two pictures later in this Introduction, and it will occupy us throughout the four Sections of the book.

II.

One of the most popular treatises on love is Leo Buscaglia's *Love*. [1] Several provocative passages in this book are worth looking at carefully. For example, Buscaglia warns us that

> we have not sufficiently celebrated the wonderful uniqueness of every individual. I would agree that personality is the sum total of all the experiences that we have known since the moment of conception . . . along with heredity. But what is often ignored is an X factor. Something within the *you* of *you* that is different from every single human being, that will determine . . . how you will see this world, how you will become a special human being. . . . Education should be the process of helping everyone to discover his uniqueness, to teach him how to develop that uniqueness, and then to show him how to share it. . . . Imagine what this world would be like if all along the way you had people say to you, "It's good that you're unique; it's good that you're different. Show me your differences so that maybe I can learn from them" (pp. 19–20).

Something is not quite right here. After all, Charles Manson has a unique personality, an idiosyncratic mixture of Satanism and allegiance to 1960s hippie flower power. Should we say to Manson, "your uniqueness is to be cherished, it is a good thing that you are unique"? Should education teach people who are similar to Manson to develop their uniqueness? I doubt that Buscaglia would agree with these implications of his view; we should assume that he realizes his educational principle needs qualification. There is, however, a more pressing issue that deserves our attention.

Many people who write about love assert, as Buscaglia does, that each person is unique. But it is difficult not only to state exactly in virtue of what each person is unique, but also to provide convincing reasons to believe that we are unique. Buscaglia says that everyone is unique in virtue of an X factor, a "something" (or another) "within the *you* of *you*." Surely we are unique in virtue of our fingerprints, for example, but that is a trivial uniqueness; and since fingerprints are not something "within" us, Buscaglia must mean that we are unique in a more significant way than that. There is something in virtue of which we are unique, he claims, but he declines to tell us what it is and to give us a hint how we can recognize it. Furthermore, there is a possible, tiny contradiction in his view: if there is an X factor that makes me unique, why does Buscaglia "agree" that my personality is the sum total of my heredity and experiences? There seems not to be any room left over for "something" else.

Buscaglia compounds the problem when he eventually (and surprisingly) suggests that our uniqueness may not play a significant role in love: "responsible love has at its universal core man's humanity. In the deepest sense, we all have a core of humanness" (pp. 166–67); "there is perhaps no greater knowledge than this, that each person in the world . . . is basically a human being" (p. 169). Buscaglia is now claiming that at our deepest existential level we are all the same. Thus he claims both that there is something unknown, an X factor, "within" each of us that makes us unique, yet we are all "in the deepest sense" and "basically" the same. Does this mean that the X factor is not our "deepest" part even though it is hidden "within" us? Or do we have two equally deep aspects, one that makes us unique and one that we share with everyone else? Suppose that Buscaglia means that in some respects we are different and in others we are the same. To make this an engaging thesis, we would have to be more specific about these two dimensions: what they are and how to tell them apart. Doing so is especially important if education, as Buscaglia claims, bears the burden of developing our uniqueness, and if, as he also claims (after all), our uniqueness does play a significant role in love: when we love someone, we attend to him or her as a unique individual.

Buscaglia's idea that loving someone involves recognizing their uniqueness is revealed in his brief discussion of the relationship between love for oneself and love for other persons. "If you know, accept and appreciate yourself and your uniqueness, you will permit others to do so. . . . [I]t all starts with you. To the extent to which you know yourself, and we are all more alike than different, you can know others. When you love yourself, you will love others" (pp. 143–44). Buscaglia here emphasizes our similarities rather than celebrates our differences. His doing so is required by his argument: my loving myself depends on knowing myself and my unique value; my loving you depends on knowing you and your uniqueness; but my knowing you is possible only if we are sufficiently similar to permit me to understand you by extrapolating from knowing myself. I wonder whether we should be convinced. After all, if what I know about myself is my uniqueness, i.e., my differences from you, then to that extent I am not permitted to assume that I am able to understand you *by* extrapolating from myself—foreign, unique creature that you also are.

Buscaglia does raise important questions about love: What role does our uniqueness play in love; what constitutes that uniqueness; and is love an emotion which at its best or by its very nature is directed at a person *qua* the unique individual he or she is? Further, what is the relationship between reflexive attitudes (self-love, self-respect, self-interest) and one's loving concern for or emotional attachment to another person? Buscaglia concludes that "when you love yourself, you will love others." Taken literally, this means that my loving myself is sufficient (all I have to do) for loving someone else. That seems false. Buscaglia may mean that my loving myself is psychologically necessary for my being able to love others. But there are reasons to challenge this claim too.

An equally well-known contemporary writer and lecturer, M. Scott Peck, more clearly advances a thesis about the role of uniqueness in love, in his *The Road Less Traveled*: "genuine love recognizes and respects the unique individuality . . . of the other person. . . . The truly loving person . . . valu[es] the uniqueness and differentness of his or her beloved. . . ."² Peck's idea is this: since, for him, love is "the will to extend one's self for the purpose of nurturing . . . another's spiritual growth" (p. 81), one cannot love another or nurture another's growth unless one knows the other as a unique individual. Being able to help the other requires knowing precisely what to do for him or her, which will be different from what one should do to foster someone else's growth. But my worries about Buscaglia's view apply also to Peck's. Does my fostering your growth depend more on my knowledge of your idiosyncratic uniqueness or on certain general facts about you? If I am concerned for your spiritual growth in particular, the answer would seem to be the latter, if your spirit is not very different from that of other people and hence what all of us need for spiritual development is roughly the same. If, as Plato and Aristotle both claim in their own ways (see Section II), my loving you is both a response to your moral virtue and leads me to help you maintain and develop that virtue, and if one's moral personality is a large part of one's "spirit," then it is not obviously true that in loving you I must attend to you as a unique individual.

Peck, like Buscaglia, also claims that there is a significant connection between self-love and love for others. I omitted something from Peck's definition of love that should now be acknowledged: "I define love thus: The will to extend one's self for the purpose of nurturing one's own *or* another's spiritual growth." Peck points out that his definition "includes self-love with love for the other." What he means is that my nurturing spiritual growth is my love for another when I aim at another's growth, and it is self-love when I aim at my own growth (p. 82). Thus Peck is providing a specific analysis of what it is to love the self. This account of "self-love" differs from other accounts, in particular the view that "self-love" refers more precisely to a person's natural tendency to favor his or her own well-being over the well-being of others. Even though, on Peck's view, self-love is more clearly associated with self-interest than it is associated, say, with self-respect, his analysis does not entail that self-love is a selfish concern for one's own interests.

Peck is of course free to define love in such a way that the concept encompasses self-love as something identical in form and nature to love for others. But his definition lends no support to one other claim he makes about the relationship between self-love and other-love, namely, that "we are incapable of loving another unless we love ourselves." Why should we believe that the will to foster another's growth psychologically presupposes the will to foster my own growth, or even that actually fostering another's growth depends on my actually fostering my own growth? It seems possible that, even when the two go hand-in-hand, I might both will to foster my growth and the growth of another without the latter requiring the former. Peck's argument is this: x cannot love y unless x loves x, "just as we are incapable of teaching our children self-discipline unless we ourselves are self-disciplined" (pp. 82–83). This argument from analogy is weak. Some of the best batting and pitching coaches in baseball are excellent teachers of those skills, yet as active players they compiled notoriously unimpressive statistics.

If self-love is the will to foster one's own growth and other-love is the will to foster another's growth, it seems inescapable that there will be conflicts between self-love and other-love. Even if Peck is right that self-love is necessary for other-love, therefore, fostering my own growth might prevent me from, or interfere with, my fostering your growth; further, sometimes abandoning or slowing down my own growth is the best way for me to maximize your growth. Peck, however, asserts that "it is actually impossible to forsake our own spiritual development in favor of someone else's" (p. 83). This amazing claim purports to solve with a single stroke one of the most perplexing puzzles about love: how to reconcile the satisfaction of our needs with the satisfaction of the needs of the other person. Peck in effect says, not to worry. If it is *impossible* to sacrifice one's own good for the sake of someone else, there is nothing to reconcile. Peck's bold assertion would be true if he meant something special by "my spiritual development," for example, if the will to attend to my own spiritual development by its very nature included or was exhausted by the will to foster your spiritual development. This is implausible and it only sidesteps, not answers, difficult questions about how to balance in a reasonable and morally acceptable way self-interest and the interests of others. That Peck implicitly makes this move is suggested by his claim that "self-love and love of others . . . ultimately are indistinguishable." If this is literally true, then of course it is impossible to do one without doing the other. But Peck's use of the term "indistinguishable" is obscure. Does he mean that self-love and other-love are indistinguishable in the way that the Morning Star and the Evening Star are indistinguishable (i.e., one and the same object—Venus)? Or does he mean that self-love and other-love are constantly and inextricably conjoined, like what is due to nature and what is due to nurture in our personalities, so that they cannot be neatly empirically separated? Or even that when we introspect, we are incapable of phenomenally distinguishing our desire for our own good and our desire for the other's good, so that the two become confusingly mixed together in our motives?

A different thesis about the connection between self-love and love for others was advanced by the ancient Greek philosopher Plato. For Plato, the desire for one's own happiness—"self-love" in one sense of that expression—is the motive behind all forms of love for other persons and things. (See Plato's *Symposium* in Section II.) Plato also claimed that we do not love other persons as unique individuals but rather as embodiments of general, meritorious properties, the sort of thing shared widely among people. (See the essays by Gregory Vlastos and L.A. Kosman in Section III.) Thus in Plato we find not only a contrary claim about the role of uniqueness in love, but also a claim about the role played by the merit of the beloved. Christians in particular have been suspicious of this latter aspect of Plato's account of love (see the essay by Anders Nygren in Section III). But not only Christians; it is possible for anyone to argue that even though love typically fastens onto the beloved via the latter's perceived merit, in some cases love may exist (as we have seen) even when the lover finds no such merit or does not respond to the merit that does exist in the beloved. The lover, instead, attributes merit on the basis of his or her love.

III.

Buscaglia writes that if one person says "I love you" to another, the latter "would have a tendency to question: 'What does he mean by that?' " (p. 90). This is a reasonable question for a beloved to ask, since people as lovers mean different things by "love." Buscaglia imagines that the beloved continues: "Does he love my body? My mind? Does he love me at this moment? Forever?" Let's try to inventory what the beloved might be asking. The beloved might be wondering, first, whether the declarer of love loves precisely her body or her mind, i.e., not *her* at all, but only a part of her. Or the beloved might be wondering whether she is loved *because* she has a fine body or a fine mind, at least as perceived by the lover. That is, our beloved can make a distinction between the *object* of her lover's love (the item that the love is directed to) and the *basis* of this love for her (*why* she is loved). Then the beloved can ask two questions, one about the object and another about the basis of love. Further, when the beloved wonders if she will be loved "forever," she might be wondering if she will be loved by her lover even after she dies,[3] or only as long as, but at least as long as, she is still alive (even if she becomes grotesque), or only as long as she remains morally and psychologically the same person. Here we have three different senses of "forever." Our beloved is wondering whether love, to be the real thing, must endure, and if so, how long, or whether it can disappear overnight yet still be love. Finally, our beloved might be wondering not only about the basis and/or object of love, on the one hand, and about the constancy of love on the other—

as if the two sets of questions were independent of each other—but also about the logical and psychological connections between the basis or object of her lover's love *and* its constancy. Thus she would like to tie together *why* she is loved (or *what* is loved) and what she can reasonably expect or hope for in terms of the durability of her lover's love.

Buscaglia's treatment of the constancy of love is quite contrary to St. Paul's "love abides" (see Section II): "Love lives the moment. . . . There is only the moment. The now. . . . Love knows this. . . . It doesn't look forward. . . . Love lives the moment; it's neither lost in yesterday nor does it crave for tomorrow. Love is now!" (pp. 104–8). Does this mean that if x and y love each other now, they do not even hope or intend that their love persist into the future? Of course there are traps to avoid, as Peck wisely recognizes: "the experience of falling in love [carries] the illusion that the experience will last forever" (p. 91). Even as we *know* love will not necessarily endure, the immediate rush of love and its confluence with sexual desire somehow causes some of us to *feel* that our love will last and last and last. But this feeling that love will last provides no reason to object to Buscaglia's claim that "love is now!" For Buscaglia is not talking about the experience of falling in love, but about what he takes to be genuine love itself. Indeed, that the experience of falling in love includes the feeling that it will last forever, which we recognize to be only an illusion, might make more credible the idea that "love is now" and does not look into the future. Peck, however, insists that genuine love is future-oriented, that it entails a constancy that is not an illusion.

"Commitment is inherent in any genuinely loving relationship. Anyone who is truly concerned for the spiritual growth of another knows . . . that he or she can significantly foster that growth only through a relationship of constancy," Peck claims (pp. 140–41). What is the source of this commitment that makes love constant? Peck reminds us that, for him, love is "the will to extend oneself for the purpose of nurturing one's own or another's spiritual growth." By the term "will" Peck does not mean "inclination" or "desire" or "need" or something "emotional." These things come and go, existing, like falling in love, in the now. Instead, for Peck, "the person who truly loves does so because of a decision to love. The person has made a commitment to be loving whether or not the loving feeling is present" (p. 119). Love is something that we choose, something "volitional," and so the commitment involved in love, or love's constancy, is the result of a deliberate mental act and one's determination to nourish endlessly another's spiritual growth. It would not be incorrect, then, to say that Peck takes very seriously one part of the marriage vow: "I promise to love." (On this locution, see the essay by Susan Mendus in Section IV.)

One problem in Peck's view is that the distinction between love as "volitional" and love as "emotional" might not make any difference for the constancy of love. The decision to love does not seem to guarantee, any better than it is guaranteed if love is emotional, that the commitment will endure. What is it about a *decision* to love that implies that one will stick to that decision? Choices are reversible, under all sorts of conditions and for all sorts of reasons, in which case love-by-decision is just as vulnerable to termination as love-as-feeling. What is there behind the decision to love endlessly, or behind a long series of decisions to keep on loving, that brings these decisions into existence or makes them possible? To answer "either other decisions or inclinations" is merely to push the question back one step (whence these other decisions?) or to grant that underlying love is desire, after all. Hence it is not clear that love is best understood as fully volitional, even though the "will" can of course play some role in love. And it is similarly unclear how the constancy of love is to be secured, if it is to be secured.

Karol Wojtyla's Roman Catholic view is close to Peck's. Love, and the marriage within which this love is to exist, must continue at least until the death of one's beloved if it is to be the genuine article, and the crucial element in love that makes it constant is "the will."[4] But even if Buscaglia's "love is now" is too weak a claim about the continuity of genuine love, Peck and Wojtyla's "love is forever" is too strong. If x has an emotion toward y for some period of time, and from all appearances (e.g., x has been intensely concerned for y's well-being during a stressful patch) this emotion seemed to be love, it is implausible to claim that just because the emotion ends, it has never been love. If x's emotion ends or x's concern for y peters out because, for example, y has become abusive or sexually promiscuous, we are not compelled to conclude that x had never loved y during the earlier time when y was still kind, honest, and faithful. Wojtyla disagrees; he asserts that genuine love shows itself by loving even more strongly when the beloved sins. After all, on his view love is not conditional on the goodness or merit of its object, and so it should endure even when its object loses its value or becomes unattractive.

Although Wojtyla claims to be describing the nature of love or establishing a logical requirement for the correct application of the term "love," I suspect that he is actually making (or is better understood as making) a moral judgment about lovers: if x's love falters when y sins, x's emotion had all along been love, but x is morally at fault for not exercising his or her will to overcome the obstacles to continuing to love. But whether we have a moral obligation to love constantly is a different question from whether love must be constant to be what it claims to be.

IV.

What is love? The complexity of this question—compare it to "what is a chair?"—is reflected in the fact that so many different answers to it exist and debates about the nature of genuine love seem impossible to resolve. But there is a methodological principle that it might be wise for us to apply in coming to grips with an answer to the question: if an assertion about what love is (or includes) entails that too many cases of what we would ordinarily call "love" are not love at all, then that is a reason (although by itself not necessarily decisive) for believing that the assertion is false. For example, Peck and Wojtyla claim that genuine love lasts "forever" or, less poetically, that it endures at least as long as the lover and beloved both exist. However, imagine that x and y love each other during their junior and senior years in college, but get jobs after graduation in different cities. They live too far apart to continue to nourish their love, which eventually fades with time. In a sense x and y, by accepting these jobs, were deciding not to continue to love each other. Here we are reluctant to say that just because their love ended, it had never been love. As much as we might like it to be true that love lasts forever, we realize that many occurrences of love come to an end yet are the real thing while they do exist. Our methodological principle would have us reject Peck and Wojtyla's thesis.

Similar uses of the principle would also show that it is implausible to assert that when x loves y, x's actions always and only serve to benefit x's beloved y; or that if x loves y, then x could not love another person z at the same time; or that when x loves y, y must also be loving x at the same time. If any of these claims were true, then the world has known very little love and we would have to revise vastly our classification of those emotional experiences we ordinarily call "love." And if we have to do that, we will have lost just about the only foundation for believing that we know what love is or for believing that we have learned with some accuracy how to use that word. We will have lost that contact with the reality of the experience that makes our talk of love meaningful and that explains why we are able to communicate with each other using the word.

The methodological principle warns us that claims of the form "love necessarily or always is, or includes, Ø" are to be treated with suspicion, and that assertions about love are more safely expressed in the form "love typically or ideally is, or includes, Ø."[5] A large number of candidates for the various Ø's that together comprise love are plausible contenders: love is usually somewhat constant, at least for conceptual reasons more constant than, for example, amusement; love manifests itself as a disposition to benefit the beloved, which often but not always leads to beneficial acts done for the sake of one's beloved; when x loves y, x is typically caused to spend a good deal of time in y's presence, or at least to want to; x typically desires to join or merge with y, although this desire for union need not be mere sexual desire[6] but also, or alternatively, a quest for intellectual or psychological intimacy; love is ideally, but not necessarily, a reciprocal phenomenon, or at least when x loves y, x hopes that y will also love x; when x loves y, x usually finds something attractive about y, or something valuable in y, that makes comprehensible x's attachment to or affection for y; and so forth.

According to this approach, the presence of all the elements mentioned (the Ø's) gives strong support to the claim that x does love y, and the absence of all of them brings into serious doubt that x loves y. Imagine your reaction to x's saying that x loved y—yet x never did anything to benefit y, never desired to talk with y, never wanted to touch y, and found absolutely nothing of value in y's personality. It is more difficult to decide whether the absence of only one Ø is sufficient for refusing to call x's attitude "love," since some Ø's might be more central to love than others. For example, if the desire to promote the well-being of the beloved is a more important feature of love than the desire to join physically with the beloved, then the absence of the former raises more serious doubts about the claim that x loves y than does the absence of the latter.

In many respects "love" is not unlike many other concepts: "work of art" comes to mind immediately. What love is, and what art is, are equally difficult questions. Yet we are able to apply "art" to a large number of noncontroversial cases, and the same is true for love. The concept "chair" seems to possess a simplicity and clarity that "art" and "love" do not have. It does so, however, only because in our kind of life making mistakes as to what counts as a chair is ordinarily not as momentous or harmful as confusing love or works of art with their pretenders.

One reason we disagree about the application of the term "love" to specific cases might be that the word refers not to one thing but to many things. Buscaglia, to the contrary, tells us that "there are not 'kinds' of love. Love is of one kind. Love is love" (p. 96). The child "loves his Pablum; he also loves his mother. . . . There are degrees of love, but there's only one kind of love." Buscaglia seems to mean that all the phenomena we call "love" have something important in common. A problem with this view is that specifying the ingredient common to all loves, that makes love just one thing, is difficult. For example, if one of the central Ø's of love is that x is concerned for the well-being of the object of x's love, it will be senseless to claim that a child loves her Pablum (let alone her mother). And although the child might very well have an inchoate desire to merge with its mother, or to remain merged, the claim that the child loves and therefore wants to merge with its Pablum (by eating it?) stretches too severely the notion of merging with one's beloved. Indeed, it might be argued (against Buscaglia) that we have trouble deciding whether a particular Ø is a part of love exactly because there are many discrete kinds of love, some of which do, while others do not, include Ø. We love chocolate, going to the movies, our country, God, the stranger, our friends, our parents and children, and each other. And these are quite distinct things.

There is, however, something irksome about this diagnosis. For even if these are discrete loves, as long as it is correct to use the word "love" to refer to them all, it seems that they must have something in common (call this element K). If so, debates as to whether love does or does not include some Ø are not futile cr pointless; they are simply debates over whether love—the phenomenon that all parties must agree has K—also has Ø. The alternative to this is simply that debates over whether love is Ø are indeed based on a deep misunderstanding, the false assumption that all the parties are discussing the same thing identifiable by at least one common denominator K. In this case, some of the phenomena we now call "love" should not be called "love" at all. The fly in the ointment, however, is that all parties to the dispute might (indeed, do) claim that the term "love" should be reserved for the item *they* are talking about and should be abandoned by the other sides; all the parties claim that they are describing genuine love while the others are describing something that does not deserve the name. [7] This metaphilosophical issue is fascinating but frustrating, and I do not propose here to make it any more manageable. It will become clear, however, that the metaphilosophical quandary is not about to disappear quietly. Many of the essays in this volume are concerned with clarifying the ideas of *eros*, *philia*, and *agape*. These are arguably either three loves that share at least one thing in common, thereby permitting the question: is one of these loves the best love? Or they are three distinct things, only one of which should be called "love."

We need to think about how to conceptualize the debate among the respective proponents of *eros*, *philia*, and *agape*. We must also apply these ancient concepts of love to the love (or loves) we experience today. Thus there are two related projects for us to carry out. The first is to compare the original formulations of the theories of *eros*, *agape* and *philia*, by studying the primary texts with which these accounts of love are associated: Plato's *Symposium*, Aristotle's *Nicomachean Ethics*, and the New Testament (see Section II). Our goal here is to lay out how these ancient writers in particular understood *eros*, *philia*, and *agape*, and to compare these historically specific accounts of love. In our second project our goal is to explain more generally what an *erosic* love is, or what an *agapic* love is; that is, to treat these ideas of love separately from their historical origins. We take the basic elements of the three concepts, weed out those aspects that the original formulations included but are logically unnecessary, and then employ these refined notions to characterize an *eros* tradition, or an *agape* tradition, to which other writers make (and have made) their own contributions. We thereby end up with less historically bound accounts of "eros-style" love, "philia-style" love, and "agape-style" love, accounts that pertain more directly to our contemporary love experiences.

The *eros* tradition, of course, begins with Plato's account of *eros* in the *Symposium*; we might even say that the exemplar of Platonic love is Socrates, someone who progressed through all four stages of Plato's ladder of love, thereby achieving Plato's ideal. The *agape* tradition begins with the many passages in the New Testament that describe God's love for humans and present the message contained both in Jesus' teachings and in the events of his life and death; here Jesus is the exemplar. Although the *philia* tradition begins with Aristotle's *Nicomachean Ethics*, it is difficult to point to an outstanding exemplar he might have had in mind while fashioning his theory of love. Perhaps we cannot do so simply because *philia* is actually a variety of *eros*. It is very close to the heavenly *eros* described early in the *Symposium* by Pausanias and to the second-level *eros* described later by Diotima. What all three have in common is the idea that in the best human love, x loves y because y is morally virtuous or otherwise displays human excellence. Thus we can understand why Gregory Vlastos ultimately contrasts *agape*, on the one hand, with both Plato's *eros* and Aristotle's *philia*, on the other hand, and judges both of the latter deficient. Only the Christian conception of love, for Vlastos, was striking out into new territory by making the beloved's virtue irrelevant.

There are many points of contrast between Plato's original *eros* and the original conception of God's *agape*, and so there are a number of ways we could analytically distinguish these loves (see Nygren's tabulation). *Eros* is acquisitive, egocentric or even selfish; *agape* is a giving love, a love that makes even the supreme sacrifice for the sake of the beloved. *Eros* is an unconstant, unfaithful love, while *agape* is unwavering and continues to give despite ingratitude. *Eros* is the manner in which humans necessarily love, by human nature itself, while *agape* is the way God necessarily by His nature loves humans. (See W. B. Yeats' poem, "For Anne Gregory," included in the Appendix.) *Eros* is a love that responds to the merit or value of its object, while *agape* creates value in its object as a result of loving it, and exists independently of, or regardless of, any merit or lack of merit in its object. *Eros* in Plato's formulation is sexual, at least for the lower levels of the ladder, and perhaps also for the higher levels in a broader sense of "sexual." Would one ever think of characterizing *agape* as including an erotic component? In *eros* the object of love is just a set of properties and not the person who possesses them, while in *agape* the object of love is a person as a distinct individual or an ontological particular rather than a sum of general properties.[8] Finally, *eros* is an ascending love, the human's route to God; *agape* is a descending love, God's route to humans.

These are, all of them, intriguing ways to distinguish the original accounts of *eros* from *agape*. (*Philia* gets caught in the cracks between or among them.) But which features of *eros* and *agape* are central? Which features are relatively dispensable to what makes *eros* what it is and *agape* what it is? For many of the features of *eros* (and the corresponding features of *agape*) are logically independent of each other. For example, from the fact that x loves y in response to y's merit, it does not follow that y is only a set of properties or that x's motive in loving y is egocentric; nor does it follow from the fact that a love exists independently of the merit of its object, and despite the object's faults, that love will be constant. Thus in characterizing eros-style love and agape-style love, we are logically free to choose any of the features mentioned above as the central feature of these two loves. But we should choose features that are the most fruitful in illuminating the differences between these styles of love and in helping us to understand our own love experiences.

My proposal is that in developing the *eros* and *agape* traditions, and therefore in applying these ancient notions of love to our present experiences, we define "eros-style" love this way: x loves y because y has attractive or valuable qualities. In "agape-style" love, then, x loves y independently of y's merit, and any merit of y's that plays a role in x's love is value that x attributes to or creates in y as a result of x's love.[9] The essential difference between the theories of *eros* and *agape* are their claims about the basis of love, not their claims about the object of love or about love's motivation. The reader should be alert to this way of distinguishing between *erosic* and *agapic* love, for this distinction either explicitly or implicitly makes its way into all the essays included in this volume. And the reader should now return to the beginning of this Introduction and ask whether it was justifiable for me to suggest that there is another difference (now seen to be derivative) between *erosic* and *agapic* love: only the former corresponds to our picture of a comprehensible, rational, unmysterious love.

NOTES

1. *Love* (New York, NY: Ballantine Books, 1982). All page numbers in the text refer to this edition.

2. *The Road Less Traveled* (New York, NY: Simon and Schuster, 1978), p. 151. All page numbers in the text refer to this edition.

3. See Søren Kierkegaard, *Works of Love* (New York, NY: Harper & Row, 1962), pp. 320–29.

4. Karol Wojtyla (Pope John Paul II), *Love and Responsibility* (New York, NY: Farrar, Straus and Giroux, 1981), pp. 91–92, 117, 123, 134–35, 185.

5. Contrast this with W. Newton-Smith's recommendation that we understand true claims about love as "g-necessary" (see his paper in Section IV).

6. On the differences between love and sexual desire, and on the relationship between them, see especially the essays below by Gregory Vlastos (the Appendix to his piece on Plato), Robert Ehman, and Joseph Diorio, as well as 1 *Corinthians* 7. Note that Newton-Smith limits, in advance, his analysis to that sort of love that does include sexual desire. This approach is different from claiming that love by its very nature includes sexual desire (Ehman). For a provocative treatment of these issues see Russell Vannoy, *Sex Without Love* (Buffalo, NY: Prometheus, 1980).

7. It might be useful to understand love as an "essentially contested" concept (see W. B. Gallie, "Essentially Contested Concepts," *Proceedings of the Aristotelian Society*, New Series 56 [1956], pp. 167–98).

8. See Martin Warner, "Love, Self, and Plato's *Symposium*," *Philosophical Quarterly* 29 (1979), pp. 329–39; and Shirley Robin Letwin, "Romantic Love and Christianity," *Philosophy* 52 (1977), pp. 131–45.

9. Brentlinger makes this proposal in his essay reprinted in Section III, and I develop it at length in my *The Structure of Love*.

Section I:

WHERE WE ARE

MANY people who have written about love or have thought about their love experiences have discerned that one major problem that threatens both the happiness of love and its very existence is the conflict between the desire for an intimate psychological union and the contrary need to maintain an independent identity. We have a need to overcome our existential or metaphysical aloneness,[1] or without an intimate union with another person we continually feel distressingly incomplete.[2] Thus we desire to join our life with the life of another person, to mingle or merge our self with the self of the other. And once this union has taken root we have a motive for continuing and nurturing the interpersonal connection that has alleviated our *Angst*. Yet, at the same time, a secure sense of ourself as a distinct individual depends on maintaining more than a semblance of separateness. We must be able to glory in the independent exercise of our abilities and to be responsible in our own right for acting in the world in accordance with our individual natures. We can often, or at least partially, satisfy both needs at roughly the same time or alternatively; yet resolving the tension between them is difficult to manage. One might say that the experience of the young child, which is not always successfully handled—the conflict between the early union with mother and a developing awareness of independence—is recapitulated in the love relationships we have as adolescents and as adults.

People disagree, of course, as to what "intimacy" and "independence" mean, and they attribute different relative importance to these contrary needs. People

1

also differ in the extent to which they are cognizant of the fact that some of their dissatisfaction in a love relationship results from the tension between togetherness and separateness, and as to what specific arrangements permit them adequately to orchestrate the satisfaction of these two needs. But these differences among people in how they conceptualize and attempt to solve the problem, or even in whether they recognize it at all, should not prevent us from aiming at a general, theoretical understanding of its origins and its implications for the possibility of happy love. A theoretical perspective will be more convincing the more it is sensitive both to individual differences among people about these matters and to the influence of ethnic background, gender, education, and level of economic well-being. Here, I think, Lillian Rubin's account of some of the problems in heterosexual love relationships is somewhat superior to Shulamith Firestone's (both accounts are included in this Section); Rubin's description of the differences between women and men in our society is less stereotypifying, even if it does border on overgeneralization.

A few years ago I was watching a movie on television and was pleasantly surprised by this dialogue, which occurred between two married men in their late thirties as they sat at a bar drinking beer:

> Man₁: Women say we have no feelings.
> Man₂: Bunch of bullweed, if you ask me.
> Man₁: Right. We have feelings like everyone else.
> Man₂: Yep.
> [silence for ten seconds as they swirl their beer]
> Man₁: So tell me. How do you *really* feel about the Cubs this year?

This joke reveals the depth and significance of the problem to which Rubin alerts us. Women and men, having different psychogenic histories, perceive themselves and relationships differently. These differences include the relative weight, in their psychologies and in their self-concepts, of the poles of detached rationality and nondetached emotionality. One consequence of these gender differences is that, whereas both men and women are vulnerable to the tension between togetherness and separateness, they conceive of this tension differently. For men, the psychic threat is an engulfing intimacy at the expense of their individuality, while for women the threat is an empty separateness at the expense of intimate union. [3] Men, according to Rubin, are able to make a loving commitment to one woman (note here a disagreement with Firestone), despite the fact that they fear engulfment in the relationship with her. But his sense of "commitment" may not be very compatible with her sense of "intimate union." A man's reluctance to probe, develop, acknowledge, and express his emotions, and even the relative lack of significance he places on that aspect of his life, continually threatens the stability of his relationships. A woman's fear of separateness, and what appears to a man as an indulgence of the emotions, also contributes to this instability. This disparity between a man and a woman, Rubin explains, has profound implications not only for the sexual dimension of their relationship but also for how they view the relative value of their careers and the love relationship itself. Clutching women and cold men do not a happy pair make.

In passing, Rubin mentions that people want to be "loved for who we really are." This very common notion is vague. What, exactly, do people want when they want to be loved in this manner? I do not think it would be fair to say that Rubin means that a man wants to be loved for who he knows he really is: a closemouthed, calculating fish; and a woman for who she knows she really is: a motor-mouth hysteric. To ask to be loved for who we really are would be asking quite a bit of other people, probably too much. And love would be impossible unless the partners loved each other *agapically*, that is, despite the glaring faults of the other. Rubin, instead, seems to mean that we want to be loved without always having to maintain a good front and without pretending that we are something we are not. There is still room, however, for exploring the question of what it is to be "loved for who we really are." Answering it might require an account of personal identity (or at least of how people conceive of their identity), in order to spell out what we "really" are. At the very least, one issue is whether the desire to be loved *for* that is a desire about the basis or about the object of love.

One specific answer is that the desire to be loved for who we really are is a negative demand regarding the truth of the beliefs that ground love: what we desire is *not* to be loved just because our lover has grossly false beliefs about us. "Idealizing" one's beloved, being out of touch with his or her true character, is a defect in the basis of love. Such love is always liable to crumble, or explode, and brings with it nary a bit of security. To the extent that the romantic phenomenon of falling in love necessarily involves idealization, we have reason to be suspicious of it. (See Geoffrey Gorer's anthropological warning, in this Section, against magnifying the significance of romantic love and taking it too seriously.) Firestone, too, condemns the idealization that can infect the basis of love, although she seems to think that men are more prone to it than women. As she puts it, men need to be able to justify to themselves their descent, in love and marriage, into a lower caste. In genuine love, for Firestone, a man would love a woman, and vice versa, as an "irreplaceable totality," not as a mere collection of attractive properties. Here we have another, perhaps not incompatible, sense of what it means to be loved "for who we really are." Firestone's critique of heterosexual love in our culture gains its energy through a comparison with what she takes ideal love to be. And in emphasizing that the object of love is an "irreplaceable totality," her view bears some resemblance to the *agape* tradition. Note that for Firestone, x's love for y *creates* the differences in x's eyes between the value of y and other people, which is also an idea much closer to *agape* than *eros*.

Although Firestone's diagnosis of what is wrong with contemporary heterosexual love is similar to Rubin's in its reliance on purported gender differences in the psychogenic production of a split between rationality and emotionality, other factors play a larger role for Firestone. Since in her view genuine love is a mutual "exchange of selves," love will be unsatisfying and turbulent to the extent that the partners are divided by an "unequal balance of power" that inevitably interferes with the mutuality of the exchange. Since men have economic, social and political power, and women in general have less of these things, Firestone concludes that men cannot make commitments, indeed cannot love, while women understandably approach relationships with men in the coldly rational, calculating manner that we commonly associate not with women's psychologies but with men's. If these are indeed the costs of our society's long-standing inequality between women and men, the very possibility of happy love depends on considering seriously this additional, implicit argument for "women's liberation."[4]

But there is something strange in Firestone's view of love: genuine love involves a mutual *exchange* of selves. Her choice of the word "exchange" was a poor one, since it leaves us with the impression that love is a business deal, in fact an equal business deal, in which the value one gives is matched by the value one receives. If so, Firestone's genuine love resembles one of Aristotle's imperfect friendships, "use-friendship," in which two people love each other simply because they are mutually, and equally, useful to each other. (See *Nicomachean Ethics* in Section II.) In this regard Karol Wojtyla's view, or his way of expressing it, may be superior to Firestone's: in genuine love, each person makes a gift of the self to the other, each surrenders the self to the other in creating their shared love.[5] There is, of course, a difference between an exchange and a gift. The latter is unconditional while the former is conditional on receiving equal value in return.

NOTES

1. See Erich Fromm, *The Art of Loving* (New York, NY: Harper and Row, 1974), pp. 6–8.
2. See Aristophanes' myth in Plato's *Symposium*, 189c–193e (not included in the selection from Plato in Section II).
3. These themes are central to much of contemporary psychology of gender. See, for example, Carol Gilligan, *In a Different Voice* (Cambridge, MA: Harvard University Press, 1982).

4. For a philosophical exploration of Firestone's and other feminist critiques of contemporary heterosexual love, see Elizabeth Rapaport, "On the Future of Love: Rousseau and the Radical Feminists," in A. Soble, ed., *Philosophy of Sex* (Totowa, NJ: Littlefield, Adams, 1980), pp. 369–88.

5. *Love and Responsibility* (New York, NY: Farrar, Straus and Giroux, 1981), pp. 95–100.

ON FALLING IN LOVE

Geoffrey Gorer

ON THE BASIS of anthropological evidence it would appear that the capacity to fall passionately in love—to feel convinced that one can only achieve bliss by the union with one unique individual—is one of those uncommon potentialities which develop spontaneously in a few individuals in all human societies that have been described.

In its distribution it seems to have the same arbitrary character as those innate potentialities which form the basis of artistic and religious creations and performances: a 'true' ear or a 'true' hand for drawing, the ability to go into deep trance and the like. It is probable that in any society which comprises more than a few hundred people there will be some man or woman with 'absolute pitch', and another with the ability to go easily into trance. Whether the people with these innate gifts will ever exercise them publicly will depend on the development and the values of their society. If there is no polyphonic music, the person endowed with absolute pitch may go to his grave without ever having been aware of, much less exercised, his gift. The person with the ability to go easily into trance will probably not escape that experience; but if the religious climate is unfavourable, he or she may well have to hide this capacity as something shameful; and, if it be discovered, he or she may well be punished or killed as a witch possessed by the devil.

This essay, originally written in 1960, is Essay IX from Geoffrey Gorer's *The Danger of Equality* (New York, NY: Weybright and Talley, 1966), pp. 126–32. Geoffrey Gorer (1905–1985) studied with Margaret Mead and Ruth Benedict, and was the author of a number of anthropological treatises.

6

The analogy between these gifts and the ability to fall deeply in love may be pushed further. The gifts in their over-powering form, so that they manifest themselves whatever the climate of opinion and the customs of the society, are statistically rare; but a large part of the population is able to develop an approximation to these abilities if the society considers them desirable and punishes their absence. Thus, there is no reason to suppose that the ability to reproduce a tune correctly, to sing in harmony, is innately more common among the Welsh than among the English or (at least in the time of Mozart) among the Czechs than among the Austrians. But because the Welsh (or the Czechs of the eighteenth century) expected every person to be able to hold a worthy part in choral singing and arranged many of their more enjoyable and respected social events around choirs, far more people developed their originally weak musical ability in these societies than they did in the neighboring ones which had neither such expectations nor such institutions.

In most modern societies trance is a generally devalued condition, may indeed be considered to demand medical or psychiatric attention, and so it only manifests itself rarely, except among spiritualists and in ecstatic religious cults. But many other societies have demanded that every person, or every person of one sex, should experience trance at least once in their lives. Among a number of American Plains Indian tribes, a male could not become a warrior or hunter until he had found his guardian spirit in a trance vision; and in some West African societies, such as Dahomey, or among the Balinese in Indonesia, a great part of the population—perhaps half—develops the ability to go into at least light trance in the appropriate religious setting.

All the anthropological evidence suggests that the ability to fall passionately in love is completely analogous in its distribution to these other gifts. Even though a society may completely devalue romantic love, it will still occur spasmodically from time to time; and if a society puts a high valuation on this behavior, the greater part of the population will be able to convince themselves that they have these feelings, in the same way as the American Indian youths could nearly all convince themselves that they had had visions of their guardian spirit.

Probably because the spontaneous ability to fall deeply in love is so rare a phenomenon statistically, very few human societies (apart from Western Europe and North America in the last two centuries) have incorporated the expectation of romantic love into their social institutions, or demanded that every young man and every young woman should manifest it, should feel it at some time in their lives. There are records of one or two small societies in the islands of Polynesia or among the American Indians who have considered romantic love a necessary prelude to marriage; but, these very rare exceptions apart, marriage has typically been considered a *social* union between two groups rather than a *private* union between two individuals. Many societies will pay some attention to the preferences of the man and woman most intimately concerned and will not force a marriage of mutual repugnance (other societies do not pay even that attention to the girl's sentiments); but what is looked for in these societies of social marriage is mutual compatibility, nothing stronger. Marriage is too important to too many people, and to society itself; it cannot be allowed, so it is argued, to depend on the whims of young people who do not know their own minds.

Consequently, in nearly all the societies of which we have record, romantic love is considered to be quite unconnected with marriage, and is usually envisaged as socially disruptive. This disruption may be tragic—probably the most common development in literate societies—it may be comic, it may be a social nuisance or an interesting topic of conversation; but in nearly every society and at nearly every period romantic love is a disruptive force outside of, and interfering with, marriage.

This is the case with the European tradition of romantic love. The ladies for whom the troubadours sung were never their own wives nor capable of becoming so; if the poets were not married to someone else, then the objects of their devotion were. Guinevere and Isolde and Petrarch's Laura were married women; Dante was a married man when he met Beatrice, and Paolo and Francesca were both married to other people. Moreover, never in romantic poetry was there a suggestion that marriage was the aim of these lovers. Love and marriage are treated as antithetical; if the two people who fall in love are by any chance unmarried, then it is a fixed convention that the families of the two lovers are completely opposed to the union, as in *Romeo and Juliet* and many lesser poems and plays. The tragic love of two young people thwarted by the wishes of their families, and culminating either in suicide or in holy resignation, is a constant theme of literature and drama throughout Asia and much of Europe. Romantic love was the disturber, the wrecker of cities, in Sophocles' phrase; and parents were to be commiserated with if their children developed such unfortunate propensities.

About the middle of the eighteenth century the situation changed rapidly in Western Europe and North America. Judging from the literary evidence—and there is little else to go on—being romantically in love changed from a potentially tragic to a potentially desirable condition; and when the loving couple were in a position to marry, public sympathy went to the young people and was withdrawn from the parents who tried to impose their more prudent plans. A number of social changes accompanied this change of attitude: American independence, the French revolution, the beginning of the "industrial revolution" and the rise in influence and the increase in numbers of the middle classes.

All these changes probably had some influence; but I should be inclined to give the most weight to the last factor, the rise of the middle classes. Both the aristocracy and the peasantry were, in their different ways, attached to specific pieces of land; and the choice of daughter-in-law (or occasionally son-in-law) was very much influenced by considerations of agriculture and of inheritance; and neither group could maintain their living standards without the ownership of land. The middle classes, on the other hand, were mobile in every sense of the word; a family's prosperity was much less dependent on marriage settlements, and children were far more easily able to earn a living without parental approval or assistance. Marriages based on romantic love were at least feasible.

Furthermore, the middle classes were the major, indeed almost the only, audience for poets and novelists; and it was the poets and novelists, above all the romantic poets of England and Germany, who preached the ecstasy of romantic love and claimed the enormous superiority of a marriage founded on love to one founded on prudential parental arrangements; and their preaching made converts.

During the nineteenth century young middle-class men and women came to expect that they would fall in love romantically, and that such falling in love was the only proper prelude to, and a guarantor of, a happy marriage. This does not seem to have been the case with the other classes in Western Europe. For the aristocracies and royalty suitability seems to have remained a far more important criterion for marriage than romantic love; and the tragedies of unsuitable and disruptive love (such as *Mayerling*) continued to occur. The urban working classes during the nineteenth century were most of them so oppressed by fatigue and poverty that they lacked both leisure and energy to search for the romantically loved one. In the novels of Dickens, the middle-class characters fall in love and eventually marry; but the pictures of working-class married life are without any suggestion of romance. Some research has been done, particularly for cities in the North Eastern United States, on the places of residence of married people before their marriage; and overwhelmingly, the married couples come from either the same small urban neighborhood or from stops on the same trolley line.

In the present century the aristocrats, the urban workers and the peasants have to a great extent abandoned their distinctive modes of life. Middle-class patterns have become increasingly widely adopted—an increase much hastened by the development of mass communications such as films, radio, and television, which offered their middle-class patterns of life to an increasingly heterogenous audience. Among these middle-class patterns none was more insistent than a demand for marriage founded on romantic love, which was the culmination of the vast majority of stories and plays offered for entertainment and as an example of proper behavior. A marriage founded on romantic love was seen as the birthright of every man and woman from Royal Princesses to seamstresses and factory hands. As far as the records go, nothing like this has ever happened before in a complex society. We know of no other society which has expected that every young man and young woman should fall deeply in love with an unmarried member of the opposite sex and should marry their love-choice; and moreover to decree that this love should occur only once in a life-time, and should be strong enough to sustain the marriage for ever after.

This expectation that everybody should feel romantic love undoubtedly puts as much strain on some individuals as the demand that everybody should sing in tune or go into ecstatic trance does on some members of other societies. As with these other rare spontaneous talents, the majority of any population can produce a sufficient approximation to the spontaneous gift to satisfy themselves and their neighbors that they feel what they ought to feel, and so to approach marriage in what they have learned is the only appropriate frame of mind. But besides the people born with a true ear there are those who are born tone-deaf; besides the people who can fall spontaneously into trance there are those whom it is impossible to hypnotize; besides the natural lovers there are people who are temperamentally incapable of romantic love.

People of such a temperament—and we have no idea how numerous they are—are put to a grave disadvantage by the present social expectations; they feel themselves, and are often looked upon by their families and friends, as inadequate, as failures. Men and women who, in earlier centuries or in other societies, would have made the most satisfactory of spouses in marriages of suitability, may well remain unmarried and unhappy in a society which considers romantic love the only proper basis for marriage.

When romantic love is considered the supreme individual value, it can still be nearly as socially disruptive as it was in earlier periods or other societies where it was not allowed for at all. Among the most ethical people of the United States and some Western European countries between the wars it was considered profoundly immoral to stay married to a spouse who had fallen in love with somebody else; and there developed the paradox of the ethical divorce, when the self-sacrificing spouse nobly broke up his or her family life rather than thwart the partner's romantic love.

As far as my information goes, the children of these ethical divorcees tend to pay much less attention to the ecstasies of romantic love and much more attention to the companionate aspects of marriage and the pleasure of parenthood. Tender, nurturing fatherhood, which is so marked a feature of the family life of the youngest adult educated men in the United States and Britain, represents a very great change in men's emotional lives, and one for which there is no precedent in history. It seems probable that it will be incompatible with the very high valuation of romantic love which distinguished their parents' and grandparents' generations.

Many signs suggest that the pleasures of parenthood are becoming the most valued aspect of marriage in prosperous Western society; and this would imply that romantic love is again being devalued, except for those few for whom it is a temperamental necessity. If this be so, it will make for a calmer and more stable society, valuing permanent domestic happiness above the temporary ecstasies of passion. And then the universal demand for romantic love of the last two centuries will pass into history as one of the strange developments of which human beings are capable, somewhat like the dancing mania of the Middle Ages, or the glossolalia, the speaking with tongues, which falls on whole congregations in some ecstatic religious cults. As with these and the other examples earlier mentioned, a rare human potentiality will have for a short period dominated whole societies.

WOMEN, MEN, AND INTIMACY

Lillian B. Rubin

INTIMACY. We hunger for it, but we also fear it. We come close to a loved one, then we back off. A teacher I had once described this as the "go away a little closer" message. I call it the approach-avoidance dance.

The conventional wisdom says that women want intimacy, men resist it. And I have plenty of material that would *seem* to support that view. Whether in my research interviews, in my clinical hours, or in the ordinary course of my life, I hear the same story told repeatedly. "He doesn't talk to me," says a woman. "I don't know what she wants me to talk about," says a man. "I want to know what he's feeling," she tells me. "I'm not feeling anything," he insists. "Who can feel nothing?" she cries. "I can," he shouts. As the heat rises, so does the wall between them. Defensive and angry, they retreat—stalemated by their inability to understand each other.

Women complain to each other all the time about not being able to talk to their men about the things that matter most to them—about what they themselves are thinking and feeling, about what goes on in the hearts and minds of the men they're relating to. And men, less able to expose themselves and their conflicts—those within themselves or those with the women in their

Excerpts from *Intimate Strangers* by Lillian Rubin. Copyright © 1983 by Lillian Rubin. Reprinted by permission of Harper and Row, Publishers, Inc. This selection includes parts of Chapters 4, 5 and 7. Lillian Rubin (b. 1924) received her Ph.D. from the University of California at Berkeley and is a practicing psychotherapist. She has also written *Worlds of Pain*.

lives—either turn silent or take cover by holding women up to derision. It's one of the norms of male camaraderie to poke fun at women, to complain laughingly about the mystery of their minds, wonderingly about their ways. Even Freud did it when, in exasperation, he asked mockingly, "What do women want? Dear God, what do they want?"

But it's not a joke—not for the women, not for the men who like to pretend it is.

> The whole goddamn business of what you're calling intimacy bugs the hell out of me. I never know what you women mean when you talk about it. Karen complains that I don't talk to her, but it's not talk she wants, it's some other damn thing, only I don't know what the hell it is. Feelings, she keeps asking for. So what am I supposed to do if I don't have any to give her or to talk about just because she decides it's time to talk about feelings? Tell me, will you; maybe we can get some peace around here.

The expression of such conflicts would seem to validate the common understandings that suggest that women want and need intimacy more than men do—that the issue belongs to women alone; that, if left to themselves, men would not suffer it. But things are not always what they seem. And I wonder: "If men would renounce intimacy, what is their stake in relationships with women?"

Some would say that men need women to tend to their daily needs—to prepare their meals, clean their houses, wash their clothes, rear their children—so that they can be free to attend to life's larger problems. And, given the traditional structure of roles in the family, it has certainly worked that way most of the time. But, if that were all men seek, why is it that, even when they're not relating to women, so much of their lives is spent in search of a relationship with another, so much agony experienced when it's not available?

These are difficult issues to talk about—even to think about—because the subject of intimacy isn't just complicated, it's slippery as well. Ask yourself: What is intimacy? What words come to mind, what thoughts?

It's an idea that excites our imagination, a word that seems larger than life to most of us. It lures us, beckoning us with a power we're unable to resist. And, just because it's so seductive, it frightens us as well—seeming sometimes to be some mysterious force from outside ourselves that, if we let it, could sweep us away.

But what is it we fear?

Asked what intimacy is, most of us—men and women—struggle to say something sensible, something that we can connect with the real experience of our lives. "Intimacy is knowing there's someone who cares about the children as much as you do." "Intimacy is a history of shared experience." "It's sitting there having a cup of coffee together and watching the eleven-o'clock news." "It's knowing you care about the same things." "It's knowing she'll always understand." "It's him sitting in the hospital for hours at a time when I was sick." "It's knowing he cares when I'm hurting." "It's standing by me when I was out of work." "It's seeing each other at our worst." "It's sitting across the breakfast table." "It's talking when you're in the bathroom." "It's knowing we'll begin and end each day together."

These seem the obvious things—the things we expect when we commit our lives to one another in a marriage, when we decide to have children together. And they're not to be dismissed as inconsequential. They make up the daily experience of our lives together, setting the tone for a relationship in important and powerful ways. It's sharing such commonplace, everyday events that determines the temper and the texture of life, that keeps us living together even when other aspects of the relationship seem less than perfect. Knowing someone is there, is constant, and can be counted on in just the ways these thoughts express provides the background of emotional security and stability we look for when we enter a marriage. Certainly a marriage and the people in it will be tested and judged quite differently in an unusual situation or in a crisis. But how often does life present us with circumstances and events that are so out of the range of ordinary experience?

These ways in which a relationship feels intimate on a daily basis are only one part of what we mean by intimacy, however—the part that's most obvious, the part that doesn't awaken our fears. At a lecture where I spoke of these issues recently, one man commented also, "Intimacy is putting aside the masks we wear in the rest of our lives." A murmur of assent ran through the audience of a hundred or so. Intuitively we say "yes." Yet this is the very issue that also complicates our intimate relationships.

On the one hand, it's reassuring to be able to put away the public persona—to believe we can be loved for who we *really* are, that we can show our shadow side without fear, that our vulnerabilities will not be counted against us. "The most important thing is to feel I'm accepted just the way I am," people will say.

But there's another side. For, when we show ourselves thus without the masks, we also become anxious and fearful. "Is it possible that someone could love the *real* me?" we're likely to ask. Not the most promising question for the further development of intimacy, since it suggests that, whatever else another might do or feel, it's we who have trouble loving ourselves. Unfortunately, such misgivings are not usually experienced consciously. We're aware only that our discomfort has risen, that we feel a need to get away. For the person who has seen the "real me" is also the one who reflects back to us an image that's usually not wholly to our liking. We get angry at that, first at ourselves for not living up to our own expectations, then at the other, who becomes for us the mirror of our self-doubts—a displacement of hostility that serves intimacy poorly.

There's yet another level—one that's further below the surface of consciousness, therefore, one that's much more difficult for us to grasp, let alone to talk about. I'm referring to the differences in the ways in which women and men deal with their inner emotional lives—differences that create barriers between us that can be high indeed. It's here that we see how those early childhood experiences of separation and individuation—the psychological tasks that were required of us in order to separate from mother, to distinguish ourselves as autonomous persons, to internalize a firm sense of gender identity—take their toll on our intimate relationships.

Stop a woman in mid-sentence with the question, "What are you feeling right now?" and you might have to wait a bit while she reruns the mental tape to capture the moment just passed. But, more than likely, she'll be able to do it successfully. More than likely, she'll think for a while and come up with an answer.

The same is not true of a man. For him, a similar question usually will bring a sense of wonderment that one would even ask it, followed quickly by an uncomprehending and puzzled response. "What do you mean?" he'll ask. "I was just talking," he'll say.

* * *

This is the single most dispiriting dilemma of relations between women and men. He complains, "She's so emotional, there's no point in talking to her." She protests, "It's him you can't talk to, he's always so darned rational." He says, "Even when I tell her nothing's the matter, she won't quit." She says, "How can I believe him when I can see with my own eyes that something's wrong?" He says, "Okay, so something's wrong! What good will it do to tell her?" She cries, "What are we married for? What do you need me for, just to wash your socks?"

These differences in the psychology of women and men are born of a complex interaction between society and the individual. At the broadest social level is the rending of thought and feeling that is such a fundamental part of Western thought. Thought, defined as the ultimate good, has been assigned to men; feeling, considered at best a problem, has fallen to women.

So firmly fixed have these ideas been that, until recently, few thought to question them. For they were built into the structure of psychological thought as if they spoke to an eternal, natural, and scientific truth. Thus, even such a great and innovative thinker as Carl Jung wrote, "The woman is increasingly aware that love alone can give her her full stature, just as the man begins to discern that spirit alone can endow his life with its highest meaning. Fundamentally, therefore, both seek a psychic relation one to the other, because love needs the spirit, and the spirit love, for their fulfillment."[1]

For a woman, "love"; for a man, "spirit"—each expected to complete the other by bringing to the relationship the missing half. In German, the word that is translated here as spirit is *Geist*. But *The New Cassell's German Dictionary* shows that another primary meaning of *Geist* is "mind, intellect, intelligence, wit, imagination, sense of reason." And, given the context of these words, it seems reasonable that *Geist* for Jung referred to a man's highest essence—his mind. There's no ambiguity about a woman's calling, however. It's love.

Intuitively, women try to heal the split that these definitions of male and female have foisted upon us.

> I can't stand that he's so damned unemotional and expects me to be the same. He lives in his head all the time, and he acts like anything that's emotional isn't worth dealing with.

Cognitively, even women often share the belief that the rational side, which seems to come so naturally to men, is the more mature, the more desirable.

> I know I'm too emotional, and it causes problems between us. He can't stand it when I get emotional like that. It turns him right off.

Her husband agrees that she's "too emotional" and complains:

> Sometimes she's like a child who's out to test her parents. I have to be careful when she's like that not to let her rile me up because otherwise all hell would break loose. You just can't reason with her when she gets like that.

It's the rational-man-hysterical-woman script, played out again and again by two people whose emotional repertoire is so limited that they have few real options. As the interaction between them continues, she reaches for the strongest tools she has, the mode she's most comfortable and familiar with: She becomes progressively more emotional and expressive. He falls back on his best weapons: He becomes more rational, more determinedly reasonable. She cries for him to attend to her feelings, whatever they may be. He tells her coolly, with a kind of clenched-teeth reasonableness, that it's silly for her to feel that way, that she's just being emotional. And of course she is. But that dismissive word "just" is the last straw. She gets so upset that she does, in fact, seem hysterical. He gets so bewildered by the whole interaction that his only recourse is to build the wall of reason even higher. All of which makes things measurably worse for both of them.

*   *   *

It should be understood: Commitment itself is not a problem for a man; he's good at that. He can spend a lifetime living in the same family, working at the same job—even one he hates. And he's not without an inner emotional life.

But when a relationship requires the sustained verbal expression of that inner life and the full range of feelings that accompany it, then it becomes burdensome for him. He can act out anger and frustration inside the family, it's true. But ask him to express his sadness, his fear, his dependency—all those feelings that would expose his vulnerability to himself or to another—and he's likely to close down as if under some compulsion to protect himself.

All requests for such intimacy are difficult for a man, but they become especially complex and troublesome in relations with women. It's another of those paradoxes. For, to the degree that it's possible for him to be emotionally open with anyone, it is with a woman—a tribute to the power of the childhood experience with mother. Yet it's that same early experience and his need to repress it that raises his ambivalence and generates his resistance.

He moves close, wanting to share some part of himself with her, trying to do so, perhaps even yearning to experience again the bliss of the infant's connection with a woman. She responds, woman style—wanting to touch him just a little more deeply, to know what he's thinking, feeling, fearing, wanting. And the fear closes in—the fear of finding himself again in the grip of a powerful woman, of allowing her admittance only to be betrayed and abandoned once again, of being overwhelmed by denied desires.

So he withdraws.

It's not in consciousness that all this goes on. He knows, of course, that he's distinctly uncomfortable when pressed by a woman for more intimacy in the relationship, but he doesn't know why. And, very often, his behavior doesn't please him any more than it pleases her: But he can't seem to help it.

That's his side of the ambivalence that leads to the approach-avoidance dance we see so often in relations between men and women.[2] What about her side?

On the surface, she seems to have little problem in dealing with closeness in a relationship. She's the one who keeps calling for more intimacy, who complains that he doesn't share himself fully enough, doesn't tell her what he's thinking and feeling. And while there's a partial truth in this imagery, the reality is more complex. Thus, when, as is sometimes the case, a woman meets a man who seems capable of the kind of intimacy she says she longs for, dreams about, we see that it's not just a matter of a woman who keeps asking for more in a relationship and a man who keeps protesting. Instead, we hear the other side of the story, as these words from a thirty-year-old patient show. Her blond curly head bent low, she sat in my office and wept bitterly:

> I can't figure out what's happening to me. I'm so anxious and churning inside I can't stand it. I try to read a book, and I find myself thinking of him. But it's not loving thoughts; it's critical, picky thoughts—anything negative, just to get me out of the relationship. Then, once I've con-

vinced myself, I wonder: Why did I love him yesterday? And, if I did, how can it feel so miserable today? I get so confused I want to run and hide just to get away. But now I understand better what I'm scared of; I know it's my problem. I can't tolerate the intimacy, but I can't just break off the relationship like I used to and justify my escape by talking about his faults and inadequacies. But, at times, I actually feel myself being torn apart by this conflict going on inside me. [Tears streaming down her cheeks] How could it be such a burden to be loved?

It would be easy, and perhaps more comfortable, to write her off as some pathological case, a study in extremes that most of us have no reason to be concerned about. In fact, she's a woman in one of our most honored professions, a competent, highly functional person whose professional and personal life would seem to most of us the very model of accomplishment—good friends, a wide range of social and cultural activities, an active and committed work life. Altogether an intelligent, appealing, personable woman. The difference between her and so many others like her is only that, in the course of her therapy, she has learned to identify the cause of the anxiety that usually remains unrecognized, therefore, nameless and formless.

Most women know when a relationship makes them uncomfortable; they just have no idea why. They blame it on something particular about the person—he's too smart or not smart enough; he's too short or too tall; he's too passive or too aggressive; he's too successful or not successful enough; he's too needy or seems too self-contained. Some good reasons, some bad. Some true, some not. More to the point is how quickly a woman will rush for her checklist, how easily she will find ways to dismiss this person whose nearness is making her uneasy.

But even those women who are more able to tolerate closeness, who have fewer problems in sustaining a long-term relationship, are not without ambivalence about just how much of themselves they want to share, and when and how they want to do it. Trying to explain to me the one thing she thought most important in the success of her thirty-four-year marriage, one woman said almost casually, "It's worked so well because we both keep very busy and we don't see that much of each other." A sentiment she was not alone in expressing.

* * *

WIFE: *I say that foreplay begins in the morning.*

HUSBAND: *It seems to me being sexual would make us closer, but she says it works the other way—if she felt closer, there'd be more sex.*

It's a common complaint in marriages—wives and husbands all too often divided as these two are. We wonder about it, ask each other questions, try to persuade the other with reason, and, when that fails, we argue. Sooner or later we make up, telling each other that we'll change. And, in the moment the words are said, we mean them. We try, but somehow the promises aren't fulfilled; somehow, without thought or intention, we slip back into the old ways. The cycle starts again; the struggle is resumed.

We're told by the experts that the problem exists because we don't communicate properly. We must talk to each other, they insist—explain what we need and want, what feels good, what bad. So "communication" has become a household word, the buzzword of the age. We think about it, talk about it, read books, take courses, see therapists to learn how to do it. We come away from these endeavors with resolutions that promise we'll change our ways, that we'll work with our partner on being more open and more expressive about what we're thinking and feeling. But too often our good intentions come to naught, especially when it comes to reconciling our sexual differences.

These are difficult issues, not easily amenable to intervention by talk, no matter how earnest, how compelling our efforts at honesty may be. One couple, aged thirty-three and thirty-five, married eight years and the parents of two children, told of these differences. Speaking quickly and agitatedly, the wife said:

> Talk, talk, talk! He tries to convince me; I try to convince him. What's the use? It's not the words that are missing. I don't even know if the problem is that we don't understand each other. We understand, all right. But we don't like what we know; that's the problem.

Her husband's words came more slowly, tinged as they were with resignation and frustration.

> I understand what she wants. She wants us to be loving and close, then we can have sex. But it's not always possible that way. We're both busy; there are the kids. It can't be like a love affair all the time, and if we have to wait for that, well [his words trailing off] . . . what the hell, it'll be a long wait.

The wife, speaking more calmly but with her emotional turmoil still evident just below the surface of her words:

> He complains that I want it to be like a love affair, but that's not it. I want to feel some emotion from him; I want an emotional contact, not just a sexual one.

The husband, vexed and bewildered:

> When she starts talking about how I'm sexual but not emotional, that's it; that's where I get lost. Isn't sex emotional, for Christ's sake?

From both husband and wife, an angry yet plaintive cry. It's not words that divide them, however. They tell each other quite openly what they think, how they feel. It just doesn't seem to help in the ways they would wish. But, if it's not a simple matter of communication, then what is it that makes these issues seem so intransigent, so resistant to resolution even with the best intentions we can muster?

Some analysts of society point to the culture, to the ideologies that have defined the limits of male and female sexuality. Certainly there's truth in that. There's no gainsaying that, through the ages of Western society, women's sexuality has come under attack, that there have been sometimes extreme pressures to control and confine it—even to deny its existence. There's no doubt either that we have dealt with male sexuality with much more ambivalence. On the one hand, it too has been the object of efforts at containment; on the other, we have acknowledged its force and power—indeed, built myth and monument in homage to what we have taken to be its inherently uncontrollable nature.

Such social attitudes about male and female sexuality, and the behavioral ideals that have accompanied them, not only shape our sexual behavior but affect our experience of our own sexuality as well. For culture both clarifies and mystifies. A set of beliefs is at once a way of seeing the world more clearly while, at the same time, foreclosing an alternative vision. When it comes to sex—precisely because it's such a primitive, elemental force—all societies seek some control over it and, therefore, the mystification is greater than the clarification. Thus, for example, Victorian women often convinced themselves that they had no sexual feelings even when the messages their bodies sent would have told them otherwise if they had been able to listen. And, even now, men often engage in compulsive sexual behavior that brings them little, if any, pleasure without allowing themselves to notice the joylessness of it. Both behaviors a response to cultural mandates, both creating dissonance, if not outright conflict, when inner experience is at odds with behavioral expectations.

The blueprint to which our sexuality conforms, then, is drawn by the culture. But that's not yet the whole story. The dictates of any society are reinforced by its institutional arrangements and mediated by the personal experience of the people who must live within them. And it's in that confluence of social arrangement and psychological response that we'll come to understand the basis of the sexual differences that so often divide us from each other.

For a woman, there's no satisfactory sex without an emotional connection; for a man, the two are more easily separable. For her, the connection generally must precede the sexual encounter:

> For me to be excited about making love, I have to feel close to him—like we're sharing something, not just living together.

For him, emotional closeness can be born of the sexual contact.

> It's the one subject we never get anywhere on. It's a lot easier for me to tell her what she wants to hear when I feel close, and that's when I get closest—when we're making love. It's kind of hard to explain it, but [trying to find the words] . . . well, it's when the emotions come roaring up.

The issues that divide them around intimacy in the relationship are nowhere to be seen more clearly than here. When she speaks of connection, she usually means intimacy that's born of some verbal expression, some sharing of thought and feeling:

> I want to know what he's thinking—you know, what's going on inside him—before we jump into bed.

For him, it's enough that they're in the same room.

> To me, it feels like there's a nice bond when we're together—just reading the paper or watching the tube or something like that. Then, when we go to bed, that's not enough for her.

The problem, then, is not *how* we talk to each other but *whether* we do so. And it's connected to what words and the verbal expression of emotion mean to us, how sex and emotion come together for each of us, and the fact that we experience the balance between the two so differently—all of which takes us again to the separation and individuation experiences of childhood.

For both boys and girls, the earliest attachment and the identification that grows from it are much larger, deeper, and more all-embracing than anything we, who have successfully buried that primitive past in our unconscious, can easily grasp. Their root is pure eros—that vital, life-giving force with which all attachment begins. The infant bathes in it. But we are a society of people who have learned to look on eros with apprehension, if not outright fear. For us, it is associated with passion, with sex, with forces that threaten to be out of our control. And we teach our young very early, and in ways too numerous to count, about the need to limit the erotic, about our fears that eros imperils civilization.

In the beginning, it's the same for children of either sex. As the child grows past the early symbiotic union with mother, as the boundaries of self begin to develop, the social norms about sexuality begin to make themselves felt. In conformity with those norms, the erotic and emotional are split one from the other, and the erotic takes on a more specifically sexual meaning.

But here the developmental similarities end. For a boy at this stage, it's the emotional component of the attachment to mother that comes under attack as he seeks to repress his identification with her. The erotic—or sexualized—aspect of the attachment is left undisturbed, at least in heterosexual men. To be sure, the incest taboo assures that future sexual *behavior* will take place with a woman other than mother. But the issue here is not behavior but the emotional structure that underlies it.

For a girl, the developmental requirement is exactly the opposite. For her, it's the erotic component of the attachment to a woman that must be denied and shifted later to a man; the larger emotional involvement and the identification remain intact.

This split between the emotional and the erotic components of attachment in childhood has deep and lasting significance for the ways in which we respond to relationships—sexual and otherwise—in adulthood. For it means that, for men, the erotic aspect of any relationship remains forever the most compelling, while, for women, the emotional component will always be the more salient. It's here that we can come to understand the depth of women's emotional connection to each other—the reasons why nonsexual friendships between women remain so central in their lives, so important to their sense of themselves and to their well-being. And it's here also that we can see why nonsexual relationships hold such little emotional charge for men.

It's not, as folklore has held, that a woman's sexual response is more muted than a man's, or that she doesn't need or desire sexual release the way a man does. But, because it's the erotic aspect of her earliest attachment that has to be repressed in childhood if a girl is later to form a sexual bond with a man, the explicitly sexual retains little *independent* status in her inner life. A man may lust after *women*, but a woman lusts after *a man*. For a woman, sex usually has meaning only in a relational context—perhaps a clue to why so many girls never or rarely masturbate in adolescence or early adulthood.

We might argue that the social proscriptions against masturbation alone could account for its insignificance in girls and young women. But boys, too, hear exhortations against masturbation—indeed, even today, many still are told tales of the horrors that will befall them. Yet, except to encourage guilt and secrecy, such injunctions haven't made much difference in its incidence among them.

It would be reasonable to assume that this is a response to the mixed message this society sends to men about their sexuality. On the one hand, they're expected to exercise restraint; on the other, there's an implicit understanding that we can't really count on them to do so—that, at base, male sexuality cannot be controlled, that, after all, boys will be boys.

Surely such differences in the ways in which male and female sexuality are viewed could account for some of the differences between the sexes in their patterns and incidence of masturbation. But I believe there's something else that makes the social prohibitions take so well with women. For with them, an emotional connection in a relationship generally is a stimulus, if not a precondition, for the erotic.

If women depend on the emotional attachment to call up the sexual, men rely on the sexual to spark the emotional, as these words from a forty-one-year-old man, married fourteen years, show:

> Having sex with her makes me feel much closer so it makes it easier to bridge the emotional gap, so to speak. It's like the physical sex opens up another door, and things and feelings can get expressed that I couldn't before.

For women, emotional attachments without sex are maintained with little difficulty or discomfort; for men, they're much more problematic. It's not that they don't exist at all, but that they're less common and fraught with many more difficulties and reservations.

This is the split that may help to explain why men tend to be fearful of homosexuality in a way that women are not. I don't mean by this that women welcome homosexual stirrings any more than men do. But, for women, the emotional and the erotic are separated in such a way that they can be intensely connected emotionally without fear that this will lead to a sexual connection. For men, where the emotional connection so often depends on a sexual one, a close emotional relationship with another man usually is experienced as a threat.

* * *

The fear that each of them experiences is an archaic one—the remnants of the separation-unity conflict of childhood that's brought to the surface again at the moment of sexual union. The response is patterned and predictable. He fears engulfment; she fears invasion. Their emotional history combines with cultural mandates about femininity and masculinity to prepare them each for their own side; their physiology does the rest.

For men, the repression of their first identification and the muting of *emotional* attachment that goes with it fit neatly with cultural proscriptions about manliness that require them to abjure the emotional side of life in favor of the rational. Sex, therefore, becomes the one arena where it is legitimate for men to contact their deeper feeling states and to express them.

Indeed, all too often, the sex act carries most of the burden of emotional expression for men—a reality of their lives that may explain the urgency with which men so often approach sex. For, if sex is the main conduit through which inhibited emotions are animated, expressed, and experienced, then that imperative and compulsive quality that seems such a puzzle becomes understandable.

But the act of entry itself stirs old conflictual desires that must be contained. This is the moment a man hungers for, while it's also the instant of his greatest vulnerability. As a woman takes him into her body, there are both ecstasy and fear—the ecstasy of union with a woman once again; the fear of being engulfed by her, of somehow losing a part of himself that he's struggled to maintain through the years.

For a woman, the repression of her first *erotic* attachment is also a good fit with the cultural proscriptions against the free expression of her sexuality. But, in childhood, there was no need to make any assault on her first identification with mother and the deep emotional attachment that lay beneath it; no need, either, to differentiate herself as fully and firmly as was necessary for a male child. In adulthood, therefore, she remains concerned with the fluidity of her boundaries, on guard against their permeability—a concern that's activated most fully at the moment of penetration.

This is one of those moments in life when the distinction between fantasy and reality is blurred by the fact that the two actually look so much alike. With entry, her boundaries have been violated, her body invaded. It's just this that may explain why a woman so often avoids the sexual encounter—a common complaint in marriages—even when she will also admit to finding it pleasurable and gratifying once she gets involved. For there are both pleasure and pain—the pleasure of experiencing the union, the pain of the intrusion that violates her sometimes precarious sense of her own separateness. Together, these conflicting feelings often create an inertia about sex—not about an emotional connection but about a sexual one—especially when she doesn't feel as if there's enough emotional pay-off in it to make it worth the effort to overcome her resistance to stirring up the conflict again.

This conflict can be seen in its most unvarnished form in the early stages of relations between lesbians. There's a special kind of ecstasy in their sexual relationship just because it's with a woman—because in a woman's arms the boundaries of separateness fall, the dream of a return to the old symbiosis with mother is fulfilled. But the rapture can be short-lived, for the wish for symbiosis belongs to the infant, not the adult. Once achieved, therefore, ecstasy can give way to fear—fear of the loss of self, which is heightened beyond anything known in the sexual bond with a man.

There's anxiety about boundaries in heterosexual sex, of course. But there's also some measure of safety that exists in this union with one's opposite. For, although sex between a man and a woman can be an intensely intimate experience, there's a limit, a boundary between them that can't be crossed simply by virtue of the fact that they're woman and man. It may, indeed, be one of the aspects of sex with a man that a woman finds so seductive—the ability to satisfy sexual need while still retaining the integrity of a separate sense of self. For, in heterosexual sex, the very physical differences help to reassure us of our separateness while, at the same time, permitting a connection with another that's possible in no other act in human life.

* * *

As I write these pages, some questions begin to form in my mind. "Is all this," I wonder, "just another way of saying that women are less sexual than men? What about the women we see all around us today who seem to be as easy with their sexuality as men are, and as emotionally detached?"

Without doubt there are today—perhaps always have been—some women for whom sex and emotion are clearly split. But, when we look beneath the behavior of even the most sexually active woman, most of the time we'll see that it's not just sex that engages her. It's true that such a woman no longer needs to convince herself that she's in love in order to have a sexual relationship with a man. But the key word here is *relationship*—limited, yes, perhaps existing only in a transitory fantasy, but there for her as a reality. And, more often than not, such relationships, even when they are little more than fleeting ones, have meanings other than sexual for a woman. For the sexual stimulus usually is connected to some emotional attachment, however limited it may be. And what, at first glance, might seem simply to be a sexual engagement is, in reality, a search for something else.

We need only listen to women to hear them corroborate what I'm saying here. When asked what it is they get in their more casual sexual encounters, even those who consider themselves the most sexually liberated will generally admit that they're often not orgasmic in such transient relationships. "When I was single, I'd sleep with someone who appealed to me right away, no problems," said a recently married twenty-seven-year-old breezily. "Did you usually have orgasms in those relationships?" I asked her. Laughing, she replied, "Nope, that was reserved." "Reserved for what?" I wanted to know. Saucily, "For the guy who deserved it." "And what does that mean?" Finally, she became serious. "I guess it means I have to trust a guy before I can come with him—like I have to know there's some way of touching him emotionally and that I can trust him enough to let him into that part of me."

"What's in it for you?" I asked all the women who spoke this way. "Why get involved at all if it's not sexually gratifying?" Without exception, they said they engaged sexually because it was the only way they could get the other things they need from a man. "What things?" I wanted to know. The answer: Something that told of their need for relationship and attachment rather than sex. They spoke of wanting "hugging more than fucking," of how it "feels good to be connected for a little while." They talked almost urgently of the "need to be held," "to feel needed by someone," of how important it is that "there's someone to give something to and take something from."

It's true, men also will speak of the need to be held and hugged. But orgasm generally is not in question and hugging is seldom an end to be desired in and for itself. In fact, it's one of the most common complaints of women that, even in the context of a stable relationship, such tender physical contact becomes too quickly transformed into a prelude to sex. "Why can't he just be happy to hold me; why does it always have to lead to fucking?" a woman complains. "I hold her and we hug and cuddle; I like it and I like her to hold me, too. But there's a natural progression, isn't there?" her husband asks, mystified.

* * *

Even before marriage, when love is likely to be felt most intensely, the conflict around love, work, and identity is experienced differently for a man and a woman, the balance between love and work, therefore, weighted differently as well—as is epitomized in this story of a young professional couple who are deeply in love and planning to marry.

They came into my office looking for help in resolving a conflict about where they would live. She has an established career on the West Coast; he has just been offered a job in the East. He started the meeting by saying:

> I know Laura's career is as important to her as mine is, and I respect that. Her ability to make that kind of commitment is part of what I value about her.

"Then what's the problem?" I asked. He replied:

> It's simple; I have a job offer in Philadelphia that I simply can't turn down, and I love her very much and want her to come with me, of course.

Laura told her side this way.

> I feel torn in two by this dilemma. I've never been happier in my life than I have been since I came here. I love my work; my career here is assured—just the kind of work life I dreamed about. I have good friends and a whole support network I can count on. When I think about giving it all up, it's so wrenching I can hardly stand it. But I love Michael, too— very much—and I want to be able to go with him. How do I resolve it?

"Is this the only job Michael can get?" I asked. He answered:

> No, but it's the best one. It's the one that will be the most advantageous for the future of my career. It's a career I've dreamed about all my life and worked very hard for. I just don't see how I can pass up an opportunity like this when it comes my way.

"What if Laura can't make this change? Will that make a difference in your plans?" His body tensed, his voice became anxious:

> I don't see how it could. I don't have a choice; I have to take this job.

"It seems to me," I said, "that's not quite accurate. If you decide to take the job even if she can't or won't go with you, then you *have* made a choice—perhaps one you regret or one you wish you didn't have to make, but a choice nevertheless. And it's important that both of you be clear about that." Looking surprised, he responded thoughtfully:

> I suppose that's true; I hadn't thought about it that way. But it doesn't *feel* like a choice. If I don't take this opportunity, I'll never know what I could have done and how far I could go. I can't pass it up; I can't. I love her desperately, and I need her, but I have to go.

"And what about you, Laura? What does it feel like to hear Michael say he has to go whether you join him or not." She listened to my words with her head in her hands, then, lifting her tear-stained face, she spoke in anguish:

> I don't know, I just don't know. I understand how he feels and I know he does have to take the job. I keep telling myself I can stake out a place for myself in Philadelphia just like I've done here.

"Have you asked Michael to take a compromise job here so that you wouldn't have to make this move?"

> Of course we've talked about it, but it's not a serious consideration. I know he can't do it without feeling abused and deprived. And what good would that be for our relationship?

"And you? How will you feel if you give up what you have here for him knowing that he couldn't do it for you?"

> That's what I'm trying so hard to decide. But, you know, it makes me very angry with myself that I can't do it with good grace. Then I get angry that

I even think that way because it's so typical of what women do. But the truth is I know it would be easier for me to do it than for him. That's just the way it still is, I guess.

Damnit, won't it ever change? Will it always be like this—men doing their damn number and we women doing ours? He says he loves me, and I know he does; I haven't any doubt about his devotion. But, if it interferes with his career plans, he knows what he has to do. And look at me, ready to throw up my life and follow him. Do I love him any more than he loves me? I don't think so. It's only that when a man puts love and work on the scale you know what loses. [Sighing deeply] I sometimes think we're doomed.

There's no denying that things have changed. Many more men than ever before are now genuinely involved in family life, just as many more women are committed to work in ways that are new. And there's no denying either that the conflicts they suffer over how their time is divided, the decisions they make when they must choose, the inner experience about what defines them and what places them in the world are still very much related to their gender. Generally, men still are best at the cognitive, rational mode that work requires, so it's where they turn for validation. Usually, women still are more comfortable in the emotional and experiential mode that interpersonal connections require, so that's where they look for fulfillment. For men, therefore, it's still work that gets their first allegiance, if not in word, then in deed; for women, it's still love.

NOTES

1. Carl Gustav Jung, *Contributions to Analytical Psychology* (New York: Harcourt, Brace & Co., 1928), p. 185.

2. Given the recent struggle to loosen traditional definitions of masculinity and femininity, we might assume that there would be differences in the intimate relations of men who are twenty-five and those who are fifty. And, although the younger men are likely to be more openly concerned with these issues, all the research evidence—my own and others'—suggests that integrating that concern into their behavior has been met with difficulties which, while usually not understood, parallel the issues I have been writing of here.

LOVE IN A
SEXIST SOCIETY

Shulamith Firestone

LOVE

HOW DOES THIS phenomenon "love" operate? Contrary to popular opinion, love is not altruistic. The initial attraction is based on curious admiration (more often today, envy and resentment) for the self-possession, the integrated unity, of the other and a wish to become part of this Self in some way (today, read: intrude or take over), to become important to that psychic balance. The self-containment of the other creates desire (read: a challenge); admiration (envy) of the other becomes a wish to incorporate (possess) its qualities. A clash of selves follows in which the individual attempts to fight off the growing hold over him of the other. Love is the final opening up to (or, surrender to the dominion of) the other. The lover demonstrates to the beloved how he himself would like to be treated. ("I tried so hard to make him fall in love with me that I fell in love with him myself.") Thus love is the height of selfishness: the self attempts to enrich itself through the absorption of another being. Love is being psychically wide-open to another. It is a situation of total emotional vulnerability. Therefore it must be not only the incorporation of the other, but an *exchange* of selves. Anything short of a mutual exchange will hurt one or the other party.

There is nothing inherently destructive about this process. A little healthy selfishness would be a refreshing change. Love between two equals would be an enrichment, each enlarging himself through the other: instead of being one, locked in the cell of himself with only his own experience and view, he could participate in the existence of another—an extra window on the world. This accounts for the bliss that successful lovers experience: Lovers are temporarily freed from the burden of isolation that every individual bears.

But bliss in love is seldom the case: For every successful contemporary love experience, for every short period of enrichment, there are ten destructive love experiences, post-love "downs" of much longer duration—often resulting in the destruction of the individual, or at least an emotional cynicism that makes it difficult or impossible ever to love again. Why should this be so, if it is not actually inherent in the love process itself?

Let's talk about love in its destructive guise—and why it gets that way, referring once more to the work of Theodore Reik. Reik's concrete observation brings him closer than many better minds to understanding the *process* of "falling in love," but he is off insofar as he confuses love as it exists in our present society with love itself. He notes that love is a reaction formation, a cycle of envy, hostility, and possessiveness: He sees that it is preceded by dissatisfaction with oneself, a yearning for something better, created by a discrepancy between the ego and the ego-ideal; that the bliss love produces is due to the resolution of this tension by the substitution, in place of one's own ego-ideal, of the other; and finally that love fades "because the other can't live up to your high ego-ideal any more than you could, and the judgment will be the harsher the higher are the claims on oneself." Thus in Reik's view love wears down just as it wound up: Dissatisfaction with oneself (whoever heard of falling in love the week one is leaving for Europe?) leads to astonishment at the other person's self-containment; to envy; to hostility; to possessive love; and back again through exactly the same process. This is the love process *today*. But why must it be this way?

Many, for example Denis de Rougemont in *Love in the Western World*, have tried to draw a distinction between romantic "falling in love" with its "false reciprocity which disguises a twin narcissism" (the Pagan Eros) and an unselfish love for the other person as that person really is (the Christian Agape). De Rougemont attributes the morbid passion of Tristan and Iseult (romantic love) to a vulgarization of specific mystical and religious currents in Western civilization.

I submit that love is essentially a much simpler phenomenon—it becomes complicated, corrupted, or obstructed by *an unequal balance of power*. We have seen that love demands a mutual vulnerability or it turns destructive: the destructive effects of love occur only in a context of inequality. But because sexual inequality has remained a constant—however its *degree* may have varied—the corruption "romantic" love became characteristic of love between the sexes.

* * *

How does the sex class system based on the unequal power distribution of the biological family affect love between the sexes? In discussing Freudianism, we have gone into the psychic structuring of the individual within the family and how this organization of personality must be different for the male and the female because of their very different relationships to the mother. At present the insular interdependency of the mother/child relationship forces both male and female children into anxiety about losing the mother's love, on which they depend for physical survival. When later (Erich Fromm notwithstanding) the child learns that the mother's love is conditional, to be rewarded the child in return for approved behavior (that is, behavior in line with the mother's own values and personal ego gratification—for she is free to mold the child "creatively," however she happens to define that), the child's anxiety turns into desperation. This, coinciding with the sexual rejection of the male child by the mother, causes, as we have seen, a schizophrenia in the boy between the emotional and the physical, and in the girl, the mother's rejection, occurring for different reasons, produces an insecurity about her identity in general, creating a life-long need for approval. (Later her lover replaces her father as a grantor of the necessary surrogate identity—she sees everything through his eyes.) Here originates the hunger for love that later sends both sexes searching in one person after the other for a state of ego security. But because of the early rejection, to the degree that it occurred, the male will be terrified of committing himself, of "opening up" and then being smashed. How this affects his sexuality we have seen: To the degree that a woman is like his mother, the incest taboo operates to restrain his total sexual/emotional commitment; for him to feel safely the kind of total response he first felt for his mother, which was rejected, he must degrade this woman so as to distinguish her from the mother. This behavior reproduced on a larger scale explains many cultural phenomena, including perhaps the ideal love-worship of chivalric times, the forerunner of modern romanticism.

Romantic idealization is partially responsible, at least on the part of men, for a peculiar characteristic of "falling" in love: the change takes place in the lover almost independently of the character of the love object. Occasionally the lover, though beside himself, sees with another rational part of his faculties that, objectively speaking, the one he loves isn't worth all this blind devotion; but he is helpless to act on this, "a slave to love." More often he fools himself entirely. But others can see what is happening ("How on earth he could love her is beyond me!"). This idealization occurs much less frequently on the part of women, as is borne out by Reik's clinical studies. A man must idealize one woman over the rest in order to justify his descent to a lower caste. Women have no such reason to idealize men—in fact, when one's life depends on one's ability to "psych" men out, such idealization may actually be dangerous—though a fear of male power in general may carry over into relationships with individual men, appearing to be the same phenomenon. But though women know to be inauthentic this male "falling in love," all women, in one way or another, require proof of it from men before they can allow themselves to love (genuinely, in their case) in return. For this idealization process acts to artificially equalize the two parties, a minimum precondition for the development of an uncorrupted love—we have seen that love requires a mutual vulnerability that is impossible to achieve in an unequal power situation. *Thus "falling in love" is no more than the process of alteration of male vision—through idealization, mystification, glorification—that renders void the woman's class inferiority.*

However, the woman knows that this idealization, which she works so hard to produce, is a lie, and that it is only a matter of time before he "sees through her." Her life is a hell, vacillating between an all-consuming need for male love and approval to raise her from her class subjection, to persistent feelings of inauthenticity when she does achieve his love. Thus her whole identity hangs in the balance of her love life. She is allowed to love herself only if a man finds her worthy of love.

But if we could eliminate the political context of love between the sexes, would we not have some degree of idealization remaining in the love process itself? I think so. For the process occurs in the same manner whoever the love choice: the lover "opens up" to the other. Because of this fusion of egos, in which each sees and cares about the other as a new self, the beauty/character of the beloved, perhaps hidden to outsiders under layers of defenses, is revealed. "I wonder what she sees in him," then, means not only, "She is a fool, blinded with romanticism," but, "Her love has lent her x-ray vision. Perhaps we are missing something." (Note that this phrase is most commonly used about women. The equivalent phrase about *men's* slavery to love is more often something like, "She has him wrapped around her finger," she has him so "snowed" that he is the last one to see through her.) Increased sensitivity to the real, if hidden, values in the other, however, is not "blindness" or "idealization" but is, in fact, deeper vision. It is only the *false* idealization we have described above that is responsible for the destruction. Thus it is not the process of love itself that is at fault, but its *political*, i.e., unequal *power* context: the who, why, when and where of it is what makes it now such a holocaust.

* * *

Men can't love. We have seen why it is that men have difficulty loving and that while men may love, they usually "fall in love"—with their own projected image. Most often they are pounding down a woman's door one day, and thoroughly disillusioned with her the next; but it is rare for women to leave men, and then it is usually for more than ample reason.

It is dangerous to feel sorry for one's oppressor—women are especially prone to this failing—but I am tempted to do it in this case. Being unable to love is hell. This is the way it proceeds: as soon as the man feels any pressure from the other partner to commit himself, he panics and may react in one of several ways:

1) He may rush out and screw ten other women to prove that the first woman has no hold over him. If she accepts this, he may continue to see her on this basis. The other women verify his (false) freedom; periodic arguments about them keep his panic at bay. But the women are a paper tiger, for nothing very deep could be happening with them anyway: he is balancing them against each other so that none of them can get much of him. Many smart women, recognizing this to be only a safety valve on their man's anxiety, give him "a long leash." For the real issue under all the fights about other women is that the man is unable to commit himself.

2) He may consistently exhibit unpredictable behavior, standing her up frequently, being indefinite about the next date, telling her that "my work comes first," or offering a variety of other excuses. That is, though he senses her anxiety, he refuses to reassure her in any way, or even to recognize her anxiety as legitimate. For he *needs* her anxiety as a steady reminder that he is still free, that the door is not entirely closed.

3) When he *is* forced into (an uneasy) commitment, he makes her pay for it: by ogling other women in her presence, by comparing her unfavorably to past girlfriends or movie stars, by snide reminders in front of friends that she is his "ball and chain," by calling her a "nag," a "bitch," "a shrew," or by suggesting that if he were only a bachelor he would be a lot better off. His ambivalence about women's "inferiority" comes out: by being committed to one, he has somehow made the hated female identification, which he now must repeatedly deny if he is to maintain his self-respect in the (male) community. This steady derogation is not entirely put on: for in fact every other girl suddenly does look a lot better, he can't help feeling he has missed something—and, naturally, his woman is to blame. For he has never given up the search for the ideal; she has forced him to resign from it. Probably he will go to his grave feeling cheated, never realizing that there isn't much difference between one woman and the other, that it is the loving that *creates* the difference.

There are many variations of straining at the bit. Many men go from one casual thing to another, getting out every time it begins to get hot. And yet to live without love in the end proves intolerable to men just as it does to women.

The question that remains for every normal male is, then, *how do I get someone to love me without her demanding an equal commitment in return?*

Women's "clinging" behavior is required by the objective social situation. The female *response* to such a situation of male hysteria at any prospect of mutual commitment was the development of subtle methods of manipulation, to force as much commitment as *could* be forced from men. Over the centuries strategies have been devised, tested, and passed on from mother to daughter in secret tête-à-têtes, passed around at "kaffee-klatsches" ("I never understand what it is women spend so much time talking about!"), or, in recent times, via the telephone. These are not trivial gossip sessions at all (as women prefer men to believe), but desperate strategies for survival. More real brilliance goes into one one-hour coed telephone dialogue about men than into that same coed's four years of college study, or for that matter, than into most male political maneuvers. It is no wonder, then, that even the few women without "family obligations" always arrive exhausted at the starting line of any serious endeavor. It takes one's major energy for the best portion of one's creative years to "make a good catch," and a good part of the rest of one's life to "hold" that catch. ("To be in love can be a full-time job for a woman, like that of a profession for a man.") Women who choose to drop out of this race are choosing a life without love, something that, as we have seen, most *men* don't have the courage to do.

But unfortunately The Manhunt is characterized by an emotional urgency beyond this simple desire for return commitment. It is compounded by the very class reality that produced the male inability to love in the first place. In a male-run society that defines women as an inferior and parasitical class, a woman who does not achieve male approval in some form is doomed. To legitimate her existence, a woman must be *more* than woman, she must continually search for an out from her inferior definition;[1] and men are the only ones in a position to bestow on her this state of grace. But because the woman is rarely allowed to realize herself through activity in the larger (male) society—and when she is, she is seldom granted the recognition she deserves—it becomes easier to try for the recognition of one man than of many; and in fact this is exactly the choice most women make. Thus once more the phenomenon of love, good in itself, is corrupted by its class context: women must have love not only for healthy reasons but actually to validate their existence.

In addition, the continued *economic* dependence of women makes a situation of healthy love between equals impossible. Women today still live under a system of patronage: With few exceptions, they have the choice, not between either freedom or marriage, but between being either public or private property. Women who merge with a member of the ruling class can at least hope that some of his privilege will, so to speak, rub off. But women without men are in the same situation as orphans: they are a helpless sub-class lacking the protection of the powerful. This is the antithesis of freedom when they are still (negatively) defined by a class situation: for now they are in a situation of *magnified* vulnerability. To participate in one's subjection by choosing one's master often gives the illusion of free choice; but in reality a woman is never free to choose love without external motivations. For her at the present time, the two things, love and status, must remain inextricably intertwined.

Now assuming that a woman does not lose sight of these fundamental factors of her condition when she loves, she will never be able to love gratuitously, but only in exchange for security:

1) the emotional security which, we have seen, she is justified in demanding.

2) the emotional identity which she should be able to find through work and recognition, but which she is denied—thus forcing her to seek her definition through a man.

3) the economic class security that, in this society, is attached to her ability to "hook" a man.

Two of these three demands are invalid conditions for "love," but are imposed on it, weighing it down.

Thus, in their precarious political situation, women can't afford the luxury of spontaneous love. It is much too dangerous. The love and approval of men is all-important. To love thoughtlessly, before one has ensured return commitment, would endanger that approval. Here is Reik:

> It finally became clear during psychoanalysis that the patient was afraid that if she should show a man she loved him, he would consider her inferior and leave her.

For once a woman plunges in emotionally, she will be helpless to play the necessary games: her love would come first, demanding expression. To pretend a coolness she does not feel, *then*, would be too painful, and further, it would be pointless: she would be cutting off her nose to spite her face, for freedom to love is what she was aiming for. But in order to guarantee such a commitment, she *must* restrain her emotions, she *must* play games. For, as we have seen, men do not commit themselves to mutual openness and vulnerability until they are forced to.

How does she then go about forcing this commitment from the male? One of her most potent weapons is sex—she can work him up to a state of physical torment with a variety of games: by denying his need, by teasing it, by giving and taking back, by jealousy, and so forth. A woman under analysis wonders why:

> There are few women who never ask themselves on certain occasions "How hard should I make it for a man?" I think no man is troubled with

questions of this kind. He perhaps asks himself only, "When will she give in?"

Men are right when they complain that women lack discrimination, that they seldom love a man for his individual traits but rather for what he has to offer (his class), that they are calculating, that they use sex to gain other ends, etc. For in fact women are in no position to love freely. If a woman is lucky enough to find "a decent guy" to love her and support her, she is doing well—and usually will be grateful enough to return his love. About the only discrimination women *are* able to exercise is the choice between the men who have chosen them, or a playing off of one male, one power, against the other. But *provoking* a man's interest, and *snaring* his commitment once he has expressed that interest, is not exactly self-determination.

Now what happens after she has finally hooked her man, after he has fallen in love with her and will do anything? She has a new set of problems. Now she can release the vise, open her net, and examine what she has caught. Usually she is disappointed. It is nothing she would have bothered with were *she* a man. It is usually way below her level. (Check this out sometime: Talk to a few of those mousy wives.) "He may be a poor thing, but at least I've got a man of my own" is usually more the way she feels. But at least now she can drop her act. For the first time it is safe to love—now she must try like hell to catch up to him emotionally, to really mean what she has pretended all along. Often she is troubled by worries that he will find her out. She feels like an impostor. She is haunted by fears that he doesn't love the "real" her—and usually she is right. ("She wanted to marry a man with whom she could be as bitchy as she really is.")

This is just about when she discovers that love and marriage mean a different thing for a male than they do for her: Though men in general believe women in general to be inferior, every man has reserved a special place in his mind for the one woman he will elevate above the rest by virtue of association with himself. Until now the woman, out in the cold, begged for his approval, dying to clamber onto this clean well-lighted place. But once there, she realizes that she was elevated above other women not in recognition of her real value, but only because she matched nicely his store-bought pedestal. Probably he doesn't even know who she is (if indeed by this time she herself knows). He has let her in not because he genuinely loved her, but only because she played so well into his preconceived fantasies. Though she knew his love to be false, since she herself engineered it, she can't help feeling contempt for him. But she is afraid, at first, to reveal her true self, for then perhaps even that false love would go. And finally she understands that for him, too, marriage had all kinds of motivations that had nothing to do with love. She was merely the one closest to his fantasy image: she has been named Most Versatile Actress for the multi-role of Alter

Ego, Mother of My Children, Housekeeper, Cook, Companion, in *his* play. She has been bought to fill an empty space in his life; but her life is nothing.

So she has not saved herself from being like other women. She is lifted out of that class only because she now is an appendage of a member of the master class; and he cannot associate with her unless he raises her status. But she has not been freed, she has been promoted to "house-nigger," she has been elevated only to be used in a different way. She feels cheated. She has gotten not love and recognition, but possessorship and control. This is when she is transformed from Blushing Bride to Bitch, a change that, no matter how universal and predictable, still leaves the individual husband perplexed. ("You're not the girl I married.")

* * *

THE CULTURE OF ROMANCE

So far we have not distinguished "romance" from love. For there are not two kinds of love, one healthy (dull) and one not (painful) ("My dear, what you need is a mature love relationship. Get over this romantic nonsense."), but only less-than-love or daily agony. When love takes place in a power context, everyone's "love life" must be affected. Because power and love don't make it together.

So when we talk about romantic love we mean love corrupted by its power context—the sex class system—into a diseased form of love that then in turn reinforces this sex class system. We have seen that the psychological dependence of women upon men is created by continuing real economic and social oppression. However, in the modern world the economic and social bases of the oppression are no longer *alone* enough to maintain it. So the apparatus of romanticism is hauled in. (Looks like we'll have to help her out, Boys!)

Romanticism develops in proportion to the liberation of women from their biology. As civilization advances and the biological bases of sex class crumble, male supremacy must shore itself up with artificial institutions, or exaggerations of previous institutions, e.g., where previously the family had a loose, permeable form, it now tightens and rigidifies into the patriarchal nuclear family. Or, where formerly women had been held openly in contempt, now they are elevated to states of mock worship.[2] Romanticism is a cultural tool of male power to keep women from knowing their condition. It is especially needed—and therefore strongest—in Western countries with the highest rate of industrialization. Today, with technology enabling women to break out of their roles for good—it was a near miss in the early twentieth century— romanticism is at an all-time high.

* * *

The Sex Privatization of Women. Eroticism is only the topmost layer of the romanticism that reinforces female inferiority. As with any lower class, group awareness must be deadened to keep them from rebelling. In this case, because the distinguishing characteristic of women's exploitation as a class is sexual, a special means must be found to make them unaware that they are considered all alike sexually ("cunts"). Perhaps when a man marries he chooses from this undistinguishable lot with care, for as we have seen, he holds a special high place in his mental reserve for "The One," by virtue of her close association with himself; but in general he can't tell the difference between chicks (Blondes, Brunettes, Redheads).³ And he likes it that way. ("A wiggle in your walk, a giggle in your talk, THAT'S WHAT I LIKE!") When a man believes all women are alike, but wants to keep women from guessing, what does he do? He keeps his beliefs to himself, and pretends, to allay her suspicions, that what she has in common with other women is precisely what makes her different. Thus her sexuality eventually becomes synonymous with her individuality. *The sex privatization of women is the process whereby women are blinded to their generality as a class which renders them invisible as individuals to the male eye.* Is not that strange Mrs. Lady next to the President in his entourage reminiscent of the discreet black servant at White House functions?

The process is insidious: When a man exclaims, "I love Blondes!" all the secretaries in the vicinity sit up; they take it personally because they have been sex-privatized. The blonde one feels personally complimented because she has come to measure her worth through the physical attributes that differentiate her from other women. She no longer recalls that any physical attribute you could name is shared by many others, that these are accidental attributes not of her own creation, that her sexuality is shared by half of humanity. But in an authentic recognition of her individuality, her blondeness would be loved, but in a different way: She would be loved first as an irreplaceable totality, and then her blondeness would be loved as one of the characteristics of that totality.

NOTES

1. Thus the peculiar situation that women never object to the insulting of women as a class, *as long as* they individually are excepted. The worst insult for a woman is that she is "just like a woman," i.e., no better; the highest compliment that she has the brains, talent, dignity, or strength of a man. In fact, like every member of an oppressed class, she herself participates in the insulting of others like herself, hoping thereby to make it obvious that *she* as an individual is above their behavior. Thus women as a class are set against each other ["Divide and Conquer"], the "other woman" believing that the wife is a "bitch" who "doesn't understand him," and the wife believing that the other woman

is an "opportunist" who is "taking advantage" of him—while the culprit himself sneaks away free.

2. Gallantry has been commonly defined as "excessive attention to women without serious purpose," but the purpose is very serious: through a false flattery, to keep women from awareness of their lower-class condition.

3. "As for his other sports," says a recent blurb about football hero Joe Namath, "he prefers Blondes."

SUGGESTED READINGS, SECTION I

Chodorow, Nancy. *The Reproduction of Mothering* (Berkeley, CA: The University of California Press, 1978).

De Rougemont, Denis. *Love in the Western World* (New York, NY: Harper and Row, 1974).

Engels, Friedrich. *The Origin of the Family, Private Property, and the State* (New York, NY: International Publishers, 1972).

Freud, Sigmund. *Sexuality and the Psychology of Love*, ed. Philip Rieff (New York, NY: Collier Books, 1963).

Fromm, Erich. *The Art of Loving* (New York, NY: Harper and Row, 1974).

Gilligan, Carol. "The Conquistador and the Dark Continent: Reflections on the Psychology of Love," *Daedalus* 113, No. 3 (1984), pp. 75–95.

Goode, William J. "The Theoretical Importance of Love," in A. Montagu, ed., *The Practice of Love* (Englewood Cliffs, NJ: Prentice Hall, 1975), pp. 120–35.

Masters, William H. and Virginia E. Johnson. *The Pleasure Bond* (Boston, MA: Little, Brown and Co., 1974).

Rapaport, Elizabeth. "On the Future of Love: Rousseau and the Radical Feminists," in A. Soble, ed., *The Philosophy of Sex* (Totowa, NJ: Littlefield, Adams, 1980), pp. 369–88.

Slater, Philip. *The Pursuit of Loneliness* (Boston, MA: Beacon Press, 1970).

Sternberg, Robert J. and Michael L. Barnes, eds. *The Psychology of Love* (New Haven, CT: Yale University Press, 1988).

Section II:

CLASSICAL
SOURCES

L O V E is constant, says the *agapist* Paul in his first letter to the Corinthians: love overcomes all obstacles and endures all threats to its existence. This might very well be a true description of God's love for humans and of Christian neighbor love at its best. But of what relevance is Paul's assertion to the more mundane loves of our everyday lives? This: some scholarly writers on love, not to mention many ordinary folk who think about such matters, look on God's love (or neighbor love) as the genuine article, believing that if an emotion or attitude one human has toward another human is to be love, it must exhibit the same constancy as *agape*. Thus, if x loves his wife y, x's love for y will persist despite y's mistakes, defects, and even ingratitude; x's love for y is put to the test by periods of marital strife, and if it is "really" love, x will always forgive y and continue to be concerned for y's well-being. Or if x loves a baseball team, x will remain loyal to it even if, season after season, the team ends up in last place and causes x profound disappointment. Genuine love is a "lost" love.

Remember that God's *agape* is not grounded in the value or merit of the humans He loves. It might be argued, then, that God's *agape* is constant precisely because the value of its object has nothing to do with the love's basis. That inference, however, is a non sequitur. True, if God's love for humans is not grounded on their merit, God's love will not fail to be constant merely because or when that merit disappears. Similarly, if x's love for his wife y is not based on y's value (say, her beauty), her losing that value (as she ages) will not be

41

the reason x's love ends. But a love's not being based on the value of its object is no guarantee that the love will be constant. God's love, as a matter of fact, is both constant and not a response to its object's merit, but it is not the former *because* it is the latter. Instead, God's *agape* is constant because God's nature is to love and to love constantly. God's nature explains both why God loves constantly and not in response to merit; these two aspects of God's *agape* flow independently from God's nature. [1] By analogy, if x loves his wife y constantly, undaunted by domestic discord, it is not merely because x's love is not based on y's merit. The constancy of x's love for y is primarily due to something about x, x's nature, and not to something about y: x's determination, for example, to continue to show concern for y's well-being despite y's misdeeds or significant disagreements about matters that affect them both.

Plato describes love in such a way that constancy is not an important feature of it, let alone a logically necessary condition. At the lowest stage of Plato's ladder of love, x loves y because y is physically beautiful. This kind of love will not be constant (we might think) because physical beauty fades with time, sometimes very quickly. But this is not exactly why, for Plato, love at this lowest stage is not constant. For Aristotle, if x loves y because y is pleasant or useful to x, x's love will not endure precisely because y's being pleasant or useful is not something that lasts (see *Nicomachean Ethics* 1156a20–1156b5, 1157a5–10). Thus in Aristotle we find the claim that because x loves y for P, x will no longer love y when P is gone. That is, for Aristotle's inferior types of friendship we find pretty much what we would expect to find in an *eros* account of love that is partially independent of its historical origin in Plato. Aristotle's position is a good example of a theory within the *eros* tradition, when that tradition is conceptualized as centrally a thesis about the basis of love. But in Plato, x's love for y, when it is based on y's physical beauty, is not constant for a different reason: x eventually realizes not only that the physical beauty possessed by y is also possessed by many other people but also that physical beauty does not hold a candle to other kinds of beauty.

There is no hint in Plato (see *Symposium* 210b–c) that x's love for y, when it is based on y's physical beauty, ends exactly when y's beauty fades. Rather, x's love for y ends even *before* that beauty fades. The lover, ideally, recognizes that y's beauty will fade and hence that this sort of beauty is inferior to other kinds. Thus x, not wanting to become overly attached to lesser beauty—since happiness does not lie here—progresses to the next level of Plato's ladder, at which a more substantial beauty provides the basis for love: moral virtue and intellectual excellence. Again, however, x realizes that even this superior type of beauty or goodness is not what x is yearning for. It, too, is widespread and fades with time (even if slowly). People die, taking their mental beauty with them, so that sort of beauty is perishable and hence inferior. Love can be constant, for Plato, only when its object is perfectly beautiful or good. This means not that its object is a kind of thing that *could* change, even if as a matter of fact it never does change, but that it is a kind of thing for which all change is impossible. This is Plato's Absolute Beauty, that which x all along had desired and which is accessible only at the highest level of the Ascent. Platonic love is, in this regard, the pagan version of the human love for the Christian God.[2]

When reading the *Symposium*, one must keep in mind the difference between (1) x loves y just because y has some attractive property P, and (2) x loves P itself. Which one is asserted by Plato (if not both)? Surely, it does not follow from x's loving y only when or because y is beautiful, that x actually loves only that beauty manifested by y and not y the person. The text suggests, however, that Plato relies on the common occurrence of cases of (1) as empirical evidence that (2) holds for all love. (See *Symposium* 205e–206b.)[3] This interpretation is supported by the fact that at the highest rung of the ladder, the Beautiful itself is the object of love, an inanimate thing like the inanimate P's of the lower stages. Thus the historically original theory of *eros* is more precisely a doctrine about the object of love, not about the basis of love, in contrast to what we have identified as being the central thesis of the later *eros* tradition: x loves y because y is (say) beautiful. Note that at the highest level of the Ascent, the distinction between the object and the basis of Platonic love may collapse altogether, since here x is loving the Beautiful just because it *is* beautiful. One thing is both the object of love and serves as the basis of love for itself.

A similar conflation of the basis and the object of love might occur in Aristotle's account of ideal friendship. He claims that x loves y because y's character is good and that this goodness is not something incidental to y but part of y's personal nature (e.g., *NE* 1156b10). But if x loves y for y's good character, and that good character is partially constitutive of y, then the good character is both the basis and (at least part of) the object of x's love. In contrast to inferior friendships based on usefulness or pleasure, Aristotle does expect ideal friendship to be constant: moral virtue is something that endures, so love that is based on goodness will be correspondingly constant. Yet Aristotle's *philia* is still, unlike *agape*, conditional on its object's remaining good (see *NE* 1165b12–22).

On the issue of the ultimate motivation underlying love, there is an obvious contrast between Paul's claim that love "seeks not its own" (*agape* is a love that desires only the best for others, even if that requires self-denial) and Plato's claim that the lover pursues the Beautiful for the sake of his or her own happiness; see *Symposium* 204e–205a. (Yet why does the Christian pursue God?) One interesting question is about the relation between love's ultimate motivation and its constancy. If love, as in Paul, does not seek its own, then x's not gaining anything from y (or from loving y) should not cause x's love for y to end. And if x, as in Plato, is always seeking a higher beauty for the sake of x's happiness, x's love for humans will not be constant because human beauty is an inferior kind of beauty. Figuring out where Aristotle stands is more difficult, since he claims both that when x has genuine *philia* for y, x wishes y well for y's sake (and acts accordingly; NE 1155b30), and that for each person his or her own good is the most important thing (NE 1159a10–12). Note that when Aristotle says that x should abandon *philia* for y if y has changed from being good to being evil, he is not asserting that x's love ends for a self-interested reason. Rather, x realizes that x can no longer do anything to benefit y.

One other difference among these three writers is their treatment of the relationship between love and sexuality. It is interesting that in Paul's letter to the Corinthians, he segregates his discussion of *agape* from his discussion of sexuality, and that throughout that portion of the letter on sexuality (Chapter 7) he never mentions "love" of any kind—only marriage. We get the impression, then, that for Paul love and sex are totally different things, or at least that *agape* has no sexual component (which makes sense) and that *agape* plays no role in the sexual lives of a married couple (which makes less sense). For Plato, by contrast, love and sexuality are intertwined. One rung of the ladder of love is occupied by sexual love inspired by physical beauty, and even though this rung is the lowest, it is not dispensable or altogether worthless. The perception of physical beauty is the first hint a person has of the Beautiful, and because the response to it is sexual, it is a powerful perception that induces a further search for Beauty. The role of sexuality in Aristotle's theory of love is not very clear. Although we might safely assume that pleasure-friendship can take the form of a sexual relationship, Aristotle never says so explicitly. (See NE 1156a31–1156b5; and note the absence of sexuality in Aristotle's list, NE 1172a1–6, a natural place to include it.) Aristotle is as silent about the place of sexuality in ideal friendship as Paul is about the role of love in the sexuality of marriage. However, Aristotle does expect those who have *philia* toward each other to live together. (This, by the way, places a limit on the number of ideal friendships a person can have; see NE 1170b20ff.) But does this mean that they will be sleeping together or engaging in sexual activity?

NOTES

1. My use of the word "explains" in this sentence should be taken with a clove of garlic. To say that God's nature, or God's being Love, explains the constancy of God's love is similar to saying that heroin's analgesic nature explains why it relieves pain. This

problem haunts the *agape* tradition. For heroin (but not God) we can dissect its nature to discover why the drug induces analgesia.

2. See Augustine, *Confessions* (New York, NY: Penguin Books, 1961), p. 55.

3. Aristotle seems to assert (2) for inferior friendships: x loves y's usefulness or y's pleasantness, not y (*Nicomachean Ethics* 1165b1–5).

SOCRATES SPEAKS AT A BANQUET

Plato

IN YOUR ORATION, my dear Agathon, I think that you were certainly right in proposing to speak of the nature of Love first and afterwards of his works—that is a way of beginning which I very much approve. And as you have set forth his nature with such stately eloquence, may I ask you further, Whether Love is by his nature the love of something or of nothing? And here I must explain myself: I do not want you to say that Love is the love of a father or the love of a mother—that would be ridiculous; but to answer as you would, if I asked, Is a father a father of something? to which you would find no difficulty in replying, of a son or daughter: and the answer would be right.

Very true, said Agathon.

And you would say the same of a mother?

He assented.

Yet let me ask you one more question in order to illustrate my meaning: Is not a brother to be regarded essentially as a brother of something?

Certainly, he replied.

That is, of a brother or sister?

Reprinted from *The Dialogues of Plato*, Vol. 1, translated by Benjamin Jowett (4th ed., 1953) by permission of Oxford University Press. This selection is taken from Plato's *Symposium*, 199c–212c; Socrates is already speaking at the very beginning of the excerpt. Benjamin Jowett was Regius Professor of Greek, University of Oxford; he died in 1893, a year after the Third Edition of his translations. Plato was born and died in Athens (ca. 428–7 to 348–7 B.C.) and was a student of Socrates.

Yes, he said.

And now, said Socrates, I will ask about Love:—Is Love of something or of nothing?

Of something, surely, he replied.

Keep in mind what this is, and tell me what I want to know—whether Love desires that of which love is.

Yes, surely.

And does he possess, or does he not possess, that which he loves and desires?

Probably not, I should say.

Nay, replied Socrates, I would have you consider whether 'necessarily' is not rather the word. The inference that he who desires something is lacking in that thing, and that he who does not desire a thing is not in lack of it, is in my judgement, Agathon, absolutely and necessarily true. What do you think?

I agree with you, said Agathon.

Very good. Would he who is great, desire to be great, or he who is strong, desire to be strong?

That would be inconsistent with our previous admissions.

True. For he who has those qualities cannot be lacking in them?

Very true.

Suppose that a man being strong desired to be strong, or being swift desired to be swift, or being healthy desired to be healthy,—since in that case he might be thought to desire something which he already has or is, I refer to the point in order that we may not be led astray—you will see on reflection that the possessors of these qualities must have their respective advantages at the time, whether they choose or not; and who can desire that which he has? Therefore, when a person says, I am well and wish to be well, or I am rich and wish to be rich, and I desire to have exactly what I have—to him we shall reply: 'You, my friend, having wealth and health and strength, want to have the continuance of them; for at this moment, whether you choose or no, you have them. And when you say, I desire that which I have and nothing else, is not your meaning that you want to have in the future what you have at present?' He must agree with us—must he not?

He must, replied Agathon.

Then, said Socrates, he desires that what he has at present may be preserved to him in the future, which is equivalent to saying that he desires something which is non-existent to him, and which as yet he has not got?

Very true, he said.

Then he and everyone who desires, desires that which he has not already, and which is future and not present, and which he has not, and is not, and which he lacks;—these are the sort of things which love and desire seek?

Very true, he said.

Then now, said Socrates, let us recapitulate the argument. First, is not love of something, and of something too which is wanting to a man?

Yes, he replied.

Remember further what you said in your speech, or if you like I will remind you: you said that the love of the beautiful set in order the empire of the gods, for that of deformed things there is no love—did you not say something of that kind?

Yes, said Agathon.

Yes, my friend, and the remark was a just one. And if this is true, love is the love of beauty and not of deformity?

He assented.

And the admission has been already made that love is of something which one lacks and has not?

True, he said.

Then Love lacks and has not beauty?

Certainly, he replied.

And would you call that beautiful which lacks beauty and does not possess it in any way?

Certainly not.

Then would you still say that Love is beautiful?

Agathon replied: I fear that I said what I did without understanding.

Indeed, you made a very good speech, Agathon, replied Socrates; but there is yet one small question which I would fain ask:—Is not the good also the beautiful?

Yes.

Then in lacking the beautiful, love lacks also the good?

I cannot refute you, Socrates, said Agathon:—Be it as you say.

Say rather, beloved Agathon, that you cannot refute the truth; for Socrates is easily refuted.

And now, taking my leave of you, I will rehearse a tale of love which I heard from Diotima of Mantinea,[1] a woman wise in this and many other kinds of knowledge, who in the days of old, when the Athenians offered sacrifice before the coming of the plague, delayed the disease ten years. She was my instructress in the art of love, and I shall try to repeat to you what she said to me, beginning with the propositions on which Agathon and I are agreed; I will do the best I can do without any help.[2] As you, Agathon, suggested,[3] it is proper to speak first of the being and nature of Love, and then of his works. (I think it will be easiest for me if in recounting my conversation with the wise woman I follow its actual course of question and answer.) First I said to her in nearly the same words which he used to me, that Love was a mighty god, and likewise fair; and she proved to me, as I proved to him, that by my own showing Love was neither fair nor good. 'What do you mean, Diotima,' I said, 'is Love then evil and

foul?' 'Hush,' she cried; 'must that be foul which is not fair?' 'Certainly,' I said.   202
'And is that which is not wise, ignorant? do you not see that there is a mean
between wisdom and ignorance?' 'And what may that be?' I said. 'Right
opinion,' she replied; 'which, as you know, being incapable of giving a reason,
is not knowledge (for how can knowledge be devoid of reason?) nor again
ignorance (for neither can ignorance attain the truth), but is clearly something
which is a mean between ignorance and wisdom.' 'Quite true,' I replied. 'Do
not then insist,' she said, 'that what is not fair is of necessity foul, or what is not   b
good evil; or infer that because Love is not fair and good he is therefore foul and
evil; for he is in a mean between them.' 'Well,' I said, 'Love is surely admitted
by all to be a great god.' 'By those who know or by those who do not know?' 'By
all.' 'And how, Socrates,' she said with a smile, 'can Love be acknowledged to   c
be a great god by those who say that he is not a god at all?' 'And who are they?' I
said. 'You and I are two of them,' she replied. 'How can that be?' I said. 'It is
quite intelligible,' she replied; 'for you yourself would acknowledge that the
gods are happy and fair—of course you would—would you dare to say that any
god was not?' 'Certainly not,' I replied. 'And you mean by the happy, those who
are the possessors of things good and things fair?' 'Yes.' 'And you admitted that   d
Love, because he was in want, desires those good and fair things of which he is
in want?' 'Yes, I did.' 'But how can he be a god who has no portion in what is
good and fair?' 'Impossible.' 'Then you see that you also deny the divinity of
Love.'

'What then is Love?' I asked; 'Is he mortal?' 'No.' 'What then?' 'As in the
former instance, he is neither mortal nor immortal, but in a mean between the
two.' 'What is he, Diotima?' 'He is a great spirit (δαίμων), and like all spirits he   e
is intermediate between the divine and the mortal.' 'And what,' I said, 'is his
power?' 'He interprets between gods and men, conveying and taking across to
the gods the prayers and sacrifices of men, and to men the commands of the
gods and the benefits they return; he is the mediator who spans the chasm
which divides them, and therefore by him the universe is bound together, and
through him the arts of the prophet and the priest, their sacrifices and mysteries   203
and charms, and all prophecy and incantation, find their way. For God mingles
not with man; but through Love all the intercourse and converse of gods with
men, whether they be awake or asleep, is carried on. The wisdom which
understands this is spiritual; all other wisdom, such as that of arts and hand-
icrafts, is mean and vulgar. Now these spirits or intermediate powers are many
and diverse, and one of them is Love.' 'And who,' I said, 'was his father, and
who his mother?' 'The tale,' she said, 'will take time; nevertheless I will tell you.   b
On the day when Aphrodite was born there was a feast of all the gods, among
them the god Poros or Plenty, who is the son of Metis or Sagacity. When the
feast was over, Penia or Poverty, as the manner is on such occasions, came
about the doors to beg. Now Plenty, who was the worse for nectar (there was no

wine in those days), went into the garden of Zeus and fell into a heavy sleep;
and Poverty considering that for her there was no plenty, plotted to have a child
c   by him, and accordingly she lay down at his side and conceived Love, who
partly because he is naturally a lover of the beautiful, and because Aphrodite is
herself beautiful, and also because he was begotten during her birthday feast, is
her follower and attendant. And as his parentage is, so also are his fortunes. In
the first place he is always poor, and anything but tender and fair, as the many
imagine him; and he is rough and squalid, and has no shoes, nor a house to
d   dwell in; on the bare earth exposed he lies under the open heaven, in the
streets, or at the doors of houses, taking his rest; and like his mother he is always
in distress. Like his father too, whom he also partly resembles, he is always
plotting against the fair and good; he is bold, enterprising, strong, a mighty
hunter, always weaving some intrigue or other, keen in the pursuit of wisdom,
fertile in resources; a philosopher at all times, terrible as an enchanter, sorcerer,
e   sophist. He is by nature neither mortal nor immortal, but alive and flourishing
at one moment when he is in plenty, and dead at another moment in the same
day, and again alive by reason of his father's nature. But that which is always
flowing in is always flowing out, and so he is never in want and never in wealth;
and, further, he is in a mean between ignorance and knowledge. The truth of
204   the matter is this: No god is a philosopher or seeker after wisdom, for he is wise
already; nor does any man who is wise seek after wisdom. Neither do the
ignorant seek after wisdom; for herein is the evil of ignorance, that he who is
neither a man of honor nor wise is nevertheless satisfied with himself: there is no
desire when there is no feeling of want.' 'But who then, Diotima,' I said, 'are
b   the lovers of wisdom, if they are neither the wise nor the foolish?' 'A child may
answer that question,' she replied; 'they are those who are in a mean between
the two; Love is one of them. For wisdom is a most beautiful thing, and Love is
of the beautiful; and therefore Love is also a philosopher or lover of wisdom,
and being a lover of wisdom is in a mean between the wise and the ignorant.
And of this, too, his birth is the cause; for his father is wealthy and wise, and his
mother poor and foolish. Such, my dear Socrates, is the nature of the spirit
c   Love. The error in your conception of him was very natural; from what you say
yourself, I infer that it arose because you thought that Love is that which is
loved, not that which loves; and for that reason, I think, Love appeared to you
supremely beautiful. For the beloved is the truly beautiful, and delicate, and
perfect, and blessed; but the active principle of love is of another nature, and is
such as I have described.'

I said: 'O thou stranger woman, thou sayest well; but, assuming Love to be
d   such as you say, what is the use of him to men?' 'That, Socrates,' she replied, 'I
will attempt to unfold: of his nature and birth I have already spoken; and you
acknowledge that love is of the beautiful. But someone will say: What does it
consist in, Socrates and Diotima?—or rather let me put the question more

clearly, and ask: When a man loves the beautiful, what does his love desire?' I answered her: 'That the beautiful may be his.' 'Still,' she said, 'the answer suggests a further question: What is given by the possession of beauty?' 'To what you have asked,' I replied, 'I have no answer ready.' 'Then,' she said, 'let me put   e the word "good" in the place of the beautiful, and repeat the question once more: If he who loves loves the good, what is it then that he loves?' 'The possession of the good.' 'And what does he gain who possesses the good?' 'Happiness,' I replied; 'there is less difficulty in answering that question.' 'Yes,'   205 she said, 'the happy are made happy by the acquisition of good things. Nor is there any need to ask why a man desires happiness; the answer is already final.' 'You are right,' I said. 'And is this wish and this desire common to all? and do all men always desire their own good, or only some men?—what say you?' 'All men,' I replied; 'the desire is common to all.' 'Why, then,' she rejoined, 'are not all men, Socrates, said to love, but only some of them? whereas you say that   b all men are always loving the same things.' 'I myself wonder,' I said, 'why this is.' 'There is nothing to wonder at,' she replied; 'the reason is that one part of love is separated off and receives the name of the whole, but the other parts have other names.' 'Give an illustration,' I said. She answered me as follows: 'There is creative activity which, as you know, is complex and manifold. All that causes the passage of non-being into being is a "poesy" or creation, and the   c processes of all art are creative; and the masters of arts are all poets or creators.' 'Very true.' 'Still,' she said, 'you know that they are not called poets, but have other names; only that one portion of creative activity which is separated off from the rest, and is concerned with music and metre, is called by the name of the whole and is termed poetry, and they who possess poetry in this sense of the word are called poets.' 'Very true,' I said. 'And the same holds of love. For you   d may say generally that all desire of good and happiness is only the great and subtle power of love; but they who are drawn towards him by any other path, whether the path of money-making or gymnastics or philosophy, are not called lovers—the name of the whole is appropriated to those whose desire takes one form only—they alone are said to love, or to be lovers.' 'I dare say,' I replied, 'that you are right.' 'Yes,' she added, 'and you hear people say that lovers are seeking for their other half; but I say that they are seeking neither for the half of   e themselves, nor for the whole, unless the half or the whole be also a good; men will cut off their own hands and feet and cast them away, if they think them evil. They do not, I imagine, each cling to what is his own, unless perchance there be someone who calls what belongs to him the good, and what belongs to   206 another the evil; for there is nothing which men love but the good. Is there anything?' 'Certainly, I should say, that there is nothing.' 'Then,' she said, 'the simple truth is, that men love the good.' 'Yes,' I said. 'To which must be added that they love the possession of the good?' 'Yes, that must be added.' 'And not only the possession, but the everlasting possession of the good?' 'That must be added too.' 'Then love,' she said, 'may be described generally as the love of the everlasting possession of the good?' 'That is most true.'

b   'Then if this be always the nature of love, can you tell me further,' she went on, 'what is the manner of the pursuit? what are they doing who show all this eagerness and heat which is called love? and what is the object which they have in view? Answer me.' 'Nay, Diotima,' I replied, 'if I knew, I should not be wondering at your wisdom, neither should I come to learn from you about this very matter.' 'Well,' she said, 'I will teach you:—The object which they have in view is birth in beauty, whether of body or soul.' 'I do not understand you,' I

c said; 'the oracle requires an explanation.' 'I will make my meaning clearer,' she replied. 'I mean to say, that all men are bringing to the birth in their bodies and in their souls. There is a certain age at which human nature is desirous of procreation—procreation which must be in beauty and not in deformity. The union of man and woman is a procreation; it is a divine thing, for conception and generation are an immortal principle in the mortal creature, and in the

d inharmonious they can never be. But the deformed is inharmonious with all divinity, and the beautiful harmonious. Beauty, then, is the destiny or goddess of parturition who presides at birth, and therefore, when approaching beauty, the procreating power is propitious, and expansive, and benign, and bears and produces fruit: at the sight of ugliness she frowns and contracts and has a sense of pain, and turns away, and shrivels up, and not without a pang refrains from procreation. And this is the reason why, when the hour of procreation comes, and the teeming nature is full, there is such a flutter and ecstasy about beauty

e whose approach is the alleviation of the bitter pain of travail. For love, Socrates, is not, as you imagine, the love of the beautiful only.' 'What then?' 'The love of generation and of birth in beauty.' 'Yes,' I said. 'Yes, indeed,' she replied. 'But why of generation? Because to the mortal creature, generation is a sort of eternity and immortality, and if, as has been already admitted, love is of the

207 everlasting possession of the good, all men will necessarily desire immortality together with good: whence it must follow that love is of immortality.'

    All this she taught me at various times when she spoke of love. And I remember her once saying to me, 'What is the cause, Socrates, of love, and the attendant desire? See you not how all animals, birds as well as beasts, in their

b desire of procreation, are in agony when they take the infection of love, which begins with the desire of union and then passes to the care of offspring, on whose behalf the weakest are ready to battle against the strongest even to the uttermost, and to die for them, and will let themselves be tormented with hunger, or make any other sacrifice, in order to maintain their young. Man may be supposed to act thus from reason; but why should animals have these

c passionate feelings? Can you tell me why?' Again I replied that I did not know. She said to me: 'And do you expect ever to become a master in the art of love, if you do not know this?' 'But I have told you already, Diotima, that my ignorance is the reason why I come to you, for I am conscious that I want a teacher; tell me then the cause of this and of the other mysteries of love.' 'Marvel not,' she said, 'if you believe that love is of the immortal, as we have several times acknowledged; for here again, and on the same principle too, the mortal nature is seeking as far as is possible to be everlasting and immortal: and this is only to be   d attained by generation, because generation always leaves behind a new and different existence in the place of the old. Nay, even in the life of the same individual there is succession and not absolute uniformity: a man is called the same, and yet in the interval between youth and age, during which every animal is said to have life and identity, he is undergoing a perpetual process of loss and reparation—hair, flesh, bones, blood, and the whole body are always changing. Which is true not only of the body, but also of the soul, whose   e habits, tempers, opinions, desires, pleasures, pains, fears, never remain the same in any one of us, but are always coming and going. What is still more surprising, it is equally true of science; not only do some of the sciences come to life in our minds, and others die away, so that we are never the same in regard to   208 them either: but the same fate happens to each of them individually. For what is implied in the word "recollection," but the departure of knowledge, which is ever being forgotten, and is renewed and preserved by recollection, and appears to be the same although in reality new, according to that law by which all mortal things are preserved, not absolutely the same, but by substitution, the old worn-out mortality leaving another new and similar existence behind— unlike the divine, which is wholly and eternally the same? And in this way,   b Socrates, the mortal body, or mortal anything, partakes of immortality; but the immortal in another way. Marvel not then at the love which all men have of their offspring; for that universal love and interest is for the sake of immortality.'

I was astonished at her words, and said: 'Is this really true, O most wise Diotima?' And she answered with all the authority of an accomplished sophist: c 'Of that, Socrates, you may be assured;—think only of the ambition of men, and you will wonder at the senselessness of their ways, unless you consider how they are stirred by the passionate love of fame. They are ready to run all risks, even greater than they would have run for their children, and to pour out money and undergo any sort of toil, and even to die, "if so they leave an   d everlasting name." Do you imagine that Alcestis would have died to save Admetus, or Achilles to avenge Patroclus, or your own Codrus in order to preserve the kingdom for his sons, if they had not imagined that the memory of their virtues, which still survives among us, would be immortal? Nay,' she said, 'I am persuaded that all men do all things, and the better they are the more they do them, in hope of the glorious fame of immortal virtue; for they desire the immortal.   e

'Those who are pregnant in the body only, betake themselves to women and beget children—this is the character of their love; their offspring, as they hope,

will preserve their memory and give them the blessedness and immortality
which they desire for all future time. But souls which are pregnant—for there
certainly are men who are more creative in their souls than in their bodies,
creative of that which is proper for the soul to conceive and bring forth: and if
you ask me what are these conceptions, I answer, wisdom, and virtue in
general—among such souls are all creative poets and all artists who are
deserving of the name inventor. But the greatest and fairest sort of wisdom by far
is that which is concerned with the ordering of states and families, and which is
called temperance and justice. And he who in youth has the seed of these
implanted in his soul, when he grows up and comes to maturity desires to beget
and generate. He wanders about seeking beauty that he may get offspring—for
from deformity he will beget nothing—and naturally embraces the beautiful
rather than the deformed body; above all, when he finds a fair and noble and
well-nurtured soul, he embraces the two in one person, and to such a one he is
full of speech about virtue and the nature and pursuits of a good man, and he
tries to educate him. At the touch and in the society of the beautiful which is
ever present to his memory, even when absent, he brings forth that which he
had conceived long before, and in company with him tends that which he
brings forth; and they are married by a far nearer tie and have a closer friendship
than those who beget mortal children, for the children who are their common
offspring are fairer and more immortal. Who, when he thinks of Homer and
Hesiod and other great poets, would not rather have their children than
ordinary human ones? Who would not emulate them in the creation of
children such as theirs, which have preserved their memory and given them
everlasting glory? Or who would not have such children as Lycurgus left behind
him to be the saviours, not only of Lacedaemon, but of Hellas, as one may say?
There is Solon, too, who is the revered father of Athenian laws; and many
others there are in many other places, both among Hellenes and barbarians,
who have given to the world many noble works, and have been the parents of
virtue of every kind; and many temples have been raised in their honor for the
sake of children such as theirs; which were never raised in honor of anyone, for
the sake of his mortal children.

'These are the lesser mysteries of love, into which even you, Socrates, may
enter; to the greater and more hidden ones which are the crown of these, and to
which, if you pursue them in a right spirit, they will lead, I know not whether
you will be able to attain. But I will do my utmost to inform you, and do you
follow if you can. For he who would proceed aright in this matter should begin
in youth to seek the company of corporeal beauty; and first, if he be guided by
his instructor aright, to love one beautiful body only—out of that he should
create fair thoughts; and soon he will of himself perceive that the beauty of one
body is akin to the beauty of another; and then if beauty of form in general is his
pursuit, how foolish would he be not to recognize that the beauty in every body

is one and the same! And when he perceives this he will abate his violent love of the one, which he will despise and deem a small thing, and will become a steadfast lover of all beautiful bodies. In the next stage he will consider that the beauty of the soul is more precious than the beauty of the outward form; so that if a virtuous soul have but a little comeliness, he will be content to love and   c tend him, and will search out and bring to the birth thoughts which may improve the young, until he is compelled next to contemplate and see the beauty in institutions and laws, and to understand that the beauty of them all is of one family, and that personal beauty is a trifle; and after institutions his guide will lead him on to the sciences, in order that, beholding the wide region already occupied by beauty, he may cease to be like a servant in love with one   d beauty only, that of a particular youth or man or institution, himself a slave mean and narrow-minded; but drawing towards and contemplating the vast sea of beauty, he will create many fair and noble thoughts and discourses in boundless love of wisdom, until on that shore he grows and waxes strong, and at last the vision is revealed to him of a single science, which is the science of beauty everywhere. To this I will proceed; please to give me your very   e best attention:

'He who has been instructed thus far in the things of love, and who has learned to see the beautiful in due order and succession, when he comes toward the end will suddenly perceive a nature of wondrous beauty (and this, Socrates, is the final cause of all our former toils)—a nature which in the first place is   211 everlasting, knowing not birth or death, growth or decay; secondly, not fair in one point of view and foul in another, or at one time or in one relation or at another place foul, as if fair to some and foul to others, or in the likeness of a face or hands or any other part of the bodily frame, or in any form of speech or knowledge, or existing in any individual being, as for example, in a living creature, whether in heaven, or in earth, or anywhere else; but beauty absolute,   b separate, simple, and everlasting, which is imparted to the ever growing and perishing beauties of all other beautiful things, without itself suffering diminution, or increase, or any change. He who, ascending from these earthly things under the influence of true love, begins to perceive that beauty, is not far from the end. And the true order of going, or being led by another, to the things of love, is to begin from the beauties of earth and mount upwards for the sake of   c that other beauty, using these as steps only, and from one going on to two, and from two to all fair bodily forms, and from fair bodily forms to fair practices, and from fair practices to fair sciences, until from fair sciences he arrives at the science of which I have spoken, the science which has no other object than absolute beauty, and at last knows that which is beautiful by itself alone. This, my dear Socrates,' said the stranger of Mantinea, 'is that life above all others   d which man should live, in the contemplation of beauty absolute; a beauty which if you once beheld, you would see not to be after the measure of gold, and garments, and fair boys and youths, whose presence now entrances you; and you and many a one would be content to live seeing them only and conversing with them without meat or drink, if that were possible—you only want to look at them and to be with them. But what if a man had eyes to see the

e   true beauty—the divine beauty, I mean, pure and clear and unalloyed, not infected with the pollutions of the flesh and all the colors and vanities of mortal life—thither looking, and holding converse with the true beauty simple and

212   divine? Remember how in that communion only, beholding beauty with that by which it can be beheld, he will be enabled to bring forth, not images of beauty, but realities (for he has hold not of an image but of a reality), and bringing forth and nourishing true virtue will properly become the friend of God and be immortal, if mortal man may. Would that be an ignoble life?'

b   Such, Phaedrus—and I speak not only to you, but to all of you—were the words of Diotima; and I am persuaded of their truth. And being persuaded of them, I try to persuade others, that in the attainment of this end human nature will not easily find a helper better than Love. And therefore, also, I say that every man ought to honor him as I myself honor him, and walk in his ways, and exhort others to do the same, and praise the power and spirit of Love according to the measure of my ability now and ever.

c   The words which I have spoken, you, Phaedrus, may call an encomium of Love, or anything else which you please.

NOTES

1.   Cf. *Alcibiades I.*
2.   Cf. *Gorg.* 505 e.
3.   *Supra,* 195 a. [Not in this volume.]

PERFECT FRIENDSHIP

Aristotle

BOOK VIII

1155ª 1 After what we have said, a discussion of friendship would naturally follow, since it is a virtue or implies virtue, and is besides most necessary with a view to living. For without friends no one would choose to live, though he had all other goods; even rich men and those in possession of office and of dominating power are thought to need friends most of all; for what is the use of such prosperity without the opportunity of beneficence, which is exercised chiefly and in its most laudable form towards friends? Or how can prosperity be guarded and preserved without friends? The greater it is, the more exposed is it to risk. And in poverty and in other misfortunes men think friends are the only refuge. It helps the young, too, to keep from error; it aids older people by ministering to their needs and supplementing the activities that are failing from weakness; those in the prime of life it stimulates to noble actions—'two going together'[1]— for with friends men are more able both to think and to act. Again, parent seems by nature to feel it for offspring and offspring for parent, not only among

Reprinted from *The Oxford Translation of Aristotle*, edited by W.D. Ross, Volume 9 (1925) by permission of Oxford University Press, and from *The Basic Works of Aristotle*, edited by Richard McKeon and translated by W.D. Ross (Random House, 1941). Included in this selection are part of Books 8 and 9 of *Nicomachean Ethics*. W. D. Ross was a well-known British philosopher, whose works included the famous treatise on ethics *The Right and the Good* (1930). Aristotle was born in Stagira (384 B. C.) and died in Greece (322 B. C.). He studied under Plato at the Academy and founded his own school, the Lyceum. (Footnotes have been renumbered.)

men but among birds and among most animals; it is felt mutually by members
of the same race, and especially by men, whence we praise lovers of their
fellowmen. We may see even in our travels how near and dear every man is to
every other. Friendship seems too to hold states together, and lawgivers to care
more for it than for justice; for unanimity seems to be something like friendship, and this they aim at most of all, and expel faction as their worst enemy;
and when men are friends they have no need of justice, while when they are
just they need friendship as well, and the truest form of justice is thought to be a
friendly quality.

But it is not only necessary but also noble; for we praise those who love their
friends, and it is thought to be a fine thing to have many friends; and again we
think it is the same people that are good men and are friends.

Not a few things about friendship are matters of debate. Some define it as a
kind of likeness and say like people are friends, whence come the sayings 'like
to like,' 'birds of a feather flock together,' and so on; others on the contrary say
'two of a trade never agree.' On this very question they inquire for deeper and
more physical causes, Euripides saying that 'parched earth loves the rain, and
stately heaven when filled with rain loves to fall to earth,' and Heraclitus that 'it
is what opposes that helps' and 'from different tones comes the fairest tune' and
'all things are produced through strife'; while Empedocles, as well as others,
expresses the opposite view that like aims at like. The physical problems we
may leave alone (for they do not belong to the present inquiry); let us examine
those which are human and involve character and feeling, e.g. whether
friendship can arise between any two people or people cannot be friends if they
are wicked, and whether there is one species of friendship or more than one.
Those who think there is only one because it admits of degrees have relied on
an inadequate indication; for even things different in species admit of degree.
We have discussed this matter previously.

2   The kinds of friendship may perhaps be cleared up if we first come to know
the object of love. For not everything seems to be loved but only the lovable,
and this is good, pleasant, or useful; but it would seem to be that by which
some good or pleasure is produced that is useful, so that it is the good and the
useful that are lovable as ends. Do men love, then, *the* good, or what is good for
them? These sometimes clash. So too with regard to the pleasant. Now it is
thought that each loves what is good for himself, and that the good is without
qualification lovable, and what is good for each man is lovable for him; but
each man loves not what is good for him but what seems good. This however
will make no difference; we shall just have to say that this is 'that which seems
lovable.' Now there are three grounds on which people love; of the love of
lifeless objects we do not use the word 'friendship'; for it is not mutual love, nor
is there a wishing of good to the other (for it would surely be ridiculous to wish

wine well; if one wishes anything for it, it is that it may keep, so that one may   30
have it oneself); but to a friend we say we ought to wish what is good for his sake.
But to those who thus wish good we ascribe only goodwill, if the wish is not
reciprocated; goodwill when it *is* reciprocal being friendship. Or must we add
'when it is recognized'? For many people have goodwill to those whom they   35
have not seen but judge to be good or useful; and one of these might return this   1156ª
feeling. These people seem to bear goodwill to each other; but how could one
call them friends when they do not know their mutual feelings? To be friends,
then, they must be mutually recognized as bearing goodwill and wishing well
to each other for one of the aforesaid reasons.   5

3   Now these reasons differ from each other in kind; so, therefore, do the
corresponding forms of love and friendship. There are therefore three kinds of
friendship, equal in number to the things that are lovable; for with respect to
each there is a mutual and recognized love, and those who love each other wish
well to each other in that respect in which they love one another. Now those   10
who love each other for their utility do not love each other for themselves but in
virtue of some good which they get from each other. So too with those who love
for the sake of pleasure; it is not for their character that men love ready-witted
people, but because they find them pleasant. Therefore those who love for the
sake of utility love for the sake of what is good for *themselves*, and those who   15
love for the sake of pleasure do so for the sake of what is pleasant to *themselves*,
and not in so far as the other is the person loved but in so far as he is useful or
pleasant. And thus these friendships are only incidental; for it is not as being the
man he is that the loved person is loved, but as providing some good or
pleasure. Such friendships, then, are easily dissolved, if the parties do not   20
remain like themselves; for if the one party is no longer pleasant or useful the
other ceases to love him.
Now the useful is not permanent but is always changing. Thus when the
motive of the friendship is done away, the friendship is dissolved, inasmuch as it
existed only for the ends in question. This kind of friendship seems to exist
chiefly between old people (for at that age people pursue not the pleasant but   25
the useful) and, of those who are in their prime or young, between those who
pursue utility. And such people do not live much with each other either; for
sometimes they do not even find each other pleasant; therefore they do not need
such companionship unless they are useful to each other; for they are pleasant
to each other only in so far as they rouse in each other hopes of something good   30
to come. Among such friendships people also class the friendship of host and
guest. On the other hand the friendship of young people seems to aim at
pleasure; for they live under the guidance of emotion, and pursue above all
what is pleasant to themselves and what is immediately before them; but with
increasing age their pleasures become different. This is why they quickly   35

become friends and quickly cease to be so; their friendship changes with the object that is found pleasant, and such pleasure alters quickly. Young people are amorous too; for the greater part of the friendship of love depends on emotion and aims at pleasure; this is why they fall in love and quickly fall out of love, changing often within a single day. But these people do wish to spend their days and lives together; for it is thus that they attain the purpose of their friendship.

Perfect friendship is the friendship of men who are good, and alike in virtue; for these wish well alike to each other *qua* good, and they are good in themselves. Now those who wish well to their friends for their sake are most truly friends; for they do this by reason of their own nature and not incidentally; therefore their friendship lasts as long as they are good—and goodness is an enduring thing. And each is good without qualification and to his friend, for the good are both good without qualification and useful to each other. So too they are pleasant; for the good are pleasant both without qualification and to each other, since to each his own activities and others like them are pleasurable, and the actions of the good *are* the same or like. And such a friendship is as might be expected permanent, since there meet in it all the qualities that friends should have. For all friendship is for the sake of good or of pleasure— good or pleasure either in the abstract or such as will be enjoyed by him who has the friendly feeling—and is based on a certain resemblance; and to a friendship of good men all the qualities we have named belong in virtue of the nature of the friends themselves; for in the case of this kind of friendship the other qualities also[2] are alike in both friends, and that which is good without qualification is also without qualification pleasant, and these are the most lovable qualities. Love and friendship therefore are found most and in their best form between such men.

But it is natural that such friendships should be infrequent; for such men are rare. Further, such friendship requires time and familiarity; as the proverb says, men cannot know each other till they have 'eaten salt together'; nor can they admit each other to friendship or be friends till each has been found lovable and been trusted by each. Those who quickly show the marks of friendship to each other wish to be friends, but are not friends unless they both are lovable and know the fact; for a wish for friendship may arise quickly, but friendship does not.

4   This kind of friendship, then, is perfect both in respect of duration and in all other respects, and in it each gets from each in all respects the same as, or something like what, he gives; which is what ought to happen between friends. Friendship for the sake of pleasure bears a resemblance to this kind; for good people too *are* pleasant to each other. So too does friendship for the sake of

utility; for the good are also useful to each other. Among men of these inferior sorts too, friendships are most permanent when the friends get the same thing from each other (e.g. pleasure), and not only that but also from the same source, as happens between ready-witted people, not as happens between lover and beloved. For these do not take pleasure in the same things, but the one in seeing the beloved and the other in receiving attentions from his lover; and when the bloom of youth is passing the friendship sometimes passes too (for the one finds no pleasure in the sight of the other, and the other gets no attentions from the first); but many lovers on the other hand are constant, if familiarity has led them to love each other's characters, these being alike. But those who exchange not pleasure but utility in their amour are both less truly friends and less constant. Those who are friends for the sake of utility part when the advantage is at an end; for they were lovers not of each other but of profit.

For the sake of pleasure or utility, then, even bad men may be friends of each other, or good men of bad, or one who is neither good nor bad may be a friend to any sort of person, but for their own sake clearly only good men can be friends; for bad men do not delight in each other unless some advantage come of the relation.

The friendship of the good too and this alone is proof against slander; for it is not easy to trust any one's talk about a man who has long been tested by oneself; and it is among good men that trust and the feeling that 'he would never wrong me' and all the other things that are demanded in true friendship are found. In the other kinds of friendship, however, there is nothing to prevent these evils arising.

For men apply the name of friends even to those whose motive is utility, in which sense states are said to be friendly (for the alliances of states seem to aim at advantage), and to those who love each other for the sake of pleasure, in which sense children are called friends. Therefore we too ought perhaps to call such people friends, and say that there are several kinds of friendship—firstly and in the proper sense that of good men *qua* good, and by analogy the other kinds; for it is in virtue of something good and something akin to what is found in true friendship that they are friends, since even the pleasant is good for the lovers of pleasure. But these two kinds of friendship are not often united, nor do the same people become friends for the sake of utility and of pleasure; for things that are only incidentally connected are not often coupled together.

Friendship being divided into these kinds, bad men will be friends for the sake of pleasure or of utility, being in this respect like each other, but good men will be friends for their own sake, i.e. in virtue of their goodness. These, then, are friends without qualification; the others are friends incidentally and through a resemblance to these.

5   5   As in regard to the virtues some men are called good in respect of a state of character, others in respect of an activity, so too in the case of friendship; for those who live together delight in each other and confer benefits on each other,

10   but those who are asleep or locally separated are not performing, but are disposed to perform, the activities of friendship; distance does not break off the friendship absolutely, but only the activity of it. But if the absence is lasting, it seems actually to make men forget their friendship; hence the saying 'out of

15   sight, out of mind.' Neither old people nor sour people seem to make friends easily; for there is little that is pleasant in them, and no one can spend his days with one whose company is painful, or not pleasant, since nature seems above all to avoid the painful and to aim at the pleasant. Those, however, who approve of each other but do not live together seem to be well-disposed rather

20   than actual friends. For there is nothing so characteristic of friends as living together (since while it is people who are in need that desire benefits, even those who are supremely happy desire to spend their days together; for solitude suits such people least of all); but people cannot live together if they are not pleasant and do not enjoy the same things, as friends who are companions seem to do.

25   The truest friendship, then, is that of the good, as we have frequently said;[3] for that which is without qualification good or pleasant seems to be lovable and desirable, and for each person that which is good or pleasant to him; and the good man is lovable and desirable to the good man for both these reasons. Now it looks as if love were a feeling, friendship a state of character, for love may be

30   felt just as much towards lifeless things, but mutual love involves choice and choice springs from a state of character; and men wish well to those whom they love, for their sake, not as a result of feeling but as a result of a state of character. And in loving a friend men love what is good for themselves; for the good man in becoming a friend becomes a good to his friend. Each, then, both loves what

35   is good for himself, and makes an equal return in goodwill and in pleasantness; for friendship is said to be equality, and both of these are found most in the friendship of the good.

1158ᵃ   6   Between sour and elderly people friendship arises less readily, inasmuch as they are less good-tempered and enjoy companionship less; for these are thought to be the greatest marks of friendship and most productive of it. This is

5   why, while young men become friends quickly, old men do not; it is because men do not become friends with those in whom they do not delight; and similarly sour people do not quickly make friends either. But such men may bear goodwill to each other; for they wish one another well and aid one another in need; but they are hardly *friends* because they do not spend their days together nor delight in each other, and these are thought the greatest marks of friendship.

One cannot be a friend to many people in the sense of having friendship of 10
the perfect type with them, just as one cannot be in love with many people at
once (for love is a sort of excess of feeling, and it is the nature of such only to be
felt towards one person); and it is not easy for many people at the same time to
please the same person very greatly, or perhaps even to be good in his eyes. One
must, too, acquire some experience of the other person and become familiar
with him, and that is very hard. But with a view to utility or pleasure it is 15
possible that many people should please one; for many people are useful or
pleasant, and these services take little time.

Of these two kinds that which is for the sake of pleasure is the more like
friendship, when both parties get the same things from each other and delight
in each other or in the same things, as in the friendships of the young; for
generosity is more found in such friendships. Friendship based on utility is for 20
the commercially minded. People who are supremely happy, too, have no need
of useful friends, but do need pleasant friends; for they wish to live with *some
one* and, though they can endure for a short time what is painful, no one could
put up with it continuously, nor even with the Good itself if it were painful to
him; this is why they look out for friends who are pleasant. Perhaps they should 25
look out for friends who, being pleasant, are also good, and good for them, too;
for so they will have all the characteristics that friends should have.

People in positions of authority seem to have friends who fall into distinct
classes; some people are useful to them and others are pleasant, but the same
people are rarely both; for they seek neither those whose pleasantness is accom- 30
panied by virtue nor those whose utility is with a view to noble objects, but in
their desire for pleasure they seek for ready-witted people, and their other
friends they choose as being clever at doing what they are told, and these
characteristics are rarely combined. Now we have said that the *good* man *is* at
the same time pleasant and useful;[4] but such a man does not become the friend
of one who surpasses him in station, unless he is surpassed also in virtue; if this
is not so, he does not establish equality by being proportionally exceeded in 35
both respects. But people who surpass him in both respects are not so easy to
find.

However that may be, the aforesaid friendships involve equality; for the 1158ᵇ
friends get the same things from one another and wish the same things for one
another, or exchange one thing for another, e. g. pleasure for utility; we have
said,[5] however, that they are both less truly friendships and less permanent. But
it is from their likeness and their unlikeness to the same thing that they are 5
thought both to be and not to be friendships. It is by their likeness to the
friendship of virtue that they seem to be friendships (for one of them involves
pleasure and the other utility, and these characteristics belong to the friendship
of virtue as well); while it is because the friendship of virtue is proof against
slander and permanent, while these quickly change (besides differing from the

10 former in many other respects), that they appear *not* to be friendships; i.e. it is
because of their unlikeness to the friendship of virtue.

7   But there is another kind of friendship, viz. that which involves an inequality between the parties, e. g. that of father to son and in general of elder to
younger, that of man to wife and in general that of ruler to subject. And these
15 friendships differ also from each other; for it is not the same that exists between
parents and children and between rulers and subjects, nor is even that of father
to son the same as that of son to father, nor that of husband to wife the same as
that of wife to husband. For the virtue and the function of each of these is
different, and so are the reasons for which they love; the love and the friendship
20 are therefore different also. Each party, then, neither gets the same from the
other, nor ought to seek it; but when children render to parents what they ought
to render to those who brought them into the world, and parents render what
they should to their children, the friendship of such persons will be abiding and
excellent. In all friendships implying inequality the love also should be propor-
25 tional, i.e. the better should be more loved than he loves, and so should the
more useful, and similarly in each of the other cases; for when the love is in
proportion to the merit of the parties, then in a sense arises equality, which is
certainly held to be characteristic of friendship.
But equality does not seem to take the same form in acts of justice and in
30 friendship; for in acts of justice what is equal in the primary sense is that which
is in proportion to merit, while quantitative equality is secondary, but in
friendship quantitative equality is primary and proportion to merit secondary.
This becomes clear if there is a great interval in respect of virtue or vice or
wealth or anything else between the parties; for then they are no longer friends,
35 and do not even expect to be so. And this is most manifest in the case of the
gods; for they surpass us most decisively in all good things. But it is clear also in
1159ª the case of kings; for with them, too, men who are much their inferiors do not
expect to be friends; nor do men of no account expect to be friends with the best
or wisest men. In such cases it is not possible to define exactly up to what point
friends can remain friends; for much can be taken away and friendship remain,
but when one party is removed to a great distance, as God is, the possibility of
5 friendship ceases. This is in fact the origin of the question whether friends really
wish for their friends the greatest goods, e.g. that of being gods; since in that
case their friends will no longer be friends to them, and therefore will not be
good things for them (for friends *are* good things). The answer is that if we were
right in saying that friend wishes good to friend for his sake,[6] his friend must
10 remain the sort of being he is, whatever that may be; therefore it is for him only
so long as he remains a man that he will wish the greatest goods. But perhaps
not *all* the greatest goods; for it is for himself most of all that each man wishes
what is good.

8 Most people seem, owing to ambition, to wish to be loved rather than to love; which is why most men love flattery; for the flatterer is a friend in an inferior position, or pretends to be such and to love more than he is loved; and being loved seems to be akin to being honored, and this is what most people aim at. But it seems to be not for its own sake that people choose honor, but incidentally. For most people enjoy being honored by those in positions of authority because of their hopes (for they think that if they want anything they will get it from them; and therefore they delight in honor as a token of favor to come); while those who desire honor from good men, and men who know, are aiming at confirming their own opinion of themselves; they delight in honor, therefore, because they believe in their own goodness on the strength of the judgment of those who speak about them. In being loved, on the other hand, people delight for its own sake; whence it would seem to be better than being honored, and friendship to be desirable in itself. But it seems to lie in loving rather than in being loved, as is indicated by the delight mothers take in loving; for some mothers hand over their children to be brought up, and so long as they know their fate they love them and do not seek to be loved in return (if they cannot have both), but seem to be satisfied if they see them prospering; and they themselves love their children even if these owing to their ignorance give them nothing of a mother's due. Now since friendship depends more on loving, and it is those who love their friends that are praised, loving seems to be the characteristic virtue of friends, so that it is only those in whom this is found in due measure that are lasting friends, and only their friendship that endures.

It is in this way more than any other that even unequals can be friends; they can be equalized. Now equality and likeness are friendship, and especially the likeness of those who are like in virtue; for being steadfast in themselves they hold fast to each other, and neither ask nor give base services, but (one may say) even prevent them; for it is characteristic of good men neither to go wrong themselves nor to let their friends do so. But wicked men have no steadfastness (for they do not remain even like to themselves), but become friends for a short time because they delight in each other's wickedness. Friends who are useful or pleasant last longer; i.e. as long as they provide each other with enjoyments or advantages. Friendship for utility's sake seems to be that which most easily exists between contraries, e.g. between poor and rich, between ignorant and learned; for what a man actually lacks he aims at, and one gives something else in return. But under this head, too, we might bring lover and beloved, beautiful and ugly. This is why lovers sometimes seem ridiculous, when they demand to be loved as they love; if they are equally lovable their claim can perhaps be justified, but when they have nothing lovable about them it is ridiculous. Perhaps, however, contrary does not even aim at contrary by its own nature, but only incidentally, the desire being for what is intermediate; for that is what is good, e.g. it is good for the dry not to become wet[7] but to come to the intermediate state, and similarly with the hot and in all other cases. These subjects we may dismiss; for they are indeed somewhat foreign to our inquiry.

* * *

BOOK IX

3   Another question that arises is whether friendships should or should not be broken off when the other party does not remain the same. Perhaps we may say that there is nothing strange in breaking off a friendship based on utility or pleasure, when our friends no longer have these attributes. For it was of these attributes that we were the friends; and when these have failed it is reasonable to love no longer. But one might complain of another if, when he loved us for our usefulness or pleasantness, he pretended to love us for our character. For, as we said at the outset,[8] most differences arise between friends when they are not friends in the spirit in which they think they are. So when a man has deceived himself and has thought he was being loved for his character, when the other person was doing nothing of the kind, he must blame himself; but when he has been deceived by the pretences of the other person, it is just that he should complain against his deceiver; he will complain with more justice than one does against people who counterfeit the currency, inasmuch as the wrongdoing is concerned with something more valuable.

But if one accepts another man as good, and he turns out badly and is seen to do so, must one still love him? Surely it is impossible, since not everything can be loved, but only what is good. What is evil neither can nor should be loved; for it is not one's duty to be a lover of evil, nor to become like what is bad; and we have said[9] that like is dear to like. Must the friendship, then, be forthwith broken off? Or is this not so in all cases, but only when one's friends are incurable in their wickedness? If they are capable of being reformed one should rather come to the assistance of their character or their property, inasmuch as this is better and more characteristic of friendship. But a man who breaks off such a friendship would seem to be doing nothing strange; for it was not to a man of this sort that he was a friend; when his friend has changed, therefore, and he is unable to save him, he gives him up.

But if one friend remained the same while the other became better and far outstripped him in virtue, should the latter treat the former as a friend? Surely he cannot. When the interval is great this becomes most plain, e.g. in the case of childish friendships; if one friend remained a child in intellect while the other became a fully developed man, how could they be friends when they neither approved of the same things nor delighted in and were pained by the

1165^b

5

10

15

20

25

same things? For not even with regard to each other will their tastes agree, and
without this (as we saw[10]) they cannot be friends; for they cannot live together.   30
But we have discussed these matters.[11]

Should he, then, behave no otherwise towards him than he would if he had
never been his friend? Surely he should keep a remembrance of their former
intimacy, and as we think we ought to oblige friends rather than strangers, so to
those who have been our friends we ought to make some allowance for our   35
former friendship, when the breach has not been due to excess of wickedness.

* * *

5   Goodwill is a friendly sort of relation, but is not *identical* with friendship;   30
for one may have goodwill both towards people whom one does not know, and
without their knowing it, but not friendship. This has indeed been said already.[12] But goodwill is not even friendly feeling. For it does not involve
intensity or desire, whereas these accompany friendly feeling; and friendly
feeling implies intimacy while goodwill may arise of a sudden, as it does   35
towards competitors in a contest; we come to feel goodwill for them and to   1167[a]
share in their wishes, but we would not *do* anything with them; for, as we said,
we feel goodwill suddenly and love them only superficially.

Goodwill seems, then, to be a beginning of friendship, as the pleasure of the
eye is the beginning of love. For no one loves if he has not first been delighted   5
by the form of the beloved, but he who delights in the form of another does not,
for all that, love him, but only does so when he also longs for him when absent
and craves for his presence; so too it is not possible for people to be friends if
they have not come to feel goodwill for each other, but those who feel goodwill
are not for all that friends; for they only *wish* well to those for whom they feel
goodwill, and would not do anything with them nor take trouble for them. And
so one might by an extension of the term friendship say that goodwill is inactive   10
friendship, though when it is prolonged and reaches the point of intimacy it
becomes friendship—not the friendship based on utility nor that based on
pleasure; for goodwill too does not arise on those terms. The man who has
received a benefit bestows goodwill in return for what has been done to him,
but in doing so is only doing what is just; while he who wishes some one to   15
prosper because he hopes for enrichment through him seems to have goodwill
not to him but rather to himself, just as a man is not a friend to another if he
cherishes him for the sake of some use to be made of him. In general, goodwill
arises on account of some excellence and worth, when one man seems to
another beautiful or brave or something of the sort, as we pointed out in the   20
case of competitors in a contest.

* * *

1169^b 9   It is also disputed whether the happy man will need friends or not. It is said
5   that those who are supremely happy and self-sufficient have no need of friends;
for they have the things that are good, and therefore being self-sufficient they
need nothing further, while a friend, being another self, furnishes what a man
cannot provide by his own effort; whence the saying 'when fortune is kind, what
need of friends?' But it seems strange, when one assigns all good things to the
10   happy man, not to assign friends, who are thought the greatest of external
goods. And if it is more characteristic of a friend to do well by another than to be
well done by, and to confer benefits is characteristic of the good man and of
virtue, and it is nobler to do well by friends than by strangers, the good man will
15   need people to do well by. This is why the question is asked whether we need
friends more in prosperity or in adversity, on the assumption that not only does
a man in adversity need people to confer benefits on him, but also those who
are prospering need people to do well by. Surely it is strange, too, to make the
supremely happy man a solitary; for no one would choose the whole world on
condition of being alone, since man is a political creature and one whose
nature is to live with others. Therefore even the happy man lives with others;
for he has the things that are by nature good. And plainly it is better to spend his
20   days with friends and good men than with strangers or any chance persons.
Therefore the happy man needs friends.

* * *

1170^b 10   Should we, then, make as many friends as possible, or—as in the case of
hospitality it is thought to be suitable advice, that one should be 'neither a man
of many guests nor a man with none'—will that apply to friendship as well;
should a man neither be friendless nor have an excessive number of friends?
To friends made with a view to *utility* this saying would seem thoroughly
25   applicable; for to do services to many people in return is a laborious task and life
is not long enough for its performance. Therefore friends in excess of those who
are sufficient for our own life are superfluous, and hindrances to the noble life;
so that we have no need of them. Of friends made with a view to *pleasure*, also,
few are enough, as a little seasoning in food is enough.
30   But as regards *good* friends, should we have as many as possible, or is there a
limit to the number of one's friends, as there is to the size of a city? You cannot
make a city of ten men, and if there are a hundred thousand it is a city no
1171^a longer. But the proper number is presumably not a single number, but anything that falls between certain fixed points. So for friends too there is a fixed
number—perhaps the largest number with whom one can live together (for
that, we found, ¹³ is thought to be very characteristic of friendship); and that one
cannot live with many people and divide oneself up among them is plain.
5   Further, they too must be friends of one another, if they are all to spend their

days together; and it is a hard business for this condition to be fulfilled with a large number. It is found difficult, too, to rejoice and to grieve in an intimate way with many people, for it may likely happen that one has at once to be happy with one friend and to mourn with another. Presumably, then, it is well not to seek to have as many friends as possible, but as many as are enough for the purpose of living together; for it would seem actually impossible to be a   10 great friend to many people. This is why one cannot love several people; love is ideally a sort of excess of friendship, and that can only be felt towards one person; therefore great friendship too can only be felt towards a few people. This seems to be confirmed in practice; for we do not find many people who are friends in the comradely way of friendship, and the famous friendships of this sort are always between two people. Those who have many friends and mix   15 intimately with them all are thought to be no one's friend, except in the way proper to fellow-citizens, and such people are also called obsequious. In the way proper to fellow-citizens, indeed, it is possible to be the friend of many and yet not be obsequious but a genuinely good man; but one cannot have with many people the friendship based on virtue and on the character of our friends   20 themselves, and we must be content if we find even a few such.

* * *

12   Does it not follow, then, that, as for lovers the sight of the beloved is the thing they love most, and they prefer this sense to the others because on it love   30 depends most for its being and for its origin, so for friends the most desirable thing is living together? For friendship is a partnership, and as a man is to himself, so is he to his friend; now in his own case the consciousness of his being is desirable, and so therefore is the consciousness of his friend's being,   35 and the activity of this consciousness is produced when they live together, so   1172ᵃ that it is natural that they aim at this. And whatever existence means for each class of men, whatever it is for whose sake they value life, in *that* they wish to occupy themselves with their friends; and so some drink together, others dice together, others join in athletic exercises and hunting, or in the study of philosophy, each class spending their days together in whatever they love most   5 in life; for since they wish to live with their friends, they do and share in those things which give them the sense of living together. Thus the friendship of bad men turns out an evil thing (for because of their instability they unite in bad   10 pursuits, and besides they become evil by becoming like each other), while the friendship of good men is good, being augmented by their companionship; and they are thought to become better too by their activities and by improving each other; for from each other they take the mould of the characteristics they approve—whence the saying 'noble deeds from noble men.'—So much, then, for friendship; our next task must be to discuss pleasure.   15

NOTES

1. *Il.* x, 224.
2. I.e. absolute pleasantness, relative goodness, and relative pleasantness, as well as absolute goodness.
3. 1156^b7, 23–33, 1157^a30, $^b4$.
4. 1156^b13–15, 1157^a1–3.
5. 1156^a16–24, 1157^a20–33.
6. 1155^b31.
7. Cf. 1155^b3.
8. 1162^b23–25.
9. 1156^b19–21, 1159^b1.
10. 1157^b22–24.
11. *Ib.* 17–24, 1158^b33–35.
12. 1155^b32–1156^a5.
13. 1157^b19, 1158^a3, 10.

SEXUALITY AND LOVE

Saint Paul

1 CORINTHIANS 7

Now concerning the things whereof ye wrote unto me: *It is* good for a man not to touch a woman.

2   Nevertheless, *to avoid* fornication, let every man have his own wife, and let every woman have her own husband.

3   Let the husband render unto the wife due benevolence: and likewise also the wife unto the husband.

4   The wife hath not power of her own body, but the husband: and likewise also the husband hath not power of his own body, but the wife.

5   Defraud ye not one the other, ¹ except *it be* with consent for a time, that ye may give yourselves to fasting and prayer; and come together again, that Satan tempt you not for your incontinency.

6   But I speak this by permission, *and* not of commandment.

7   For I would that all men were even as I myself. But every man hath his proper gift of God, one after this manner, and another after that.

This version of Paul's letter is from the King James edition of the New Testament, reprinted from a volume supplied to A. S. by The Gideons International. (Footnotes added by A. S.) Paul the Apostle, originally a Jew, was born in what is now Turkey (date unknown) and died in Rome (ca. 62–68 A.D.). The student should take note of *Matthew* 22: 37–39, "Thou shalt love the Lord thy God with all thy heart, and with all thy soul, and with all thy mind. This is the first and the great commandment. And the second is like unto it, Thou shalt love thy neighbor as thyself."

8   I say therefore to the unmarried and widows, It is good for them if they abide even as I.

9   But if they cannot contain, let them marry: for it is better to marry than to burn.[2]

10   And unto the married I command, *yet* not I, but the Lord. Let not the wife depart from *her* husband:

11   But and if she depart, let her remain unmarried, or be reconciled to *her* husband: and let not the husband put away *his* wife.

12   But to the rest speak I, not the Lord: If any brother hath a wife that believeth not, and she be pleased to dwell with him, let him not put her away.

13   And the woman which hath an husband that believeth not,[3] and if he be pleased to dwell with her, let her not leave him.

14   For the unbelieving husband is sanctified by the wife, and the unbelieving wife is sanctified by the husband: else were your children unclean: but now are they holy.

15   But if the unbelieving depart, let him depart. A brother or a sister is not under bondage in such *cases*: but God hath called us to peace.

16   For what knowest thou, O wife, whether thou shalt save *thy* husband? or how knowest thou, O man, whether thou shalt save *thy* wife?

17   But as God hath distributed to every man, as the Lord hath called every one, so let him walk. And so ordain I in all churches.

18   Is any man called being circumcised? let him not become uncircumcised. Is any called in uncircumcision? let him not be circumcised.

19   Circumcision is nothing, and uncircumcision is nothing, but the keeping of the commandments of God.

20   Let every man abide in the same calling wherein he was called.

21   Art thou called *being* a servant? care not for it: but if thou mayest be made free, use *it* rather.

22   For he that is called in the Lord, *being* a servant, is the Lord's freeman: likewise also he that is called, *being* free, is Christ's servant.

23   Ye are bought with a price; be not ye the servants of men.

24   Brethren, let every man, wherein he is called, therein abide with God.

25   Now concerning virgins I have no commandment of the Lord: yet I give my judgment, as one that hath obtained mercy of the Lord to be faithful.

26   I suppose therefore that this is good for the present distress. *I say*, that *it is* good for a man so to be.

27   Art thou bound unto a wife? seek not to be loosed. Art thou loosed from a wife? seek not a wife.

28   But and if thou marry, thou has not sinned: and if a virgin marry, she hath not sinned. Nevertheless such shall have trouble in the flesh: but I spare you.

29   But this I say, brethren, the time *is* short: it remaineth, that both they that have wives be as though they had none;[4]

30 And they that weep, as though they wept not: and they that rejoice, as though they rejoiced not: and they that buy, as though they possessed not:

31 And they that use this world, as not abusing *it:* for the fashion of this world passeth away.

32 But I would have you without carefulness. He that is unmarried careth for the things that belong to the Lord, how he may please the Lord:

33 But he that is married careth for the things that are of the world, how he may please *his* wife.

34 There is difference *also* between a wife and a virgin. The unmarried woman careth for the things of the Lord, that she may be holy both in body and in spirit: but she that is married careth for the things of the world, how she may please her husband.

35 And this I speak for your own profit; not that I may cast a snare upon you, but for that which is comely, and that ye may attend upon the Lord without distraction.

36 But if any man think that he behaveth himself uncomely toward his virgin, if she pass the flower of *her* age, and need so require, let him do what he will, he sinneth not: let them marry.

37 Nevertheless he that standeth stedfast in his heart, having no necessity, but hath power over his own will, and hath so decreed in his heart that he will keep his virgin, doeth well.

38 So then he that giveth *her* in marriage doeth well: but he that giveth *her* not in marriage doeth better.

39 The wife is bound by the law as long as her husband liveth; but if her husband be dead, she is at liberty to be married to whom she will; only in the Lord.

40 But she is happier if she so abide, after my judgment: and I think also that I have the Spirit of God.

* * *

1 CORINTHIANS 13

THOUGH I speak with the tongues of men and of angels, and have not charity, I am become *as* sounding brass, or a tinkling cymbal. 5

2 And though I have *the gift of* prophecy, and understand all mysteries, and all knowledge: and though I have all faith, so that I could remove mountains, and have not charity, I am nothing.

3 And though I bestow all my goods to feed *the poor,* and though I give my body to be burned, and have not charity, it profiteth me nothing.

4 Charity suffereth long, *and* is kind; charity envieth not: charity vaunteth not itself, is not puffed up.

5   Doth not behave itself unseemly, seeketh not her own, is not easily pro-
voked, thinketh no evil;

6   Rejoiceth not in iniquity, but rejoiceth in the truth;

7   Beareth all things, believeth all things, hopeth all things, endureth all
things.

8   Charity never faileth: but whether *there be* prophecies, they shall fail;
whether *there be* tongues, they shall cease; whether *there be* knowledge, it shall
vanish away.

9   For we know in part, and we prophesy in part.

10   But when that which is perfect is come, then that which is in part shall be
done away.[6]

11   When I was a child, I spake as a child, I understood as a child, I thought
as a child: but when I became a man, I put away childish things.

12   For now we see through a glass, darkly; but then[7] face to face: now I know
in part; but then shall I know even as also I am known.

13   And now abideth faith, hope, charity, these three; but the greatest of these
is charity.

NOTES

1.   Paul means, I think: do not lie to your spouse or make excuses for refusing to engage in
sexual activity. Refusing is permissible only for "fasting and prayer."

2.   Paul probably means: it is better to marry and engage in licit sexual activity with one's
spouse than to remain unmarried and be painfully aflame with unsatisfied sexual
desire, which might lead one into illicit sexual activity (fornication).

3.   Such a husband does not believe in Christ.

4.   Paul's claim seems to be: even if one is married, there is no reason to engage in sexual
activity with one's spouse and to procreate. The Day of Judgment is around the corner,
and one should be more concerned to prepare oneself for that. If so, we can understand
why it is a fault (see line 33, below) to please one's spouse (sexually?)—doing so is a
distraction (line 35) from the preparation. See Søren Kierkegaard, *Works of Love*, pp.
117–18: "the person who in love belongs to a woman shall first and foremost absolutely
belong to God, shall not first seek to please his wife, but shall strive first that his love
may please God."

5.   By "charity" we should understand "*agapic* love."

6.   I cannot avoid reading this line *pace* Hegel: all partial truths vanish in the wholeness of
the Absolute.

7.   When the perfect, i.e., God, comes the second time.

SUGGESTED READINGS, SECTION II

Aristotle, *Politics*
Augustine, *City of God*
Augustine, *Confessions*
Plato, *Lysis*
Plato, *Phaedo*
Plato, *Phaedrus*

Section III:

EXPLORING
THE CLASSICS

M OST of us at some time in our lives have said to a person who was showering us with attention and affection[1] (or we thought quietly to ourselves): "you do not love *me*, you only love my φ"—one of my properties or qualities. Or we phrased the accusation quite differently, perhaps not fully realizing that we were employing a different category: "you do not love me *for* myself, you only love me for my φ." In the first case, we are indignant that the *object* of the person's love is (in some sense) not us but only one or more features of us, while in the second case we are bothered by the possibility that the *basis* of the person's love for us is merely one aspect of us rather than (in some sense) us. What both accusations have in common is that they rebuke the person for loving in a defective or second-rate way. It occurs to us that if we were genuinely loved, we would not be loved *for* φ, nor would the person love φ itself. We also suspect that underlying the person's focusing on φ rather than on us are egocentric motives: the person is attending to φ because φ satisfies his or her desires or because φ provides certain advantages and pleasures. Further, if we are loved in such a narrow way the person is not substantially giving himself to us. In attending only to the φ part of us, he is also withholding part of himself, and so his love is self-protective in a way incompatible with its being the genuine article.

When these two accusations are stated in such abstract terms, however, it is difficult to assess their validity. One question is whether the accusations have force when the variable φ refers to certain properties or qualities, but amount

77

only to an incoherent or pointless complaint when ф refers to yet other properties. Or are these accusations valid no matter what properties are used to fill in "ф"? Another question concerns the alternative styles of loving presupposed by the accusations. If one claims that x's loving y *for* y's ф, or x's loving ф itself, is a defective style of love, then one must be able to describe accurately some superior style of loving. What, exactly, would it be for our lover to love *us* rather than our ф; what would it be for our lover to base his or her love *on* us rather than on our ф? (This is why in my initial statements of the accusations I inserted the phrase "in some sense.") Our being told what can go wrong with, or what to avoid in, love is insufficient; we also want to be told what we should be striving for.

One solution goes like this: properties, when considered as the basis of love, can be divided into two types, P and Q. Then a distinction can be made between x's loving y for a P property and x's loving y for a Q property. The difference between these two styles of loving is that x's loving y for Q is a superior love; or x's loving y for Q is more of what it means to love than is x's loving y for P. For example, suppose that the beauty of one's face or body, one's income or wealth, or one's power and position, are P properties, while intelligence, grace, wit, and moral virtue are Q properties. Then x could love y for her beautiful hair and her sexual attractiveness, but if x loved her instead (or in addition) for her intelligence and courage, x's love would be superior or the genuine article. Why might it be the case that loving for Q properties is a superior style of love? Several answers come to mind. (1) x's loving y for Q means that x is loving y for properties more closely associated with who y is (Q properties are central to y's identity while P properties are incidental). (2) x's loving y for Q is more likely to produce constancy in x's love, thus showing it to be the real thing, while x's loving y for P is unlikely to endure. Or (3) if x's love is based on Q rather than on P, then x can be expected to exhibit more reliably the behaviors connected with love—especially, say, being unselfishly concerned for the well-being of the beloved.

This solution is similar to Pausanias' position in the *Symposium*, where he distinguishes between "vulgar" and "heavenly" *eros*. That is, the solution interprets the accusation ("you only love me for my ф") entirely in *erosic* terms. Both the force of the accusation and the alternative superior style of loving it presupposes depend on viewing love as an *eros* phenomenon. What the accusation really means is this: "you only love me for my P, when you should be loving me for Q—if you really wanted to love me." When the accusation is about the object of love rather than its basis, it means: "you only love my P, not my Q, and if you wanted to love me properly, you would focus on Q and not on P." Using our examples of the different kinds of properties, these complaints would be: love my mind, not (merely) my body; or love me *for* my mind, not (only) for my body. As John Brentlinger suggests, the beloved is not complaining that the basis or object of her lover's love is a property *simpliciter,* but that her lover has settled on the wrong properties. If she is loved for the "right" properties, she has less reason to worry that her lover is motivated by egocentric considerations: if x's loving y for her sexy body smacks of self-interest, x's loving y for her intellect and virtue is less vulnerable to that charge.

This solution, despite the fact that it is commonsensical, might not do the trick. Even if a love based on or aimed at Q properties is superior to a love based on or aimed at P properties, we need to take seriously the suggestion that there is a style of love that is superior to both. If x loves y for, say, y's intelligence, x is still loving y for only a part of y; and if x loves y's intelligence itself, x is still loving only a part of y, not y the "whole" person. The protagonist of Rebecca Goldstein's *The Mind-Body Problem* recognizes this point and then tries to talk herself out of it:

> Did I ever love Noam? It's a question I've considered continuously these past months. Did I ever love anything beyond his position in that special world, the only world that's ever mattered to me? Did I ever . . . focus on the person who occupied that position? I know I never considered the person behind the genius—if there was such a person. Noam's personal identity was, at least for me, entirely absorbed by his genius. All the properties he had were defined in relation to his genius. But that would be okay, wouldn't it? If one can love someone for the curve of her nose or thigh, the charm of his laugh or his manner of smoking, why can't one love someone for his genius?[2]

Gregory Vlastos' major criticism of Plato's *eros* is that in Plato's view the object of love is not a person in all of his or her individuality and humanity (including faults and weaknesses), but only "that abstract version of persons which consists of the complex of their best qualities." Further, even if x loves y for Q properties, the mere fact that something valuable about y is the basis or object of x's love shows that the love is egocentric. This is Anders Nygren's major criticism of Plato's *eros.* He says that "like all acquisitive love, Eros necessarily directs itself to an object which is regarded as valuable. . . . Only that which is regarded as valuable can become an object of desire and love." Why that which is valuable?—because only such an item can bring the lover the happiness he or she ultimately is seeking. If x loves y for y's intelligence rather than y's beautiful body, it is only because that Q property brings x pleasure.

For both Vlastos and Nygren, the best style of love does not merely focus on some properties rather than on others. It repudiates the significance of properties as either basis or object altogether. In the best love, x loves y "for himself," not in virtue of any property, and x loves y the "whole" person, not just a part of y. The alternative superior style of love presupposed by the accusations is a kind of love fashioned along the lines of *agape*. The love we should strive for is an unconditional acceptance of the other person. Only then is the "whole" of us loved, and loved for who we really are; only then will x's love avoid egocentric motivation. Note that for Vlastos, Aristotle's *philia* comes close to this ideal, but is still insufficient. To love, as Aristotle claims, is to wish another person well for his or her own sake, and this excludes self-interested motivations. Yet Aristotle thought that this benevolence should be directed only at *good* people, i.e., that it is conditional on their merit. For Vlastos, such love must not be parceled out selectively.

John Brentlinger attempts to defend Plato against the objections voiced by Nygren and Vlastos. It does not follow from Plato's account of *eros*, he claims, that love is acquisitive, egocentric, or "impersonal." For Plato, love always does include desire. But, says Brentlinger, not all desire is acquisitive, in particular the desire to benefit another person. If x desires sexual pleasure from y, x wants that pleasure to be his, x wants to possess it. But if x desires y's welfare, or desires that y's well-being be enhanced, x's desire is not acquisitive in any robust sense. Brentlinger also points out that even if desires are *self-interested*, that does not mean the lover is *selfish*. If x loves y because y's jokes satisfy x's desire to be amused, but x never cares one whit about y's well-being and becomes cold to y when the jokes run out, x's love is offensively self-interested. But if x's strongest desire is to enhance y's welfare, that x seeks the satisfaction of this desire does not mean x is offensively self-interested. If it makes x happy to make y happy, that does not condemn x as selfish. Finally, Brentlinger argues that if x loves y for having P, it need not be the case that x loves only P itself; hence x need not be loving y "impersonally." The distinction between the basis and the object of love, for Brentlinger, saves Plato's theory from the objection that it never secures love for y the person.

Brentlinger's defense of Plato, however, is not totally convincing. He overcomes the objection that Plato's *eros* is acquisitive and egocentric by supposing that the lover's desire is to benefit the beloved. But this desire plays a role in Plato's *eros* only—if at all—at the second level of Plato's ladder, the stage at which Plato's *eros* bears some resemblance to Aristotle's *philia*. At the other levels a desire to benefit the beloved seems to play no essential role at all. And remember that the ultimate goal of the Platonic person is to achieve his or her own happiness at the highest level of the ladder. If so, what Brentlinger has accomplished is more modest. Perhaps he has successfully defended the *eros* tradition as it was developed after Plato, but not Plato's specific version of *eros*. For similar reasons, Brentlinger's conclusion that Plato's *eros* is not "impersonal" is questionable. It is true that if x loves y for P, it does not follow that x impersonally loves only P itself. Hence the *eros* tradition—understood as a thesis primarily about the basis of love—is protected against this objection. But it is not clear that in Plato's own brand of *eros* the crucial feature is x's loving y *for* y's beautiful P. Rather, as I suggested earlier (p. 43), Plato's theory might be more immediately about the object of love (namely, beauty) and not about its basis.

Aryeh Kosman employs a quite different tactic to defend Plato against the objection that his *eros* is impersonal. In effect, Kosman admits that in Plato's *eros* x does love P itself (or that if, in Plato's *eros*, x loves y for P, x still ends up loving P itself). But, Kosman argues, the fact that x loves some property-set S of y does not necessarily mean that x does not love the person y. In some circumstances, if the set S is the object of x's love, then the person y is also the object of x's love. In particular, when x loves S then x is automatically loving the person y if the properties making up the set S are none other than the properties that constitute y's identity. For example, if x loves y's mathematical talent, sense of humor, and delicately formed nose, then x's love is not impersonal, even though properties are the object of x's love, if y's mathematical talent, sense of humor, and unique nose are the properties that make y the person y is. If y is simply identical to the set S, then x's loving S is precisely x's loving the person y. There are not two objects of love here, but only one, which is at the same time the person y and the property-set S.

Like Brentlinger, Kosman also defends Plato's *eros* against the objection that it is viciously self-interested. It should be pointed out, however, that even if these defenses are not successful, we might be able to turn the tables on proponents of *agapic* love—by showing that that sort of love can similarly involve unacceptable egocentrism. For example, consider a person y who *desires* to be loved by x unconditionally or agapically. This means that y wants to be loved by x no matter what good or bad traits y has and no matter what nice or nasty things y has done to x. This person y is no fine specimen of a giving creature.[3] Similarly, the *agape* tradition might not be able to secure love "for the person" any more reliably than does the *eros* tradition. As both Kosman and Neera Badhwar argue, if x agapically loves y regardless of y's properties, it becomes difficult to understand not only why x selects y (rather than z) to be x's beloved, but also how y himself could be the object of x's love. If none of y's properties—or only the ubiquitous property of being a human being—plays a significant role in the fact that x's love gets attached to y, how is it that the person y, so stripped of all individuating qualities, could be the object of x's love? There is an inexplicable gap here between x's love and y the person.

Badhwar goes this far with Kosman but no further. She denies that Plato's *eros* can be salvaged by supposing that as long as x loves the set S of y's identity properties, the Platonic lover achieves love for the person y. Badhwar's reason is that in her view there is no room within Plato's metaphysics for conceiving of persons as constituted by essential properties; persons, in Plato's view, do not have the sort of personal nature presupposed by Kosman's solution. Instead, Badhwar argues, the notion that x loves the person y just when x loves y for the properties that constitute y's identity is an idea central to Aristotle's conception of *philia*. If so, Kosman's ingenious argument (like Brentlinger's) ends up defending only some versions of the theory of *eros* but not specifically Plato's.

Badhwar's analysis of love begins with her assumption (she calls it an "intuition") that if x genuinely loves y, the object of x's love is y *as* a unique and irreplaceable individual.[4] Neither Plato's theory of *eros* nor the Christian theory of *agape*, she argues, have the philosophical resources to explain this truth about the object of love. A theory of love derived from Aristotle's conception of *philia*, however, does account for this intuition. For Badhwar, x can love y "as an end" (a notion similar to x's loving y "for herself") if x loves y in virtue of those properties that "define" the person y. In this sort of love, x does not love y as a means or "instrumentally" (that is, merely as a source of pleasure or because y is useful) but as having her own intrinsic value. Since x loves y for y's identity properties, x loves y as a unique and irreplaceable person; y is both of the latter at least because y's identity properties are nonrepeatable. Thus Buscaglia's "something within the *you* of *you*" (see above, p. xiii) that makes each of us unique should be understood simply as the property-set that makes us who we are. It is certainly not the ubiquitous something that all objects of indiscriminate *agapic* love have, nor is it something valuable that is in principle repeatable among the various potential objects of *erosic* love.

As attractive as Badhwar's proposal is, it does involve two claims that are controversial enough to cause us to raise our eyebrows: the assumption, first, that y's identity properties make y unique in some significant way and, second, the assumption that it is in virtue of *these* properties that y is loved as having intrinsic rather than instrumental value. The problem is not merely that some of our useful properties might very well constitute our identity and thus that x's loving y for y's identity properties may be x's loving y as a means rather than as an end. There is a deeper problem, one that plagues any theory of love according to which in genuine love, x loves y for her identity properties. How do we determine which of y's many properties are essential to y's personal nature and which are only incidental to who she is?

A person's nature, for Badhwar, consists of both "qualities" *and* "their style of expression." That is, the essential nature of a person is not just a set of properties S, but necessarily includes the way x manifests S. It follows that if x loves y *only* for S, or if x loves y *only* for the style of expression of S, x is not loving y for who y is. If this is right, both qualities alone and style alone are something incidental to y. But then it is incoherent for Badhwar to claim that y's personal nature "includes the way his *fundamental* qualities are expressed." For no quality can *be* "fundamental" unless or until it is expressed by y's style. Where is the clear distinction that we need between "fundamental" and "not fundamental" properties? Perhaps what Badhwar has in mind is this. If, when P is joined with y's style, it *would* be part of y's personal nature, then P is fundamental; otherwise it is incidental. But if so, we are free to assert that some of y's instrumentally valuable properties are essential precisely when they are expressed by y's style. This conclusion can be avoided if it is shown that style is logically incapable of expressing merely useful properties, but I see no prospect for a successful demonstration of *that*.

Badhwar's idea—that identity consists of both qualities and style—is, I think, intended to sidestep the argument that no one is nontrivially unique because our properties cannot sufficiently do the job of differentiating us (properties other than, say, our fingerprints and the like). If identity also includes style, however, then the repeatability of mere properties may be no bar to uniqueness. But I still wonder: are there sufficiently different styles to make us nontrivially unique? This question is important because Badhwar admits in passing that x's style can be construed as just another one of x's *properties*. It is not clear, then, that Badhwar has adequately supported her "intuition" that people are nontrivially unique.

NOTES

1. If we have not said such things to another person who has declared love for us, we have probably heard them said to us by others whom we professed to love.

2. New York, NY: Random House, 1983, pp. 95–96.

3. See Michael Ignatieff, "Lodged in the Heart and Memory," *Times Literary Supplement* (London), April 15–21, 1988, pp. 411–13.

4. Beware of a terminological problem in Badhwar's essay: she explicitly defines "target" of love to mean what I mean by "object," and she defines "object" of love to mean what I mean by "basis." However, she does not consistently use "object" according to her own definition. Sometimes her "object" means (my) "basis," but in several passages it means (her) "target." In the long run this might not make much difference, since in her view the basis of genuine love is identical to its object: x loves y for y's identity properties, yet y *is* those properties.

AGAPE AND EROS

Anders Nygren

THE CONTENT OF THE IDEA OF AGAPE

OUR INQUIRY HAS NOW reached the point where it is possible for us briefly to describe the content of the Christian idea of love in so far as it concerns Divine love. Its main features can be summarized in the following four points:

(1) *Agape is spontaneous and "unmotivated."* This is the most striking feature of God's love as Jesus represents it. We look in vain for an explanation of God's love in the character of the man who is the object of His love. God's love is "groundless"—though not, of course, in the sense that there is no ground for it at all, or that it is arbitrary and fortuitous. On the contrary, it is just in order to bring out the element of necessity in it that we describe it as "groundless"; our purpose is to emphasize that there are no extrinsic grounds for it. The only ground for it is to be found in God Himself. God's love is altogether *spontaneous*. It does not look for anything in man that could be adduced as motivation for it. In relation to man, Divine love is *"unmotivated."* When it is said that God loves man, this is not a judgment on what man is like, but on what God is like.

Reprinted from *Agape and Eros*, by Anders Nygren; translated by Philip S. Watson. First published in Great Britain by SPCK, and in the U.S.A. in 1953 by The Westminster Press, Philadelphia, PA. Reprinted and used by permission of Westminster Press and SPCK, London. Anders Nygren was the Bishop of Lund, Sweden. (Reprinted are pp. 75–80, 175–81, and 208–210 of the combined 1953 edition; footnotes have been renumbered when retained.)

It is this love, spontaneous and "unmotivated"—having no motive outside itself, in the personal worth of men—which characterizes also the action of Jesus in seeking out the lost and consorting with "publicans and sinners." It was precisely in this action, which from the point of view of legal relationships was inexplicable and indefensible, that He knew Himself carrying out the Father's work and revealing His mind and will. When fellowship with God is conceived of as a legal relationship, Divine love must in the last resort be dependent on the worth of its object. But in Christ there is revealed a Divine love which breaks all bounds, refusing to be controlled by the value of its object, and being determined only by its own intrinsic nature. According to Christianity, "motivated" love is human; spontaneous and "unmotivated" love is Divine.

This being so, we can see why Jesus was bound to attack a religious relationship conceived in legal terms. Had He been concerned only to claim a place for the idea of *love in the most general sense* within the religious relationship, He could have secured it even within the legal scheme. There was no need to smash the legal scheme in order to do that. The love for which there is room in this scheme, however, is the "motivated" love that is directed to the righteous, to those who deserve it. But Jesus is not concerned with love in this ordinary sense, but with the spontaneous, unmotivated love that is Agape; and for this there is fundamentally no place within the framework of legal order. To go back once more to the words of Jesus in Matt. ix. 17, we may say that *Agape is the new wine which inevitably bursts the old wineskins.* Now we see also why there had to be a revolutionary change of attitude towards the righteous and the sinner. If God's love were restricted to the righteous it would be evoked by its object and not spontaneous; but just by the fact that it seeks sinners, who do not deserve it and can lay no claim to it, it manifests most clearly its spontaneous and unmotivated nature.

(2) *Agape is "indifferent to value."* This does not really add anything new to what has already been said; but in order to prevent a possible misunderstanding, it is necessary to give special emphasis to one aspect of the point we have just made. When Jesus makes the righteous and sinners change places, it might at first sight appear as if this were a matter of simple transvaluation, or inversion of values; but we have already said enough to show that it is a question of something far deeper. It is not that Jesus simply reverses the generally accepted standard of values and holds that the sinner is "better" than the righteous. True as it is to say that He effected a "transvaluation of all values," yet the phrase can easily give rise to a false impression. Actually, something of far deeper import than any "transvaluation" is involved here—namely, the principle that *any thought of valuation whatsoever* is out of place in connection with fellowship with God. When God's love is directed to the sinner, then the position is clear; all thought of valuation is excluded in advance; for if God, the Holy One, loves the sinner, it cannot be because of his sin, but in spite of his sin. But when

God's love is shown to the righteous and godly, there is always the risk of our thinking that God loves the man on account of his righteousness and godliness. But this is a denial of Agape—as if God's love for the "righteous" were not just as unmotivated and spontaneous as His love for the sinner! As if there were any other Divine love than spontaneous and unmotivated Agape! It is only when all thought of the worthiness of the object is abandoned that we can understand what Agape is. God's love allows no limits to be set for it by the character or conduct of man. The distinction between the worthy and the unworthy, the righteous and the sinner, sets no bounds to His love. "He maketh His sun to rise on the evil and the good, and sendeth rain on the just and the unjust" (Matt. v. 45).

(3) *Agape is creative.* When we seek to analyze the structure of the idea of Agape, what first attracts our attention is its spontaneous and unmotivated character. This, as we have described it above, shows that we are dealing with a love of a quite unique kind. The deepest reason for its uniqueness, however, has not yet been stated. What is ultimately decisive for the meaning of Agape can only be seen when we observe that it is *Divine* love and therefore shares in the creativeness that is characteristic of all the life of God. Agape is creative love. God does not love that which is already in itself worthy of love, but on the contrary, that which in itself has no worth acquires worth just by becoming the object of God's love. Agape has nothing to do with the kind of love that depends on the recognition of a valuable quality in its object; Agape does not recognize value, but creates it. Agape loves, and imparts value by loving. The man who is loved by God has no value in himself; what gives him value is precisely the fact that God loves him. *Agape is a value-creating principle.*

We have now reached the deepest and ultimately decisive feature of the idea of Agape—a feature which it must be said has been very much obscured in modern theology. Ever since Ritschl's time it has been common for theologians to speak of "the infinite value of the human soul" as one of the central ideas of Christianity, and to connect it with the idea of "God's fatherly love." Thus A. von Harnack, in *Das Wesen des Christentums*, claims that the teaching of Jesus as a whole can be grouped under three heads, each of such a nature as to contain the whole; and one of these he entitles "God the Father and the infinite value of the human soul."[1] To this, however, we can rightly object that the idea of "the infinite value of the human soul" is by no means a central idea of Christianity. Only a false exegesis has made it possible to find support for this idea in the oft-quoted passage: "What doth it profit a man, to gain the whole world, and forfeit his life (A. V. soul)? For what should a man give in exchange for his life (A. V. soul)?" (Mark viii. 36 f.). Moreover, Harnack's statement that "all who bear a human face are of more value than the whole world"[2] shows very clearly that the thought of an infinite value of this kind as belonging to man by nature has its roots elsewhere than in Christianity.

What chiefly interests us here, however, is the destructive effect that this idea has had on the conception of Divine love. The suggestion that man is by nature possessed of such an inalienable value, easily gives rise to the thought that it is this matchless value on which God's love is set. Even though the Divine spark may seem to have been wholly quenched in a man sunk in sin, it is nonetheless present in "all who bear a human face," and its potentialities are capable of being actualized in everyone. Viewed in this light, God's forgiveness of sins means merely that He disregards the manifold faults and failings of the outward life and looks only at the inward, imperishable value which not even sin has been able to destroy. His forgiving love means that He sees and values the pearl of great price, regardless of the defilement that happens at present to cling to it. He overlooks the defects and imperfections and concentrates on the essence of the personality which wins His approbation. [3]

If this interpretation of Divine forgiveness and love were correct, God's love would not in the last resort be spontaneous and unmotivated but would have an adequate motive in the infinite value inherent in human nature. The forgiveness of sins would then imply merely the recognition of an already existing value. But it is evident enough that this is not the forgiveness of sins as Jesus understands it. When He says, "Thy sins are forgiven thee," this is no merely formal attestation of the presence of a value which justifies the overlooking of faults; it is the bestowal of a gift. Something really new is introduced, something new is taking place. The forgiveness of sins is a *creative work of Divine power* (ἐξουσία) which Jesus knows Himself called to carry out on earth, and which can be put on a level with other Divine miracles, such as His healing of the paralytic (Mark ii. 5–12).

(4) *Agape is the initiator of fellowship with God.* Not only does Agape determine the essential and characteristic content of Christian fellowship with God, but in virtue of its creative nature it is also important for the initiation of that fellowship. In the relations between God and man the initiative in establishing fellowship lies with Divine Agape. If we consider the implications of the idea of Agape, it becomes very plain that all the other ways by which man seeks to enter into fellowship with God are futile. This is above all true of the righteous man's way of meritorious conduct, but it is no less true of the sinner's way of repentance and amendment. Repentance and amendment are no more able than righteousness to move God to love.

In this connection also the advent of Agape is completely revolutionary. Hitherto the question of fellowship with God had always been understood as a question of the way by which man could come to God. But now, when not only the way of righteousness but also that of self-abasement and amendment is rejected as incapable of leading to the goal, it follows that *there is from man's side no way at all that leads to God.* If such a thing as fellowship between God and man nevertheless exists, this can only be due to God's own action; God must Himself come to meet man and offer him His fellowship. There is thus no way for man to come to God, but only a way for God to come to man: the way of Divine forgiveness, Divine love.

* * *

THE CONTENT OF THE IDEA OF EROS

The account we have so far given of Plato's conception of Eros, drawn mainly from the *Phaedrus* and the *Symposium*, has been largely of a mythological character; but it is not difficult to discern the underlying rational idea. It now remains for us to fix more precisely the content of the idea of Eros, or to show the distinctive features of the Platonic conception of love. The chief points to be noticed here can be summed up under three heads: (1) Eros is the "love of desire," or acquisitive love; (2) Eros is man's way to the Divine; (3) Eros is egocentric love.

(1) *Eros as acquisitive love.* When giving a closer definition of Eros, Plato says it is intermediate between having and not having. The most obvious thing about Eros is that it is a desire, a longing, a striving. But man only desires and longs for that which he has not got, and of which he feels a need; and he can only strive for that which he feels to be valuable. Hence love, as Plato sees it, has two main characteristics: the consciousness of a present need and the effort to find satisfaction for it in a higher and happier state. The sense of need is an essential constituent of Eros; for without a sense of need acquisitive love would never be aroused. An Eros that was rich, and had everything it wanted, would be a contradiction in terms; and the same is true, fundamentally, of any thought of Eros as freely giving anything away. G. Simmel is right when he says: "The Greek Eros is a Will-to-possess, even when it carries the nobler sense of possessing the beloved object as a recipient of ideal instruction and morally improving attention. That is why love can be for him [Plato] the middle state between having and not having; and the logical consequence is that love must inevitably die away when the possession of its object is secured."[4] It should be specially noted that even where Eros seems to be a desire to give it is still in the last resort a "Will-to-possess"; for Plato is fundamentally unaware of any other form of love than acquisitive love.

By classifying Eros as a type of acquisitive love, Plato has fixed the limits within which we must look for Eros-love. Like all acquisitive love, Eros necessarily directs itself to an object which is regarded as valuable. Love and value belong together here; each suggests the other. Only that which is regarded as valuable can become an object of desire and love. From this it is plain that there can be no room in Plato for any spontaneous and unmotivated love: for acquisitive love is motivated by the value of its object. Eros, however, is not adequately defined by being simply described as acquisitive love. For there is a kind of acquisitive love that drags the soul downwards and only binds it the more firmly to things temporal; and that is sensual love. In contradistinction from this, Eros is a love that is *directed upwards*; it is the soul's upward longing and striving towards the heavenly world, the world of Ideas.

It would, of course, be an undue simplification to assert that this difference in the direction of the love was entirely without influence on the structure of the love itself. The plain fact is rather that the character of the desire varies with the quality of the desired object. "Desire for something different is a different desire" (Simmel).[5] It is not the same desire that is directed in the one case downwards and in the other case upwards. Yet however great the difference, it cannot alter the fact that even upward-directed Eros-love has an acquisitive aim.

(2) *Eros as man's way to the Divine.* Plato's description of Eros as an intermediate thing has also a religious significance. Eros is the mediator between Divine and human life. It is Eros that raises the imperfect to perfection, the mortal to immortality. In this connection Plato can speak of love as something Divine, though only in the sense that it unites man with the gods, *not in the sense that the gods feel love.* The gods live their blessed life wanting for nothing. They do not need to love. "Man loves and desires only that which he wants and has not got," Plato says;[6] for "who in the world would desire what he already has?"[7] Since the gods have everything and need nothing, there can be no question of their feeling love. The only relation they can have to love is to be the objects of love. In virtue of its beauty the Divine sets all things in movement towards itself; but the Divine itself is unmoved; it is absolute rest. "A god holds no intercourse with a man," Plato says, "but by means of this intermediary [Eros] all intercourse and discourse between gods and men is carried on."[8] Love, as activity and movement, belongs exclusively to man's side. For love is always the desire of the lower for the higher, the imperfect for the perfect. *Eros is the way by which man mounts up to the Divine, not the way by which the Divine stoops down to man.* This is the simple consequence of the twofold presupposition of Eros-love—namely, the recognition of a value in the loved object and the consciousness of needing this value.

The direction of love towards the super-sensible is constitutive of the Platonic idea of Eros. It has often been stated that there is a sharp contrast between the pessimistic outlook on the world which we find in the *Phaedo* and the optimistic view which prevails in the *Symposium* and the *Phaedrus.* The ethical program of the *Phaedo* is one of sheer flight from the world. The right attitude to the sense-world is to turn one's back upon it. The things of sense merely drag the soul downwards. In this world we have only dim shadow-images of true being. The soul is held in the body as in a prison-house, and waits for the hours of its deliverance. But in the *Phaedrus* and the *Symposium* we find a quite different aesthetic-ethical program. The sense-world is given a positive value. Sensible beauty is a reminder of the Absolute Beauty, and the thought of the beautiful provides a connecting link between the Ideal world and the sense-world. The sharp dualism is overcome and a more harmonious world-view is attained.

Now the difference of tone between these Dialogues is certainly not to be denied; but to conclude from this that the fundamental dualism of Plato's world-view is overcome by the Eros-doctrine of the *Symposium* and the *Phaedrus* is completely to misapprehend the facts of the case.[9] The sharp dualism between the two worlds is not done away by the doctrine of Eros, for this doctrine only shows man how he is to be saved out of the one world into the other. That there was a practicable way of escape from the sense-world to the super-sensible Plato never doubted; but this does not imply any weakening of the dualistic opposition between the two worlds. Furthermore, Eros is in no sense an affirmation or acceptance of the sense-world; on the contrary, it is the turning of the soul away from it. *Eros is itself a form of flight from the world.* It is not beautiful things as such that are the object of love and desire. It is only because of the memory they awaken of the higher world that they have any place in the scheme of Eros. Plato's interest in them attaches, not to their singularity and individuality, but to their being "paradigms," particular instances, which "participate in" the universal beauty. They exist for him only as stepping-stones to this universal. "Beauty in one body," he says, "is sister to the beauty in any other body; and therefore, as our purpose is to seek after the Idea of the beautiful, it would be very unreasonable not to regard beauty as always one and the same."[10] Hence the *ordo salutis* of Eros, as Plato teaches it, is as follows: from one beautiful body to all beautiful bodies, from these to the beauty of the soul, from this to the beauty in human laws and institutions, then to the beauty of the sciences, and finally to that which is absolutely beautiful, the Idea of beauty itself. Not even in the doctrine of Eros do we find any other way of salvation than this: escape from the sense-world.

(3) *Eros as egocentric love.* The entire structure of Platonic Eros is egocentric. Everything centers on the individual self and its destiny. All that matters from first to last is the soul that is aflame with Eros—its Divine nature, its present straits while it is in bondage to the body, its gradual ascent to the world above, its blessed vision of the Ideas in their unveiled glory. The very fact that Eros is acquisitive love is sufficient to show its egocentric character: for all desire, or appetite, and longing is more or less egocentric. But the clearest proof of the egocentric nature of Eros is its intimate connection with *eudaemonia*.[11] The aim of love is to gain possession of an object which is regarded as valuable and which man feels he needs. Plato is specially concerned to emphasize this point. "It is by the acquisition of good things [*i.e.*, advantageous, satisfying things]," he says, "that the happy are made happy."[12] And since all men wish to

be happy, the same point can be made by saying that all men love the good. Who would not strive to obtain that which was advantageous to himself? To love the good, therefore, is the same as to desire to possess the good and to possess it *permanently*. Love is therefore always a desire for immortality. But in this desire, too, the egocentric will is in evidence.

If we still had any doubt about the egocentric character of the love in question here, it certainly would be removed by such passages of Plato as the following: "Do you think that Alcestis would have died for Admetus, or Achilles have followed Patroclus to death, or that your own Codrus would have sacrificed himself to preserve the kingdom for his sons, if they had not believed that they would win thereby an immortal renown—as in fact they have? Nay, most certainly not. On the contrary, I believe that all men will do anything to win immortal fame and such glorious renown, and the better they are, the more eager they are about it: for they love the immortal."[13] Of such a love it could scarcely be said that it "seeketh not its own." Wilamowitz-Moellendorff comments on the passage thus: "But the motive alleged for the self-sacrifice of Alcestis, Achilles and Codrus is not, we hope, to be taken as Plato's real meaning."[14] It may be readily admitted that the egocentric interest appears here in a particularly startling form, which brings it into immediate proximity with the lower egoism. But there is no fundamental reason for dismissing this passage on account of its egocentric coloring; for never in any circumstances, not even in its highest form as yearning for the Divine, does Eros shed its egocentric habit of mind.[15] In order to prevent any misunderstanding, however, let it be clearly stated that the word "egocentric" is not used here in any derogatory sense. It expresses neither approval nor disapproval, but is simply descriptive of the type of love to which Eros belongs.

* * *

TABULATION OF THE ESSENTIAL POINTS OF CONTRAST

We have seen the contrast between Eros and Agape widen out into a fundamental opposition between two whole attitudes to life. With this we have reached the point which has all along been the main purpose of our study. We stated already in the Introduction that we were not, strictly speaking, concerned with a comparison of two isolated historical phenomena. Such a comparison would easily lead to all kinds of arbitrariness. Indeed, it is questionable whether there would be any possibility of comparison; for Eros and Agape grew up in such different circumstances that they are bound to appear incommensurable when set over against one another in their simple historical form. In this connection we may recall the saying of Wilamowitz-Moellendorff about Plato and Paul, that "they could have learnt something from one another here, but, being what they were, they would not have done so."[16] What reason is there, then, for taking Plato as the starting-point for a discussion of Paul's outlook, or Paul for a discussion of Plato's? In the present instance, however, as has been said, we are not concerned simply with two such historical individuals and their views, but with two fundamentally different attitudes which set their mark on the whole of life. We are concerned with two competing fundamental motifs, two contrary ideals, or conceptions of what life means. This entirely alters the situation, and provides much more favorable conditions for the purposes of comparison and contrast.

For a comparison to be possible, the objects to be compared must, of course, have something in common as well as their points of difference; and this appears to revive our difficulty. For what could Eros and Agape have in common? There seems in fact to be no possibility of discovering any idea common to them both which might serve as a starting-point for the comparison; for at every point the opposition between them makes itself felt. It is, however, unnecessary to look for anything common to them in that sense. What is common in a case like this, where we are dealing with fundamental motifs, is the question to which they are answers. The common question furnishes a common denominator, so to speak, for the answers, despite all differences between them. Both Eros and Agape claim to give expression to man's relation to the Divine, and both exercise a formative influence on his ethical life. It is these ultimate, universal questions that concern us here. We can speak of Eros-religion and Agape-religion, of Eros-ethics and Agape-ethics; and it is the content of these general concepts that we have to try to determine.

One further observation must be made. When we are comparing and contrasting two general attitudes to life, it is easy to slip over from the consideration of facts to an appraisal of values. The terms that are used to describe the different attitudes to life are then taken as indicative of the value attached to them. For example, when we describe the contrast between Eros and Agape by saying that Eros is egocentric love, Agape unselfish love, or that Eros means self-assertion, Agape self-sacrifice, we readily associate the idea of unselfishness and self-sacrifice with that of something estimable, and the idea of self-assertion and egocentric conduct with that of something unestimable. It is owing to the transvaluation wrought by Christianity that this has come to seem natural and inevitable to us. To the men of antiquity, however, self-assertion and egocentric conduct were not less obviously estimable. We have thus two ultimate standards of value confronting one another here, and it is our purpose simply to describe them, not to act as judge between them. In setting Agape and Eros side by side, *our aim is to bring out a difference in type, not a difference in value.*

Bearing this in mind, we may now go on to ask what are the characteristic features of the Eros-attitude and the Agape-attitude respectively. The principal and ultimately decisive contrast between them has already been clearly brought out in the preceding pages. In order to sum up and conclude our account of the two fundamental motifs and their contrary tendencies, we append here a tabular survey. The various particulars it contains have, of course, emerged here and there in the course of our investigation, but now we are less concerned with these details as such, than with the antithetical arrangement of them, which will enable us to see how the difference in type is manifested throughout.

Eros is acquisitive desire and longing.	Agape is sacrificial giving.
Eros is an upward movement.	Agape comes down.
Eros is man's way to God.	Agape is God's way to man.
Eros is man's effort: it assumes that man's salvation is his own work.	Agape is God's grace: salvation is the work of Divine love.
Eros is egocentric love, a form of self-assertion of the highest, noblest, sublimest kind.	Agape is unselfish love, it "seeketh not its own," it gives itself away.
Eros seeks to gain its life, a life divine, immortalized.	Agape lives the life of God, therefore dares to "lose it."
Eros is the will to get and possess which depends on want and need.	Agape is freedom in giving, which depends on wealth and plenty.
Eros is primarily *man's* love; God is the *object* of Eros. Even when it is attributed to God, Eros is patterned on human love.	Agape is primarily *God's* love; God *is* Agape. Even when it is attributed to man, Agape is patterned on Divine love.
Eros is determined by the quality, the beauty and worth, of its object; it is not spontaneous, but "evoked," "motivated."	Agape is sovereign in relation to its object, and is directed to both "the evil and the good"; it is spontaneous, "overflowing," "unmotivated."
Eros *recognizes value* in its object—and loves it.	Agape loves—and *creates value in its* object.

NOTES

1. A. v. Harnack, *Das Wesen des Christentums*, 1913, pp. 33 and 40 ff.; E.T., *What is Christianity?* pp. 51 and 63 ff.

2. *Op cit.*, p. 43; E.T., p. 67.

3. *Cf.* the similar argument in F. C. Krarup, *Livsforstaaelse*, 1915, pp. 97 ff.

4. G. Simmel, "Fragment über die Liebe," in *Logos*, vol. x., 1921–22, p. 27.

5. *Op. cit.*, p. 53.

6. *Symposium* 201; *cf.* 200.

7. *Ibid.*, 200.

8. *Ibid.*, 203.

9. Even in the *Phaedrus* the body is described as the prison-house of the soul (250). *Cf. Theaetetus* 176 f.: "Evil cannot exist among the gods, but must of necessity dwell in our mortal nature and in our lower world. *Therefore we must seek as quickly as possible to fly from it and escape thither.* But to fly thither is the same thing as to become as

much as possible like God."—"World-flight" and the doctrine of Ideas are simply inseparable from one another.

10. *Symposium* 210. For the religious significance of the aesthetic in Plato, see H. Ording, *Estetikk og kristendom*, 1929, pp. 14–25.

11. Socrates' conversation with Diotima in the *Symposium* (204 f.) is instructive on the point: "Tell me, Socrates, what does he desire who loves the good?—He desires to possess it, said I.—And what does he gain who possesses the good?—That is easier to answer, I replied, he gains happiness.—Yes, she said, it is by the acquisition of good things that the happy are made happy. And now there is no need to go on and ask what a man desires who is happy; for we have already reached finality.—You are right, I replied.—Do you now think that this desire and this love is common to all men, and that all wish to have the good always in their possession, or what do you think?— Indeed, said I, I think the desire is common to all."

"Finality" is thus reached only when love is referred back to the egocentric quest for happiness that is common to all men.

12. *Symposium* 205.

13. *Symposium* 208.

14. *Platon*, vol. ii, 1919, p. 173.

15. Further evidence of the egocentric nature of Eros is found in Plato's description of the endeavor of souls to rise to the higher world as a chariot-race, in which each "strives to get in front" of the rest (*Phaedrus* 248). Cf. what is said of friendship in the *Lysis*. There cannot be friendship without desire. The good cannot be the friend of the good, since the good man, "in so far as he is good, is self-sufficient" (214). The object of friendship is to gain some good for oneself. The sick man is a friend to the physician in order that by his aid he may gain health (218 f.). Thus egocentric desire is the basis of friendship (220 f.). *"The ground of friendship*, then, *is purely and simply desire*. A man desires that which is lacking to him, yet is necessary to him (for his existence or the fulfillment of his appropriate tasks); in other words, that which is peculiarly his own."—F. Überweg, *Grundriss der Geschichte der Philosophie*, vol. i., *Die Philosophie des Altertums*, 12th ed., ed. K. Praechter, 1926, p. 238.

16. *Platon*, I, 1919, p. 384.

THE INDIVIDUAL AS AN
OBJECT OF LOVE
IN PLATO

Gregory Vlastos

φιλεῖν = Love

I

"LET φιλεῖν BE DEFINED," writes Aristotle in the *Rhetoric*, "as wishing for someone what you believe to be good things—wishing this not for your own sake but for his—and acting so far as you can to bring them about."[1] The same thing is said about φίλος in the essay on friendship in the *Nicomachean Ethics*: "They define a φίλος as one who wishes and acts for the good, or the apparent good, of one's φίλος, for the sake of one's φίλος; or as one who wishes for the existence and life of one's φίλος, for that man's sake."[2] In the standard translations of these passages φίλος comes through as "friend," φιλεῖν as "friendly feeling," and φιλία as "friendship." This blunts the force of Aristotle's

"The Individual as an Object of Love in Plato" and Appendix II of that essay ("Sex in Platonic Love") are taken from Gregory Vlastos, *Platonic Studies*. Copyright © 1973 by Gregory Vlastos. Excerpts, pp. 3–34 and 38–42, reprinted with permission of Princeton University Press. This is the complete and unaltered text of the essay and Appendix II, which below is called "Appendix." The Bibliography that appears after the Appendix is based on Vlastos' more complete Bibliography in *Platonic Studies*. Professor Vlastos was born in 1907 (Istanbul), received his Ph.D. at Harvard University, and has had a long and distinguished career, holding positions at Cornell University, Princeton University, and Berkeley. Following the Bibliography is a guide prepared for this volume by Edward Johnson; the guide transliterates and translates the Greek that occurs in Vlastos' text, and also translates the French. Professor Johnson was born in 1950 in Lincoln, Nebraska, received his Ph.D. from Princeton University, and now teaches at The University of New Orleans.

Greek, as should be clear from one of his illustrations: maternal affection is one of his star examples of φιλεῖν and φιλία;[3] would "friendly feeling" do justice to what we normally have in view when we speak of a mother's love for her child? Or again, consider the compounds: φιλάργυρος, φιλότιμος, φιλόνικος, φιλόκαλος, and so forth: twenty-two columns of them in Liddell and Scott. φιλάργυρος is Greek for "miser." A man would need to have something considerably stronger than "friendly feeling" for money to live up (or down) to that name. Much the same would be true in the case of the vast majority of the other compounds. "Money-lover," "honor-lover," etc. would be the best that we could do to approach the natural sense of the Greek words. "Love" is the only English word that is robust and versatile enough to cover φιλεῖν and φιλία.[4] Nor is there any difficulty in seeing why Aristotle should undertake to define "love" in order to elucidate the meaning of "friendship": he thinks of friendship as a special case of interpersonal love.

So what Aristotle is telling us is that to love another person is to wish for that person's good for that person's sake, doing whatever you can to make that wish come true. This is not meant to be a run-of-the-mill definition. Its purpose is not to explain all uses of φιλεῖν but only those that answer to what Aristotle takes to be its "focal meaning"[5]—to capture the kind of love we can have only for persons and could not possibly have for things, since in their case it would make no sense to speak of wishing for their own good *for their own sake:* "It would be absurd, no doubt," says Aristotle, "to wish good for wine; if one wishes it at all, it is that the wine may keep, so that we may have it for ourselves."[6] He says this, knowing quite well that love for persons *could* be just like love for inanimates in this crucial respect. This is how Swann loves Odette in *Swann's Way.* At the height of his infatuation he is so far from wishing for her good for her own sake, that he is scarcely capable of thinking of her at all except as an adjunct to his own existence. A chance remark about her from someone who had seen her in an outfit she had never worn for him comes as a shock: "It upset him because it made him realize all of a sudden that Odette had a life which was not wholly his."[7] Aristotle recognizes two varieties of this kind of love, admitting them as φιλίαι of an incomplete, imperfect kind: "φιλία δι' ἡδονήν, φιλία διὰ τὸ χρήσιμον,"[8] "pleasure-love," "utility-love," affective bonds with men or women whose good we want because they serve our need, or interest, or pleasure, and for no other reason.

But suppose we do wish for someone's good for his own sake. Must we then forfeit utility and pleasure? Not necessarily, Aristotle would insist, and not at all when the relation is "complete" or perfect φιλία. In friendships with good and noble men one who is himself good and noble will find both profit and delight;[9] so he will love his friends for his own sake as well as for theirs. This is the only kind of love that gets a high rating in Aristotle's design of life. What then of that mother, in one of his examples, whose children, separated from her, do not know her, while she loves them, wishes for their good and works for it, yet gets nothing from them in return, and expects nothing (1159A27–33)? Though he cites this as evidence (σημεῖον) that "love is thought to consist more in loving than in being loved,"[10] it will not fit his concept of "perfect" φιλία. So what could he have made of it? He does not say. Either he fails to see that his concept of φιλία makes no provision for this and other hard cases or, if he does, the discrepancy does not disturb him. The only love of persons as persons that really interests him is that between the members of a social élite, each of whom can afford disinterested affection for his peers, assured in advance that he will normally have theirs in return, so that "in loving the friend each will love what is good for himself."[11] That Aristotle's notion of "perfect" love should be so limited is disappointing.[12] But this does not spoil it for my purposes in this essay. All I need here is to find a standard against which to measure Plato's concept of love—a standard from his own time and place, so that I would not have to risk gross anachronism by going with Anders Nygren[13] so far afield as the New Testament. This standard Aristotle does supply. That to love a person we must wish for that person's good for that person's sake, not for ours—so much Aristotle understands. Does Plato?

II

I start with the *Lysis*—one of those earlier dialogues where Plato's thought still moves within the ambit of his Socratic heritage.[14] What does Socrates here make of φιλία? Consider this exchange:

> And shall we be dear [φίλοι] to anyone, and will anyone love us [φιλήσει], in those respects in which we are unprofitable [ἀνωφελεῖς]?
>
> Of course not, he said.
>
> So your father does not love [φιλεῖ] you now, nor do others love anyone so far as he is useless [ἄχρηστος]?
>
> Evidently not, he said.
>
> So if you become wise [σοφός], my boy, everyone will love you and all will be your οἰκεῖοι[15]—for you will be useful and good—otherwise no one will love you[16]: Neither your father nor your mother nor your οἰκεῖοι. (210CD)

"Useful" and "profitable" in Plato—as in Greek usage generally—must not be given the narrow sense these adjectives ordinarily have in English. Plato uses them to cover any attribute—physical, economic, aesthetic, intellectual, or moral—that makes the one who has it a valuable asset. It is as broad as "good-producing," with no strings on the kind of good produced; and with Socrates as the speaker we can count on a bias in favor of moral and spiritual good. Socrates then is saying that a person will be loved if, and only if, he produces good. Produces it *for whom?* Jowett translated as though our text had said that A will love B only if B produces good *for* A. [17] If that were right, what Socrates calls "love" would coincide with Aristotle's utility-love: the Socratic lover would look on those he loves simply as sources of benefits to him. But the text does not say this. For all that is said there to the contrary, A might love B because B produces benefits for a third person or for a group or groups of persons or, for that matter, for B himself. So far, then, Socrates has said nothing which could fairly be said to endorse the egocentricity of utility-love. Yet neither has he made a place, even marginally, for what we found at dead center in Aristotle's conception of love: wishing another person's good *for that person's sake.* Nothing of this is said or even hinted at in our passage. There is not a word here to imply that Lysis' father and mother love him when he is "wise" because they see how beneficial it would be *for Lysis* if he were wise, and that they wish this for him just because their loving him *means* wishing for his own good for his own sake. What Socrates says of their love for the boy would have been perfectly true even if they had happened to be arrant egoists who wanted their son to be sensible and well-behaved only because of the trouble this would spare them and the credit it would bring on them. So egoistic love is not excluded though, so far, neither is it implied.

But as we go on reading in the dialogue we find that it is implied, in effect, after all. [18] This happens when Socrates goes on to argue (213E ff.) that if A loves B, he does so because of some benefit *he* needs from B and for the sake of just that benefit: The sick man loves his[19] doctor for the sake of health (ἕνεκα ὑγιείας, 218E); the poor love the affluent and the weak the strong for the sake of aid (τῆς ἐπικουρίας ἕνεκα, 215D); "and everyone who is ignorant has affection and love for the one who has knowledge" (*loc. cit.*) This is straightforward utility-love: the doctor, the rich, the wise are loved by one who needs them for what *he* can get out of them, and no reason is offered why we could love anyone except for what we could get out of him. The egoistic perspective of "love," so conceived becomes unmistakable when Socrates, generalizing, argues that "if one were in want of nothing, one would feel no affection, . . . and he who felt no affection would not love."[20] The lover Socrates has in view seems positively incapable of loving others for their own sake,[21] else why must he feel no affection for anyone whose good-producing qualities *he* did not happen to need?[22]

Socrates then goes on to argue that just as we love the doctor for the sake of health, so we love health for the sake of something else; hence, short of an infinite regress, there must be a πρῶτον φίλον, οὗ ἕνεκα καὶ τὰ ἄλλα φαμὲν πάντα φίλα εἶναι—a "first [i.e., terminal] object of love, for whose sake, we say, all other objects are loved" (219D), this being the only thing that is "truly" (ὡς ἀληθῶς) or "really" (τῷ ὄντι) loved—or, more precisely that *should be* so loved. There is danger, Socrates warns, that "those other objects, of which we said that they are loved for *its* sake, should deceive us, like so many images[23] of it" (219D2–4). So unless a man we loved actually *was* this πρῶτον φίλον, it would be a mistake to love him "for his own sake," to treat him, in Kant's phrase, as "an end in himself."[24] We would then stand in need of a philosopher, like Socrates, to cure us by his dialectic, to break the illusion, and make us see that what we "really" love is something else.[25] What is it then, this sovereign πρῶτον φίλον? All Socrates seems to be prepared to say is that it is "the good";[26] and "the good for any given person" Socrates understands to mean: what makes that person happy.[27] For something more definite we must go to the dialogues of Plato's middle period. Only there do we find the new theory of love which we can call distinctively Plato's.

III

The ideal society of the *Republic* is a political community held together by bonds of fraternal love.[28] The Allegory of the Metals which epitomizes its ethos pictures all citizens as children of the same mother, the Earth (= the polis). They are told: "You are all brothers in the *polis* . . . , all akin. . . ."[29] They are expected to have the same solicitude for the welfare of the polis which men ordinarily feel for that of their own family. Those appointed to govern must excel not only in intelligence and all-around ability but also in their concern for the welfare of the polis, which is said to be a function of their love for it: "One is most concerned for what one loves" (κήδοιτο δέ γ' ἄν τις μάλιστα τούτου ὃ τυγχάνει φιλῶν, 412D). Radical institutional innovations are to insure that this affection will be wholehearted, undistracted by economic self-interest, on the one hand, by special attachments to kith and kin, on the other. The whole of the ruling class now becomes a single communal family, where no one is an "outsider"[30] and everyone is "a brother or sister or son or daughter" or other kin "to everyone he meets."[31] The maxim of this extended family is that "φίλοι have all things in common, so far as possible."[32] The last four words explain why the same institutions are not laid down for the producers in spite of the fact that, as the Allegory of the Metals so clearly implies, all of the members of the polis are expected to be φίλοι: if the communistic property and family arrangements do not apply to them, this must be due only to the fact that Plato does not think these institutions would be practicable in their case, however desirable ideally for all.[33] But there can be no doubt of his confidence that they too will feel love for their motherland and for their rulers, who are their "saviors and helpers" (463B) and think of them as "φίλοι and sustainers"

(547C). In a postscript which gives in a nutshell the rationale of the beneficent subjection of the producers to the philosophers we are told that those who are "naturally weak in the principle of the best" (i.e., of reason) ought to be governed by those who are strong in this principle "so that we may all be alike and φίλοι so far as possible, all governed by the same principle."³⁴ Subjection³⁵ to another's will is justified on the assumption that it may not only coexist with, but also promote, φιλία.

Since we are given no formal definition of φιλία and φίλος in the *Republic*, let us try out what we heard from Socrates in the *Lysis*. "You will be loved," Socrates had told Lysis there, "if and only if you are useful." Does this fit the *Republic?* It fits perfectly. The institutions we find here appear designed from start to finish to make it possible for people to have each others' affection if, and only if, each "does his own,"³⁶ i.e., performs to the best of his ability that complex of activities through which he is best fitted by nature and nurture to make his greatest possible contribution to his polis. In doing this he would fulfill the Platonic norm of δικαιοσύνη: he would discharge all of his obligations, and earn all of his rights. For our present purpose the latter is the important point. Whatever a man can rightly claim from others in the *Republic* is tied to the performance of his job. He can claim no benefit for himself except insofar as it would enable him to be a better producer.³⁷ This principle, upheld in the name of δικαιοσύνη, dovetails into a conception of φιλία according to which one is loved so far, and only so far, as he produces good. And here the question we raised a moment ago in the *Lysis*—"produces good for whom?"—answers itself: Good for the whole community, which plays no favorites, distributing the social product to its producers with scrupulous impartiality, taking from each according to his ability and giving to each according to the needs of his job.

This moral philosophy Sir Karl Popper has called "collectivist or political utilitarianism." "Plato," he writes, "recognizes only one ultimate standard [of justice], the interest of the state. . . . *Morality is nothing but political hygiene* [his italics]."³⁸ But for Plato, as for Socrates before him, the supreme goal of all human endeavor is the improvement of the soul—and that means its *moral* improvement.³⁹ So the interest of the state would count for nothing unless it were strictly subordinate to this end.⁴⁰ The excellence of a state, its very legitimacy, would be judged by that standard:

> The sum and substance of our agreement comes to this: By what means can the members of our community come to be good men, having the goodness of soul that is proper to men? . . . This is the end to whose attainment all serious effort must be directed throughout life. Nothing which could hamper this should be given preference. In the end one should rather overturn the state, or else flee from it into exile, rather than

consent to submit to the servile yoke of baser men—one should endure any fate rather than suffer the state to change to a polity which breeds baser human beings. (770C–E)[41]

To be true to what Plato says so explicitly here and assumes throughout the *Republic*, one would have to say not that morality is political hygiene but that politics is moral hygiene. Yet even so what Popper says is not entirely without foundation. One feels intuitively that something is amiss in Plato's ultra-moralistic polity. But just what? The present analysis suggests an alternative diagnosis:

Consider what would happen in this utopia if someone through no fault of his own were to cease being a public asset. One of the philosophers, let us say, becomes permanently disabled and can no longer do his job or any other work that would come anywhere near the expected level of productive excellence. And to plug a possible hole in the hypothesis, let us preclude any higher spin-offs from the misfortune. It is not the case, for instance, that the man's character has been so purified during his illness that those who now come to visit him leave his bedside morally braced and elevated: that would be tanta-mount to shifting him to another job, the propagation of virtue. Our hypothesis is that neither in this nor in any other way can this man recoup his place as a producer. What may he then claim, now that he may no longer ground his claims on the needs of his job, but only on the value of his individual existence? As I read the *Republic*, the answer is: Nothing. In Book III Asclepius is pictured as follows:

> He would rid them of their disorders by drugs or by the knife and tell them to go on living as usual, so as not to impair their civic usefulness [ἵνα μὴ τὰ πολιτικὰ βλάπτοι]. But where the body was diseased through and through he would not try, by diet and by finely graduated evacuations and infusions, to prolong a miserable existence. . . . Treatment, he thought, would be wasted on a man who could not live in his ordinary round of duties and was thus useless to himself and to the polis. (407DE; translation after Cornford)

What are we to say? That this "political Asclepius" (497E) is not the divinity we know from other sources, the culture-hero of a vocation pledged to "love of mankind" (φιλανθρωπία)?[42] This would be true. But it would miss the point that Plato could say exactly what he did and still credit his reconditioned Asclepius with φιλανθρωπία. If men are to be loved for their productiveness and for no other reason, why should there be breach of love in the refusal of medical treatment to the unproductive?

For another sidelight on what is morally disquieting about φιλία in the

Republic, consider what would happen to the individual's freedom in that utopia. We know how highly this was prized in Plato's Athens. We know the current estimate of the positive side of freedom: guaranteed participation in the process by which political decisions were reached. "There is no better way to define the proper sense of 'citizen,' " says Aristotle, "than in terms of having a share in judgment and office."[43] He holds that to deny a man such a share would be to treat him as though he were no better than an alien or a slave.[44] And we know how highly the negative side of freedom—the right to protected privacy—was esteemed. In Thucydides Pericles boasts that daily life in Athens is free from censorious constraint,[45] and Nicias, calling on his commanders to do their utmost for Athens in her hour of supreme peril,

> reminded them that their fatherland was the freest in the world and that in it everyone had the right to live his daily life without orders from anyone.[46]

What would be left of all this in the *Republic?* Participatory democracy vanishes without a trace. So does free speech and, what Plato realizes is at least as important, free song, free dance, free art.[47] The rulers lose all right to personal privacy. Even their sex-life belongs to the state. For the greater part of their adult years intercourse is permitted them only for purposes of eugenic breeding, with partners assigned them by state officials. The end in view is the communizing—one might almost say the homogenizing—of their value-preferences, their likes and dislikes:

> Can we say that anything would be a greater evil for a polis then what breaks it up and makes it many instead of one? Or any good greater than what binds it together and makes it one?
>
> We can not.
>
> And is not the community of pleasure and of pain that binds it together—when so far as possible all the citizens are pleased or pained alike on the same occasions of gain or loss?
>
> Quite so.
>
> Whereas it is the privatization[48] of these feelings that breaks the bond—when some are intensely pained, while others are overjoyed at the very same things befalling the polis or its people?
>
> Yes indeed.[49]

Plato's community is to approach the unity of affective experience in a single person: When a man hurts his finger, we don't say that his finger feels the pain, but that *he* "feels the pain in his finger"; so too in "the best ordered polis . . . , when any citizen is affected for good or ill, this kind of polis will feel the affection as its own—all will share the pleasure [συνησθήσεται] or pain [συλλυπήσεται]" (462D–E).

Now that persons who love each other should respond sympathetically to each others' mishaps and triumphs, that each should rejoice when his fellows have cause for joy and grieve when they have cause to grieve, is only what we would expect. So from the fact that A and B are φίλοι we may expect that A will be pleased at B's pleasure and pained at B's pain. But to say this is not to say that each will be himself pleased or pained at those (and only those) things which please or pain the other.[50] Let A admire and B dislike the mixolydian mode and Sappho's lyrics. Then some things in their world which thrill A will chill B. Would it follow that they cannot be friends or lovers? Why should it? Why should not personal affection imply tolerance, even tender regard, for such differences? So it would, if it did mean wishing another's good for his own sake. For then A would have good reason for wishing that B should have what B himself deems material to the fulfillment of his own unique personality— pleased at the thought of B's having it, though A himself would only be pained if it were forced on him. To work out a *modus vivendi* in which such differences are respected might well involve practical difficulties. It would call for reciprocal adjustments and concessions. But these would be felt as implementations of mutual love, not as denials of it. This possibility does not occur to Plato. He takes it for granted that diversity of valuational response—"privatization" of feelings—would be a disruption of the love-bond,[51] a sign of mutual indifference or hostility. So the constraint on personal freedom at its deepest level— the freedom to feel whatever it be one wants to feel, whose suppression would justify that of so many other kinds of freedom—becomes not only compatible with what Plato understands by φιλία, but its indispensable ideal condition. He could not have reached this result if he had thought of love as wishing another person's good for just that person's sake, looking upon the loved one's individual being as something precious in and of itself.

IV

If—to recall the diction of the *Lysis*—we may not accord to any person we love the status of πρῶτον φίλον, whom, or what, may we "really" and "truly" love? The sections of the *Republic* I have so far discussed give no more of an answer than does the passage about the πρῶτον φίλον in the *Lysis*. Only when we come to the treatise on metaphysics and epistemology, which starts with the introduction of the Theory of Ideas in the latter part of Book V, do we get at long last what we have been looking for.[52] We get it when Plato starts talking of the philosophers as lovers of the Ideas.[53] He uses for this purpose not only φιλεῖν (479E, with ἀσπάζεσθαι), but also ἐρᾶν which is so much stronger.[54] From just these data in the *Republic* we could have inferred that now the πρῶτον φίλον is the Idea. But we have also the *Symposium* and the *Phaedrus*, either of which would confirm this inference to the hilt. I shall be content to work with the former, and there only with the metaphysical core of the dialogue—the part in which the priestess-prophetess, Diotima, instructs Socrates in "the things of love."[55] She begins with things Socrates says he knows already:

> We love only what is beautiful.
>
> In loving it we desire to possess it in perpetuity.
>
> We desire to possess it because we think it good and expect that its possession would make us happy.[56]

Then she goes on to ask (206B1–3):

> This being the aim of love,[57] in what way and by what activity is it to be pursued if the eagerness and intensity of the pursuit is to be (properly) called "love"?

Socrates has no idea of what she is driving at.[58] She tells him: "Birth in beauty" (τόκος ἐν τῷ καλῷ). She explains:

> We are all pregnant[59] in body and in spirit, and when we reach maturity our nature longs to give birth. But this we can do only in the presence of beauty, never in that of ugliness.[60] There is something divine about this. In pregnancy and in birth the mortal becomes immortal. (206C)

Beauty stirs us so deeply, Plato is saying, because we have the power to create and only the beauty we love can release that power. He puts this, to begin with, into his interpretation of physical, heterosexual, love. Being himself an invert, with little appreciation of passionate love between the sexes for purposes other than procreation,[61] all he sees in feminine beauty is the lure to paternity. He accepts this as an authentic, if lowgrade, form of creativity. Then, turning to other ranges of experience, he holds that what we love in each of them is always some variety of beauty which releases in us the corresponding power of "birth in beauty." Living in a culture which accepts the pederast[62] and does not constrain him, as ours did Proust, to falsify the imaginative transcript of his personal experience, transvesting Alfred into Albertine, Plato discovers a new form of pederastic love,[63] fully sensual in its resonance,[64] but denying itself consummation,[65] transmuting physical excitement into imaginative and intellectual energy. At the next level, higher in value and still more energizing, he puts the love of mind for mind, expecting it to prove so much more intense than skin-love that mere physical beauty will now strike the lover as a "small," contemptible, thing.[66] Still higher in ordered succession come the beauty of poetry, of political constitutions, of science, and of philosophy. Ascending relentlessly, the lover will come to see at last "a marvelous sort of Beauty" (210E)—the Platonic Idea of Beauty. "And all our previous labors," says Diotima, "were for this."[67] All previously encountered objects—bodies, minds, institutions, works of the imagination or of science—were loved as a means of moving closer step by step to this "marvellous sort of Beauty."

Here we find ourselves in the thick of Plato's ontology, so let us stop to get our bearings. For every generic character which spatio-temporal objects may have in common, Plato posits an ideal entity in which particular things "participate" so long as they have that character. We are thus offered a tripartite ontology:

1. the transcendent, paradigmatic form: say, the Form of Justice;
2. the things in our experience which may have or lack the corresponding character—the persons, laws, practices, states, which may or may not be just;
3. the character of those things—the justice they instantiate if they are just.[68]

That (1) is radically distinct (or, as Aristotle was to put it, "exists separately")[69] from (3) I take to be the crux of this ontology. But what exactly does this "separation" mean? Plato never made this fully clear. Had he done so, he would surely have seen how treacherous is one of the ways in which he tends to represent it in his middle dialogues, thinking of the Form as differing from its empirical instances not only categorially—as incorporeal, eternal, intelligibles would differ from corporeal, temporal, sensibles—but also as would an ideal exemplar from imperfect "resemblances" of it.[70] This kind of language, if meant literally, would burden the Platonic Form with the logical difficulties of "self-predication"[71]—an assumption which could not be generalized without contradiction, for then, e.g., the Form, Plurality, would have to be plural, and the Form, Motion, would have to be moving, contrary to the stipulation that each Form is unitary and immutable. Did Plato ever walk into this trap? The question has been hotly debated, and this essay is not the place to pursue the controversy. All I need say here is this: If Plato's ontology had been fashioned for narrowly logical semantic, and epistemological purposes, he would have had no use whatever for exemplarism and we would have to read the language which suggests it as pure metaphor, freeing it from any self-predicative commitment. Suppose that just this had been Plato's intention. What would have been the consequence? A more coherent ontology, certainly—but a less fruitful one for other uses to which Plato put his Ideas, for his theory of love most of all. If Plato had seen in the Idea of Beauty just the character, not the paradigmatic instance of the character, then it would not have been for him the absolutely[72] and divinely[73] beautiful object of Diotima's discourse; it would not even have been beautiful—no more beautiful than ugly, as the character, Whiteness, being an abstract universal, a purely logical entity, is itself neither white nor of any other color. How then could it have been love object par excellence in a theory which so strictly conditions love on beauty? What inspired that theory was a paradigm-form so splendidly and shamelessly self-exemplifying that its own beauty outshines that of everything else.

I cannot here formulate, let alone try to answer, the many questions that spring to mind when one ponders this theory that has done so much to mold the European imagination from Plotinus to Dante and from Petrarch to Baudelaire. A proper study of it would have to take account of at least three things about its creator: He was a homosexual,[74] a mystic, and a moralist. So to reach a balanced understanding of Platonic love—of the true original, not of that caricature confused with it by the illiterate and not infrequently by literati— one would need to pursue at the very least three complementary investigations:

First, a clinical study of the effect which Plato's inversion would be likely to have on one who saw anal intercourse as "contrary to nature,"[75] a degradation not only of man's humanity, but even of his animality: even to brutes, Plato believes, "nature" ordains heterosexual coupling.[76] This thought would poison for him sensual gratification with anticipatory torment and retrospective guilt. It would tend to distort his overall view of sexual fulfillment, while leaving him with raw sensitiveness to male beauty and heightening his capacity for substitute forms of erotic response.

Second, a study which would connect his theory of love with his religious mysticism, exploring the implications of the momentous fact that while Plato retains traditional deities and sets high above them in the *Timaeus* a creator-god of his own devising, none of these personal divinities stirs either awe or love in his heart, while the severely impersonal Ideas evoke both, but especially love, so much so that he speaks repeatedly of communion with them as an act of blissful and fertile conjugal union.[77]

Third, a study of the place of love in the pattern of inter-personal relations recommended in his moral philosophy.

Realizing what folly it would have been to spread myself in a single essay all over these three areas, I chose to concentrate on the third. That is why I started off with Aristotle, and then approached the *Symposium* via the *Lysis* and the *Republic.* My reason may be now apparent: What needs to be stressed most of all in this area is that Plato's theory is not, and is not meant to be, about personal love for persons—i.e., about the kind of love we can have only for persons and cannot have for things or abstractions. What it is really about is love for place-holders of the predicates "useful" and "beautiful"—of the former when it is only φιλία, of the latter, when it is ἔρως. In this theory persons evoke ἔρως if they have beautiful bodies, minds, or dispositions. But so do quite impersonal objects—social or political programs, literary compositions, scientific theories, philosophical systems and, best of all, the Idea of Beauty itself. As objects of Platonic love all these are not only as good as persons, but distinctly better. Plato signifies their superiority by placing them in the higher reaches of that escalated figure that marks the lover's progress, relegating love of persons to its lower levels. Even those two personal attachments which seem to have meant more to him than did any others in his whole life—his love for Socrates in his youth and, later on, for Dion of Syracuse[78]—would be less than halfway up to the summit in that diagram. This is what we must keep in view, if we are to reach a fair assessment of Plato's conception of love, acknowledging its durable achievement no less than its residual failure.

V

Let me speak first of the achievement. Plato is the first Western man to realize how intense and passionate may be our attachment to objects as abstract as social reform, poetry, art, the sciences, and philosophy—an attachment that has more in common with erotic fixation than one would have suspected in a pre-Freudian view of man. So far as we know no earlier Greek had sensed this fact, though language had pointed the way to it by sanctioning as a matter of course the use of ἐρᾶν, no less than φιλεῖν, for something as impersonal as love of country.[79] It is left to Plato to generalize this kind of ἔρως and to see that it may reach a mad[80] obsessive intensity which is commonly thought peculiar to sexual love. He discerns, as the link between such disparate involvements, the sense of beauty. He understands how decisive a role in the motivation of the most abstruse inquiry may be played by such things as the elegance of a deduction, the neatness of an argument, or the delight which floods the mind when a powerful generality brings sudden luminous order to a mass of jumbled data. He sees that the aesthetic quality of such purely intellectual objects is akin to the power of physical beauty to excite and to enchant even when it holds out no prospect of possession. And, instead of undertaking, as did Freud, to explain the attractiveness of beauty in all of its diverse manifestations as due to the excitation of lust, open or disguised, Plato invokes another drive, the hunger to create, and argues that this is what we all seek to appease in every activity propelled by beauty. That Plato's explanation is onesided does not damn it. So is Freud's. Where comprehensive insight is denied us even partial glimpses of the truth are precious.

But, second, to return to Plato's view of that kind of love whose immediate object is a man or a woman, we can get out of it a subordinate thesis which has not only psychological but also moral validity. When he speaks of ἔρως for a person for the sake of the Idea, we can give a good sense to this at first sight puzzling notion, a sense in which it is true. It is a fact that much erotic attachment, perhaps most of it, is not directed to an individual in the proper sense of the word—to the integral and irreplaceable existent that bears that person's name—but to a complex of qualities, answering to the lover's sense of beauty, which he locates for a time truly or falsely in that person. I say "truly or falsely" to call attention to a feature of Platonic love which has never been noticed, to my knowledge, in the rich literature on this subject. This feature can best be appreciated by contrast with romantic love—at any rate, with that brand of it whose textbook example is Rousseau.

"There is no real love without enthusiasm," he writes in the *Émile*, "and no enthusiasm without an object of perfection, real or chimerical, but always existing in the imagination."[81] So if we do want "real love," we must buy it with illusion. We must transfigure imaginatively the necessarily imperfect persons in whom we vest our love. We see in the *Confessions* that this is the recipe Rousseau followed himself in what he calls there "the first and only love of my life, whose consequences were to make it unforgettable for the rest of my life and terrible in my recollection."[82] What excited that high-temperature passion was scarcely the plain[83] and unremarkable young woman, Madame d'Houdetot. She served him only as a mannequin to wear his fantasies. A mood of frustration and self-pity had settled on him in his middle forties and had thrown him back, so he tells us, "into the land of chimeras":[84]

> Finding nothing in existence worthy of my delirium, I nourished it in an ideal world which my creative imagination soon peopled with beings after my own heart. . . . Forgetting completely the human race, I made for myself societies of perfect creatures, as heavenly in their virtues as in their beauties.[85]

Presently Madame d'Houdetot moves into his private landscape. He had been "intoxicated with a love without an object." She provided one. "Before long I had no eye for anyone but Madame d'Houdetot, but reclothed with all the perfections with which I had come to adorn the idol of my heart."[86]

It would be a blunder to call this affair "Platonic love," which it in fact was in the vulgar sense of the term—technically there was no infidelity[87]—and which it also approached as love for an ideal object. But no Platonist could have confused the idol of *his* heart with a Madame d'Houdetot. Even in the heat of passion the Platonic Idea does not lend itself to this kind of mistake. We see in the *Phaedrus* what keeps Plato's head clear even when his senses are enflamed.[88] It is the ontology of the paradigm-form. That harshly dualistic transcendentalism, which enraged Aristotle by its "separation" of Forms from things and which nowadays drives analytical philosophers to despair when they try to make logical sense out of it, proves a sterling asset in this area. It sustains a kind of idealism less addicted to the pathetic fallacy than are most other kinds.

It makes for a more truthful vision of that part of the world which we are all most tempted to idealize and so to falsify—the part we love. And it makes for a gain of another, no less important, kind: Freedom from the tyranny which even the unidealized love-object can exercise over a lover. Swann did not long idealize Odette. [89] But his love for her made a tortured, degraded, slave out of him while it lasted, and disabled his spirit for the rest of his life. If there is any place at all in Plato's diagram for a creature like Odette, it would be at just one level short of the bottom. At the next higher level Swann would have been once again free and whole.

But a sterling asset may be bought at a heavy cost. Plato's theory floods with the most brilliant light a narrow sector of its theme, and there points the way to authentic spiritual achievement. Beyond those limits the vision fails. Plato is scarcely aware of kindness, tenderness, compassion, concern for the freedom, respect for the integrity of the beloved, as essential ingredients of the highest type of interpersonal love. Not that Platonic eros is as "egocentric" and "acquisitive" as Nygren has claimed;[90] it is only too patently Ideocentric and creative. But while it gives no more quarter to self-indulgence than would Pauline *agape* or Kantian good will, neither does it repudiate the spiritualized egocentricism of Socratic *philia*.[91] That first description of the aim of eros in Diotima's speech—"that one should possess beauty for ever"—is never amended in the sequel in any way which would make egoistic eros a contradiction or even an anomaly.[92] It is not said or implied or so much as hinted at that "birth in beauty" should be motivated by love of persons—that the ultimate purpose of the creative act should be to enrich the lives of persons who are themselves worthy of love for their own sake. The preceding analysis shows that Diotima's failure to say or to suggest anything of the kind is no accidental oversight, but an integral feature of the structure of Plato's theory.

As a theory of the love of persons, this is its crux: What we are to love in persons is the "image"[93] of the Idea in them.[94] We are to love the persons so far, and only insofar, as they are good and beautiful. Now since all too few human beings are masterworks of excellence, and not even the best of those we have the chance to love are wholly free of streaks of the ugly, the mean, the commonplace, the ridiculous, if our love for them is to be only for their virtue and beauty, the individual, in the uniqueness and integrity of his or her individuality, will never be the object of our love. This seems to me the cardinal flaw in Plato's theory. It does not provide for love of whole persons, but only for love of that abstract version of persons which consists of the complex of their best qualities. This is the reason why personal affection ranks so low in Plato's *scala amoris*. When loved as congeries of valuable qualities, persons cannot compete with abstractions of universal significance, like schemes of social reform or scientific and philosophical truths, still less with the Idea of Beauty in its sublime transcendence, "pure, clear, unmixed, not full of human flesh and color and other mortal nonsense" (*Smp.* 211E1–3). The high climactic moment of fulfillment—the peak achievement for which all lesser loves are to be "used as steps"[95]—is the one farthest removed from affection for concrete human beings.

Since persons in their concreteness are thinking, feeling, wishing, hoping, fearing beings, to think of love for them as love for objectifications of excellence is to fail to make the thought of them as *subjects* central to what is felt for them in love. The very exaltation of the beloved in the erotic idyll in the *Phaedrus* views him from an external point of view. Depicting him as an adorable cult-object, Plato seems barely conscious of the fact that this "holy image"[96] is himself a valuing subject, a center of private experience and individual preference, whose predilections and choice of ends are no reflex of the lover's[97] and might well cross his at some points even while returning his love. Transposing this from erotics to politics we see the reason for the tragedy of the *Republic*; we see why its effort to foster civic love obliterates civil liberty. The fashioner of this utopia has evidently failed to see that what love for our fellows requires of us is, above all, imaginative sympathy and concern for what they themselves think, feel, and want. He has, therefore, missed that dimension of love in which tolerance, trust, forgiveness, tenderness, respect have validity. Apart from these imperatives the notion of loving persons as "ends in themselves"[98] would make no sense. No wonder that we hear of nothing remotely like it from Plato. Had such a thought occurred to him, his theory could have seen in it only conceptual error and moral confusion. On the terms of that theory, to make flesh-and-blood men and women terminal objects of our affection would be folly or worse, idolatry, diversion to images of what is due only to their divine original. We are a prey to this error, Plato would say, because of our carnal condition, burdened with incompleteness which fellow-creatures have power to complete;[99] were we free of mortal deficiency we would have no reason to love anyone or anything except the Idea: seen face to face, it would absorb all our love. Here we see the polar opposite of the ideal which has molded the image of the deity in the Hebraic and Christian traditions: that of a Being whose perfection empowers it to love the imperfect; of a Father who cares for each of his children as they are, does not proportion affection to merit, gives it no more to the righteous than to the perverse and deformed. Not even Aristotle had any inkling of such a notion[100]—indeed, he less than Plato, whose God is impelled by love for Beauty to create and thereby to share his own goodness with his creatures,[101] while Aristotle's Prime Mover remains eternally complete in the stillness of his own perfection. Discerning the possibility of a kind of love which wishes for another's existence, preservation, and good for that other's sake, Aristotle thought only men could have it and only few men for few. To universalize that kind of love, to extend it to the slave, to impute it to the deity, would have struck him as quite absurd.

Though so much of what I have said here has been critical of Plato, this was only incidental to the effort to understand him. And since he is a philosopher whose separate ventures must be seen in the context of his synoptic vision, let me point out in closing how Plato's speculation structures love in the same way as it does knowledge in epistemology, the world-order in cosmology, the inter-relations of particular and universal, time and eternity, the world of sense and the world of thought in ontology. In each of these areas the factors of the analytic pattern are the same: the transcendent Form at one extreme, the temporal individual at the other, and, in between, the individuals' immanent characters, projections of eternity on the flickering screen of becoming. And everywhere Plato gives the Form preeminence. In epistemology it is *the* object of knowledge; sensible particulars can only be objects of that low-grade cognitive achievement, opinion. In cosmology only the Forms represent completely lucid order; physical individuals, enmeshed in brute necessity, are only quasi-orderly, as they are only quasi-intelligible. In ontology there are grades of reality and only Forms have the highest grade. So too in the theory of love the respective roles of Form and temporal individual are sustained: the individual cannot be as lovable as the Idea; the Idea, and it alone, is to be loved for its own sake; the individual only so far as in him and by him ideal perfection is copied fugitively in the flux. [102]

NOTES

1. *Rhet.* 1380B35–1381A1: . . . τὴν φιλίαν καὶ τὸ φιλεῖν ὁρισάμενοι λέγωμεν. ἔστω δὴ τὸ φιλεῖν τὸ βούλεσθαί τινι ἃ οἴεται ἀγαθά, ἐκείνου ἕνεκα ἀλλὰ μὴ αὑτοῦ, καὶ τὸ κατὰ δύναμιν πρακτικὸν εἶναι τούτων.

2. *N.E.* 1166A2–5: τιθέασι γὰρ φίλον τὸν βουλόμενον καὶ πράττοντα τἀγαθὰ ἢ τὰ φαινόμενα ἐκείνου ἕνεκα, ἢ τὸν βουλόμενον εἶναι καὶ ζῆν τὸν φίλον αὑτοῦ χάριν.

3. The second citation runs on: "as mothers do for their children. . . ." Parental affection is used to illustrate φιλία already in the first chapter of the Essay on φιλία (N.E. VIII. 1). Cf. my reference to 1159A27–33 in the third paragraph of this essay.

4. As is shown, e.g., by the fact that the translator is compelled to use "love" when translating the verb φιλεῖν and that the commentators shift without apology to "love" and "beloved" when they gloss φιλεῖν and φίλον in the *Lysis*. I say that "love" *covers* these Greek terms, bearing in mind that its connotation is considerably broader, since it does also the work of ἐρᾶν, which overlaps with φιλεῖν, but differs from it in three respects: (i) it is more intense, more passionate (cf. Plato, *Lg.* 837A: ὅταν δὲ ἑκάτερον [*sc.* φίλον] γίγνηται σφοδρόν, 'ἔρωτα' ἐπονομάζομεν); (ii) it is more heavily weighted on the side of desire than of affection (*desire, longing*, are the primary connotations of ἔρως, *fondness* that of φιλία); (iii) it is more closely tied to the sexual drive, (though φιλεῖν may also refer to sexual love [*LSJ* s.v. φιλεῖν, 3]):

for nonincestuous familial love one would have to turn to φιλία in lieu of ἔρως (cf. Plato, *Symp.* 179C: Alcestis had φιλία for her husband, Admetus, and so did his parents; but "because of her ἔρως for him she so surpassed them in φιλία" that she was willing to die in his place, while they were not.)

5. A useful term we owe to G. E. L. Owen (1960, p. 169) for what Aristotle calls πρὸς ἓν λεγόμενον (a phrase applied to the definition of φιλία in the *Eudemian Ethics*, 1236A16–B27,) on which see below *JHR*, n. 60.

6. 1155B29–31. The parenthesis which Bywater closes here in the Oxford text should rather close at the end of the immediately following remark which explains the point of the example: τῷ δὲ φίλῳ φασὶ δεῖν βούλεσθαι τἀγαθὰ ἐκείνου ἕνεκα).

7. "Ce simple croquis bouleversait Swann parce qui'il lui faisait tout d'un coup apercevoir qu'Odette avait une vie qui n'était pas tout entière a lui, . . ." *A la recherche du temps perdu*, Vol. I of the *Pléiade* Edition (Paris, 1954), 240.

8. N.E. 8. 3–5, 1156A6 ff. These are φιλίαι κατὰ συμβεβηκός, 1156A17–18. They are called φιλία "by similitude" (καθ' ὁμοιότητα, 1157A31–32; cf. ὁμοίωμα ἔχει, 1157A1) of the kind which is "truly" (ὡς ἀληθῶς), "primarily" (πρώτως), and "strictly" or "chiefly" (κυρίως) φιλία (*loc. cit.* A24 and 30–31), the only kind Aristotle considers "complete" or "perfect" (τελεία) φιλία (1156B34, 1158A11).

9. This is implied unambiguously in his discussion of what he calls "τελεία φιλία" in 1156B7ff, "μάλιστα φιλία" in 1157B1–1158A1.

10. N.E. 1159A27–28, [φιλία] δοκεῖ . . . ἐν τῷ φιλεῖν μᾶλλον ἢ ἐν τῷ φιλεῖσθαι εἶναι.

11. N.E. 1157B33, καὶ φιλοῦντες τὸν φίλον τὸ αὑτοῖς ἀγαθὸν φιλοῦσι.

12. Cf. n. 100, below.

13. *Agape and Eros* (English translation by P. S. Watson, Harper Torchbook edition, New York, 1969)—a distinguished, influential, and very one-sided book, whose treatment of the "Greek" idea of love fails to reckon with the elementary fact that *philia* is a near-synonym of *agape*, and that, regardless of what their philosophers said, Greeks, being human, were as capable of genuine, non-egoistic, affection as are we. Ignoring *philia* (save for a passing notice of the *Lysis* on p. 180, where Nygren translates the word by "friendship" and uses the dialogue as further evidence "of the egocentric nature of Eros" in Plato, 181, n. 3), he fails to take the slightest cognizance of Aristotle's conception of it.

14. See Appendix I to this essay, below, pp. 35 ff. [Deleted in this volume.]

15. Literally *"in* [or *of*] *the house"*; here "family-relation, kinsman" in the extended sense of "intimate," "near and dear."

16. Good examples in this citation of the unavoidability of the resort to "love" when translating the verb *philein*.

17. His rendering for 210C5–8 reads: "And shall we be friends to others, and will any others love us, in matters where we are useless *to them?*—Certainly not—Then neither does your father love you, nor does anybody love anybody else, in so far as he is useless *to him?*" The italicized words answer to nothing in the Greek text. Similar mistranslation of the second sentence in the Pléiade translation by Robin (1950), "En consequence, ton père non plus, dans la mesure où tu ne *lui* es bon à rien, n'a donc pas d'amitié pour toi. . . ." (My emphasis). The passage had been correctly translated in the Budé translation by A. Croiset (1956).

18. It must have been an unconscious anticipation of this sequel that led Jowett to mistranslate the earlier passage.

19. The pronoun is not in the text. But the reflexive reference is definitely implied in the context. Thus Socrates observes at 217A that "no one, while healthy, loves a doctor for the sake of health": so when persons "love a doctor for the sake of health" it must be for the sake of the health *they* have lost and wish, with *their* doctor's aid, to regain. And cf. the next note.

20. 215BC: ὁ δὲ μή του δεόμενος οὐδέ τι ἀγαπῴη ἄν . . . οὐδ' ἂν φιλοῖ. This is reinforced by the general formula in 218D7–9: When A loves B it is always for the sake of (ἕνεκά του) something, x, and because of something (διά τι), y, where x ranges over goods and y over "evils" remedied by the appropriate values of x. The "evil" here stands for a remediable deficiency in A which B has power to remedy: ". . . that which desires, desires that of which it is in want. . . . Hence that which is in want loves that of which it is in want . . ." (221D7–E2). This is Socrates' last word on this aspect of the topic (and, therefore, reassures us that the question in 215C3–4, "But tell me, Lysis, in what way [πῇ] have we gone off the track? Are we perchance wholly mistaken?" is not meant to invalidate everything in the preceding paragraph and, in particular, is not meant to impugn the statement that "if one were in want of nothing one would feel no affection.")

    This feature of the theory of *philia* in the *Lysis* is conserved and elaborated in what I take to be the Socratic component in the theory of eros expounded in the *Symposium*, i.e., in Socrates' dialogue with Agathon (199C–201C) and in the first part of his dialogue with Diotima (201D–206A): what we learn about love here is that it is caused by a deficiency in the lover and expresses the lover's longing for the good whose possession will relieve the deficiency. (For the shift in perspective at 206B, cf. Marcus in n. 56 below, and paragraph 1 of Section IV of the present essay and n. 58). This notion finds its complement in the thesis, emphasized in both dialogues (more briefly in the *Lysis* [216D–217A], at greater length in the *Smp.* [201B–204C]), that the lover is in a condition intermediate between goodness and evil, or beauty and ugliness, hence *qua* lover neither good nor evil, neither beautiful nor ugly: if he were wholly the former, he would have no need to love.

21. It might be objected that Socrates cannot mean to endorse this view of love, for it would belie his own profession of love for his fellow-citizens: he says that he loves them (*Ap.* 29D), but does not impute to them either wisdom (just the opposite!) nor any other quality which would elicit utility-love. But what does this prove? Can't a man be better than his theory? And what precisely *is* the "love" which Socrates professes for his fellows? Does it measure up to the Aristotelian definition? I do not think so, but to argue out the point would require an extended discussion which I cannot pursue here. Cf. n. 91 below.

22. R. A. Gauthier and J. V. Jolif take no account of this passage when they see the *Lysis* as an expression of "l'amour de bienveillance où amour désintéressé" (1970, 671; cf. 726). Since they do not argue for this extraordinary suggestion, one is reduced to surmise as to how it ever occurred to them that this is the message of the *Lysis*. What apparently suggested it to them is the example in 219E2–220B5 (cf. n. 23 below): they quote this passage in full (670–71) and cap the citation with a remark which shows that they are taking the father's love for the wine and his love for the son to stand respectively for "amour de concupiscence" and "amour désintéressé," without a word of explanation or argument to convince us that this is what Plato is illustrating in this passage. What he *says* he is illustrating is concern for an object which is valued not for its own sake, but for the sake of another (πᾶσα ἡ τοιαύτη σπουδὴ οὐκ ἐπὶ τούτοις ἐστὶν ἐσπουδασμένη, ἐπὶ τοῖς ἕνεκά του παρασκευαζομένοις, ἀλλ' ἐπ' ἐκείνῳ οὗ ἕνεκα πάντα τὰ τοιαῦτα παρασκευάζεται, 219E7–220A1). One wonders if they are confusing the difference between instrumental and intrinsic value

(which is the immediate point of the example) with that between egoistic and non-egoistic valuation, losing sight of the fact that the former difference would be as valid for the egoist as for anyone else: there is no reason in the world why an egoist should not attach intrinsic value to certain things, desiring them as ends (*his* ends), not as mere means.

23. Or "phantoms" (εἴδωλα). In the terms of the accompanying example (219D5ff.), the mistake would be to put such a value on wine as to refuse it to one's son when he is in mortal need of it, having drunk hemlock for which the wine is the only available antidote. In the analogy the father's love for the wine stands to love for his son as would love for a particular person to love for the πρῶτον φίλον. It would be hard to think of a stronger way of making the point that in our love for persons we should *not* treat them as "ends in themselves" (cf. the next note).

24. For an interpretation of this phrase see Vlastos 1962, 48–49, and notes. Aristotle's "wishing another's good for his sake, not for yours," though still far from the Kantian conception of treating persons as "ends in themselves," is the closest any philosopher comes to it in classical antiquity.

25. Just as "it is not altogether true [οὐδέν τι μᾶλλον οὕτω τό γε ἀληθὲς ἔχῃ]" that we set great stock by money, since we give it up readily when we find things we want to buy with it, so too "it is only in a manner of speaking [ῥήματι . . . λέγοντες] that we say we 'love' what is loved for the sake of something else; it looks as though what is really loved [φίλον . . . τῷ ὄντι] is that very thing in which all of these so-called loves terminate [ἐκεῖνο αὐτό . . . , εἰς ὃ πᾶσαι αὗται αἱ λεγόμεναι φιλίαι τελευτῶσιν]" (209A2–B3). To say of another person that he or she is what we *really* and *truly* love would be to lapse, like the miser, into moral fetishism.

26. ". . . hence the good is loved? [ἀλλ᾽ ἄρα τὸ ἀγαθόν ἐστιν·φίλον;]" (220B7)—a surprisingly casual and elliptical answer: it does not *say* that the good is the πρῶτον φίλον, though this is doubtless what is meant. Socrates must think the proposition that the good is the πρῶτον φίλον so truistic that it does not even call for a formal statement, let alone defense, in the present context. His attitude is perhaps understandable, given his standing conviction that the good is the only (real) object of desire (*Grg.* 467C5–468C7, which concludes, "for we desire those things which are good, . . . while those which are neither good nor evil we do not desire, nor yet those which are evil"; cf. *Meno* 77C1–E4), and his present contention that "desire is the reason (αἰτία) for love, and we love that which we desire and when we desire it" (221D2–4).

27. This is regarded as axiomatic in the Socratic dialogues, though never formally spelled out. It shows up, e.g., in the *Meno* (77C ff.), where the thesis that no one can desire evil things knowing that they are evil is proved by arguing that "no one desires to be wretched and miserable" (78A4–5), or in the *Euthydemus* (278E2–282D: the protrepsis to philosophy), where it is argued that wisdom is the greatest of all goods because it alone enables us to use any other good in such a way as to make us happy (εὐδαιμονεῖν, εὖ πράττειν), the presupposition of the argument being that anything will be good for any person if, and only if, it makes that person happy.

28. Though one would hardly guess this from much that has been written about Plato's social theory. Not a word about political *philia* in Plato in T. A. Sinclair, *Greek Political Theory* (London, 1951); in the Index under *philia* there are references to Protagoras and five other authors, but none to Plato. Sheldon Wolin, in his acute critique of Plato's political philosophy, *Politics and Vision* (Boston, 1960), duly reports (47) the doctrine of the *Politicus* that "the end of the royal art was . . . a community bound together in 'a true fellowship by mutual concord and by ties of

friendship' " (311B9–C1); but nine pages later he says that "it required the Christian notion of *agape* before there could be an idea of love as a force fusing together a community." He evidently has no inkling of the fact that Plato expects *philia* to be just such a force. The same is true of the study of Plato's contribution to social theory, *Enter Plato* (New York, 1964), by the sociologist, Alvin W. Gouldner. He says that while Plato "speaks well of friendship" (244), he "removes love from the Pantheon of virtues . . . strip[s] it of moral relevance" (246). One wonders how so imaginative a student of Plato's social theory could say such things in view, e.g., of the fact that in the *Laws* the three goals that are to guide all legislation are that the state should be intelligent, free, and "ἑαυτῇ φίλη" (693B–E, 701D; cf. also 628A–C, 697C, 698C, 699C, and especially 743C and 759B). Part of the trouble seems to be that he gets Plato *via* the Jowett translation, where φίλη is turned into "harmonious" or "at unity with itself" and φιλία into "friendship." Yet even the Jowett translation might have given Gouldner reason to doubt that "friendship" is what Plato means here. Thus in 698C one should be able to tell just from the context that Jowett's "spirit of friendship" is a feeble understatement of what is being talked about: the embattled comradeship, the fraternal solidarity, that flared up among the Athenians at the time of the Persian invasion.

29.   ἐστὲ μὲν γὰρ δὴ πάντες οι ἐν τῇ πόλει ἀδελφοί . . . ἅτε οὖν συγγενεῖς ὄντες πάντες . . . (415A2–8). And cf. 414E5–6, καὶ ὑπὲρ τῶν ἄλλων πολιτῶν ὡς ἀδελφῶν ὄντων (δεῖ) . . . διανοεῖσθαι.

30.   A. Bloom's happy rendering of ἀλλότριος (antonym of οἰκεῖος).

31.   463BC.

32.   424A; cf. 449C.

33.   Cf. *Laws* 739C–740B, where thoroughgoing communism in both property and family is proclaimed as the ideal (it represents "the best polis and laws, the most excellent constitution"), but private allotments and private families are accepted since the pure ideal would be "beyond the capacity of people with the birth, rearing and training we assume" (740A).

34.   590C–D. Cornford, for once, misses the sense by a mile when he translates ὅμοιοι here by "equal" (as I did too in *SPT*, [292], in 1941: I have corrected to "alike" in the reprint): the word could, of course, mean equal in certain contexts; but equality between subject and ruler is the last thing Plato would tolerate, let alone commend; and that "alike" in the sense here follows directly from its use in C8, ὑπὸ ὁμοίου ἄρχηται to which τῷ αὐτῷ κυβερνώμενοι in D8 alludes.

35.   Which Plato accents strongly by using the word δοῦλος, without meaning, of course, that the producers in the *Republic* are to be the slaves of the philosophers (cf. below, *SPT*, [292] and n. 25).

36.   Cf. *JHR*, Sections II and III.

37.   Thus the Guardians are denied individual property-rights because they would be "more excellent craftsmen at their own job" (421C1–2) without, than with, such rights. Cf. *JHR*, III. 2.

38.   *The Open Society and Its Enemies*, Vol. I of the Fourth edition (Princeton, 1963), 107 (and cf. 119). There have been many replies to this indictment. But it is not easy to rebut its thesis without endorsing antitheses which are still further from the truth. Thus R. B. Levinson (*In Defense of Plato* [Cambridge, Mass., 1953], 517) caps his critique (much of it pertinent) by calling on us to "recognize Plato's altruistic concern for the welfare of the individual"; we are to see in "every Platonic dialogue . . . a monument erected to his belief that individual men are important."

39. *Lg.* 707D: ". . . unlike the majority of mankind, we do not regard mere safety and survival as matters of greatest value, but rather that men may become and be as virtuous as possible as long as they do survive."

And 705E–706A: "For I lay it down that only that law is rightly enacted which aims, like an archer, at this and this alone: how beauty [τὸ καλόν] should come about in consequence of it, passing over every other consideration, be it wealth or anything else devoid of beauty and virtue."

40. *Lg.* 630BC: ". . . every legislator worth his salt will legislate with no other end in view than to secure the greatest virtue [of the citizens]."

41. And see the preamble to the laws in the opening paragraphs of *Lg.* V, where the rationale of the legislation is explained. (Here and in the preceding notes I have drawn on the *Laws* where much that is implicit in the tightly constructed argument of the *Republic* is spelled out at length.)

42. Hippocrates, *Precepts* (παραγγελίαι), 6: "for if there is φιλανθρωπίη, there is bound to be φιλοτεχνίη."

43. *Pol.* 1275A22–23, πολίτης δ' ἁπλῶς οὐδενὶ τῶν ἄλλων ὁρίζεται μᾶλλον ἢ τῷ μετέχειν κρίσεως καὶ ἀρχῆς. By κρίσις Aristotle must mean here effective judgment in political and legislative, no less than judicial, decisions (cf. *Thuc.* 2,40,2, ἤτοι κρίνομέν γε ἢ ἐνθυμούμεθα, where the latter "must here be used of those who originate proposals," the former of those who judge [i.e., vote for or against] them [A. W. Gomme, *ad. loc.*]; also κριταί, 3,37,4, and κρῖναι in 6,39,1). Aristotle goes on to explain (23–31) that under ἀρχή he includes that of the juror and of the ecclesiast, no less than that of the magistrate and of a member of the Council. Cf. 1275B 18–20 (much the same in 1278A 35–36, where "μετέχ[ειν] τῶν τιμῶν" = "sharing in ἀρχή" here).

44. *Pol.* 1275A7–8.

45. ἐλευθέρως δὲ [1] τά τε πρὸς τὸ κοινὸν πολιτεύομεν καὶ [2] ἐς τὴν πρὸς ἀλλήλους τῶν καθ' ἡμέραν ἐπιτηδευμάτων ὑποψίαν, οὐ δι' ὀργῆς τὸν πέλας, εἰ καθ' ἡδονήν τι δρᾷ, ἔχοντες, οὐδὲ ἀζημίους μέν, λυπηρὰς δὲ τῇ ὄψει ἀχθηδόνας προστιθέμενοι. ἀνεπαχθῶς δὲ τὰ ἴδια προσομιλοῦντες . . . (2,37, 2–3). The sense of ὑποψίαν in this context I take to be "censorious watchfulness" (*LSJ s.v.*, II). λυπηρὰς τῇ ὄψει ἀχθηδόνας refers directly to "dirty looks" at those who choose a different style of life for themselves (Croiset, "regards chargés de blâme"), indirectly to all those informal, extra-legal, pressures by which their life could be made miserable. ἀνεπαχθῶς τὰ ἴδια προσομιλοῦντες reinforces the notion of private life free from oppressive intolerance. For the recognition of [1] and [2] as distinct, though complementary, aspects of freedom, cf. Aristotle's account of liberty as the "postulate" (ὑπόθεσις) of democracy: "one [kind] of freedom is to rule and be ruled in turn. . . . The other mark of democracy is to live as one wishes [τὸ ζῆν ὡς βούλεταί τις]" (*Pol.* 1317 B2–12).

46. *Thuc.* 7, 69, 2. Cf. Plato's account of the democratic ethos in *Rep.* 557B: there men are "free and the polis is full of freedom and free speech, and one has the liberty to do what he likes. And where this liberty exists it is clear that each will make his own life according to his own private design—that which pleases him." And cf. Aristotle in the preceding note.

47. The rulers "must take the greatest care not to overlook the least infraction of the rule against innovation in gymnastic and in music counter to the established order. . . . For a new form of music is to be feared as endangering the whole [of the social order]: for nowhere are the modes of music altered without affecting the most fundamental political usages. . . . Here, in music, our guardians it seems must build their guard-

house" (424B–C). Conceding that Homer is "the first and most poetic of the tragic poets," we must banish him from our state: "if you allow the honied Muse in song or verse, pleasure and pain will be king in your polis instead of law and consensus about the highest good" (607A).

48. No such word exists in English, as probably there was none in Greek when Plato wrote ἰδίωσις here (no other occurrence is listed in *LSJ*). Shorey and Robin translate "individualization," which is close enough. Cornford resorts to periphrasis: "when such feelings are no longer universal"; so does Lee: "When feelings differ between individuals."

49. 462A9–C1. And cf. *Laws* 739C–D: the implementation of the maxim, κοινὰ τὰ τῶν φίλων would require ideally "driving out by every means what is called 'private' [ἴδιον] out of life, and contriving, if it were possible, that even things which nature made private should somehow become common—thus eyes and ears and hands would be expected to see and hear and act in common, and men would be as united as they could possibly be in what they praise and blame, rejoicing and grieving at the same things."

50. The notion that friends are those who share each others' pleasures and pains is accepted by Aristotle, but only with the proviso which expresses what he himself considers definitive of φιλία: "Your φίλος is he who shares your pleasures at what is good [τὸν συνηδόμενον τοῖς ἀγαθοῖς] and grief at what is painful [συναλγοῦντα τοῖς λυπηροῖς] *for your sake, not for the sake of something else*" (*Rhet*. 1381A4–6).
   The all-important phrase I have italicized is not present, in *N.E.* 1166A6–8: "And some [define the φίλος] as one who consorts with another and shares his preferences [τὸν συνδιάγοντα καὶ ταὐτὰ αἱρούμενον], or as one who shares the pains and pleasures of the one he loves [τὸν συναλγοῦντα καὶ συνηδόμενον τῷ φίλῳ]." But note that there is no indication here that this formula would be acceptable to Aristotle as a *definition* of φιλία. The evidence of the *Rhet*. shows that it would not: of the two formulae in 1166A2–10 only the first (A2–5, quoted in n.2, above) would be acceptable to Aristotle, since only this one states the condition which Aristotle uses to define φίλος in *Rhet*. 1380B35–1381A1 (quoted in n. 1, above), a context which leaves no doubt that Aristotle is speaking *in propria persona* (cf. ὁρισάμενοι λέγωμεν here with οἱ δὲ [τιθέασι] in *N.E.* 1166A6). That this remains the crucial condition of "perfect" φιλία in the *N.E.* is clear e.g. at 1156B9–10, "οἱ δὲ βουλόμενοι τἀγαθὰ τοῖς φίλοις ἐκείνων ἕνεκα μάλιστα φίλοι."

51. As breaking up (διασπᾷ) the community, making it "many" rather than "one" (462AB); the same implication in *Laws* 739C–D, where the citation in n. 49 goes on to speak of laws which maximize identity of pleasure and pain among the citizens as "making the polis one so far as possible" (739D3–4).

52. 474C ff. Cf. below, *MP*, pp. 43 ff.

53. 501D: the philosophers are the "lovers [ἐρασταί] of being and truth," i.e., of the Ideas; 490B: the philosopher's ἔρως for the Idea will lead him to a union with it which will give birth "to intelligence and truth" (a passage which states in miniature the experience of the vision of the Idea of Beauty and union with it in *Smp*. 210E–212A).

54. Cf. above, n. 4 (i).

55. ἡ δὴ καὶ ἐμὲ τὰ ἐρωτικὰ ἐδίδαξεν, 201D5. τὰ ἐρωτικά is used repeatedly throughout the discourse to refer to its theme.

56. 204D–205A; 205E–206A11; 207A2. Nygren (*op. cit.*, 180, n. 1) cites this passage to prove the "egocentric" and "acquisitive" nature of Platonic eros, taking no account of

the fact that what Diotima has said so far is not meant to be the whole story: as yet she has not stated, has scarcely hinted at, that distinctive feature of Platonic eros which she proceeds forthwith to explain as "birth in beauty" (to be discussed directly in the text above). For a corrective see R. A. Markus (1955, 219–30); Markus (225 ff.) calls attention to "the radical change of perspective" when "the new picture" of love "as a begetting or procreating" is introduced. However, Markus goes a bit too far in the other direction when he remarks that while this new conception of love "is at first grafted onto the original metaphor of desire-and-fulfilment, it very soon achieves independence" (*loc. cit.*). Diotima never cuts loose from the original description of eros as desire for one's perpetual possession of the good (ἔστιν ἄρα συλλήβδην ὁ ἔρως τοῦ τὸ ἀγαθὸν αὐτῷ εἶναι ἀεί, 206A11–12); she brings in "birth in beauty" to fill out, not to amend, that description (see next note), even asserting (206E8–207A2) that "birth in beauty" *follows* (and "necessarily"!) from that agreed-upon description. She claims that only through the immortalizing effect of "birth in beauty" can one fulfill the desire to possess the good in perpetuity; how seriously she takes this implication shows up in her treatment of the Alcestis story: Alcestis' readiness to give her life for that of Admetus, which Phaedrus had explained as due to the intensity of her love for her husband (ὑπερεβάλετο τῇ φιλίᾳ διὰ τὸν ἔρωτα, 179C1), Diotima explains as due rather to her desire to win immortal fame for herself (208C–D). (A further point that should not escape notice is the force of the possessive pronoun in the [above cited] phrase in 206A11–12 and in the parallel phrase [to be cited in the next note] in 207A2. This is brought out well in Suzy Groden's translation of the two phrases: "love is for the good to always belong to oneself," "love is for the good to be eternally one's own." It gets lost in the usual translations. Thus, to render the first phrase "love is of the eternal possession of the good" [so Jowett, and similar renderings in Hamilton, Robin, Apelt & Capelle], fails to make it clear that what the lover desires is *his* possession of the good.)

57. Following Bury (against Burnet, Robin, and others) I accept Bast's emendation (favored by Hermann and Schanz among others) of τοῦτο of the codices to τούτου, since the sense makes it clear that the reference of the pronoun in διωκόντων αὐτό is not ἔρως itself, but its aim (love is the pursuing—not the object of the pursuit, which is the eternal possession of the good); and cf. 207A2, εἴπερ τοῦ ἀγαθοῦ ἑαυτῷ εἶναι ἀεὶ ἔρως ἐστίν, where the object of ἐστίν is quite explicitly the aim of ἔρως, not ἔρως itself.

58. He replies, "If I could [tell you the answer], Diotima, I should not be marvelling at your wisdom and coming to you to learn of this very matter." This suggests that Plato is now introducing a doctrine which cannot be credited to the historical Socrates (cf. his use of a similar device in *Meno* 81A: Socrates learns of the doctrine of transmigration from "priests and priestesses.") I see no justification for the view (F. M. Cornford, "The Doctrine of Eros in Plato's *Symposium*," in *The Unwritten Philosophy* [Cambridge, 1950], 75) that "the limit reached by the philosophy" of Socrates is indicated no earlier than in 209E4. If Plato had wanted to imply such a thing why should he have represented Socrates as stumped already at 206B?

59. πάντες κυοῦσιν ἄνθρωποι. For this striking image of male pregnancy there is no known precedent in Greek literature. The nearest thing to it is in Apollo's argument in the *Eumenides* (661 ff.) that the father is the true progenitor (τοκεύς), the mother serving only as "nurse of the new-sown pregnancy [τροφὸς . . . κύματος νεοσπόρου]"—a kind of human incubator.

60. Excising ἡ γὰρ ἀνδρὸς καὶ γυναικὸς συνουσία as a gloss: cf. Bury *ad loc*. I find the defense of the text in S. Rosen, *Plato's Symposium* (New Haven, 1968), 247, n. 125, incomprehensible: "it has the obvious function of serving as transition from homosex-

ual to heterosexual generation"—how so, when there has been absolutely no reference to homosexual *generation* at all?

61. At least in the middle dialogues. There is a passage in the *Laws* (839AB) which suggests a better appreciation of conjugal love: one of his reasons there for prohibiting every other form of sexual gratification is that the restriction would make men fonder of their own wives (γυναιξί τε ἑαυτῶν οἰκείους εἶναι καὶ φίλους). Cf. G. Grube, *Plato's Thought* (London, 1935), 118–19.

62. On this see Dover, 1966, 31–42, and Appendix II, below. [This Appendix reprinted below, pp. 124–128.]

63. I say "new" because the doctrine σώφρων ἔρως (in which, it has been claimed, "Euripides anticipates Plato," [Helen North, 1966, 73 ff. *et passim*], is a doctrine of self-control, *not* of abstinence. The Uranian Aphrodite of Pausanias' speech in the *Symposium* is not meant to rule out intercourse, but to restrict it to a context in which intellectual and spiritual values prevail. Cf. Dover: "But both good and bad [eros in Pausanias' speech] aim at the physical submission of the boy. . . . [T]he difference . . . lies in the whole context of the ultimate physical act, not in the presence or absence of the act itself" (34).

64. See Appendix II, below. [Reprinted below, pp. 124–128.]

65. This is not said in the *Symposium* (cf. Grube, *op. cit.*, 103–4) but it is suggested in the rebuff to Alcibiades' all-out attempt at seduction in 219B–D. It is unambiguously clear in *Phdr.* 250E and 255E–256E, as well as in R. 403BC. The latter is not contradicted by μηδενὶ ἐξεῖναι ἀπαρνηθῆναι ὅν ἂν βούληται φιλεῖν as a prize for military prowess in 468BC. The assumption that here Plato is "allowing sexual license, a completely free pick of sexual partners" to valorous athletes (Gouldner, 335) is based on a misreading of the text: φιλεῖν does not mean "intercourse" in this context (or in any other in Greek prose, to my knowledge)—for that Plato would have used συγγίγνεσθαι (as in 329C2, 329C4, 360C1, 459D8, 560B5); φιλεῖν and ἅπτεσθαι are specifically allowed to chaste lovers in 403BC, where intercourse is clearly ruled out, as also in *Phdr.* 255E, where ἅπτεσθαι, φιλεῖν, and even συγκατακεῖσθαι are proper and will stop short of intercourse in the case of the "victorious" lovers (256AB). (It should be noted that this interpretation of 468BC is entirely consistent with "opportunity of more frequent intercourse with women" (460B) as an incentive to military prowess: this has to do not with φιλεῖν but with eugenic breeding [ὡς πλεῖστοι τῶν παίδων ἐκ τῶν τοιούτων σπείρωνται].)

66. τὸ περὶ τὸ σῶμα κάλλος σμικρόν τι ἡγήσεται εἶναι, 210C (a remarkable thing to say, considering the extreme susceptibility to physical beauty revealed in a passage like *Phdr.* 250C–E); and cf. κατεφρόνησεν καὶ κατεγέλασεν τῆς ἐμῆς ὥρας in *Symp.* 219C4.

67. 210E; cf. also 210A1 and 211C2.

68. Cf. *RC*, pp. 76 ff., below.

69. Cf. *Metaph.* 1039A25 ff., and the references in Bonitz, *Index Aristotelicus*, 860A35–38.

70. For sensible instances "resembling" their Form "defectively" see *Phdo.* 74E1–4, ἐνδεῖ δὲ καὶ οὐ δύναται τοιοῦτον εἶναι οἷον ἐκεῖνο, ἀλλ' ἔστιν φαυλότερον . . . προσεοικέναι μέν, ἐνδεεστέρως δὲ ἔχειν. Cf. also: we cannot expect the just man πανταχῇ τοιοῦτον εἶναι οἷον ἡ δικαιοσύνη (R. 472B); we must believe that the visible movements of the heavens τῶν ἀληθινῶν πολὺ ἐνδεῖν (R. 529D) and that the physical bed is not the "real" Bed, ἀλλά τι τοιοῦτον οἷον τὸ ὄν and ἀμυδρόν τι πρὸς ἀλήθειαν (R. 597A).

71. The assumption that the Form corresponding to a given character has that character; cf. below, *UVP*, n. 97.

72. *Symp.* 211A1–5.

73. *Symp.* 211E3 αὐτὸ τὸ θεῖον καλόν.

74. The evidence tells strongly against classifying Plato as a bisexual (as, e.g., in R. B. Levinson, *op. cit.*, 118, n. 109, "Plato . . . like others of the bisexually inclined Athenians"). In every passage I can recall which depicts or alludes to the power of sexual desire the context is homosexual. For some examples see D. F. Ast (1835), *s.v.* παιδικά (to which R. 474D–E and 485C should be added); also *Symp.* 211D, and *Phdr.* 250D ff. And cf. Appendix, below.

75. *Phdr.* 251A1, L. 636–7. And see next note.

76. *Lg.* 636B4–6, καὶ δὴ καὶ παλαιὸν νόμιμον δοκεῖ τὸ ἐπιτήδευμα τὰς κατὰ φύσιν περὶ τὰ ἀφροδίσια ἡδονὰς οὐ μόνον ἀνθρώπων, ἀλλὰ καὶ θηρίων, διεφθαρκέναι (England's text, defended by him *ad loc.*): "And then again this ancient usage is thought to have corrupted the pleasure of sex which is natural not only for men but even for brutes." *Lg.* 836B8–C6, "If one were to follow nature in enacting the usage [observed] before Laius, stating that it was right to refrain from the same intercourse with men and boys as with women, calling to witness the nature of wild beasts and pointing out that male has no [such] contact with male, since it is contrary to nature. . . ." (I agree with de Vries [1969, 153] that Dover's explanation of "contrary to nature" here by "against the rules" will not do: something far stronger is intended.) The same indictment of παρὰ φύσιν ηδονή occurs in *Phdr.* 250E–251A, where the sight of the beautiful boy incites the depraved lover to homosexual intercourse. The point of this passage has been blunted by mistranslation. Thus Hackforth takes τετράποδος νόμον βαίνειν ἐπιχειρεῖ καὶ παιδοσπορεῖν to mean "essays to go after the fashion of a four-footed beast, and to beget offspring of the flesh" (the same misconstruction of the sense in every translator and commentator I have consulted); hence Plato is thought to be making here "a contemptuous reference to heterosexual love" (Hackforth, 1952, 98), which would be sharply at variance with the whole notion of "birth in beauty" in the *Smp.* But βαίνειν here is "to mount" (cf. de Vries [1969] *ad loc.*: he refers to LSJ, *s.v.* A, II, 1). As for παιδοσπορεῖν, this means only "to sow generative seed" (what is "contrary to nature" is precisely that this "sowing" cannot generate: cf. *Lg.* 841D4–5, σπείρειν . . . ἄγονα ἀρρένων παρὰ φύσιν); and "the way of the four-footed brute" alludes to the posture in anal intercourse (so portrayed in pottery: see, e.g., Jean Marcadé [1962], plates 136 and 147). The context is purely homosexual, and the passage was so read in antiquity: Plut. *Amat.* 751D–E, leaves no doubt on this point.

77. For the references see note 53 above *sub fin.*; and cf. *MP*, pp. 50–51, below.

78. On the latter see P. Shorey, *What Plato Said* (Chicago, 1933), 45. I see no good reason to doubt the authenticity of the epigram on Dion's death *ap.* Diogenes Laertius, 3, 30 (accepted by Shorey, *loc. cit.*, and by U. v. Wilamowitz-Möllendorff [1948, 509]; defended by C. M. Bowra, *A.J.P.* 59 [1936] 393–404) whose terminal line is ὦ ἐμὸν ἐκμήνας θυμὸν ἔρωτι Δίων (cf. ἐκμήνας here with the definition of love as μανία in the *Phdr.* 265A–266A *et passim*; cf. note 80 below).

79. Cf. Aristophanes, *Birds* 1316, κατέχουσι δ' ἔρωτες ἐμᾶς πόλεως. Thuc. 2, 43, 1, ἐραστὰς γιγνομένους αὐτῆς [sc. τῆς πόλεως], with Gomme's comment *ad loc.*

80. Had I been able to work more intensively on the *Phdr.* in this essay I would have taken a crack at the extraordinary fact that here ἔρως is not only described, but *defined*, as μανία by our ultra-rationalist, Plato, and is associated as μανία in the closest terms

with philosophy no less than with the mystic cults (which had been done also, though only in passing, in *Smp.* 218B, τῆς φιλοσόφου μανίας τε καὶ βακχείας [of Socrates]). This convergence of μανία and νοῦς in love does not seem to intrigue commentators. Few of them notice the paradox at all or, if they do, they seem bent on explaining it away (thus J. Pieper [1964, 49 ff.] gives μανία in the *Phdr.* a theological twist which hardly does justice to its psychological meaning; and even *qua* theology it is too onesided: Pieper objects to "madness" as the sense of μανία because that "suggests ties with the orgiastic Dionysian rites.") But even the above citation from the *Smp.* (not to refer to further evidence, which exists in abundance) would show that those "orgiastic Dionysian rites" could not have been entirely uncongenial to Plato.

81. *Œuvres Complètes*, vol. IV of the Pléiade Edition (Paris, 1969), 743. He goes on, a little later: "Not all is illusion in love, I admit. But what is real consists of the sentiments with which it animates us for the true beauty it makes us love. This beauty is not in the object we love, it is the work of our errors. Well, what difference does that make? Would we be less willing to sacrifice all those base sentiments to this imaginary model?" For more statements, some of them quite remarkable, to the same effect elsewhere in Rousseau see M. Eigeldinger, *Jean Jacques Rousseau et la realité de l'imaginaire* (Neuchatel, 1962), Chapter 4, "L'Amour et le pays des chimères."

82. *Œuvres Complètes*, vol. I of the Pléiade Edition (Paris, 1959), 439. The references in the next five notes are to this volume.

83. "Mad. la Comtesse de Houdetot . . . n'étoit point belle. Son visage étoit marqué de la petite vérole, son teint manquoit de finesse," etc., 439. Compare Zulietta, 318–20.

84. 427. Erotic fantasy had been a habit of his since adolescence, 41.

85. *Loc. cit.*

86. 440.

87. I.e., no genital intercourse. That there was physical contact of other sorts in abundance is stated openly enough in the *Confessions* (443–45; and see also the passages from the Correspondence in H. Guillemin's study, *Un Homme, Deux Ombres* [Geneva, 1943], Chapter IV, "Fausse Route"). But there is plenty of this in Platonic love too: cf. note 65 above. Rousseau says that "though at times carried away by my senses I sought to make her unfaithful, I never really desired this" (444); the lover depicted in *Phdr.* 254A ff. would not be human or truthful if he did not say the same *mutatis mutandis*.

88. Not that the lover in the *Phaedrus* is less combustible: the exaltation of the erotic object depicted here outruns anything in the *Confessions* or, to stick to Plato's own culture, anything in the whole of Greek prose and almost the whole of surviving Greek verse as well; it is matched only in Sappho (with whom Plato openly invites comparison, 235C3: cf. Fortenbaugh, 1966, 108): "[when he encounters the youth], first there comes upon him a shuddering and a measure of that awe which the [transcendental] vision had once inspired, then reverence as at the sight of a god: did he not fear being taken for a madman he would offer sacrifice to his boy-love as to a holy image and a god . . ." (251A2–7; the translation mainly after Hackforth's).

Even so, the lover is in no danger of confusing the boy with the Idea or of decking him out with pseudo-attributes. In particular, there is no magnification of his moral or intellectual virtues, which are apparently not out of the ordinary, and the lover is not required to make believe that they are. His physical beauty is itself the "divine" (θεοειδές, 251A2) thing in him, and this suffices.

89. Seeing her first as "bonne, naïve, éprise d'idéal," almost incapable of untruth (239), he soon discovers that she is cruel, sly, devious, deceitful, mercenary. Yet he remains as helplessly in love as before.

90. Cf. note 56 above.

91. Cf. Section II above and note that in the last analysis Socrates has just one reason for moral conduct: the perfection of his soul. In the *Crito*, his final reason for refraining from an unjust act (breaking jail) is that to commit injustice would corrupt his soul (47C–48D). Cf. the argument against Polus and Callicles in the *Grg.*: against Polus he argues that one should abstain from wrong-doing because this would make one's own soul evil; also that when one has done wrong, one should welcome punishment which purges the evil in the soul, because the man with unpurged evil has suffered the greatest possible harm and is most wretched of men (477A–478E). Similarly he argues against Callicles that "wrong-doing is the greatest of evils to the wrong-doer" (509B) because it ruins his soul and, with one's soul ruined, one would be better off dead than alive (511E–512B). Plato never repudiates this motivation for moral conduct. He supports it to the hilt in the great argument that "justice pays" in the *Republic*.

92. Cf. note 56 above.

93. This is most explicit in the *Phaedrus* (250E1 ff.), but also clear enough, by implication, in the *Symposium* also. This is all love for a person could be, given the status of persons in Plato's ontology.

94. Section IV above, the terminal paragraph.

95. ὥσπερ ἐπαναβασμοῖς χρώμενον, 211C3—an image for the idea that every other love is a means to the attainment of this one (an idea expressed no less than three times in two Stephanus pages, 210A–212B: cf. n. 67 above).

96. 251A6.

97. Which is what the boy's love turns out to be (255A ff.); he wants what his lover wants "only more feebly" (255E2–3).

98. Cf. n. 24 above.

99. This is the point of Aristophanes' myth in the *Symposium*, as has often been noticed, and it is picked up and emphasized in another way in Diotima's speech (cf. n. 20 above).

100. Aristotle's conception of "perfect φιλία" does not repudiate—does not even notice— what I have called above "the cardinal flaw" in Platonic love. His intuition takes him as far as seeing that (a) *disinterested affection for the person* we love—the active desire to promote that person's good "for that person's sake, not for ours"—must be built into love at its best, but not as far as sorting this out from (b) *appreciation of the excellences instantiated by that person*; (b), of course, need not be disinterested and *could* be egoistic. The limits of Aristotle's understanding of love show up in his failure to notice the ambiguity in "loving a person for himself" (φιλεῖν τινα δι' ἐκεῖνον— a phrase which may be used to express either (a) or (b): thus in *Rhet.* 1361B37 and 1381A5–6 δι' ἐκεῖνον is used to express exactly the same thing which is conveyed by ἐκείνου ἕνεκα in 1380B36. But there are passages in which it is clearly used to express *only* (b): so, e.g., in *N.E.* 1157B3 οἱ δ'ἀγαθοὶ δι' αὑτοὺς φίλοι· ἦ γὰρ ἀγαθοί: here "A and B are good men and A loves B for B's self" implies "A loves B because B is a good man and in so far as he is a good man."

101. *Ti.* 29E–30B.

102. A slightly revised form of an address at the University of Montana on May 5, 1969, at a celebration honoring the retirement of Professor Edwin L. Marvin, who had served the university with distinction as a teacher and founder of its department of philosophy. I have read drafts to other groups and profited from their criticism. My greatest debt is to the members of the Philosophical Discussion Club of Cornell University, and most particularly to Norman Kretzmann and William Nelson, who helped me detect a confusion from which no earlier draft had been free. I must also express thanks to Charles Kahn, Richard Rorty, and Terry Irwin for suggestions and criticisms which enabled me to correct other mistakes.

APPENDIX

Sex in Platonic Love

According to the *Concise Oxford Dictionary of Current Usage* (1954), Platonic love is "purely spiritual love for one of the opposite sex."[1] If we are to concede that this is what the term has come to mean today—we need not dispute the dictionary's authority—we should at least be careful to notice how far it has strayed away from what it meant for Plato. The first deviation—the notion that interpersonal eros is "purely spiritual love"—passes unnoticed in the scholarly literature; so far from calling attention to it, some recent studies have actually endorsed it. Thus Gould (1963, 119) writes:

> If they [the amorous couple in the *Phaedrus*] are truly lovers of wisdom, the only intercourse which will appeal to them is rational exploration together, to be companions in the adventures of the life of the mind.

And Irving Singer (1966, 80):

> In the *Phaedrus* . . . the harmony of black and white finally yields to a purely spiritual bond from which all sexuality has been exorcised.

Such statements seem to have gone unchallenged, and it may not be amiss to point out that they are out of line with the clear implications of Plato's text.

Consider what happens in the passage these statements have in view: when the man first chances on the beautiful youth the "erotic vision" provokes libidinous impulse in "the whole" of his psyche: all of it—charioteer and white horse, no less than the black—is "enflamed," is "filled with the ticklings and pricklings of desire" (253E5–254A1).[2] The white horse (and *a fortiori* the driver) is "held back by shame from leaping on the beloved" (254A2–3): the impulse is checked, not dissipated. Unchecked in the black horse, "terrible and lawless deeds" would have ensued on the spot, were it not that the driver, falling back like a racer at the barrier, with a still more violent jerk breaks the bit from the shameless horse's teeth, bespattering its railing tongue and jaws with blood, throws it down on its legs and haunches, and punishes it. (254E)

This happens "many times" (254E6) before the lecherous horse gives in.

Now would it be reasonable to think that Plato expects this liaison to start with such raw, all-but-overpowering, lust, and then become totally desexualized as it matures? If so, why does he tell us (255E) that the boy, when he comes to return the lover's passion, "wants to see, touch, kiss, and share his couch," a desire which "ere long, as one might guess, leads to the act," so that we now find the pair "sleeping together"? Are we to suppose that such a thorough job of mortifying the flesh has intervened that kissing, embracing, and sleeping together now leaves the couple physically undisturbed—that a Masters and Johnson record of their intimacies would register no sign of genital excitement? What comes next in Plato's story is not favorable to the hypothesis: the black horse in the boy's soul "swells with desire" (σπαργῶν, 256A2) when he embraces and kisses; he "would not refuse to do his part in gratifying the lover's entreaties" (256A4–5) were it not that the white horse and driver resist. So physical desire is still there in the boy, and *a fortiori* in the lover. It takes "Olympic wrestling" (256B4–5) to keep it in check.

To put my thesis positively: that form of passionate experience invented by Plato, which should count as the original, and always primary, sense of "Platonic love," is a peculiar mix of sensuality, sentiment, and intellect—a companionship bonded by erotic attraction no less than by intellectual give-and-take. Body-to-body endearment is one of its normal features, though always subject to the constraint that terminal gratification will be denied. And this interdict is itself only an ideal requirement; sternly mandatory for philosophers, it is applied more leniently to others. In lovers of the "ambitious and less philosophic" way of life (256B–C) Plato expects lapses: "When drunk or in some other careless hour, the insolent horses in their souls may catch them off their guard . . . and they may then choose and do what the vulgar take for bliss." If this happens infrequently and against their best resolves, Plato's eschatology will not damn them—which means, among other things, that they still qualify as Platonic lovers:

Those who have once got started on the heavenward journey no law would send to the dark pathways under the earth. But they shall walk together in a life of shining happiness and, when the time comes, they shall grow wings together because of their love. (256D)

Now let me take up the other point where the dictionary parts company with Plato on "Platonic love": "love for one of the opposite sex." Here scholars have gone to the other extreme, suggesting that for heterosexual love Platonic eros has no place at all. Some of the finest studies have implied as much. J. A. Symonds, the Victorian invert, whose monograph cracked open Greek homosexuality for Englishmen of his generation, saw Platonic love as "veiled sodomy" (1901, 54). Kenneth J. Dover, in his admirable monograph—as precise and sophisticated a piece of scholarship on its theme as has ever appeared in any language—says that "Plato exploited exclusively homosexual emotion for his philosophical theory of eros" (1966, 39). I submit that this goes too far. Admittedly it fits everything in the *Phaedrus* and also *most* of what Plato put into the *pièce de resistance* of the *Symposium,* the speech of Diotima: boy-love forms the base of that escalated figure along which the lover rises to ever higher forms of love; he starts with the love of "beautiful bodies," and if one reads attentively one will see that, sure enough, these bodies are male.[3] However, when Diotima undertakes to state the most general condition which the pursuit of Beauty has to meet to qualify as eros, her phrase "birth in beauty,"[4] is all too patently a generalization of procreative—hence necessarily *heterosexual*—love. Let me dwell on this formula, for it is surely the most profound thing in the dialogue. Just before she had got Socrates to agree that eros is desire to possess the good, believing that it would bring its possessor happiness. One might have expected her to construe this along commonplace, hedonistic, lines—that what we want in love is pleasure and that beauty lures by promising pleasure. That is where she surprises us. For the picture of man as pleasure-chaser she substitutes an image of man as creator, producer, new-maker: ever "pregnant,"[5] carrying a burden for which he craves release, he thrills to Beauty because only in its presence can he find the longed-for deliverance.

This understanding of love has plainly a heterosexual paradigm. In the drive to reproductive coupling Plato recognizes the archetypal expression of eros, its most elemental and universal form. And he does not understate the emotional force of the drive:

> Don't you see how all living creatures, birds and brutes, in their desire of procreation are in agony when they take the infection of love, which begins with the desire of intercourse and then passes to the care of offspring, on whose behalf the weakest are ready to battle the strongest to the last and die for them, and will suffer the torments of hunger, or make any other sacrifice, to tend their young? (207B–C)

What is it then that prompted Symonds' and Dover's remarks and led that erudite philistine, John Jay Chapman, to stigmatize the *Symposium* as

The *vade mecum* of those who accept and continue the practice it celebrates . . . a sort of lurid devotional book—the sulphurous breviary of the pederast? (1934, 133)

At most this: conjugal love, however intense, would still remain in Plato's scheme a spiritual dead end[6]—an impulse fully spent in reaching its immediate goal, generating no surplus energy to fuel flights into the empyrean. Suppose the man in the *Phaedrus*, long before meeting that boy, had loved a beautiful girl with whom he had reared in harmonious domesticity a brood of splendid children. There is not one word in Plato to suggest that this relation could have been at any point for the man, or for the girl, the start of a *vita nuova*—the take-off for the ascent diagrammed in the escalated figure. Platonic—as also, later, courtly, and still later, romantic—love is meant to be a life-transforming miracle, a secular analogue to religious conversion, a magical change of perspective that opens up new, enchanted, horizons. For Plato, for whom the spirit comes to life in words, the first decisive sign of the mutation would be a sudden loosening of the tongue, a new-found flair for intellectual talk. When do we hear of this? When the man who is "pregnant in soul" encounters a "noble and well-nurtured" soul housed in a beautiful body, he then "embraces the two in one, and in this man's company he straightway finds facility of speech about virtue and about what a good man ought to be and practice."[7] This is what starts him off on the ascent whose terminus is the face-to-face encounter with the Idea of Beauty. There, at the peak, the homosexual imagery is dropped. Communion with the Idea is consummated in conjugal intercourse which "will bring forth not images of beauty but realities" (212A). What started as a pederastic idyll ends up in transcendental marriage.

NOTES

1. Much the same, though in more guarded terms, in Webster's.

2. 253E5–254A1, . . . τὸ ἐρωτικὸν ὄμμα πᾶσαν αἰσθήσει διαθερμῆναν τὴν ψυχήν, γαργαλισμοῦ τε καὶ πόθου κέντρων ὑποπλησθῇ. I have followed Stallbaum's emendation, διαθερμῆναν for διαθερμήνας of the MS. Spurned by later editors, it seems to me justified by the sense: the MS. reading would make "the charioteer" the subject of the participle, and Plato could scarcely have put reason in the position of "heating up the whole soul by means of sensation," while he would find it very natural to speak of the stimulus, τὸ ἐρωτικὸν ὄμμα, as having just this effect. However, my argument in no way depends on the acceptance of this emendation; the quoted parts of the translation I give above will do in either case.

3. The καλὰ σώματα in 210A are male: cf. γεννᾶν λόγους καλούς here with the "fine words about virtue" induced by erotic passion at 209B, where boy-love is clearly in view; note παιδαρίου κάλλος in 210D2 and ὀρθῶς παιδεραστεῖν in 211B5–6.

4. *Smp.* 206B ff.

5. Plato gets hold of this image in 206C (quoted above, first paragraph of Section IV), and keeps returning to it all through the sequel.

6. Cf. the concluding lines in Dover (1966, 40).

7. *Smp.* 209A–C; cf. 210C1–3.

BIBLIOGRAPHY

Apelt, O. *Platonis "Symposium,"* translated with notes (Leipzig, 1926). Revised edition by Annemarie Capelle (Hamburg, 1960).

Ast, D. Friedrich. *Lexicon Platonicum* (first edition, 1835; reprinted, Berlin Hermann Barsdorf, 1908).

Bloom, A. *The REPUBLIC of Plato,* translated with notes and an interpretive essay (New York, 1968).

Bonitz, H. *Index Aristotelicus* (vol. 5 of the Prussian Academy edition of Aristotle), (Berlin, 1870).

Bowra, C.M. *American Journal of Philology,* 59 (1936).

Burnet, J. *Plato's PHAEDO* (Oxford, 1911).

Chapman, John Jay. *Lucian, Plato, and Greek Morals* (Boston, 1934).

Cornford, F.M. *The REPUBLIC of Plato,* translated with introduction and notes (New York, Oxford University Press, 1945).

Cornford, F.M. "The Doctrine of Eros in Plato's *Symposium,*" in *The Unwritten Philosophy,* ed. W.K.C. Guthrie (Cambridge, 1950).

De Vries, G.J. *A Commentary on the PHAEDRUS of Plato* (Amsterdam, 1969).

Dover, K.J. "Eros and Nomos," *Bulletin of the Institute of Classical Studies,* No. 11 (1966), 31–42.

Eigeldinger, M. *Jean Jacques Rousseau et la réalité de l'imaginaire* (Neuchâtel, 1962).

Fortenbaugh, W. "Plato *Phaedrus* 235C3," *Classical Philology* 61 (1966), 108–9.

Gauthier, R.A., and J.Y. Jolif. *L'Ethique à Nicomaque,* Tome II, Commentaire, Deuxième Partie, Livres VI–X, Deuxième Edition (Louvain, 1970).

Gomme, A.W. *Historical Commentary on Thucydides, Book I* (Oxford, 1956).

Gouldner, Alvin W. *Enter Plato: Classical Greece and the Origins of Social Theory* (New York, 1965).

Grube, G.M.A. *Plato's Thought* (New York, 1964).

Guillemin, H. *Un Homme, Deux Ombres* (Geneva, 1943).

Hackforth, R. *Plato's PHAEDRUS* (Cambridge, 1952).

Hamilton, W., translation, *Plato, the SYMPOSIUM* (Baltimore, 1951).

Lee, H.D.P. Plato: *The REPUBLIC*, translated with introduction (Baltimore, 1955).

Levinson, R.B. *In Defense of Plato* (Cambridge, Mass., 1953).

Markus, R.A. "The Dialectic of Eros in Plato's *Symposium*," *Downside Review*, 73, 1955 (reprinted in *Plato*, Vol. II, ed. by Gregory Vlastos, New York, 1971, 132–43).

Mercadé, Jean. *Eros Kalos* (Geneva, 1962).

North, Helen. *Sophrosyne* (Ithaca, 1966).

Nygren, Anders. *Agape and Eros* (English translation by P.S. Watson, Harper Torchbook edition, New York, 1969).

Owen, G.E.L. "Logic and Metaphysics in Some Earlier Works of Aristotle," in *Aristotle and Plato in the Mid-Fourth Century*, ed. by I. Düring and G.E.L. Owen (Goteborg, Almquist & Wicksell, 1960), pp. 163–90.

Pieper, J. *Enthusiasm and Divine Madness*, English translation by Richard and Clara Winston (New York, 1964).

Popper, Karl. *The Open Society and Its Enemies*, Vol. I (Fourth Edition, Princeton, 1963).

Robin, L. *Platon, Oeuvres Complètes*, Tomes I, II: the Pléiade translation (with the collaboration of T. Moreau).

Rosen, S. *Plato's Symposium* (New Haven, 1968).

Shorey, P. Translation, *Plato: The Republic*, 2 volumes (London, 1930 and 1935).

Shorey, P. *What Plato Said* (Chicago, 1933).

Sinclair, T.A. *Greek Political Theory* (London, 1951).

Symonds, J.A. *A Problem in Greek Ethics, Being an Inquiry into the Phenomenon of Sexual Inversion Addressed Especially to Medical Psychologists and Jurists* (printed for private circulation, London, 1901).

Vlastos, G. "Justice and Equality," in *Social Justice*, edited by R. Brandt (Englewood Cliffs, N.J., 1962). A slightly corrected version of the first two sections of this essay has appeared in *Human Rights*, edited by A.I. Melden (Belmont, Calif., 1970).

Wilamowitz-Moellendorff, U.V. *Platon* (reissue of the Third Edition, Berlin and Frankfurt, 1948).

Wolin, Sheldon. *Politics and Vision* (Boston, 1960).

ABBREVIATIONS

In his essay, Vlastos uses these abbreviations:

Ast   See Ast, D. Friedrich, above.

Budé   Plato's dialogues, Société d'Edition "Les Belles Lettres" (Paris), Association Guillaume Budé.

LSJ   *Greek-English Lexicon* by H.G. Liddell and R. Scott, New Edition by H.S. Jones (Oxford, 1925–40).

Pléiade   See Robin, L., above.

JHR, MP, RC, SPT, UVP are references to other essays written by Vlastos that are included in *Platonic Studies*; respectively: "Justice and Happiness in the *Republic*" (p. 111), "A

Metaphysical Paradox" (p. 43), "Reasons and Causes in the *Phaedo*" (p. 76), "Slavery in Plato's Thought" (p. 147), and "The Unity of the Virtues in the *Protagoras*" (p. 221).

There are also many abbreviated references to the dialogues of Plato and to the works of Aristotle. See *LSJ*, "Authors and Works," *s.v. Aristotle, Plato*.

GLOSSARY FOR VLASTOS

Edward Johnson

SECTION A: TEXT

96 *philein:* to love, loving
philos: lover, friend
97 *philarguros:* money-lover, miser
philotimos: honor-lover, ambitious
philonikos: victory-lover
philokalos: beauty-lover
98 *sēmeion:* sign, evidence
philia: love
philia: love
philoi: loved, dear
philēsei: will (someone) love
anōpheleis: unprofitable
philei: loves
achrēstos: useless
sophos: wise
99 *heneka hugieias:* for the sake of health
tēs epikourias heneka: for the sake of aid
prōton philon, hou heneka kai ta alla phamen panta einai: first (or primary) love, for whose sake, we say, the others are (loved)
100 *hōs alēthōs:* truly
tō(i) onti: really, in fact
prōton philon: first (or primary) love
kēdoito de g' an tis malista toutou ho tugchanei philōn: one is most concerned for what one happens to love
philoi: friends
101 *philia:* love
philos: loved, dear, friend
dikaiosunē: justice, righteousness
102 *hina mē ta politika blaptoi:* in order not to harm political matters (or things)
philanthrōpia: love of humankind
philia: love
104 *sunēsthēsetai:* share sensation
sullupēsetai: share pain
philoi: friends

> *modus vivendi:* way of living [LATIN]
> *philia:* love
> *prōton philon:* first (or primary) love
> *philein:* to love
> *aspazesthai:* to welcome, to be glad
> *eran:* to love (erotically)

105 *prōton philon:* first (or primary) love
tokos en tō kalō(i): birth in beauty

107 *philia:* love
erōs: (erotic) love

108 *eran:* to love (erotically)
philein: to love

110 *scala amoris:* hierarchy of love [LATIN]

SECTION B: NOTES

1. *tēn philian kai to philein horisamenoi legōmen. estō dē to philein to boulesthai tini ha oietai agatha, ekeinou heneka alla mē hautou, kai to kata dunamin praktikon einai toutōn:* . . . we say having defined love and loving. Let loving, then, be wishing for someone those things one thinks good, for the sake of that one but not for one's own, and bringing them about as far as one can.

2. *titheasi gar philon ton boulomenon kai prattonta tagatha ē ta phainomena ekeinou heneka, ē ton boulomenon einai kai zēn ton philon autou charin:* We consider a friend one who wishes and brings about goods, or what appear (to be goods), for another's sake, or one who wishes a friend to exist and to live, for his sake.

3. *philia:* love

4. *philein:* to love, loving
philon: loved, dear, friend
eran: to love (erotically)
hotan de ekateron [namely, *philon*] *gignetai sphodron, 'erōta' eponomazomen:* whenever each (friend) becomes intense, we call it love
philia: love
eros: (erotic) love

5. *pros hen legomenon:* said with regard to one (thing)
philia: love

6. *tō(i) de philō(i) dein boulesthai tagatha ekeinou heneka:* in love they say it is necessary to wish goods for the other's sake

8. *philiai kata sumbebēkos:* friends by circumstance, by accident
kath' homoiotēta: by similitude, by similarity
homoiōma echei: bears a likeness
hōs alēthōs: truly
prōtōs: primarily
kuriōs: strictly, chiefly
teleia: complete, perfect

9. *teleia philia:* complete love
   malista philia: most love, greatest love

10. *[philia] dokei . . . en tō(i) philein mallon ē en tō(i) phileisthai einai:* love seems . . . to be in loving rather than in being loved

11. *kai philountes ton philon to autois agathon philousi:* and loving the friend they will love what is good for themselves

17. *Robin's mistranslation:* Consequently, to the extent that you are good for nothing *to him,* your father has had no more love for you.

20. *ho de mē tou deomenos oude ti agapō(i)ē an . . . oud' an philoi:* someone who didn't lack anything would not feel affection for anything . . . nor would he love

    heneka tou: for the sake of
    dia ti: because of something

22. *l'amour de bienveillance ou amour desinteressé:* benevolent love or disinterested love [FRENCH]
    amour de concupicence: love involving desire
    amour desinteressé: disinterested love
    pasa hē toiautē spoudē ouk esti toutois estin espoudasmenē, epi tois heneka tou paraskeuazomenois, all' ep' ekeinō(i) hou heneka panta ta toiauta paraskeuazetai: all such regard is set not on those things procured for the sake of something, but on that for the sake of which all such are procured

23. *eidōla:* images, icons, idols, phantoms
    prōton philon: first (or primary) love

25. *ouden ti mallon houtō to ge alēthes echē(i):* it is not altogether true
    hrēmati . . . legontes: manner of speaking
    philon . . . tō(i) onti: really loved
    ekeino auto . . . eis ho pasi hautai hai legomenai philiai teleutōsin: that itself in which all these so-called loves end (or are completed)

26. *all' ara to agathon estin philon?:* But then the good is loved?
    prōton philon: first (or primary) love
    aitia: reason, cause
    eudaimonein, eu prattein: to flourish, do well, be happy

28. *heautē philē:* dear to itself
    philē: loved, dear
    philia: love

29. *este men gar dē pantes hoi en tē(i) polei adelphoi . . . hate oun suggeneis ontes pantes:* for you are all brothers in the city-state . . . all being akin
    kai huper tōn allōn politōn hōs adelphōn ontōn (dei) . . . dianoeisthai: and it is necessary to think of the other citizens as being brothers

30. *allotrios:* alien, outsider
    oikeios: familiar, domestic, proper

34. *homoioi:* alike
    hupo homoiou archētai: be ruled by a like
    tō(i) autō(i) kubernōmenoi: governed by the same

35. *doulos:* slave, servant

39. *to kalon:* the beautiful, beauty

42. *paraggeliai*: instructions, doctrines, precepts
     philanthrōpiē: love of humankind
     philotechniē: love of craft, ingenuity

43. *politēs d' haplōs oudeni tōn allōn horizetai mallon ē tō(i) metechein kriseōs kai archēs*: a citizen in general is defined in no way better than in having a share in judging and ruling
     krisis: judging
     ētoi krinomen ge ē enthumoumetha: either we judge or we form plans
     kritai: judge
     krinai: judge
     archē: rule, beginning
     metechein tōn timōn: having a share in honors

45. *eleutherōs de ta te pros to koinon politeuomen kai es tēn pros allēlous tōn kath' hēmeran epitēdeumatōn hupopsian, ou di' orgēs ton pelas, ei kath' hēdonēn ti dra(i), echontes, oude azēmious men, lupēras de tē(i) opsei achthēdonas prostithemenoi. anepachthōs de ta idia prosomilountes*: Freely we act as citizens in matters of common concern, and in the watchfulness of everyday pursuits involving each other, not getting upset with the neighbor if he acts according to his pleasure, nor imposing harmless but unpleasant annoyed looks. Busying ourselves about private matters without offence . . .
     hupopsian: censorious watchfulness
     lupēras tē(i) opsei achthēdonas: unpleasant annoyed looks
     regards chargés de blâme: blameful looks [French]
     anepachthōs ta idia prosomilountes: busying ourselves about private matters without offence
     hupothesis: hypothesis, postulate
     to zēn hōs bouletai tis: to live as one wishes

49. *koina ta tōn philōn*: the things of friends are common
     idion: private

50. *philia*: love
     philos: friend
     ton sunēdomenon tois agathois: one who shares pleasure in goods
     sunalgounta tois lupērois: one who shares suffering in pains
     ton sundiagonta kai tauta hairoumenon: someone who consorts with one and shares one's preferences
     ton sunalgounta kai sunēdomenon tō(i) philō(i): one who shares pains and pleasures with a friend
     philia: love
     in propria persona: in his own voice [LATIN]
     horisamenoi legōmen: we say, by way of definition
     hoi de (titheasi): some consider
     hoi de boulomenoi tagatha tois philois ekeinōn heneka malista philoi: those wishing goods for their friends for the sake of those are friends most of all

51. *diaspa(i)*: breaks up
     erastai: lovers
     erōs: (erotic) love

55. *hē dē kai eme ta erōtika edidaxen*: she taught me erotic matters, the things of love

56. *estin ara sullēbdēn ho erōs tou to agathon hauto(i) einai aei*: eros is a desire for the good to be one's own always, a desire for one's perpetual possession of the good

huperebaleto tē(i) philia(i) dia ton erōta: she exceeded on account of erotic love for her loved one

57. *touto:* this
    toutou: of this
    diōkontōn auto: pursuing it
    erōs: (erotic) love
    eiper tou agathou heautō(i) einai aei erōs estin: if indeed eros is (desire) for the good to be always one's own

59. *pantes kuousin anthrōpoi:* all humans are pregnant
    tokeus: progenitor
    trophos . . . kumatos neosporou: nurse of the new-sown pregnancy

60. *hē gar andros kai gunaikos sunousia:* the being together of man and woman

61. *gunaixi te heautōn oikeious einai kai philous:* suitable and loving to their wives

63. *sōphrōn erōs:* wise eros

65. *mēdeni exeinai aparnēthēnai hon an boulētai philein:* it is not permitted to anyone, whom he might wish to love, to refuse
    philein: to love, love
    suggignesthai: (sexual) intercourse
    haptesthai: touch, grasp
    sugkatakeisthai: lie with
    hōs pleistoi tōn paidōn ek tōn toioutōn speirōntai: as many children as possible to be engendered by such (fathers)

66. *to peri to sōma kallos smikron ti hēgēsetai einai:* (think) the body's beauty to be a small thing
    katephronēsen kai kategelasen tēs emēs hōras: he scorned and mocked my young manhood (or bloom of youth)

70. *endei de kai ou dunatai toiouton einai oion ekeino, all' estin phauloteron . . .*
    proseoikenai men, endeesterōs de echein: it fails and is not able to be like that, but is more worthless . . . it resembles, but in a less degree
    pantachē(i) toiouton einai hoion hē dikaiosunē: to be in every way like justice
    tōn alēthinōn polu endein: to fall far short of the truth
    alla ti toiouton hoion to on: but something like what is
    amudron ti pros alētheian: something murky in the direction of truth

73. *auto to theion kalon:* divine beauty itself

74. *paidika:* darling boy

76. *kai dē kai palaion nomimon dokei to epitēdeuma tas kata phusin peri ta aphrodisia hēdonas ou monon anthrōpōn, alla kai thēriōn, diephtharkenai:* And then again this ancient usage seems to have corrupted the pleasures of sex according to nature, not only for humans but also for beasts.
    para phusin hēdonē: unnatural pleasure
    tetrapodos nomon bainein epicheirei kai paidosporein: in the quadruped way he attempts to mount and to sow generative seed
    bainein: to mount
    paidosporein: to sow generative seed
    sperein . . . agona arrenōn para phusin: to sow . . . a contest of males, against nature

78. *o emon ekmenas thumon erōti Dion:* o my Dion, you maddened my heart with love
    ekmenas: you maddened
    mania: madness

79. *katechousi d' erōtes emas poleōs:* they possess/occupy my city-state in the manner of lovers
      erastas gignomenous autēs [namely, *tēs poleōs*]: become lovers of her (i.e., of the city-state)

80. *erōs:* (erotic) love
      mania: madness
      tēs philosophou manias te kai bakcheias: "this philosophical frenzy, this sacred rage" [Paul Shorey's rendering; Plato refers to the religious rites sacred to the worship of Bacchus]
      nous: mind, intellect

83. The Countess de Hondetot . . . wasn't pretty. Her face was marked from smallpox, her complexion lacked finesse. [FRENCH]

88. *theoeides:* divine in form

95. *hōsper epanabasmois chrōmenon:* used as steps

100. *philia:* love
      philein tina di' ekeinon: to love someone on account of that (person)
      di' ekeinon: on account of that one
      ekeinou heneka: for the sake of that one
      hoi d'agathoi di hautous philoi; hē(i) gar agathoi: the good are loved on account of themselves; insofar as they are good

SECTION C: APPENDIX

125 *spargōn:* swells
127 *vita nuova:* new life [ITALIAN; reference to Dante]
127(n.2) *to erōtikon omma pasan aisthēsei disathermēnan tēn psuchēn, gargalismous te kai pothou kentron hupoplēsthē(i):* the erotic vision heating up the whole soul by means of sensation, he is filled with the ticklings and pricklings of desire
128(n.3) *kala sōmata:* beautiful bodies
      gennan logous kalous: to generate fine words
      paidariou kallos: beauty of a young child
      orthōs paiderastein: to love boys correctly

THE NATURE OF LOVE

John A. Brentlinger

PHILOSOPHERS WHO HAVE written on love—and as Plato noticed in his day, they are very few—have mainly discussed four issues: (1) the objects of love, and whether loved objects are one sort of thing or diverse; (2) the sort of state love is—whether it is a sensation or feeling, an attitude, an emotion, a belief, a desire, or some combination of these; (3) the relation between love and desire (which may, or may not, be answered under the previous topic); and (4) the relation between love and valuation. I shall briefly discuss the first three of these issues, but my main concern shall be the last.

The question concerning the objects of love is actually several issues which are sometimes confused. Many thinkers have held that there is one proper sort of love object which is not, however, always or exclusively loved by everyone. Such thinkers have to allow that what people actually love, and what they would love if they were moral or prudent, may be different. In this category I would place Plato and Freud. Both hold that we can be mistaken in our love objects, and experience great frustration and despair because of such mistakes. Another distinction must be made. There are thinkers who would insist that, though we may actually love an object that is not worthy of love, we could not

Reprinted from *The Symposium of Plato*, Suzy Q Groden, tr., John A. Brentlinger, ed. (Amherst, MA: University of Massachusetts Press, 1970), pp. 113–29; copyright © 1970 by The University of Massachusetts Press. John Brentlinger is in the philosophy department, The University of Massachusetts at Amherst.

love the object unless we *believed* it was worthy of love. Plato, again, is an instance of this position. Freud and certain Christian philosophers, for example St. Augustine, are instances of thinkers who hold, on the contrary, that there is a certain sort of object which is worthy of love, and that people may mistakenly love things not of that sort, *and* that they need *not* think what they love to be of that sort.

The things people actually love and, Plato notwithstanding, what people think worthy of love, are as various—indeed more various—than one can imagine. Whether there is one *proper* sort of object of love, for example, sexually gratifying objects (Freud), God (St. Augustine), good things (Plato), pleasant things (Mill), happiness-giving things (I would say), is a question I cannot discuss. Though this is one central issue for a complete theory of love, it overshadows it entirely. Indeed one reason that so few philosophers write about love is that what people *actually* love cannot be determined philosophically without grotesque oversimplification; and the *proper* object of love is considered in a division of philosophy all its own: ethics and value-theory.

All writers on love have agreed that loving something necessarily implies valuing it. Perhaps we can best see the sort of psychological state love is if we begin with this. Love, then, can be thought of as a form of valuation. Clearly many valuations do not involve love: I value my car and I do not love it. Is there a form of valuation such that we can say, when someone values something in that way, they love that object? The concept of intrinsic value is immediately suggested. Can we hold that people love that which they value intrinsically, that is, what they value in and of itself;[1] and conversely, that whatever they love, they value for its own sake?

An objection to this is that love involves emotional attachment, or affection, and that many cases of intrinsic valuation do not. This is especially clear (the objection goes) when the object of my valuation is general, for instance, the welfare of mankind. In such a case, surely, it makes no sense to speak of emotional attachment, hence there is no love.

My reply is that there is more than one sort of love, and that many kinds of love (at least relations we now call 'love') cannot conceivably involve emotional attachment. Thus, I would say, the objection which is brought against some forms of intrinsic valuation being love applies equally to some forms of love; and this shows that the objection fails to understand the connection between love and emotion and feeling.

I assume that a basic distinction in love is according to whether its object is individual or general. In the former case there is an emotional attachment, of one person to another thing (person or nonperson), in the latter there is not. For distinctions' sake let us say that in the former case there is a presupposition of affection. This concept is vague and broad—enough to stretch from the love of inanimate things, and animals, to those friendships which are serious enough to involve love, through the feelings of parent and child, through the most emotional, sexual, relationships, and at an opposite extreme, to sexual relationships which are comparatively free of other interest or involvement.

In all of these cases, I suggest, besides intrinsic valuation there is the direction of feeling upon an individual. We can roughly characterize the kinds of love by the kinds of feelings and emotions and their intensity and duration, yet the distinctions are very rough and unclear, so much so that people often cannot compare and distinguish their own relationships. Nor can we single out one feeling or emotion which alone constitutes a type of love relationship: any feeling or emotion, *under the appropriate circumstances*, may be expressive of love *or* the absence of love. It is the *pattern* of feeling and behavior, in their circumstances, which tells us whether love exists and what sort, in ourselves or in others. And the possible patterns are infinitely various and complicated. Thus we cannot define the kinds of love which fall within this broad class, nor can we define the class itself beyond saying that it requires positive intrinsic valuation and positive emotional attachment directed toward an individual. In practice, when we require more specific or exact distinctions, we usually classify our relationships by their *objects* rather than by sorting and describing our feelings.

Yet we also recognize a form of love which is more generalized: the love of mankind, of animals or kinds of animals, of kinds of activities (chess, skiing), of kinds of things (flowers, the sea). In these cases the attitude manifests itself largely in the willingness and cheerfulness with which we engage in certain kinds of behavior, and by our preferences—the things we choose to do, to concern ourselves with, to nurture, as opposed to those which we ignore, neglect, or forget. We find ourselves pleasantly occupied with these things, and feel a sense of loss when we are kept from being engaged with them for great lengths of time. Some might question the term 'love' as applied to such things. Can we find anything importantly similar between the love of gardening and the love of humanity, and between both of these and the love of a man for his wife? I am not ashamed to see, even in such different cases, one centrally important feature: high intrinsic value placed upon an element of one's life. To this extent, the common use of the term 'love,' to cover such diverse cases, seems entirely justified.

Of course when the object of love is general, a *kind* of thing, the quality and intensity of feeling or emotion is very different. But even for these cases, feeling cannot be completely absent. For example, consider a philanthropist (literally, a lover of mankind) who shows by acts of generosity that he values the well-being of others intrinsically. (For instance, he uses his money to alleviate suffering.) Such a man may not have feelings of tenderness or affection toward those he assists, nor any emotion whatever. Much less will he long to be with them, to live with them, or have sexual feelings about them. Thus according to the first conception of love he would not be said to love them. Even so people must be able to act upon his feelings. One who feels nothing when he sees a picture of a starving child, or reads about the suffering of needy people, should not be counted a lover of mankind. Those who lack feelings in such circumstances, and still act in ways which promote the welfare of the suffering, may do so out of a sense of duty or in order to *appear* concerned. They may be *benefactors* of mankind. But they are not, I believe, *lovers* of mankind even in the most abstract sense, nor do they consider the benefits they confer to be intrinsically worthwhile. Their concern is with the imperatives of duty or custom, or the benefits philanthropy brings to *them*.

This suggests there is more in common between the two kinds of love—love of individual, as opposed to general, objects—than one might expect, for both require feelings of some sort, under some circumstances, as a condition of love. Further, we cannot define conditions which decisively test the presence or absence of either sort of love. In both cases a very wide variety of feelings, in all sorts of different circumstances, may be relevant as indications of its presence or absence. The mistakes people make by giving undue importance to one sort of feeling, in one sort of circumstance, are, of course, notorious!

I shall assume, then, that love must contain a valuational and emotional element, and since both of these admit of great difference of kind and of degree, love too may vary greatly in the value it places on its object, and the feelings it has about it, both in kind and in degree. And I shall assume that people love that which they value intrinsically, and that whatever they love, they value intrinsically. These assumptions are controversial, but I have gone as far as I can in this context to indicate my reasons for them.

A major disagreement among writers on love and the topic I want mainly to discuss, concerns the *relation* of valuation and love. When we love something we value it intrinsically: do we love it *because* we value it, or do we value it *because* we love it? In the former case we must believe the object of our love to have certain value properties, as a precondition of loving it. In the latter case our love is a precondition of the objects' having value to us.

Christian *agape* is a concept of the latter sort. It is held that God's love for man is not *due* to the value of man, God does not love man *because* of a value possessed by human beings; rather, the love of God is bestowed as a gift, and human beings have value through this bestowal. Also, though man's love for God cannot be thought of in this way, men may love one another with *agape*: "Freely give, as freely ye have received." It is also held that this sort of love is higher: it is *better* to love without a reason, than with a reason. It is also held that one cannot love another person *as a person* unless one loves unconditionally, or for no reason, and thus with *agape*.[2]

Platonic *eros*, on the contrary, is the concept of love as motivated by the belief that the object of love is good or beautiful or valuable in some other way.[3]

I want first to discuss certain fallacious criticisms of the Platonic view. Then I will try to formulate considerations which will allow us to settle the dispute between the two theories.

In the literature on love one often sees arguments against Platonic love of this sort:

1) All *eros*-love is acquisitive/egocentric/nonpersonal;
2) There is a very important sort of love which is not acquisitive/ egocentric/nonpersonal; therefore,
3) There is a very important sort of love which is not *eros*.

I shall show that Platonic love is quite capable of being nonacquisitive, nonego-centric, and personal, thus that the first premise of this argument is false. There is no such simple way of deciding between *eros* and *agape*.

One criticism of *eros* is that since *eros* is desire, or at least cannot exist without desire,[4] it is acquisitive, in a sense intended to be incompatible with the selfless, bestowal characteristics of *agape*. For instance, Nygren writes:

> even where Eros seems to be a desire to give it is still in the last resort a "Will-to-possess"; for Plato was fundamentally unaware of any other form of love than acquisitive love. (*Agape and Eros*, p. 176)

And in his book *The Nature of Love*, Irving Singer says:

> For desire is always acquisitive, and its object a mere commodity designed to satisfy. As Platonic eros is the organism striving to overcome deficiencies, so too is desire an attempt to eliminate a state of need or want . . . as an interest in the object itself, one that refuses to treat the object as merely a means to satisfaction, love is not reducible to *any* desire. (p. 89)

These writers can only make the charges they do by ignoring a very large class of desires. Desire is not acquisitive in those cases in which the object of my desire is the welfare, happiness, or satisfaction of some other person or group of people. Nor is it incompatible with my having an interest in the object itself, in such cases as when I desire and take satisfaction in another's happiness for his sake (and *not* because his achieving happiness allows me to realize my desire for his happiness!).

A similar mistake is made in the charge that *eros* is egocentric. Since *eros*-love is founded on the value of the love-object, it is assumed to follow that the lover seeks to aggrandize himself through his love. To quote Nygren again:

But the clearest proof of the egocentric nature of Eros is its intimate connection with *eudaimonia*. The aim of love is to gain possession of an object which is regarded as valuable and which man feels he needs. . . . Plato is especially concerned to emphasize this point. "It is by the acquisition of good things," he says, "that the happy are made happy." . . . To love the good, therefore, is the same as to desire to possess the good and to possess it *permanently* . . . but in this desire, too, the egocentric will is in evidence. (p. 180)

Nygren also writes:

all desire, or appetite, and longing, is more or less egocentric. (p. 180)

To call all desires "egocentric" is to deprive the term of all (but its pejorative) meaning. What matters is the *object* of the desire. Desires differ as their objects differ. My desire for a drink is egocentric, since it concerns *my* having a drink. My desires for the betterment of mankind, an end of poverty, a permanent peace, and so on, concern myself indirectly or not at all. It is sophistry to say that my interest in these matters derives from an interest in my own welfare. What if it does? I still have a genuine interest in them, in my present state: they are what I desire, and my desire is satisfied by virtue of someone else attaining something valuable to them. An egocentric man rates the satisfactions of other people lower than his own; it is in his system of values and the accompanying desires that he is egocentric. All men are alike in trying to satisfy their desires, and thus it shows nothing about the egocentricity of a concept of love to show that it involves desire. According to Plato men desire beauty and goodness everywhere: in the world of change they seek to create it as artists and statesmen; as educators they create it in other souls and themselves; they admire and contemplate it in the unchanging world of forms. In this they find happiness. But there is no reason to conclude that they view this beauty and goodness simply as means to their happiness or satisfaction. [5] For people do find satisfaction in contemplating that which they consider desirable for its own sake.

Platonic *eros* is often criticized as being incompatible with the love of persons. The assumption behind this criticism is a general principle of this form: if a person loves x because he believes x to have the property G, he must be using x as a means to acquiring G.

Take, for initial consideration, an ordinary, nonemotional sort of instance. I love a certain wine; I love it *because of* its taste, aroma, and color. Does it follow that I use the wine as a means to enjoying its taste, aroma, and color? Not at all. The idea of means and end, so used, is completely inappropriate. If I desire something only as a means, I care about it only because it may be used to cause something else which I love per se. My loving a wine because it has certain properties, could mean that I love the properties per se and the wine only because it brings me that which I love. Yet it has a more natural interpretation: the properties are what it is *about* the wine, which is the basis of my love for *it*. On the first interpretation, we are asked to suppose that people love properties, and objects only as means, whenever their love has a reason. It is more plausible, I suggest, that when people love for a reason, they love objects, but conditionally upon believing that their reason is satisfied. When I say that I love *x* because it is G, I am giving an *explanation* of my love for *x* by the reference to G. I am saying, in effect, that I am moved to love anything which is G, insofar as it is G; and since *x* is a G, I love *x*. Notice that in the conclusion the object of my love is *x*, not the property G (my reason for loving *x*).

Thus it does not follow from Plato's claim that we love persons (or anything else) because we believe them to be beautiful and good, that we really love the properties of beauty and goodness per se, and do not really love persons per se. In making this statement he is arguing that our love follows a general pattern: it occurs only where we believe something to be good, and it is the stronger where we believe greater good to be present. Now it is certainly true that Plato believed that we loved the Good and the Beautiful more than anything else, and that other things are loved because they resemble the Good and the Beautiful. Yet the Good and the Beautiful are themselves good and beautiful things loved *because of* their goodness and beauty. Also, they are loved more than other things only because they are held to be more beautiful than other things. Further, the relation of lower things to the Good and the Beautiful is not the relation of thing to property, but of imitation to reality, copy to exemplar.

This mistake is difficult to stamp out. We are familiar with the perennial but not very bright complaint: you don't love *me*, you just love my G (for 'G' may be substituted 'money,' 'body,' 'brains,' and so forth). The basis of the unhappiness expressed by this remark, however, is being loved for the *wrong* qualities, not the wish for the lover to be indifferent to *all* the beloved's qualities! In the case of Plato the plausibility of this mistaken principle has a different source. We think the love of persons is the highest form of love, and we feel that Plato is deeply wrong when he says that (1) other people are loved because of a resemblance they bear to the Good and (2) the Good is more valuable, and more satisfying to love, than persons. And Plato is wrong in these two points. Yet it is not a consequence of this system of values, that there can be no genuine love of persons per se.[6] Plato's hierarchy is not a hierarchy of merely instrumental goods leading to the Good; it is a hierarchy of intrinsic goods. Each member of the hierarchy is less good, hence less worthy of love, than any member above it; and each depends on the highest good for what goodness and beauty it has. Yet since each is beautiful and satisfying (in its limited, imperfect way), each is (in its limited, imperfect way) intrinsically good.

The conclusion to be drawn from these arguments is that *eros* is not distinguishable from *agape* by being egocentric, acquisitive, or nonpersonal. If they are correct I believe there is no possibility of singling out cases which are definitely examples of *agape* but not of *eros* by the sort of interest involved. For both *eros* and *agape* are valuational. And we cannot point to cases of nonacquisitive, nonegocentric, personal love and say: that is *agape*, not *eros*. It is usually assumed that the reverse is possible: we can distinguish cases of *eros* from *agape*, as, for instance, where sexual love occurs completely divorced from other interests in the partner. Yet this assumption is merely another form of the first mistake just discussed: it is simply prejudice that sexual love must be exploitative, or use its object as a means to selfish enjoyment. Sexual love can be as spontaneous and unmotivated as *agape* traditionally conceived; it too can creatively bestow value on its object. The essential feature of *agape* is its being a love which does not follow criteria but creates them in the love itself. This may be a feature of pure sexuality as much as in the less physically directed forms of love. But where sexual love is exploitative, where it uses the object simply as a means of satisfaction, there is no *eros* present and indeed, no love properly so-called; for it was laid down earlier in this paper that all love views its object as valuable for its own sake and not merely as a means.

These moral considerations show no distinction between *agape* and *eros*. Either sort of love is as capable of dignifying its object as the other. Nor should this surprise us, after all, when we consider that we did not distinguish the two by a moral criterion. We have said that we must decide whether love creates a valuation (*agape*) or proceeds from one (*eros*), not whether love uses a certain sort of valuative criterion for its objects (thereby including some sorts of things and excluding others). Our concern is with the relation between love and valuation generally.

We may make a fresh approach by considering a classic text for this issue, the discussion in Plato's *Euthyphro*. In this dialogue Euthyphro has defined Piety as that which all of the gods love (7A); Impiety as that which all of the gods hate (9E). Further Socrates and Euthyphro agree that the gods love the Holy because it is holy—they agree that it is *not* holy *because* it is loved (10C). Socrates then points out a fault in the definition:

> It seems, Euthyphro, when you were asked to say what Piety is, you did not wish to make plain its nature and told instead something which has been done to it, namely that it pertains to Piety to be loved by all of the gods. But you did not say what its *being* is. Do not hide it from me, if you please, but starting again from the beginning tell me what Piety is, and never mind whether it is loved by the gods, or anything else has happened to it. (11A–B)

Socrates' distinction between what Piety really is, and what belongs to it by virtue of an act of approval or love, may give one key to the difference between Plato and St. Paul. For to Plato it is incidental to the pious, something which merely pertains to it, that the gods love it. And this presupposes that the value characteristics of things are independent of the approval or disapproval of the gods, that the gods approve that which they *find* to be worthy of their approval. For Plato, then, value characteristics exist *prior* to the beliefs of either gods or men.

To Plato the creative activities of men and god presuppose an ideal or model which guides the act of creation. One of the highest forms of creative activity in men is legislation, but the man-created laws and rules which guide life are not basic value principles but "recipes" by which men may be guided in patterning themselves after the higher realities. The human statesman gazes at the ideals of Justice, Wisdom, and Courage, and like a painter forms his creation, the human state, in their likeness (*Republic* 500C–501A). And when Plato describes the creation of the world he speaks of god as contemplating and copying in as much detail as possible an uncreated model of the world (*Timaeus* 30C–D). To Plato thought is always and essentially directed to externally existing objects (*Parmenides* 132B–C, *Republic* 478B). And action and feeling, in their highest form, are guided by thought.

Christian thought takes a major initiative in its doctrine of creation, according to which God not only makes the world out of nothing, but in his act of creation gives the standards by which the world and everything in it are to be judged. The love of the Christian god, according to Nygren (and in Paul's epistles and the parables of Jesus) is not measured out in terms of some antecedently given scale of values. The values of things, in relation to God, are dependent, in this sense: the love of God creates the intrinsic value which belongs to the objects of his creation. It is not something which merely pertains to good things, that they should be loved by God. Being good and being God-loved, are essentially the same. Of course for men in this interpretation, the value characteristics are prior—exist independently of *their* beliefs and attitudes. For this reason it might be thought that human love could not confer value on its object in the same manner as the divine, hence could not be *agape*.[7]

Here is a difference between the Platonic and Christian points of view which may elucidate the difference between *eros* and *agape*. Can we say that philosophers who accept the *eros* view of love do so *because* they believe value properties to exist independently of the attitudes and beliefs of persons (divine and human)? And that philosophers who believe that values are relative are inclined for that reason, to accept the concept of *agape* over that of *eros*? This, I believe, is the basic difference in the two concepts of love. If so then the issue of whether *eros* or *agape* is the correct conception of love reduces to the question of whether values are objective or relative (either to man or to the will of God).

However, there is a way of construing the emphasis on *eros* rather than *agape* which does not assume objective values. Rather, this second way assumes the primacy of value *beliefs* over *feelings*. For one element in the concept of *eros* is that the *beliefs* the lover has in the value of the object causes his love for the object. Thus while earlier we stated that *eros* involved a prior recognition that its object is intrinsically valuable, we may now define it solely by reference to the lover's beliefs. So defined the concept of *eros* no longer carries a presupposition of the objectivity of values. By contrast, *agape*, on this model, would be a love in which the (spontaneous, unreasoned) feeling of the lover for the object causes him to believe the object has intrinsic value. The controversy then centers around whether value-beliefs and reasons cause love-feelings, or conversely, whether love-feelings cause value-beliefs.[8]

It seems to me that if we redefine the issue between *eros* and *agape* as we have done, *neither* concept is by itself sufficient to explain all cases of love. Rather, some lovers and loves will be cases of *eros* and some of *agape*. An important difference exists between those who let their emotions be guided by their beliefs and whose love thus has an ethical or prudential cast, and those whose love is unmotivated by reasons. Though both sorts of person will value the object of their love intrinsically, a very important difference obtains in their *reasons* for ascribing value to the object of love. On the one hand, the beloved is thought to be valuable because certain value-making conditions are thought to be fulfilled, for example, it is intelligent or beautiful. In the second case, the value-making condition is the love itself, which does not in turn exist for a reason that the lover can offer. Since no value-making condition exists or at least is operative as a belief of the lover, it is proper to say that the love itself creates the value belief.

I think that both have existed and hence that both are possible. The question which remains is whether one sort is preferable, and hence whether we should cultivate one form—at least in some circumstances—in preference to the other. The answer is clearly that an unqualified preference for either sort would be wrong. No general answer is possible since the causes of love, whether feelings or beliefs, *may* be either destructive or constructive in their effects. A person who bases his love on reasons may take as his reasons a selfish and short-term consideration, or a false assessment of the character of the beloved; and a love founded on "pure" emotion may be morbid or temporary or exploitative. In other cases important values may attach to a spontaneous, unmotivated love, or to the rational assessment of its object prior to a full emotional commitment. There is no empirical warrant for saying that human love must follow either course if it is to be "true love," and no basis for holding up either form as the highest since excesses are possible in the direction of rationalization or feeling.

In summary: My concern has been to survey the question of love as it now exists for us, to bring out the issues involved in it, and suggest answers to some of these issues. One issue is the nature of the object of love. I am much more cautious than Plato (and many other earlier writers) in attempting to give a general characterization of the actual objects or motives of human love. It is possible, I think, to achieve a theory of the proper objects of human love, but it is not possible to circumscribe human love within the limits of propriety! A second issue is a general description of the sort of psychological state love is. I suggested that love is not to be identified with any emotion or feeling, but rather with valuation. I hold that love is the same as intrinsic valuation, and that its relation to emotion and feeling (1) varies immensely according to the *sort* of love we are concerned with, and (2) is such a complex relationship, so dependent upon circumstances, that neither love in general nor any particular sort of love can be defined by the pattern of feelings involved in it. A third issue is the relation of love to desire. Here, I believe, Plato is entirely right: there is no love without desire for the object. Critics of Plato have either misunderstood Plato's claim (thinking that he was identifying love and desire) or misunderstood the nature of desire (thinking that desire is egocentric). The fourth issue, the connection of love and valuation, has in modern times been debated as an issue between *eros* and *agape*. My main concern has been to define this issue, which has never been properly understood. I argue that it has nothing to do with the supposed egocentricity of *eros* versus the supposed selflessness of *agape*. The real distinction is between two attitudes toward values: whether value-properties exist objectively, independently of human decisions or attitudes or feeling, as in the classical, Platonic conception of the world; or whether they are relative to human or divine conventions or attitudes or feelings. A second conception of *eros* and *agape* is also of importance, however, and concerns the causal priority of beliefs or feelings in bringing about the attitude of love. [9]

NOTES

1. I shall not try to define the concept of intrinsic value, but shall assume it to be sufficiently clear for my discussion of love. Roughly, I mean by intrinsic value, the property an object has of being worthy of choice independently of its consequences for other experiences of the agent or other persons; and by intrinsic disvalue, the property of being worthy of avoidance independently of the object's consequences for other experiences of the agent or other persons. Plato makes this distinction in *Republic* II (357B). The opposite of intrinsic value is ordinarily called 'instrumental value.'

2. The most influential work, advancing a distinction between *agape* and *eros*, is the three-volume study by Anders Nygren, *Agape and Eros*, first published in 1929; references and quotations in this article are all to the latest English translation, by Philip S. Watson

(Philadelphia: The Westminster Press, 1953). The study is the starting point of the studies of Denis De Rougemont, *Love and the Western World*, trans. by Montgomery Belgian (New York: Harcourt, Brace and Co., 1940), and M. C. D'Arcy, *The Mind and Heart of Love* (London: Faber, 1945), and gives important background for two other worthwhile studies, *The Nature of Love: Plato to Luther* by Irving Singer (New York: Random House, 1966), and *Platonic Love* by Thomas Gould (New York: The Free Press, 1963). I have no space to discuss these works here in detail, though I will attempt to correct certain misunderstandings of Plato which are current in some of them. Nygren's conception of *agape*, as opposed to *eros*, is stated by him in the following terms: (1) "Agape is spontaneous and 'unmotivated' " (p. 75); (2) "Agape is 'indifferent to value' " (p. 77); (3) "Agape is creative" (p. 78), that is *agape* creates value in the object of love; (4) "Agape is the initiator of fellowship with God" (p. 80), that is, *agape* is the basis of the relationship of man and God. In contrast, according to Nygren, (1) "Eros is the 'love of desire,' or acquisitive love"; (2) "Eros is man's way to the divine—as opposed to God's approach to man; (3) "Eros is egocentric love" (p. 175).

3. Platonic *eros*, in one sense, involves a great deal besides: Plato's views on knowledge, reason, and desire; his dualism of being and becoming; his claim that the form of the Good is the highest object of love. I shall not be concerned here with this, but only one part of his theory, and a part which many would accept who disagree with him on other matters: that a belief in the value (the goodness, beauty, or other) of the object of love, is a precondition of love. The traditional Christian philosophy is Platonistic on many of these other points. I am concerned here only with the contrast between *eros* and *agape*.

4. The latter, and not the former, is actually Plato's stated position in the *Symposium*: Love, he says, desires its object (200A). He does not say that love is a desire, much less that love and desire are the same. That Love desires its object means, in nonfigurative language, that whoever loves something, desires that which they love. The strongest interpretation, which I do not believe can be justifiably attributed to Plato, is that whoever desires something, loves that which they desire. It should also be noted, in interpreting Plato, that his claim that there is no love without desire does not imply (a) that love is *nothing but* desire, nor (b) that love is directed to what we do not have or possess. For Plato specifically points out that we can desire what we have; for this means that we desire to continue to have it. Thus assuming that people desire to continue to have what they love, we will not find any cases in which people have and love something, but contrary to Plato's theory, do *not* desire it.

5. In the *Republic* Socrates says that the best things are those which are desirable both for their consequences and in themselves. And he argues that people who attain these things without their (normal) consequences, are happier than people who attain their (normal) consequences without the things themselves. Thus Plato rates as the happiest existence that in which the self contemplates things, valuable in themselves, without reference to their consequences. Thus clearly he does not think that we find them valuable *because of* their consequences.

6. Singer claims that it is: "Plato emphasizes that love for another person is primarily a desire for the goodness which is in him. In other words, it is not the other person as a person that the Platonic lover cares about. He loves his beloved, not in himself, but only for the sake of goodness or beauty. The Platonic lover does not love anyone: he loves only the Good" (*The Nature of Love*, p. 87).

7. Nygren claims as much, for instance, *Agape and Eros*, p. 125.

8. We may take two views of this characterization of *eros*. Either we may suppose the lover believes the value of his love-object is objective or not. If the former, then the lover believes (1) that the object of his love is intrinsically valuable, (2) that it has this value

objectively, and (3) these beliefs cause him to love this object. If the latter, then we leave out condition (2). In the former alternative our concept of *eros* no longer commits us to the existence of objective intrinsic values, but only to the belief in their existence. In this case, if the belief is false or unprovable, *eros* would involve a kind of illusion not unlike the sort of illusion Kant felt existed in our inescapable belief in an external, intelligible world. In the second alternative we are no longer committed even to this illusion. To make this clearer consider the ethics of Jean-Paul Sartre. He holds that each man creates his own system of moral rules and correlated values, hence he denies the objective status of values. Yet within each man's system, so viewed, a distinction between intrinsic and nonintrinsic values may be made. *Agape* may be similarly defined in two ways. Either one may maintain that the lover has a love-feeling for an object which causes him (1) to believe the object is intrinsically valuable and (2) to believe this value is objective, or one may hold that the love-feeling simply causes the value-belief as in (1) with the omission of the condition stated in (2).

9.   I am grateful to Ann Brentlinger and Alex Page for helpful criticisms of earlier drafts of this essay.

PLATONIC LOVE

L. A. Kosman

IT IS NOT surprising that love, like other concepts which seem to have their first home in individual and personal contexts, should have assumed for Plato cosmic and mythic proportions. Throughout the dialogues may still be heard the voices of Hesiod and Empedocles, the voices of poets, philosophers, and myth-makers for whom the human soul is a miniature of the world soul and Eros and Philia principles of cosmic magnitude.

In Plato, the cosmic dimensions of love are most explicitly articulated in the early *Symposium* speeches, in Erixymachus' invocation of Eros as a principle operative not simply "ἐπί ταῖς ψυχαῖς τῶν ἀνϑρώπων, in the dealings of human life," but "ἐπὶ πᾶν, everywhere in the universe, in all matters human and divine alike,"[1] in Agathon's pompous and cliché-ridden account of Eros as that by which all living things are begotten and come forth, a principle governing alike the Muses, Apollo, Hephaestus, Pallas Athene, and Zeus himself, who by love attained "the governance of gods and men."[2] These cosmic descriptions of love are not simple mythological atavisms which Plato overcomes in directing his philosophical attention to the moral questions of human intercourse. For in general, even in the earlier and middle dialogues,

Reprinted from *Facets of Plato's Philosophy*, edited by W. H. Werkmeister (Assen, Amsterdam: Van Gorcum, 1976), pp. 53–69, with the permission of Professor Kosman. Louis Aryeh Kosman received his Ph.D. at Harvard University and is Professor of Philosophy at Haverford College in Pennsylvania. (This is a corrected version of the essay that appeared in Werkmeister's volume.) Appended to the essay is a guide to Kosman's Greek, prepared for this volume by Edward Johnson.

the apparently local moral concerns have much broader and more ambitious overtones, metaphysical and epistemological in nature, every bit as much as does the much later search for the Sophist.

Nor is this a feature of those concepts alone which have clear and determinate histories as mythic personalities in Homer or Hesiod. Justice, as much as Eros, is writ small, so to speak, in the human soul, and although finally it may be that habitat which most concerns Plato in the *Republic*,[3] δικαιοσύνη is undeniably a principle by which the universe itself is apportioned according to the virtues of its parts, a principle by which the good distributes itself properly into forms and then into particulars, and thus perhaps the fundamental metaphysical principle according to which each thing is itself in conformity to its true nature. The ultimate justice is thus the justice of appearance to being, i.e. of the "lower" to the "higher" world.[4]

So with Eros; as each thing in the world of appearance strives to incorporate its nature, i.e. to 'imitate' its true form, it exhibits and acts out that world's erotic striving toward the world of being. But appearances are not outlandish; they are citizens, ambassadors perhaps, sometimes in exile, but citizens nonetheless of that higher world, and their striving is thus revealed to be, as it were, auto-erotic, the eros of a world in love not with some alien empire, but with its own true order, that which is to it φύσει οἰκεῖον.

I

None of this is surprising given the proximity of Plato's to an older and still vital, if already ironically appropriated mythopoeic view of the world. Indeed what philosophers have found disturbing about Plato's views is not that they are confined to those contexts of interpersonal love which most of us would take as paradigmatic instances of love, but that it is precisely those contexts which they fail to give an adequate account of or positively exclude.

Two basic objections to Plato's theory of love are by now commonplace in the literature, and both find that theory inadequate precisely in so far as it fails to account for the love between persons, the love between parent and child, man and woman, lover and lover, friend and friend.

(1) Love in Plato's theory is basically egoistical and selfish. A person cannot, according to Plato, love or desire another for the sake of that other, i.e. for the other's good, but only for his own sake, that is, for whatever good that other might provide him; indeed as Gregory Vlastos writes:

> if A loves B, he does so because of some benefit he needs from B and for the sake of just that benefit . . . no reason is offered why we could love anyone except for what we could get out of him. The egoistic perspective

of "love" so conceived becomes unmistakable when Socrates, generalizing, argues that "if one were in want of nothing, one would feel no affection; . . . and he who felt no affection would not love."[5]

(2) Proper love in Plato's view is not love of an individual person, but either (ideally) love of beauty itself, love of that unchanging, ungenerated, perfectly proportioned καλόν revealed veiledly in the final ἐποπτικά of Diotima's speech, or at best love of the cluster of beautiful and desirable qualities instantiated in the individual.

> This seems to me the cardinal flaw in Plato's theory. It does not provide for love of whole persons, but only for love of that abstract version of persons which consists of the complex of their best qualities. This is the reason why personal affection ranks so low in Plato's scala amoris.[6]

> The Platonic lover does not love *anyone:* he loves only the Good, either in abstraction or in concrete manifestations.[7]

These objections are independent of one another, though sometimes they're confused, and sometimes merged into a portmanteau objection, according to which Plato's theory allows as the object of legitimate love only the collection of egoistically useful characteristics which merely happen to be instantiated in an individual. But that the two are independent is clear. A theory of love might fail to allow individual persons as appropriate objects of love without being egoistic. A theory e.g. which assimilated love to worship either of gods or of impersonal and admirable universals might maintain that the love of individual persons is idolatrous, without locating the origin of love for an appropriate object in the benefit which such love or that object might occasion for the lover.

Conversely, a theory of love might recognize individuals as proper and appropriate objects of love while still being egoistic, that is, while still maintaining that the love of another is only for the benefit or advantage which might accrue to the lover. It may be that such a theory ought ultimately to be described as deficient in that the individual is not loved for his own sake; but to make that out, it will be necessary to add some argument to the effect that individuals are being loved *qua* individuals only when they are being loved for their own sake, and that argument couldn't be generated from the concept of an individual alone.

The two objections might be thought to be connected in the following way: it is precisely because of the egoistic nature of Plato's love, precisely, that is, because the love is directed toward and conditional upon specific qualities which are instantiated in the beloved and considered to be advantageous to the lover, that the beloved individual is, so to speak, bypassed.

> We cannot love another person for himself, but only as a vehicle and partial embodiment of what we really want—the Good. By seeing that this is the real object of his love, the Platonic philosopher disintoxicates himself from the interest in persons as such. For what is a person but a conglomeration of accidental properties that chance and nature have thrown together? No, Plato would say, to love anyone is really to love the goodness which is in him. [8]

But it is not a condition of this bypassing occurring that the qualities for which and conditional upon which the individual is said to be loved should be advantageous to the lover. To generate the paradox that conditional love of the individual is not love of the *individual*, it is necessary only that the love be conditional, that is, bestowed in response to and on the condition of qualities which the individual happens to have, whatever the independent relation of these qualities to the lover. To say of a theory that it understands love to be determined by or conditional upon the worth of the beloved is thus not the same as to say that the theory is egoistical. A non-egoistical theory might distinguish between worthy and unworthy objects of love in such a way as to generate the same difficulties. This makes clear that if we're to escape the difficulties attributed to Plato's theory we shall need something more than a non-egoistical theory of love; we shall need a theory in which love is unconditional, given regardless of the worth or worthlessness of the object. As long as love is in response to or conditional upon the object's worth, or in general its being *lovable*, then it would seem to be those features in virtue of which the object is lovable which constitute the true and proper objects of love, not the individual who happens to have them. Note that this is a feature of a theory of love which is the result not of it being a theory of *love*, but rather of the demand that it be an *individual* who is the object of love. What we are asking for is some axiological analogue of *de re* necessity. We are demanding, so to speak, *de re* and not *de dicto* valuation; but valuation seems possible only under some description, and then it doesn't seem to be of the individual, who only *accidentally* enjoys that description. If then we wish love of an *individual*, it seems that we had best resign ourselves to dispensing with the valuation.

In fact, it is in accordance with just such reasoning that the second criticism has been directed against Plato, contrasting the Platonic theory unfavorably with what Nygren and others have characterized as the agapic, Christian view, a view according to which love is not conditional and contingent upon worth, but unconditional and creative, spontaneous, uncaused, indifferent to human merit. [9]

There may be much to be said in favor of a love of this sort, but it doesn't seem to me that one of the things which can be said is that it restores the individual as the proper object of love. For what is demanded when we demand that an individual person be the object of love is not simply that love be directed toward the individual, *per accidens*, but that it be directed toward the individual *qua* that individual, that is, that love recognize the individual as particular and unique and as loved for being precisely who he is. But wholly unconditional love cannot provide this recognition; it is again only *accidental* that *I* am loved. Since there's nothing about me which has occasioned the love, there's no important respect in which I, in contrast to the person who happened along in this place at this moment, am loved. I have become, so to speak, the recipient of an erotic lottery.

The difficulty of articulating a theory of love which recognizes the individual *qua* individual as object of love thus seems perplexingly to infect any theory, whether it views love as conditional or unconditional. The individual frustrates our efforts by a maddening transparency. Insofar as I love him for his qualities, the qualities seem to constitute the proper object of my love; insofar as I love him irrespective of his particular qualities, it becomes unclear in what sense I may be said to love, specifically, *him*.

The problem may be put in another way; we want a theory which will account for our prereflective paradoxical demands that love be charitable and unconditional, yet not independent of features of the beloved which the lover recognizes and values. We want our lovers at once to accept us as we are and admire us for what we are. In theology, this is the problem of reconciling God's merciful love and demanding judgment, a problem which, as the prophets testify, even God was not comfortable with. We may wish, if we find the demand finally an impossible one, to choose for other reasons in favor of what Plato's critics have characterized as agapic love; but we ought not to characterize this as a choice in favor of a love which recognizes individuals.

II

In the *Symposium*, Socrates' speech introduces a fundamental shift in the direction and understanding of the nature of eros. In the first place, beginning with the conversation with Agathon, [10] Socrates reveals or first makes explicit a) the intentional, object-saturated character of love, and b) the separation of love from its object, the fact, that is, that the object which defines and determines love is always something which love lacks. These facts, in the second place, lead to an important shift in the description of the nature of eros, a shift strikingly represented in the mythological account of Eros no longer as a god, but as a daimon poised in metaxy, in intermediate state, between being and non-being, and thus not itself good and beautiful, but of, that is in love with, the good and beautiful.[11] This shift, finally, is connected with a change in rhetorical strategy, as Socrates turns from a praise of love to a praise of love's object, a praise which culminates in the moving if problematic description of αὐτὸ τὸ καλόν with which Socrates' speech ends.[12] The importance of this last move may be overlooked. If love is intentional of an object not yet realized, then the love or praise of love will constitute a project essentially selfcontradictory in nature, for in constituting love with the opacity of an object, it will frustrate the intentional transparency which love must have toward *its* proper object. The love of love, the establishment as a *goal* of the unconsummated erotic stance, constitutes a project represented in the worse elements of the courtly love tradition, a project to whose dangers and attractiveness the Greek philosophical sensibility was always sensitive.[13] Much of the brilliance of the *Symposium* rests in the subtlety with which we are led to the very threshold of this position, and at the last minute averted by Socrates' rhetorical transformation, his move from a *praise* of love, an encomium of eros in λογῶ, to an exhibition of love, an encomium of eros in ἐργῶ, in the form of a speech praising the beautiful.

The metaxy of eros does not come upon us completely by surprise in the dialogue; it has run as an undercurrent in several of the previous speeches, and is most importantly prefigured by the startling statement of Socrates at the beginning of the evening that the subject of τὰ ἐρωτικά is the one subject on which he is an expert.[14] This claim does not contradict his more usual profession of ignorance; for that profession is essentially a claim to be situated between ignorance and wisdom, a claim to be a philosopher, a lover of wisdom, where that love is revealed in and constituted by the recognition of ignorance, the recognized separation from and desire of wisdom. These two states of intermediateness are brought together in the earliest part of Diotima's reported conversation.[15]

I have rehearsed these obvious features of Socrates' speech as preparatory to focusing attention upon the important question, what according to Plato is the proper object of eros? Two further points must be made prior to turning directly to that question, one methodological, one a minor point of phrasing.

The methodological point is this: no unambiguous answer to the question, what did Plato hold, can be obtained by mere attention to the views put forward by Socrates. I say this not because of a difference between the views of the historic Socrates and the historic Plato, a difference often thought to be signaled in the *Symposium* by the presence of Diotima and her warning that Socrates may not understand fully the "higher mysteries,"[16] but because of the differences of view between the fictional Socrates and the authorial Plato. Plato is a philosophical poet, which means that the arguments we encounter are mimetic; they are imitation arguments, not of Plato, but of the fictional Socrates, Theaetetus, Lysis and so on. The reasoning in favor of and consequences of this claim, which I think are of the utmost importance to understanding Plato, would take us far afield here. But as a methodological principle I shall try to avoid taking the speech of Socrates, especially at the end of the *Symposium*, as unqualifiedly and in its totality representing Plato's position. [17]

The second is a minor point, but one which opens up the important question of love's proper object. Plato's love is sometimes described as desire for an object not possessed. But this is a seriously misleading representation of the view found in the dialogues. It is true that in the *Symposium* eros is characterized as loving that which it loves when it doesn't have it: οὐκ ἔχων αὐτὸ οὗ ἐπιθυμεῖ τε καὶ ἐρᾷ. [18] But that characterization does not specify an essential feature of love's object; it specifies rather an accidental consequent of a stronger feature, namely that love is the desire for that of which the love is ἐνδεής, the desire for what one *lacks*. [19]

That of which one is ἐνδεής is not simply that which one does not have, nor which one wants in the sense of desires, but that which one *lacks*, or wants in the sense of needing, missing and requiring for the fulfillment and completion of some nature. That of which a person is ἐνδεής is thus something to which he has, under some description and relative to it, a claim or right. Only relative, of course, to that description: a person might desire something upon which he had no claim, which in no sense belonged to him, and still, relative to that desire, be ἐνδεής of the means of acquiring it.

When we understand that, an important and perplexing discussion in the *Lysis* becomes somewhat clearer, though far from clear. In the course of the complex and important discussion of whether like loves like, Socrates and Menexenus have been led to say that that which is neither wholly good nor wholly bad loves what it loves for the sake of the good because of the bad which it despises. For the sake of health, for example, we love the art which leads to health, the τέχνη ἰατρική. But then, of course, we must love health, and if so, we must love *it* for the sake of some good, and we thus stand at the edge of one of the dizzying and wearying regresses which so fascinated Plato and Aristotle after him. Mustn't there then be, Socrates concludes, some πρῶτον φίλον, a first love for the sake of which we love all else that we love and of which all our other loves are εἴδωλα, images, and which alone is ἀληθῶς φίλον or τῷ ὄντι φίλον, which is alone our sole *true* love?

The argument, after a short interlude, proceeds with Socrates' claim that what desires, desires that of which it is ἐνδεές, and therefore loves that of which it is ἐνδεές. Suddenly three further conclusions materialize as if out of the air: 1) that which lacks lacks that which has been taken away from it, 2) eros, love and desire are therefore (sic!) of that which is φύσει οἰκεῖον, that which naturally belongs to us, and so 3) the φύσει οἰκεῖον is seen to be that which we necessarily love. [20]

The logic here is sketchy, as the perplexity of Lysis and Menexenus attests to and the "rapturous blushing" of Hippothales ironically underscores. But the conclusion is clear and interesting, for it suggests that the πρῶτον φίλον is that of which we may be said to be *properly* ἐνδεεῖς, and this is our own true but fugitive nature, that which is for us φύσει οἰκεῖον, even if we are separated from it.

The proper object of erotic love is thus understood by Plato to be τὸ οἰκεῖον, that which belongs naturally to oneself, but from which one has been separated. Erotic love is thus primarily for Plato *self-love*, for it is finally our true self which is at once native to us and lacked by us. "Self-love" does not here mean love of *love*, like the understanding of understanding in the *Charmides*, but one's love of one's *self*. Nor does it mean *selfish* love, the vanity and egocentricism which is assailed in Book V of the *Laws*.[21] It means at the human level that erotic self-striving which characterizes all being: the desire of each thing to become what it is.

As is generally true in Plato, a manifold of false images of the true understanding is possible. Just as there is a wide variety of ways to misunderstand the sense in which the philosopher practices the art of dying, so there might be a wide variety of ways to misunderstand the sense in which the philosopher's love is self-love. I take it that in part Phaedrus, Agathon, perhaps above all Alcibiades, represent, in ways that would be interesting to spell out, modes of that false understanding.

The most striking articulation of this view of eros as self-love is in the speech of Aristophanes.[22] Aristophanes' myth invokes for us in comic fashion the fugitive sense of that dearer self we see in dreams and in rare moments of lucid vision or action. The force of the myth lies in its claim that that self is *my* self, the self which I am not but am (as Sartre might say) in the mode of always being about to become. Central to Plato's vision as articulated comically in Aristophanes' myth is that the self which I am about to become, my "ecstatic self," is ideally no mere projection of my fantasies or desires, but is my true nature from which I am only in some accidental sense, by a willful and jealous act of the gods, alienated.

To recognize my erotic striving as fundamentally directed toward my true being is to recognize, with Aristophanes, Eros as that "great god who leads us εἰς τὸ οἰκεῖον . . . , εἰς τὴν ἀρχαίαν φύσιν, who restores us to our native selves, to our true and original nature.[23]

III

That human eros is most properly auto-erotic is only an instance of the fact that for Plato the world itself is auto-erotic. But if this is true, three questions arise. (1) Why is it that in the final sober sections of the *Symposium*, that is, in the speech of Socrates, it is the beautiful and the good, αὐτὸ τὸ καλόν and αὐτὸ τὸ ἀγαθόν, which is described as the proper object of philosophic love. (2) What does it mean anyway to talk of one's "true self." (3) What after all about the love of others?

The first two questions can be answered only provisionally. *Good* as we know is an *incomplete predicate*, as is *beautiful*. To say of something that it is good must always be relative to some description under which the entity said to be good is specified. In the most revealing cases, cases of the sort which greatly interested Plato, one and the same individual may be good and bad under alternative descriptions. One and the same copper is at once a good conductor and a bad insulator; one and the same pickpocket a good thief and a bad person to be standing next to. Predications of good take the form "x is a good Ø," where "Ø" specifies some description which provides the criteria for determining the truth of the predication, the description in terms of which the entity is said to be good. There is then, as Aristotle was quick to note, [24] no being good neat, any more than there is just being. Where we employ predications of the form "x is good" (period), these stand (just as with being) for more replete predications of the form, "x is a good Ø," where "Ø" states what x is essentially. 'Abromowitz is a good philosopher,' '. . . is a good backgammon player,' '. . . is a good lover,' are clear. 'Abromowitz is good' neat, means generally, I suggest, 'Abromowitz is a good *person*' (except in contexts—in the classroom, over the board, in bed— which make clear that some other description is implicitly understood). So with *beautiful*, except that here we are more ready to link the predicate with an essential description, more reluctant to conditionalize by some qualifying accidental description. 'She's beautiful' will have a different descriptive content depending on whether she is a crystal formation, a giraffe, or a woman who has taken my fancy. The concept of my being beautiful is dependent upon and specified by my being *what* I am. [25] To love the beautiful in me is thus to love my essential being, my 'realest' self. Alternatively, that is beautiful in me which is my essential self, and which is that which I properly love. Philosophy, as the discipline which trains us in seeing things as they are, is thus at the same time the discipline which trains us to know what to love in ourselves, i.e. teaches us what we really *want* by teaching us what we really *are*. Thus it is philosophy which is that therapeutic art of which Erixymachus speaks, [26] the art which teaches us what is proper and improper in our loves, which by teaching us what is good in us, teaches us how to and what to love in ourselves.

Provisionally and within the context of self-love, I suggest then that talk of beauty as the proper object of eros is talk of eros as directed toward what is truly native to us, and that in turn (i.e. circularly) may be thought of as the self which manifests our good and beautiful nature, i.e. the nature which we love.

The fact of my being and not being my true self, like the fact of two sticks being and not being equal, is the source of the fallenness of the world, the source of the separation (but also of the nonalienness) of being and appearance, of the world of forms and the world of particulars. It is also, at some deep level, the source of the recurrent motif throughout the *Lysis* and *Symposium* of the aporiai concerning love and its relation to the like and the unlike. In self-love, lover and beloved are one; but such love is always love of the "ecstatic" self. What is loved, the self, that is, which one is not but is always about to become (given the notion of a true nature which one ought to or would truly love to become, given, that is, a Platonic rather than Sartrean view) is at once like and unlike the lover. The self is thus itself a metaxy, poised between, so to speak, that which it just "is" and that which it *is*. [27]

IV

I've said that one central kind of erotic love is self-love, where that means the desire to become what one truly is, to be that self descriptions of which one can find throughout Plato, a self which being like and unlike the self which loves, constitutes at once the true φίλον of the *Lysis* and the archaic οἰκεῖον nature of Aristophanes, as corrected by Diotima:[28] lovers aren't looking for any old other half, but the good, the better half, as we might once have said.

What now about other people? If erotic love is desire for the possession of that which one lacks, then the only rationale for the erotic love of another in this strict sense could be comic and mythic as in Aristophanes. For otherwise the erotic love of another would constitute seeing the other as part of oneself which one is desirous of possessing and making one's own. I have no doubt that love often enough takes that pathological form with others. But if the criticism of Plato's theory is that it makes impossible erotic love of other individuals in *this* sense, and of *this* sort, then it strikes me as strange we should count it a criticism.

It now becomes possible to say something about the claim that Plato's theory of love is egoistical. Plato's theory is said to be egoistical since according to it, A loves B only insofar as B produces some good for A. But surely a theory which holds that A *loves* B insofar as or because B produces some good for A is not an egoistic theory in any normal sense unless we make one of the following qualifications: 1) A *desires* B only insofar as B produces some good for A, or 2) A loves B only insofar as *loving* B produces some good for A. Without one or another of these qualifications, A's loving B for some good B produces for A could no more be said to be egoistic than could A's thanking or rewarding or praising B for some good B produces for A. But (1) has now been ruled out, and (2) represents simply the *general* problem of egoism in moral theory.

That's a problem I've never quite understood, but it does strike me as odd, as it struck Bishop Butler and others, to claim that because I fulfill a desire of *mine* in wishing or doing good for another it somehow fails to be the case that the wishing or doing has been real. For years I've wanted to give you, because I love you and know how much you love Dante and Rauschenberg, a prohibitively expensive edition of Rauschenberg's illustrations of the *Comedy*. One day, trying to counter melancholy, I decide to give myself a present which I have long since denied myself and which will give me great pleasure. I give you the Dante illustrations. The genuine love of others can satisfy selfish needs, as can genuinely altruistic acts on their behalf. Indeed, we should feel some apprehension if we thought our lovers didn't get satisfaction from their love of us. I don't mean by this that all love needs to be requited (this may or may not be true), but that A's love of B is cause for concern if loving B does not itself give A satisfaction.

If I love A because of Ø, is what I love in A the object of my love and different from A in such a way that what I really love is Ø and not A? Is there any way to escape the difficulty concerning love of the individual of which we spoke earlier? Here I want to translate what we said concerning self-love to the love of others. If I love A because of Ø or love the Ø in A, I should not be said to love something other than A if Ø is *what* A is. Thus to love A for its beauty is to love A for itself. 'You only love me because of my money (body, connections, whatever)' means 'that's not what I am; you don't love me for *myself*.' But loving another for himself is not totally unconditional agapic love, because in loving A for himself, I don't love what A *happens* to be, but A *qua* beautiful, and this means loving A for what he *is*, in spite of what he may happen to be, or for the mode of his being what he is. My love is the condition of my asking the other that he be himself, i.e. the self which I love and which I recognize as in the accidental being of that other, even perhaps in the mode of nonpresence.

Love on this view is *recognition*; it is seeing another as what that other might be, not in the sense of what he might be other than himself, but how he might be what he is. It is, in other words, coming to recognize the *beauty* of another. (Compare great portrait painters, who evoke the beauty of their [often plain] subjects not by artifice or camouflage, but by their skill in capturing the subject in just that attitude, in just that light, in which their true beauty is revealed.) The love which does not unconditionally accept another's accidental being, so to speak, but calls the other to be his true self, is a love which at once recognizes and bids the other to his true virtue and beauty. [29]

This is the thrust, in comic and half-understood form, of Aristophanes' myth, and in more serious and subtle form (though in imagery no less sexual) of the first part of Socrates' speech. Love is the power by which, recognizing the beauty in another, we bring forth that beauty by eliciting it, calling it forth. We thus call forth the other's true *virtue*, for virtue is, as we know, ontologically like goodness and beauty; it is the mode of an entity's *being itself well*. So cosmically love is that principle which draws the world toward *itself*, not just, as Erixymachus claimed, toward something else, but toward its own good and beautiful being.

To see that love recognizes the present but unrealized beauty and virtue of another and bids him to the impersonation of that beauty is to see love's generative power and the proper telos of that power. It is here that Aristophanes' myth is transcended in a typically Platonic fashion, the archaeology of love taken up in its teleology.[30] This is the force of Diotima's insistence that love is not simply a bringing forth upon the beautiful, but is itself directed toward, is a longing for that conception and bringing forth.[31] Love, as Aristotle clearly recognized, is thus a virtue, not merely a passion. We need to ask not simply what leads us to love another, but what is the discipline by which we might learn to love another. How may we develop the virtue which elicits beauty, which brings virtue to birth? In this respect it is important to recall that the majority of those we love—parents, family, children, perhaps above all one's self—are not people we are necessarily attracted to or choose, but people in whose lives we find ourselves implicated, whom we discover ourselves fated to love and must learn to love. So, I think Plato would say, with the world itself.

The philosophical nature begins, as we know from the *Republic*, with a love of spectacle, and is, in its more refined form, simply a love of τὰ ὄντα, of the world as it truly is.[32] Just as proper self-love is merely a special instance of the universal erotic striving of the universe for itself, so authentic personal love is merely a particular, special instance of the philosophical love of the world in its true being. To recognize shining through this world the world of forms, to see the world aright through that discipline of philosophical κάθαρσις which is generated by and results in love of the world's true nature, this is according to Plato the task and goal of the philosopher; proper self love and love of others is simply this visionary and accepting power focused upon human beings in the world. These two loves are not unconnected. Eros as self-love, in recalling us to our own true nature, frees us from the desire to practise homophilia upon our friends and loved ones, that is, frees us to give them in our heterophilia (whether homo- or hetero-sexual) their own other, being, frees us to the shared joy we experience when those we love are capable of erotic self-love.

The beautiful is the description under which τὰ ὄντα are given insofar as they constitute the object of our desire and love. Like *true* and *good*, *beautiful* is thus an intentional description: in the case of *beautiful*, of love's object. To describe the philosopher as coming to love *beauty*, or *the beautiful*, as Diotima does in her revelation to Socrates, is thus to describe him as coming to understand what *is* beautiful, i.e. as learning to love things as they are. Loving things as they are, the philosopher will then not be seduced by the appearances of beauty, exchanging one beauty for another. As in the *Phaedo*,[33] true virtue consists not in the exchanging of one pleasure for another, but in the kathartic wisdom which detaches the philosopher from pleasure and pain, and allows him to accept but transcend his pleasures and pains, so true philosophic love is the result of a katharsis which allows the philosopher to exhibit the detached, non-erotic love of the saint. It is this love which is true "agapic" love, a love in which the philosopher, by transcending the world to a vision of its perfect form, is able to accept it as an appearance and manifestation of that form.

The ascent to this vision and detached love is the ascent which Diotima speaks of. It is part at once of the genius and of the mystery of her description that the practice of eros is an important element of the κάθαρσις which leads to this state, and not, as we might be tempted to think, its sublimation. As Descartes courts doubt to transcend doubt in that calm certainty which can accept doubt, and as in general philosophers of various persuasions have realized that salvation from finitude can come only in the joyous acceptance of finitude, so Plato shows us eros as the ladder to that state in which eros is transcended, but transcended in the mode of acceptance. To deny eros, to flee from it into the arms of false chastity, is, as Hippolytus learned, to flee into its destructive snares; Cypris is benign only to those who pay her homage.

The ascent described in Diotima's higher mysteries is that typically Platonic ascent out of the cave and into the real world, that is, into this world seen aright, and thus seen as beautiful, recognized for what it is, and consequently to be loved. If then we feel called upon to say that for Plato "the Idea, and it alone is to be loved for its own sake; the individual only so far as in him and by him ideal perfection is copied fugitively in the flux,"[34] we must remember that that fugitive copying, which other traditions have called incarnation, is the highest mystery. Understood, it reveals the deceptive fact that the luminous world of forms is this world seen aright. That seeing (itself fugitive)[35] is accomplished by the katharsis which makes appearance transparent, which allows the world itself to shine through its appearances. The philosopher, unlike the sophist, recognizes the world as image, that is, as its own appearance, and loving it, thus calls it to itself.

I shall end with a remark now almost traditional in discussions of Platonic eros. Several scholars in their accounts of Plato's views have directed our attention to the similarities between the erotic ascent described in Diotima's speech and the poet's upward journey at the end of Dante's *Commedia*, a journey whose motive principle and goal are also love, that love which, just as it moves the poet's will and desire, moves the sun and other stars.[36]

These similarities are invoked on the supposition that ascent—ascent from the cave, the ascent in the *Symposium*, the poet's ascent from purgatory to paradise—are ascents to abstract visions of a transcendental being beyond the world around us, the world so cunningly called *this* world. But it is important to remember the nature of the poet's final vision in *Paradiso*, for it is not a vision of the sphere, but a vision of the sphere incorporate in the image, a vision, that is, of nothing less than the incarnation. Anything short of such a vision might be wondrous, but would hardly be a mystery. And surely it is such a mystery to which Diotima alludes: the mystery of loving being itself incorporate in the world, of loving in my very beloved himself humanity incarnate. [37]

NOTES

1. *Symposium* 186A.

2. *Symposium* 197A-B.

3. As we learn at *Republic* 443D and 592A.

4. Cf. *Republic* 361A.

5. Gregory Vlastos, "The Individual as an Object of Love in Plato," in *Platonic Studies* (Princeton, 1972), p. 4. [Reprinted in this volume, pp. 96–135.]

6. Vlastos, p. 31.

7. Irving Singer, *The Nature of Love: Plato to Luther* (New York, 1966), p. 87.

8. Singer, p. 72.

9. Anders Nygren, *Agape and Eros* (English Translation, New York, 1969); cf. Vlastos. *op. cit.*

10. *Symposium* 199Dff.

11. *Symposium* 202Cff.

12. *Symposium* 211Aff. But see the qualification below, toward the end of section IV.

13. Because of its fundamental concern with making means transparent to ends (appearance transparent to being). A discussion in full of how this operates in Plato, which would involve a discussion of the relation between the philosopher and the sophist, would, I think, reveal the heart of Plato's thought. I have touched on this theme in "Aristotle's Theory of Motion" *Phronesis*, XIV. p. 60 ff.

14. *Symposium* 177D9. This claim is echoed elsewhere, e.g. *Lysis* 204C2.

15. *Symposium* 202A. This point is highlighted by the fact that the description of eros in Socrates' speech is a description of Socrates himself, i.e. of the philosopher. Cf. Diskin Clay, "Socrates' Mulishness and Heroism," *Phronesis*, XVII, p. 58, n. 12. In fact, each speaker describes eros as he would wish to see or describe himself.

16. *Symposium* 210A1.

17. I do not fully exploit this principle here; a full spelling out of the view which I am suggesting in this essay would demand a careful and detailed study of all the speeches of the *Symposium* and their relation to one another in light of such a principle.

18. *Symposium* 200A5.

19. *Symposium* 200C9, *Lysis* 221D–222A.

20. *Lysis* 218D–222B.

21. *Laws* V 731E.

22. *Phaedo* 64B.

23. *Symposium* 193D.

24. At *Nicomachean Ethics* I.6, 1096a23ff inter alia.

25. I mean 'what' to be a translation of 'τί' in 'τί ἐστί.'

26. *Symposium* 186D.

27. Much of the conversation concerning like and unlike takes place in a context in which homosexual love makes problematic the condition of otherness which is seen to be essential to eros. I take it, that is, that a problem for homosexual love is how to constitute the beloved as an *other.* This is to be sure no less a *problem* for heterosexual love, in that we are always tempted to devour the other, and to transform heterophilia into homophilia. But homosexual love often founds itself on the promise of escaping that problem, hoping that homosexuality by erasing a fundamental mode of complementary alienness, will guarantee homophilia and thus avoid the issue of otherness.

28. *Symposium* 205D–E.

29. This is the meaning of Diotima's definition of love as 'τόκος ἐν καλῷ' at *Symposium* 206B7. Love calling the beloved to his own beauty and virtue is mirrored in the recurrent theme throughout the *Symposium* of love's engendering of αἰσχύνη, shame. The centrality of this theme in the dialogue, first introduced at 178D and interestingly articulated by Alcibiades at 216B, was called to my attention by Sara Ruddick.

30. I mean 'taken up' to English 'aufgehoben.' Here, as elsewhere, I am indebted to Sara Ruddick.

31. *Symposium*, 206E.

32. *Republic* 475Dff., 501D.

33. *Phaedo* 68Dff.

34. Vlastos, op. cit. p. 34

35. As the love of which I'm speaking is fugitive and difficult; Alcibiades is always in the wings.

36. *Paradiso*, XXXIII. 144.

37. This essay was originally presented at a symposium in memory of Robert Miller. I did not know Robert Miller during his lifetime, but I have learned something of him from knowing those he loved, including Plato, and from the considerable love others had for him. What I know makes me honored to dedicate this essay to his memory.

GREEK GLOSSARY FOR KOSMAN

Edward Johnson

149. *epi tais psuchais tōn anthrōpōn:* among human souls
     epi pan: among all (things)
150. *dikaiosunē:* justice, righteousness
151. *kalon:* beauty, fineness, nobility
     epoptika: survey of mysteries
154. *auto to kalon:* beauty, the beautiful itself

155. *ouk echōn auto hou epithumei te kai era(i):* not having the thing itself which it
desires, it loves
endeēs: in need
technē iatrikē: medical art or skill
prōton philon: first (or primary) love
eidōla: images, icons, idols, phantoms
alēthōs philon: truly loved
tō(i) onti philon: loved in fact, really loved
endees: in need
phusei oikeion: proper by nature
to oikeion: what is properly one's own
eis to oikeion . . . eis tēn archaian phusin: to the proper . . . to the ancient (or ruling)
nature
auto to kalon: the beautiful itself, beauty
auto to agathon: the good itself, goodness
160. *ta onta:* the facts, reality
katharsis: purgation, purification, catharsis
163(n. 25)   *ti esti:* what (it) is
(n. 29)   *tokos en kalō(i):* birth in beauty
aischunē: shame

FRIENDS AS ENDS
IN THEMSELVES

Neera Kapur Badhwar

I. Introduction

I define friendship as a practical and emotional relationship of mutual and (roughly) equal goodwill, affection and pleasure.[1] In a general discussion of friendship I would unpack and defend this broadly Aristotelian definition. But my concerns in this paper can be addressed without doing so. My chief concern is to give an analysis of end love in friendship, distinguishing it from means love, as well as from other notions of end love I regard as unjustifiable. I discuss love outside of friendship only insofar as it has a bearing on love in friendship.

I shall give a preliminary sketch of my topic by invoking widely-held intuitions about end friendship as that in which the friend is loved for her essential, not incidental, features; as an intrinsic, not instrumental, value; and as a unique and irreplaceable individual; and by showing how these intuitions fit in—or not—with the common but ill-understood distinction between conditional and unconditional love. The explication of these intuitions will follow in later sections as part of the analysis of end friendship.

Reprinted from *Philosophy and Phenomenological Research* 48, No. 1 (1987), pp. 1–23, by permission of that journal and Neera K. Badhwar. The essay in its present form includes about ten revisions of the original article. Neera Badhwar did her graduate work at the University of Toronto and teaches philosophy at the University of Oklahoma.

1) Ends and Means Friendships.

The best, most complete friendships are those in which friends love and wish each other well as ends in themselves, and not solely, or even primarily, as means to further ends—social advancement, amusement, the promotion of some cause, or even mutual edification or improvement. In such friendships, the friends value each other's separateness—the fact that each has, and gives importance to, her own life and perspective, no matter how similar this life and perspective to the other's; and take pleasure in being together primarily because of the persons they are. The other's usefulness in bringing about a desired end may, of course, be the initial spark of the friendship, and most friendships *are* useful in many ways. Indeed, if friends were not useful in times of need, they would not be friends. But in the best friendships, the central feature of the friendship is simply that the friends love, and wish each other well, as ends in themselves, whereas in lesser friendships, the central feature is the instrumental or means value of each to the other. The friends value each other's life and perspective only to the extent that it is useful to do so; and each takes pleasure in the other primarily as a means to a further end. [2]

The two kinds of friendship differ in their *object* or *focus* as well as in their attitudes. Part of what it means to love something as an end, say a certain work of literature, is that one loves it for the features that make it the work it is. In friendship, too, then, part of what it means to love a friend as an end is that one loves her for the features that make her the person she is. As Aristotle puts it, those who are "most truly friends" love each other "by reason of their nature," i.e., for being the persons they are. [3] The friend is seen as lovable on account of what she essentially is, and not just on account of incidental features that make her useful or pleasurable. In instrumental friendships, by contrast, the object of love is primarily or only the other's incidental features.

How far must the person *seen* as intrinsically or non-instrumentally lovable be *actually* thus lovable by objective standards of human worth, [4] if the love is to count as genuine end love in friendship? It is at least necessary that she *be* an end in herself (Sec. III below), and have the dispositions and qualities that are needed for being a good friend. (Whether a person can combine these good dispositions towards her friends with nasty dispositions towards everyone else—thus be grossly deficient in human worth—is not a question I can pursue here. Here I shall assume that someone who is deficient in this way is also deficient in her capacity for the best kind of friendship, the friendship that is an end in itself.)

In end friendship, then, the friends are ends in themselves, and love each other as ends in themselves, i.e., non-instrumentally, and by virtue of their essential features. Because the friends are not primarily means to each other's ends, they cannot—logically cannot—be replaced by more efficient means, or abandoned on the achievement of the end. It is this irreplaceability that most obviously marks off end friendship from means or instrumental friendship, in which the friends *are* thus replaceable or dispensable.

Is it possible to love someone who is an end for her essential features, but also, primarily, as a means to an end, say, to the end of self-improvement? The two sets of attitudes and emotions are psychologically incompatible, but it is surely possible for a person to have psychologically conflicting attitudes towards someone. In such a case, however, the friendship in question is neither fully instrumental, nor fully an end in itself. Accordingly, when I discuss the objects of the two kinds of friendship, I shall assume that the object of end love is always the other's essential features, the object of instrumental love, the other's incidental features.

2) Loving Someone as a Good to Oneself.

Friendships are generally recognized to involve pleasure. In end friendships, friends are a source of pleasure or happiness by virtue of their intrinsic worth or lovability. They are thus a good to each other, and love each other as such. A strong, opposing view, however, is that so long as one loves another as a good to oneself, then whether the source of this good is the other's intrinsic worth or instrumental worth, one loves her as a means to an end. A recent proponent of this idea is George Nakhnikian, [5] whose target is Aristotle's theory of friendship, a theory which shares in its essentials the view of end love I have sketched. Nakhnikian argues that love of another because of his "admirable character traits," is no less "transactional" or instrumental than love of another "because of his usefulness," for both are "supposed to rebound to the satisfaction or benefit of the one who loves . . ." (p. 287). We love a person non-instrumentally, according to Nakhnikian, only when we love him *for whatever he is*, i.e., "undemandingly" or unconditionally. In such a love, there can be "no thought of expected returns and no requirement that the person loved be a good [or lovable] human being" (p. 294). To love him as a good to ourselves is necessarily to love him instrumentally. According to this line of thought, then, loving another non-instrumentally *cannot* imply loving him as a good to oneself, thus as a source of pleasure or happiness.

This exclusion of pleasure in the other from the phenomenon of love is, however, false to experience, at least so long as "love" is used in the usual emotional-practical sense, and not in Kant's rarefied purely practical sense. One can *admire* a person's admirable qualities without getting any pleasure from them: witness Salieri's bitter, grudging admiration of Mozart's genius in *Amadeus*. One can delight in a person's *accomplishments*, without getting any pleasure from the *person* as the cause and bearer of these accomplishments: witness Salieri's delight in Mozart's music, coupled with his hate-filled resentment of Mozart for being the one "chosen" to produce such sublime sounds. And one can wish a person well, and even want to spend time with her to

love despite who they are

Unpassionate love ?.

benefit her, without getting any pleasure from her company. But one cannot *love* a person without delighting in her under some aspect—in the end love of friendship, without delighting in her as being the person she is. Hence end love is also necessarily a good to the one who loves. But it is not thereby, I hold, instrumental. These conclusions are further supported in Section II by an analysis of what it means to love someone as an end.

Some people might be inclined to dismiss the view I am discussing—that the presence of pleasure or satisfaction necessarily makes love instrumental—as a simple-minded confusion between pleasure being the *result* of loving some-one, and pleasure being its *goal*. But simple-minded confusions do not have the long and tenacious life that this view has had. Hence it is not surprising that it has not disappeared in spite of Bishop Butler's exposure of a similar confusion at the heart of the argument for psychological egoism. For what Butler's argument leaves untouched is the further possibility that even if self-benefit (satisfaction, pleasure, or whatever) is only an unintended *result* of a certain kind of activity, it may well be that the tacit *expectation* of self-benefit—based on past experi-ence, or even just on the natural teleology of our biological constitution—is necessary for *sustaining* the activity. It is this worry that leads Kant to say that we can never be sure that "the dear self" is not intruding even when we think our only motive is duty. And it is this possibility in personal love that is thought to make it instrumental, and to distinguish it from the unconditional love— agape—with which God is said to love us, and which in us is called neighborly love. This argument, however, will not concern me here, as I do not believe that the good to oneself that I have identified as delight in the other is only an unintended *result* of love. Nor do I believe that its presence distinguishes personal love from agape. Rather, I believe it is an essential *element* of end love, in agape—in so far as it is conceivable as a form of love—no less than in friendship and in other forms of personal love. So either loving another as a good to oneself does not necessarily make personal love instrumental, or else agape is also instrumental.

3) The Friend as the Unique, Irreplaceable Individual.

Those who believe that only unconditional love makes it as non-instrumental love, but have not wanted to condemn friendship out of hand as mere instru-mental love, might be attracted by Nakhnikian's suggestion that the best kinds of friendship be understood as a combination of unconditional and instrumen-tal love. But can friendship love be accurately characterized as a combination of these, or in some way be explained by reference to these? If it cannot, then there is good reason to suppose that not all non-instrumental love is uncondi-tional, and not all love of the other as a good to oneself is instrumental.

The main problem in trying to explain friendship in terms of unconditional and instrumental love, is that each, in its own way, does violence to the intuition that in end friendship the object of love is the unique, irreplaceable individual. If I love you unconditionally, I love you regardless of your individual qualities—your appearance, your temperament, your style, even your moral character. So you are no different from anyone else as the object of my love, and my love for you is no different from my love for anyone else. But then in what sense are *you* the object of my love? On the other hand, if I love you instrumentally, for the benefit I derive from certain of your qualities,[6] then your value to me is entirely dependent on my needs or ends, and you are dispensable as soon as I have achieved them or relinquished them or found someone else who can better serve them. So again, in what sense is it *you* that I love? In the first you lose your *qualitative* identity, in the second your *numerical* or *historical* identity. Thus in agape, the exemplar of unconditional love, although the *target* of love—that which the love is directed to or at—is, indeed, the particular, numerical individual, the focus or *object*[7] of love—that *for* which or *as* which the target is loved—is not that which makes him the unique person he is, but that which he shares with everyone else: his substantial, metaphysical identity as a human being. Every individual is loved equally and indifferently as a Speck of Humanity among other Specks in the Ocean of Humanity. Thus every individual is *phenomenologically replaceable* by any other as the object of love. In the Platonic view, the exemplar of instrumental love, although the target of love is only that individual who has the qualities beneficial to the lover, the object of love is not the person, not *that individual with those qualities*, but rather *those qualities in any individual*.[8] The individual is loved for his qualitative identity as an instantiation of the abstract Idea of Beauty, and is a means to this ultimate object of love. Hence the individual is both *phenomenologically and numerically replaceable* in the lover's journey to this ultimate object. Thus both agape and Platonic love have as their objects the universal and nonindividual in the individual target. Their difference is only that in one the individual target is regarded as an end, in the other, as a means. But in neither is the individual loved for the unique character or personality that make him the distinct *person* he is, as he must be in the end love of friendship.

Can this double failure be compounded into a single success, as suggested by some? I suspect not. On the one hand, my love for you, who are my friend, is not love if it alters *whenever* it alteration finds. Hence it cannot be of qualities as such, qualities you happen to manifest—as it is in instrumental love. But neither is my love for you, the unique person, love for *you* if it remains unaltered through *all* alterations of your qualities (as if "you" = "bare particular")—as it is in unconditional love. The object of my love must be you, the person, in your concrete individuality, not "Human Being" or "Instance of (some) F." The question, then, is: What is essential to your being the person you are? When are you no longer you? We need an analysis of the person or self in friendship that allows us to accommodate the idea that friendship love is dependent on the qualitative identity of the friend, yet not such as to make her numerically or phenomenologically replaceable by any individual with those qualities—that such love is of the numerically irreplaceable individual, yet not such as to persist independently of her qualitative identity. In other words, we need an analysis of the object of friendship love which preserves both the qualitative and the numerical identity of the individual.

Before proceeding, I want to make three points of clarification.

First, although I have used the words "historical identity" and "numerical identity" interchangeably, it is only *generally* true, not *necessarily* true, that numerically (spatiotemporally) different individuals have different histories. For instance, identical twins raised in the same environment will probably have the same histories in all essential respects: find the same events crucial, make essentially the same responses. Therefore they will probably also have essentially the same qualities, hence be essentially alike as persons. (It is also, of course, logically possible—though highly improbable—that genetically unrelated people, raised in different environments, turn out to have essentially the same histories and qualities as well.) What is necessarily true is that *historically* distinct individuals be distinct as persons. All of this further implies a qualification of my claim that in the end love of friendship, the object of love is the unique, irreplaceable person. For if in end love one loves the other for the person he is, then if one twin is loved for what he is, so must the other, and both be loved in exactly the same way. They remain *numerically* irreplaceable, not being means to an end, but not *phenomenologically* irreplaceable. Thus in Shakespeare's *Twelfth Night* Olivia's romantic love for the disguised Viola is automatically transferred to her twin Sebastian. But since most people are not personality twins, the thesis that in the end love of friendship, the object of love is the person for what he essentially is, will generally also mean that the object of love is irreplaceable both numerically and phenomenologically. It has sometimes been suggested that if friends are unique and irreplaceable, it is only by virtue of their incidental qualities, or of fortuitous differences in the circumstances of the friendship. But if I am right, for most of us, our differences are deeper and richer than *that* (see Sec. III below).

Secondly, my concern with that which is essential to a person has to do entirely with that constellation of fundamental, empirical, mental qualities—moral, psychological, aesthetic, intellectual—that constitutes an individual's self or personality, and not with any Metaphysically Changeless and Simple Essence. What is empirically essential or fundamental to a person is both dynamic and ambivalent. Most people change over their lifetimes in some of their fundamental qualities—in aspects of their selves—and an individual can change enough to have what Derek Parfit calls "later" and "earlier" selves. Thus it is possible to love an individual as an end, but not forever. Most people also harbor ambivalences in their fundamental qualities, and an individual can be ambivalent enough to have simultaneously more than one self. Thus it is possible to love an individual as an end, but not wholly. (These facts explain some of the tragic conflicts that beset friendships.) But even an individual with a single self may be loved as an end but not wholly. For the self is multi-faceted, and no one friend can love—or even evoke—every facet. (This explains, in part, why friendship is not a transitive relationship.) So which changes in the self are crucial to a friendship depends, in part, on what the friends in question find important in each other and in themselves.

Thirdly, as the central aim of this paper is to provide an analysis of the object of love in end friendship, I shall not address myself to the other elements of friendship, e.g., that of mutual and equal goodwill; nor to its "background conditions"—the psychological and social circumstances that explain *why* people make the friends they do.

In the following section, using agape as the paradigm of unconditional love, I shall argue that in one interpretation, unconditional love is conceptually impossible; on the other, possible but irrelevant to friendship. The first argument will show that the idea of loving someone for her intrinsic worth—and thus as a good to oneself—is necessary to the end love of friendship as well as to agape. Hence the difference between agape and the end love of friendship must lie elsewhere. The second argument will show that the difference between the two is that in friendship the worth in question is *empirical*, in agape, *transcendental*. But there is no transcendental worth. Again, since loving the friend for her intrinsic worth is necessary to end friendship, the difference between instrumental and end friendship cannot be that the former is based on valuable qualities, the latter not. In Sec. III I shall analyse the distinction already made between them in terms of incidental qualities (qualities that in one way or another fail to define the person) and essential qualities (qualities that do define the person). I will then show that essential qualities can neither be, nor be understood, apart from an individual's numerical or historical identity. This will serve to distinguish my position from any position, Platonist or anti-Platonist, that identifies love of the person with love of his historical *rather than* qualitative identity.

II. Loving a Friend as an End vs. Unconditional Love

1) *Agape as Completely Unmotivated.*
Agape is God's love for human beings and, through Him, our love for our neighbors.[9] Anders Nygren points out that the life which is organized on the principle of agape is completely different from the life which is organized on the principle of eros, the principle that love is of the good or lovable: eros and agape are opposite "general attitudes to life."[10] Thus agape has no direct

bearing on the nature of friendship. But it does have an indirect bearing if it is an ideal that friendship ought to approach, or if it is an element in all forms of love, as Kierkegaard, Nakhnikian, and perhaps others, believe. According to Kierkegaard, Christian love "can lie at the base of and be present in every other expression of love. . . . It is . . . [or] can be in all of them, but this love itself you cannot point out": it is like the "man" in all men.[11]

What, then, is the nature of agape? Following Luther's interpretation, Anders Nygren summarizes its main features thus: agape is spontaneous and "unmotivated"; it is "indifferent to value"; and it is creative.[12] It stands *"in contrast to all activity with a eudaemonistic motive,"* and *"in contrast to all legalism."*[13] Agape gives with no thought of gain. Being "indifferent to value," it needs no encouragement from, or justification by, the perceived value of the target of love. To love someone for his worth is to love him acquisitively, not agapeistically.[14] Christian love is "a lost love," "the direct opposite of rational calculation" (p. 514). In Kierkegaard's words, "love to one's neighbor makes a man blind in the deepest and noblest and holiest sense, so that he blindly loves every man . . ." (p. 80).

Can such a love be the foundation of friendship? or perhaps the mortar that holds it together? It is hard to see how a love which is in principle blind can be the foundation of a relationship which is in principle cognitive, a response to the perceived value of the other. But perhaps it is agape under its positive, creative aspect which serves this function. Agape's indifference to value has as a corollary its creativeness: it *creates* value by loving. In Luther's words, agape is "an overflowing love . . . which says: I love thee, not because thou art good . . . for I draw my love not from thy goodness (Frommigkeit) as from an alien spring; but from mine own well-spring . . ." (in Nygren, p. 512, n. 1).

Now it may seem that agape under this creative aspect enters into friendship as the generosity and abundance which are characteristic of friendship: I forgive your faults, or shower you with gifts, not because you *deserve* any of this, but as an expression of my love. But the semblance is misleading. For the love which motivates such generosity is itself a response to the friend's value, whereas agape on this strictly unconditional interpretation cannot be linked to any recognition of value. Whatever it means, then, to love a friend as an end, it cannot mean to love him with the unconditionality of agape. Indeed, on this Lutheran interpretation, the denial that the worth or lovability of the individual has anything to do with the love, is precisely the denial that the individual is loved for "himself." So while agape is non-instrumental love, it is not, so far, end love. But this radical interpretation of agape renders it mysterious why agape is selectively *directed* at human beings, given that it is not *motivated* by them.[15] To dispel the mystery, the Christian must at least concede that human beings are loved qua human beings, hence that humanity as such—the good or God in each individual, in Augustine's words—is worth loving.[16] Agape can, consistently, be unconditional in the sense of being independent of the individual's *personal* nature and worth—of that which distinguishes him from other persons—but not of his *human* nature and worth—of that which distinguishes him from non-humans. Agape also, in other words, must be of the individual for what he is, even though only qua *human being*, and not qua *person*. At least God's agape for us must, then, be a form of end love.[17] But now, if loving someone for his worth is logically necessary for loving him as an end, then loving someone as a means cannot be explicated in terms of loving him for his worth, simpliciter. Both end love and instrumental love are directed at the other as lovable or worthy.

2) Happiness as Goal of Love and Happiness as Intrinsic to Love.
It may still be argued, following Nygren, that in loving something as lovable or good we must love it only as a means, even if the love aims only at the possession and contemplation[18] of the loved object, and not at any further advantage. And this because in such possession and contemplation we attain happiness, so that the love remains but a means [conscious or unconscious] to our happiness.[19] If Nygren is right, we are caught in a contradiction: to love x as an end is necessarily to love him for his worth; to love him for his worth is necessarily to love him as a means; hence to love x as an end is to love him as a means. But Nygren's view depends upon his distinction between the love of x, and the happiness we gain from the attainment and contemplation of x. Is this a viable distinction? *Must* love be a separable *means* to the happiness contained in the attainment and contemplation of the loved object? It would have to be construed thus if it were such as to come to an end on the attainment of the happiness,[20] as the desire at a particular time for, say, the sight of green valleys, comes to an end on seeing them.[21] But love is not quenched by the happiness we get from the contemplation of the loved object. Rather, if love is a response to the perceived value of the other, then its contemplation must further *evoke* the love, not extinguish it;[22] and because the happiness afforded by this is itself a value, the happiness must serve to perpetuate the love of the other who is its source. The relationship of loving to the happiness we get from loving is not, then, modeled by the relationship of the desire to see to the pleasure of seeing.

This in itself, however, is not enough to show that end love and happiness are not related as means to goal. For even if y's love for x is not extinguished by happiness, it may yet be the case that it is wholly conditional on the happiness y gets from the satisfaction of her goals by x: anyone with x's ability could take his place.[23] To show that in end love, love is not a means to happiness, it must be the case that here the happiness cannot be adequately specified independently of the love, such that in loving you as an end, my happiness is to the love, not as the *desire to see x* to seeing x, but as the *pleasure of seeing x* to seeing x.

We have seen that essential to loving someone as an end is perceiving and responding to her as lovable by her very nature, however this is to be defined. Hence pleasure or delight is intrinsic to perceiving and responding to someone as lovable by her very nature[24]—to contemplating the person loved.[25] Happiness is related to end love not as goal to means, but rather, as element to complex whole. So when x is loved as an end, the happiness cannot, logically, exist apart from the love: different end loves bring different forms of happiness. By contrast, when x is loved as a means, the happiness is a further goal of the love, and can, logically, exist without it: different means loves can bring the same form of happiness. For it is in the satisfaction of her own ends that y takes pleasure and delight, and only derivatively, i.e., by virtue of x's ability to fulfill these ends, in x.

It is important to remember that the happiness that is intrinsic to end love, whether in agape or in friendship, is not the only kind of happiness afforded by such love. Happiness comprehends different kinds of pleasures and satisfactions, and the happiness which consists in loving x may cause the happiness which consists in, say, philosophizing well. It is a common enough experience for happiness in one area of one's life to spread into other areas by motivating one to do well—act successfully, hence pleasurably—in those other areas. Besides, as I remarked earlier, end friendships usually are useful in many ways, and friends must at least *aim* to be useful in certain ways if they are to be real friends. They remain end friendships, however, because what is central to them is the happiness that is intrinsic to the love, and not the happiness that results from the satisfaction of one's goals.

Someone may object to making happiness intrinsic to the end love of friendship on the grounds that one may regard the other not with pleasure and delight but with pain and frustration as, for instance, when his life is fraught with pain and disappointment; and this precisely because in loving him one shares in his pain. This is obviously true. I would still maintain, however, that insofar as the love is a response to the other's worth, one cannot fail to regard him with pleasure, even if the pleasure is outweighed by the pain. If he changes in a way which destroys the possibility of such a response, as when the frustrations of his life not only make him unhappy and "not much fun to be with" but also, say, self-pitying and self-centered, one may indeed keep up "friendly relations" out of a sense of loyalty, one may even feel a kind of love out of pity, but the emotion is no longer the value response necessary to end love.

3) Irreplaceability as Criterion of End Love in Friendship.

I stated earlier that it is irreplaceability that most obviously marks off end friendship from means friendship. A friend who is loved as an end is numerically irreplaceable in the sense that she is not a means to a happiness which can be better or as well served by another. It can now be stated more clearly how and why she is also phenomenologically irreplaceable. She is thus irreplaceable in the precise sense that loving and delighting in her are not completely commensurate with loving and delighting in another, not even when this other is loved as an end. This is confirmed by the fact that if the happiness we got from different friends were completely commensurate, there would be no qualitative differences among our friendships, and we would not, e.g., desire to spend an evening with x rather than with y, but rather only "with a friend." Again, when someone who is loved as an end ceases to be loved, the loss cannot be completely made up by acquiring a new friend—the loss of the old friend is a distinct loss, the gain of the new friend, a distinct gain. Even when one ceases to *feel* the loss, because of the passage of time, and the presence of other enriching activities and experiences in one's life, it remains true that different end friendships engender different forms of love and happiness. In instrumental friendships, on the other hand, anyone who fulfills my goals as well as x, is a potential replacement for x: different friendships engender the same love and happiness. The friend may, indeed, never be replaced, but only for contingent reasons, as when circumstances conspire to make her uniquely qualified to promote my ends.[26] Thus there can be a lifelong friendship which is enacted entirely in pubs over shared beers—but which would have ended on one of the friend's going off beer. This is why mere permanence is not sufficient for end friendship.[27] Neither is it necessary. For if the essential qualities of one of the friends change, such that either you are no longer the person who evoked my love, or I am no longer the person who loved you—then, barring the happy possibility that the other one of us undergoes a parallel or complementary change, the love must disappear because its *object* or its *subject* have disappeared.[28]

My account might give rise to the objection that the person who is loved as an end cannot, contrary to my claim, be irreplaceable. For when someone who affords greater happiness than x comes along, she must displace x. But this criticism is either misleading or not an objection at all. It is misleading insofar as it suggests that x's *intrinsic* value to me is displaced by the new friend. For this is not possible: the pleasure I get from x is different from the pleasure I get from the new friend, even if the latter is greater.[29] Given that time is finite, the greater friendship will certainly limit and change my *practical* relations with x. In particular, it will displace x's instrumental value; for instance, x will no longer be my primary support in times of trouble. But this is hardly an objection to my account of end love.

To summarize this part of the discussion: loving x as an end in himself requires explication in terms of x's worth or lovability, whether the lovable object be x the unique and irreplaceable person, as in friendship, or x the human being, as in agape. Insofar as happiness is intrinsic to such love, and not its goal, one necessarily loves x as a good to oneself without loving him as a means. So if x ceases to be such a good, he ceases to be loved as an end. The attempt to interpret end love as an unconditional love which is completely independent of the other's worth or lovability, and of its relation to one's own happiness, thus fails. There is no such love.

4) Agape as Motivated by a Necessary Human Worth.
When agape is interpreted as a love which is motivated by the good in each individual, then it is compatible with end love in friendship. Is it, however, in any way *relevant* to it? It is often thought so. Erich Fromm states: "In essence, all human beings are identical. We are all part of One; we are One. This being so, it should not make any difference whom we love."[30] All human beings qua human beings are equally worthy of love.

But what is the evidence for this common humanity, this equal potential for worth or virtue that we all, supposedly, share? There seems to be no *empirical* evidence. Experience indicates that there *are* people who are completely lacking in moral capacities—the criminally insane, the thoroughly wicked, the psychopathically amoral. Hence the only way to sustain belief in a universal potential for goodness is by means of a transcendental metaphysics of the person (in the religious version, the idea of man as created in the image of God; in a well-known secular version, the idea of man qua moral agent as a noumenal being). Without this transcendental assurance of a necessary potential for goodness in all human beings, the goodwill we bear to those we are unacquainted with can be based only on the fact that most human beings do have some actual or potential moral worth. Now such a goodwill or "love of humanity" *is* related to friendship. It is, in Aristotle's words, "a beginning of friendship [philia], as the pleasure of the eye is the beginning of love [eros]" (NE 1167a3–4). But since the assumption on which the goodwill is based is defeasible with respect to any given individual, so is the goodwill itself. Thus the goodwill presupposed by friendship is not unconditional love. We may conclude, therefore, that unconditional love is neither an element of, nor an ideal for, friendship love. The object of the former is Humanity, the "God in the neighbor," that of the latter, the person, the qualitatively and numerically unique individual.

III. LOVING A FRIEND AS AN END VS. INSTRUMENTAL LOVE

It is time now to discuss the difference between the objects of love in end and means friendships. In Sec. I, I stated that instrumental friendships are based on incidental qualities, qualities that in one way or another fail to define the person, whereas end friendships are based on essential qualities, qualities that do define the person. Further, in end friendships the friend is, and is regarded as, an end in himself. How do we pick out the qualities that define a person? And what does it mean for someone to *be* an end in himself?

1) The Object of Love in End Friendship.

Defining is a process of selecting the qualities we regard as essential: the qualities we think are ontologically fundamental in, and best explain, the constitution and behavior of the thing defined.[31] But in trying to define a person, our selection of fundamental qualities is complicated not only by their dynamism and ambivalence (see pp. 7–8 above), but also by the feature of *reflexiveness*. For unlike other things, our personal nature is given not just in what we are, as expressed in the goals, values, and abilities we act upon, but may or may not endorse as good or important; but also in what we would be, as expressed in our still-born ideals and aspirations—those we merely endorse, but do not act upon.[32] For even in merely endorsing something we exercise our discrimination and judgment, and express this endorsement, however inconsistently, in the pattern of our evaluations.[33] In defining ourselves we may pick out as fundamental only the values and abilities we merely endorse, leaving out entirely those we act upon. Then our self-definition shows that we have a false self-image. Nevertheless, since this very selection expresses a higher-order value-judgment (*"This* is what I most value, and want to be valued for [and to emulate]"), our self-definition necessarily constitutes and reveals something of our value-scheme and standards, hence of our nature. Or it can go the other way: we may pick out as fundamental in ourselves only the values and abilities which explain our actual goals and actions, leaving out entirely the ideals and aspirations we do not act upon, either because we are unable to articulate them accurately or because we disavow them and are, to that extent, living in bad faith. Nevertheless, insofar as our self-definition is a true statement of the values we actually live by, it necessarily reveals something of our value-scheme and standards, hence of our nature. In *The Doll's House*, Nora defines herself in terms of her husband's needs as part amusing plaything, part obedient wife, disavowing her aspirations to autonomy. Her self-definition, as shown by her subsequent development, is inadequate. Yet it does reveal something of her nature.

Is it logically possible for just anyone to be loved non-instrumentally? A paradox lurks within any analysis of end friendship that allows this possibility. Consider the case of someone who lives and defines himself as an instrument of another's ends, not because he is ignorant or self-deceived about any contrary aspirations, but because he is simply lacking in them. The goals he pursues are his neither in the sense that he endorses them, nor even in the sense that *his* desires select them. What he desires and endorses—if he endorses anything—is his own instrumentality, and it is this instrumentality that is his fundamental trait. The paradox in allowing that even such a person can be loved as an end is this. In an end friendship, the friends love and wish each other well non-instrumentally, and by virtue of what they essentially are, and thus irreplaceably. But if someone is essentially an instrument of another's ends, then loving him for what he essentially is, must entail loving him as an instrument of those ends,[34] and thus as replaceable by anyone who can fill that role. It follows that such a person cannot be loved as an end.

A person can fail to be an end in himself even if he does not live or define himself as an instrument of others' ends. Consider the case of someone who acquires his goals and values, including his friendships, through imitation of significant others, although he does not live or define himself as an instrument of their ends. Such a person also pursues goals that are his neither in the sense that he endorses them, nor even in the sense that *his* desires select them: his *self* is engaged at neither level of discrimination and judgment. All he desires and endorses is the safety and acceptability he expects through imitation—*this* is what is essential to his self. As an imitator of others, he is eminently duplicable and replaceable by those others. This captures some of the content of the intuitive idea that a person can be an end in himself only if the goals and values he pursues are his in some substantive sense, the products of his own encounters with the world. Only then do they express his sense of himself as someone *worthy* of living quite apart from his utility to others' ends, and *able* to live by his own judgment and effort. To be loved for being the person he is, he must *be* a person in his own right, neither an instrument of others, nor their imitator: someone who is essentially a means to another's ends, or who is incapable of living by his own judgment, encounters the world and acquires a self through the goals and judgments of others.[35] (What exactly it means, in concrete terms, to view oneself as worthy and able to live, what restrictions this imposes on the content of one's goals, can probably be adequately specified only with the help of a literary narrative, and not by a philosophical analysis alone. For our present purposes it is enough to note that we do distinguish between those who live by their own judgment and values, and those who live second-hand, whether as devotees of some one individual or, in the words of the poet, as "the epitome of all mankind.")

2) *The Essential and the Accidental: Two Views.*
My characterization of the object of end love in friendship has still to meet an indirect metaphysical challenge. I have talked about end love in terms of essential qualities. But as is well known, at the third step of the Platonic ladder of love, the other is loved for what at least *seem* to be his essential qualities, his "fair and noble and well-nurtured soul,"[36] even though he is, at the same time, loved only as a means to the *proton philon*, the abstract Form of Beauty. *The paradigm of instrumental love turns out to be based on essential qualities.* I shall show that this comes about only because of Plato's peculiar conception of qualities and their relation to the individual. On the conception I am defending, a person's essential qualities are inseparable from his numerical or histori-

cal identity, both in fact and as object of cognition and love. In trying to see why Platonic love of essential qualities is instrumental, we can also take a deeper look into what is involved in love of essential qualities in end friendship.

Recall, first, that a person's goals and aspirations, thus his fundamental qualities, are the result of his encounters with the world, whether at first-hand, or in imitation of others. Thus his fundamental qualities are inevitably colored by his particular, historical, existence. Conversely, his goals and aspirations are expressed in, and contour, his particular existence. A personal essence is not a set of qualities detached from one's particular existence, but qualities which express, and are expressed in, this existence. Thus a person's essence, that which makes him what he is, includes the *way* his fundamental qualities are expressed, i.e., his *style:* as Buffon noted, the style is the man. Thus, for example, Cyrano de Bergerac would not be the person he is without his poetic wit and physical daring. [37] His wit and daring constitute *his* particular stylization of his qualities: his independence of mind, his courage and loyalty, his passion for the "white plume of freedom . . . "—as well as his tragic conviction that he is too ugly for a woman's love. What makes these qualities uniquely *his*, is the style of their expression. Equally, what makes his poetic wit and physical daring uniquely *his*, is the qualities they express. [38] The distinction between qualities and style, however, is only a relative one: the style in which one expresses certain qualities can itself be described as a set of qualities, and the qualities expressed can be described as a style of facing life. [39] Those who love Cyrano for one or the other do not love him for what he essentially is. [40] Thus the hangers-on in Ragueneau's bakery, delighting in Cyrano's wit, fail to see it as an expression of his deepest moral passions; [41] and we can imagine some earnest devotee of Cyrano who loves him for his "moral nobility," while failing to see his wit as an essential expression of this nobility.

In Plato's conception of essential qualities, of course, the earnest devotee would be right. The proper object of love is the qualities of soul as abstracted from their mode of expression in the individual's life. For the fairness and nobility of the well-nurtured soul are reflections of "beauty absolute, separate, simple, and everlasting . . . " (*Symposium*, 211b), the true and ultimate object of love, whose instantiation in the individual's life is but an unfortunate entanglement. It is this kind of detachment of an individual's qualities from their concrete manifestation in his life that makes the Platonic ladder of love a metaphor for instrumental love. The individual as a numerical particular becomes a mere vehicle for these qualities, the concrete events of his life which give them shape and expression mere accidents. That which is *essential* in an individual is universal; that which is *unique* and *personal* in him, is accidental: there are no individual essences, no truly *personal* natures. Thus the noble character of one individual is identical with the noble characters of other individuals, and love of a given individual for what he essentially is, implies love of all instantiations of this universal essence. Such a love is therefore not only compatible with, but *requires*, regarding him as replaceable with like others, and with regarding his particular existence as but a means to a further goal. To regard him as irreplaceable, as an end rather than a means, is to lose sight of the true object of love, to distort reality.

Thus in Plato's theory this abstraction of qualities from their concrete manifestation is a moral recommendation to the lover which comes backed by an elaborate metaphysics. The qualities of the individual—the *what* he is—can and should be divorced from their expression in his life—from the *how* he is what he is—because doing so brings one closer to seeing them as they are in themselves, to seeing them as they are in their original and pure form. But this belief (in certain of) the individual's *qualities* as essential, and the *style* in which they are manifested as accidental, is neither required nor possible in a non-transcendental metaphysics. For here, particulars—material objects as well as individuals—are not instantiations of abstract, preexisting qualities; rather, qualities come into being, persist and change in particulars, and can be abstracted from them only mentally or conceptually. An individual's *history*, as such, is no more accidental than his *qualities*: the essential-accidental distinction is a distinction *within* the individual's historical-qualitative identity. Thus an individual cannot be known or loved as an end if he is seen as a set of qualities divorced from their expression in his life.

Plato's metaphysical fiction yields a psychological and moral truth. It shows that a love which is motivated primarily by a need to fulfill a deficiency must be a means love. Even when it purports to be directed to the other's fundamental qualities, its view lacks the *richness* and *depth* necessary to capture the essential person.

3) The Historical Dimension of Love.

The attempt to defend personal love against the Platonistic impulse sometimes takes the form of contrasting love of the *person* with love of his *characteristics*. But in this form the defence implicitly accepts the Platonic premise of the separability of the two. To quote Robert Nozick:

> An adult may come to love another because of the other's characteristics; but it is the other person, and not the characteristics, that is loved. The love is not transferable to someone else with the same characteristics, even to one who "scores" higher for these characteristics. . . . One loves the particular person one actually encountered. Why love is historical, attaching to persons in this way and not to characteristics, is an interesting and puzzling question.[42]

But in a non-transcendental metaphysics, this puzzle cannot even be legitimately formulated. The characteristics that motivate the love are not the type of which various individuals are tokens, so that love's non-transferability should generate a puzzle. No description of an individual's characteristics which abstracts from their style of expression in his particular existence can capture the *person*. And neither can any explanation of love as historical which excludes reference to the characteristics that are revealed in, and shape, this history. Insofar as love is historical, it is also of the individual's characteristics as expressed in this history. Love may, indeed, endure "through changes of the characteristics that gave rise to it" (Nozick, p. 168). But this in itself does not imply that characteristics are irrelevant to the continuation of love. After all, love may *not* endure through such changes—indeed, a "love" that endures through a loss of *all* valued characteristics is not love, but obsession or routine. For then its object is not the *person*, but a "bare particular," the numerical individual who happened to be the one initially encountered and loved. When love does endure through changes of the characteristics that gave rise to it, it could be either because the subject of love has also changed in a complementary way, or because he comes to love the other for *other* characteristics initially unperceived.

The value of a shared history—of the historical dimension of love—lies chiefly in its epistemic and creative functions, both of which have to do with characteristics. A shared history is usually required for *knowledge* of each others' characteristics, and knowledge is essential to love. When a shared history reveals characteristics that make people lovable to each other, then it leads to or strengthens love. A shared history can also contribute to the mutual *creation* of characteristics. And when it is "shared" emotionally and cognitively, a shared history contributes to the creation of the very *object* of love. Under this creative aspect, a shared history is a source of the uniqueness and irreplaceability of the object of love. A shared history, in short, both *reveals* and, in part, *constitutes*, the object of love. In neither case is it a dimension of love *independently* of characteristics.

IV. CONCLUSION

I have argued that to love a friend as an end is to love her for her intrinsic worth, for the worth that is hers by virtue of her personal nature, and not unconditionally. For the object of unconditional love is the universal and non-individual, that of end love in friendship, the unique and irreplaceable. I have also argued that in instrumental love, the object of love is qualities which fail to define the person, or which define her as essentially an instrument of others' ends, whereas in the end love of friendship, the love is necessarily based on qualities which do define the person, and define her as an end in herself. Finally, I have argued that these qualities can neither be, nor be understood, apart from a person's historical and numerical identity.

The fact that loving someone as an end implies loving her as a good to oneself points to the possibility that morality can likewise be regarded as an end which is also a good to oneself. This possibility challenges the canonical distinction between teleological and deontological moralities, according to which morality is *either* related to human good, *or* is an end in itself.[43]

NOTES

1. Hence a friendship can exist between lovers, siblings, parent and child, as well as between those who are related only as friends.

2. This does not mean that instrumental friendships are inherently exploitative or unjust: they could not count as friendships if they were. What makes a relationship exploitative is not the mere fact that it serves an end beyond itself, but that it violates the rightful expectations and obligations of one or both parties, where "rightfulness" is itself determined by wider moral criteria. And elements of such injustice are present in practically all relationships.

3. *Nicomachean Ethics* (hereafter NE), 1156a18–19.

4. The notion of intrinsic worth is often construed Platonically, i.e., as a worth which is independent of any valuer, even potential valuer. But this interpretation is necessary only for that which is conceived as a value because it is the source of all value—the Good or God. This must, logically, have a value which is independent of any valuer. But it is possible as well as more plausible to hold that all other values, including intrinsic values, are *relational*, the other term of the relation being that for which it is a value (cf. NE, 1097a1–22). What makes something a value is its actual or possible relation to a valuer as an ultimate end (an end in itself), or means to such an end. If it were not even a *possible* end in itself, or means to it, it could not be a value, any more than something which is not even a possible object of perception could be perceptible. (It should be clear from the analogy with perception that the question of the objectivity or rationality of our value choices and judgments is independent of the ontological claim that values are relational.) What makes something an *intrinsic* value is that it is valued just for being what it is, for its very nature, not for its usefulness in bringing about some other valued state of affairs. But valuing something for its very nature is only a necessary condition of valuing it intrinsically or non-instrumentally: for some things are *by their nature* tools or instruments (see Sec. III.1 below).

5. George Nakhnikian, "Love in Human Reason," *Midwest Studies in Philosophy*, Vol. III, ed. P. French, T. E. Uehling, Jr., H. K. Wettstein (Minneapolis: University of Minnesota Press, 1980).

6. All instrumental love is not, of course, self-regarding—it can be a means to Utility, to the imperatives of Pure Practical Reason, to the Idea of Beauty. The logic of the objection, however, remains the same.

7. I borrow the distinction between target and object of love from Amélie Rorty, "Explaining Emotions," in *Explaining Emotions*, ed. A. O. Rorty (Berkeley: University of California Press, 1980).

8. Or for that matter, in *anything*—laws, institutions, theories et al. As Gregory Vlastos remarks in "The Individual as an Object of Love in Plato," "as objects of Platonic love, all these are not only as good as persons, but distinctly better," *Platonic Studies* (Princeton: Princeton University Press, 1973), p. 26. Vlastos goes on to state that "the cardinal flaw in Plato's theory" is that it "does not provide for love of whole persons, but only for love of that abstract version of persons which consists of the complex of their best qualities" (p. 31). Vlastos equates love of the whole person with love of the individual but, typically, picks out Christian unconditional love as its exemplar (p. 33). [Reprinted in this volume, pp. 96–135.]

9. See A. Nygren, *Agape and Eros*, Part II, Vol. II, trans. P. S. Watson (New York: The Macmillan Company, 1939). Agape, he says, is "primarily God's own love." "In faith he [the Christian] receives God's love, in love he passes it on to his neighbour. . . . The love which he can give is only that which he has received from God" (p. 516).

10. A. Nygren, cited in *Philosophies of Love*, ed. D. L. Norton and M. F. Kille (Totowa: Rowman and Allanheld, 1983), p. 157. Cf. Martin C. D'Arcy, S. J., in the same collection: "All our actions are to some extent affected by our central love . . ." p. 168.

11. S. Kierkegaard, *Works of Love*, trans. H. and E. Hong (New York: Harper & Row, 1962), p. 146.

12. Nygren, cited in Norton and Kille, pp. 158–60.

13. Nygren, *Agape and Eros*, pp. 508, 509. All further references to Nygren are from this book.

14. Nygren notes disapprovingly of Augustine that "when he speaks of God's love for the sinner, he is anxious to explain that it is not strictly love for the sinner himself, but for the good which, in spite of sin, still remains in him, and for the perfection which he can still attain. The idea that love has still something to hope for, something to gain, in the sinner, thus supplies the final motive when all other motives have disappeared. Luther, on the other hand, is anxious to eliminate even this last motive" (pp. 513–14).

15. This question is raised by any noncognitivist view of love, the view that love is not *motivated* by the other's lovable qualities, but rather that it *bestows* these qualities on him. With respect to God's love for humans, we can, perhaps, answer the question— if we are willing to ignore the problems it raises for the Christian concept of God. Imagine the following scenario (and ignore the problems). God, lonely and needing to love, creates human beings. He could have loved anything at all, for love is part of His nature. But in a playful mood he creates human beings and, according to plan, loves them. His love, then, is completely unmotivated, but nevertheless, explicably selective.

16. Even if this worth or lovability is only a *consequence* of God's arbitrary choice to love them—despite my scenario, a moot point ever since the *Euthyphro's* "Do the gods love the pious because they are pious, or are they pious because the gods love them?"

17. Agape between humans may or may not be an end love. According to Augustine, our love for all things except God *ought* to be an "uti" or instrumental love.

18. In the Greek and medieval traditions "contemplation" refers to a state of awareness distinguished from other states of awareness by having no end beyond itself: one contemplates not for the sake of clarification or information or action or production—

although contemplation may indirectly aid us in all these—but for its own value. It is a state of receptive awareness, of "listening to the essence of things," as Heraclitus put it (v. Joseph Pieper, *Leisure the Basis of Culture* [New York: Random House, 1963], p. 26), which takes as its object that which is similarly self-sufficient, serving no end beyond itself. Such an object is obviously God. But such are also all objects that are valuable by their very nature.

19. Thus Nygren says of Augustine's view of our love for God: the love of the *summum bonum* is a means to the happiness and blessedness we derive from its possession, "the blessedness does not consist in *loving*—that is, desiring and longing for the highest good—but in *possessing* it" (pp. 292–93).

20. This is, in fact, Nygren's interpretation of Augustine's view of our love for God: "We have reached our goal; eternal rest (quies) is here; and the very meaning of this quies is that desire is for ever quenched: man no longer needs to seek his 'bonum,' but possesses it. Perfect fruitio Dei means in principle the cessation of love" (p. 293).

21. One can, of course, desire to *keep seeing* them. More generally, as Socrates's question to Agathon shows, desire can be for *keeping* what we already have, not only for what we *lack* at the time of the desire: "[W]hen you say, I desire that which I have and nothing else, is not your meaning that you want to have what you now have in the future?" *Symposium*, 200d, trans. M. Joyce in *The Collected Works of Plato*, ed. E. Hamilton and H. Cairns (Princeton: Princeton University Press, 1963).
    Nevertheless, a desire for keeping something we already have is purely future-directed: in any given moment it is satisfied—quenched—for that moment. But love does not get "satisfied." So love cannot be mere desire, not even an on-going desire for keeping what we have.

22. As Augustine, who seems to hold two opposing views, points out: the better we know God, the better we must love him, hence it is precisely when we have obtained the *summum bonum* that our love grows (v. Nygren, p. 293).

23. To illustrate by means of an analogy: I love this knife only because it enables me to slice onions quickly and easily, even though in so doing, it further *evokes* my love for it.

24. To be lovable is to be valuable, but to be valuable is not necessarily to be lovable. Hence there is no necessary connection between taking pleasure in something and valuing it, simpliciter. E.g., someone who accepts the Kantian view of morality as categorically commanded, as an "end in itself" in the special Kantian sense of "serving no empirical end," may well derive no joy from his success in performing his duty, from achieving "the right." But he may still value this success. On the other hand, if one does not have joy in the attainment of something regarded as an end in itself, then the awareness of it is not contemplation, and it is not an object of love. For between happiness and the value-response called love there *is* a necessary connection.

25. As Amélie Rorty writes, ". . . in contemplating our friends' lives, we become aware of them as forming a unity," and by "such reflection, we take pleasure in their *existence*, in their life as the unimpeded exercise of an activity," "The Place of Contemplation in Aristotle's Ethics," *Essays on Aristotle's Ethics*, ed. A. O. Rorty (Berkeley: University of California Press, 1980), pp. 379, 390. In a similar vein, Ortega y Gasset states: "Love . . . is involved in the affirmation of its object . . . it is like recognizing and confirming at each moment that they [its objects] are worthy of existence. . . . To hate someone is to feel irritated by his mere existence," *On Love: Aspects of a Single Theme* (London: Jonathan Cape, 1967), p. 17. But some have *contrasted* contemplation with pleasure. Thus Harold Osborne, who contrasts aesthetic contemplation as "a mode of awareness in which a thing is apprehended for its own sake," with aesthetic pleasure, *Aesthetics*, ed. H. Osborne (Oxford: Oxford University Press, 1972), p. 14. If this contrast is well-

made, then pleasure cannot be intrinsic to love. But it is hard to see what aesthetic pleasure is, if it is not pleasure in an object apprehended as an end in itself.

26. Just as the knife of the example in n. 23 above may turn out to be uniquely qualified to slice my onions.

27. It is true, of course, that an instrumental friendship is less likely to be permanent than an end friendship. For circumstances and incidental qualities are more variable than essential qualities; and the love and concern based on these, being relatively narrow in focus, are far sooner and easier undermined by the wear and tear of friendship than a love and concern based on a person's essential qualities.

28. Frederic C. Young has objected to this view as implying that friendship cannot even survive a fundamental change in the other which is due to unhappy chance, such as, e.g., Alzheimer's disease; an implication that is clearly false, since love and acts of friendship can and do survive such tragedies. My response is that the continuing love in such a case is like the love for a dead friend—a love based on the memory of the person loved, and a homage to that memory; and likewise, the continuing acts of friendship—the help, the care and so on. But clearly such one-sided love and acts of friendship do not constitute friendship in the full sense of the word, whether the friend is dead, or alive but bereft of the powers that make mutual delight and caring possible.

29. This implies, contrary to the usual thought on the matter, that there is a sense in which even unique, irreplaceable values, including pleasures, may be comparable. What makes them irreplaceable is that they have a different *meaning* to the valuer, are *experienced* differently. Thus x has a value to me for being the person he is that is different, phenomenologically, from the value of y: there is no deeper, neutral pleasure or other mental state to which these values can be reduced, and made exchangeable. Yet x's value to me may be comparatively greater, insofar as x's character or personality answers to more facets of my own. So at least some irreplaceable values can be compared on the scale of one's overall happiness or well-being.

30. Erich Fromm, *The Art of Loving* (New York: Harper and Row, 1956), p. 47. In the case of erotic love he acknowledges that it does make a difference whom we love for, although "[w]e are all One—yet every one of us is a unique, unduplicable entity. . . . [and] erotic love requires certain specific, highly individual elements which exist between some people but not between all" (pp. 47–48).

31. See R. Harré and E. Madden, "Natural Powers and Powerful Natures," *Philosophy* 48 (1973), and C. McGinn, "A Note on the Essence of Natural Kinds," *Analysis* 35 (June 1975), for a discussion of the concept of the nature or fundamental properties of a thing as that which explains that thing's other properties and behavior. This analysis is compatible with the view that a thing's nature or essence is, in part, relative to our epistemological interests. Cf. R. de Sousa's criticism of the contrary, absolutist view in "The Natural Shiftiness of Natural Kinds," *Canadian Journal of Philosophy* 14 (Dec. 1984).

32. And conversely, our personal nature is also given in what we *would not* be, as expressed in our *disavowals* of the values and abilities we act upon.

33. Cf. H. Frankfurt, "Identification and Externality," *The Identities of Persons*, ed. A. O. Rorty (Berkeley: University of California Press, 1976), especially pp. 247–51, on the role of attitude and decision in establishing that some desire or passion that a person has is *his*.

34. Just as loving the aforementioned knife for what it is, entails loving it as a means to slicing onions quickly and easily.

35. Putting it thus allows one to say both that a person can freely and independently

choose to live as an instrument of another, and that by doing so she surrenders her own self or identity.

36. Plato, *Symposium*, 210c.

37. Edmond Rostand, *Cyrano de Bergerac*, trans. Brian Hooker (London: George Allen and Unwin Ltd., 1953).

38. Such descriptions, of course, are not enough to uniquely pick out Cyrano, even barring the logical possibility of a personality twin. In general, no *description* can individuate a person—only a presentation in drama or narrative, with its setting and incident. The point of my descriptions is only to illustrate the claim that a person's essence consists of both qualities and their style of expression. It is the two together that explain, e.g., why Cyrano decides to defend Lignière (out of admiration for Lignière's having "once in his life . . . done one lovely thing," p. 39), singlehandedly against a hundred men.

39. Thus Cyrano's wit and daring and poetic genius are expressed perfectly in his victorious duel with Valvert, in the course of which he composes a Ballade perfectly timed to the action. Likewise, Cyrano's independence and courage and loyalty constitute his style of facing life, his determination to "carry . . . [his] adornments on . . . [his] soul" (p. 27), to "make [himself] . . . in all things admirable!" (p. 34).

40. Even among those who love Cyrano for what he is, only Le Bret, Christian, and Roxane know him—from differing perspectives—as the passionate and tragic lover. One can, of course, have a *true* view of someone even in the absence of a *full* view: if one knows someone in his fundamental aspects, then what one might discover about him fits in, makes sense, in terms of what one already knows. So those who don't know about Cyrano's love for Roxane are not necessarily in the same position as Torvald with respect to Nora.

41. They love him, as Aristotle would put it, only incidentally, and "not as being the man he is . . ." (1156a18). For the wit without the qualities it expresses would be a superficial thing, varying independently of Cyrano's essential qualities. (It is important to note that there is no one invariable set of properties which can be marked off as incidental, as Aristotle seems to think when he states that those who love their friends for their ready-wit, love them only incidentally. *Any* property which varies, or can vary, independently of a person's essential qualities is, under that description, incidental.)

42. Robert Nozick, *Anarchy, State and Utopia* (New York: Basic Books, 1974), p. 168. See also Susan Mendus, "Marital Faithfulness," *Philosophy* 59 (1984), p. 246: "the person who promises to love and to honour only on condition that there be no such [i.e., radical] change in character . . . was never committed in the appropriate way at all." [Reprinted in this volume, pp. 235–244.]

43. I have benefited from Ronald de Sousa's many and detailed comments on this paper, and from Alan Soble's commentary at the Society for the Philosophy of Sex and Love. I also received helpful criticisms from Tom Hurka, Raymond Martin, and Wayne Sumner; from members of the Philosophy Departments at Rice University and Texas Tech University; and from the audiences at the American Association for the Philosophic Study of Society, the Canadian Philosophical Association and the Canadian Society for Women in Philosophy. The Institute of Humane Studies, Virginia, generously paid for my travel expenses to the meeting of the American Association for the Philosophic Study of Society.

SUGGESTED READINGS, SECTION III

Annas, Julia. "Plato and Aristotle on Friendship and Altruism," *Mind* 86 (1977), pp. 532–54.

D'Arcy, Martin C. *The Mind and Heart of Love* (New York, NY: Holt, Rinehart and Winston, 1947).

Gould, Thomas. *Platonic Love* (London, Eng.: Routledge and Kegan Paul, 1963).

Kierkegaard, Søren. *Works of Love* (New York, NY: Harper and Row, 1962).

Kraut, Richard. "Egoism, Love, and Political Office in Plato," *The Philosophical Review* 82 (1973), pp. 330–44.

Letwin, Shirley Robin. "Romantic Love and Christianity," *Philosophy* 52 (1977), pp. 131–45.

Levy, Donald. "The Definition of Love in Plato's *Symposium*," *Journal of the History of Ideas* 40 (1979), pp. 285–91.

Lewis, C.S. *The Four Loves* (New York, NY: Harcourt, Brace, Jovanovich, 1960).

Morgan, Douglas N. *Love: Plato, the Bible and Freud* (Englewood Cliffs, NJ: Prentice Hall, 1964).

Nussbaum, Martha. *The Fragility of Goodness* (Cambridge, Eng.: Cambridge University Press, 1986).

Outka, Gene. *Agape. An Ethical Analysis* (New Haven, CT: Yale University Press, 1972).

Price, A.W. "Loving Persons Platonically," *Phronesis* 26 (1981), pp. 25–34.

Rist, J.M. *Eros and Psyche. Studies in Plato, Plotinus, and Origen* (Toronto, Can.: University of Toronto Press, 1964).

Rosen, Stanley. *Plato's Symposium*, 2nd edition (New Haven, CT: Yale University Press, 1987).

Santas, Gerasimos. "Plato on Love, Beauty and the Good," in D. J. Depew, ed., *The Greeks and the Good Life* (Fullerton, CA: California State University, 1980), pp. 33–68.

Singer, Irving. *The Nature of Love, Vol. I. Plato to Luther,* 2nd edition (Chicago, IL: University of Chicago Press, 1984).

Smedes, Lewis B. *Love Within Limits: A Realist's View of 1 Corinthians 13* (Grand Rapids, MI: Eerdmans Publishing Co., 1978).

Soble, Alan. "Love is Not Beautiful: *Symposium* 200e–201c," *Apeiron* 19 (1985), pp. 43–52.

Warner, Martin. "Love, Self, and Plato's *Symposium*," *Philosophical Quarterly* 29 (1979), pp. 329–39.

Section IV:

CONTEMPORARY ANALYSIS

IMAGINE that you buy a lottery ticket, which you put safely in a drawer at home. Later, while riding the subway and reading the newspaper, you come across an announcement of the winning number—and you recognize it to be yours. As a result, you immediately experience excitement. You also feel happy at the prospect of being wealthy and relief at being able to pay overdue bills. When you arrive home and retrieve your ticket, however, you are shocked to see that you had remembered its number incorrectly. *Now* you experience grief, disappointment, and annoyance. There are at least two philosophical lessons to be learned from this story. First, which emotion a person experiences is a function of the beliefs the person has. When you believed (falsely) that your ticket was the winner, you experienced delight, but when you believed (correctly) that your ticket was not the winner, you experienced depression. Indeed, the change from delight to depression was directly due to a change in belief. Second, there is no doubt that while you believed falsely that your ticket was the winner, your excitement and relief were real, that is, genuine instances of these emotions. The mere fact that a person's emotion is dependent on a false belief does not mean that the emotion is bogus or some other emotion pretending to be that emotion. Emotions, we can say, are *intentional*: they depend on beliefs and these beliefs need not be true.

To this point in our study of love we have mostly ignored intentionality, even when defining the *eros* and *agape* theories about the basis of love. In *erosic* love, we said, x loves y because y has a set S of attractive or valuable properties, while in *agapic* love the merit of the object is irrelevant. But now we must take into account the complications surrounding intentionality suggested by our lottery ticket story. We should characterize *erosic* love more precisely this way: x loves y because x believes or perceives that y has S. In the sequence leading from y's having S to x's loving y in virtue of S, we have to insert between them x's belief or perception that y has S. *Erosic* love is necessarily intentional. By contrast, there is no point incorporating "x believes that y has S" into our characterization of *agapic* love, since in this tradition y's having S is irrelevant to the basis of love. This is not to say that intentionality does not figure at all in *agapic* love (perhaps x must believe that y exists), but intentionality will clearly play a much less significant role in *agapic* love than it does in *erosic*. If x loves y because x believes that y has S, whether x's belief is true or false might very well influence our assessment of x's love, but x's believing falsely that y has S means nothing if x loves y *agapically*.

There are a number of ways in which the truth or falsity of x's beliefs about y might affect how we judge x's *erosic* love for y. *First*, x's belief that y has S might be due to a suspicious or pathological psychological process, e.g., rationalization, projection, or idealization. (See W. Newton-Smith's discussion of Stendhal's "crystallization" theory of romantic love, below.) In this case, x's love-grounding belief is not only likely false but also irrationally-formed, and x's love is to this extent defective. At least, we expect this "blind" love to dissipate as soon as x wakes up to the reality. Indeed, Susan Mendus proposes a neat distinction between genuine love and one of its variants, infatuation: the latter sort of love is typically the result of the lover's too quickly and falsely believing that y has S.[1] Recall that Vlastos (in his essay in Section III) argued that idealization plays no role in Plato's version of *eros*; that x's love is directed at a truncated object—i.e., the set of y's best qualities—does not mean that x has magnified these properties out of proportion to their reality. In fact, it is the Platonic lover's clear vision that y is not so darn perfect that induces him or her to search for better manifestations of beauty.

Second, perhaps x believes falsely that y has S not as a result of psychological pathology but (which might be just as common) because y has deliberately deceived x into believing that y has S. Here if x's love ends when x wakes up to the reality, we are more prone to blame y than x and to judge y immoral for the deception.[2] People who verbally exaggerate their own merits or who do so nonverbally (by their actions and appearance) are often attempting to induce love in another person. Of course this tactic is not usually successful in the long run. It is a curious thing about our society, however, that both x and y know in advance that each will be trying to impress the other (especially on a first date), specifically by hiding their faults. Hence, outright deception in this circumstance is probably impossible; neither x nor y, if they are both rational and acculturated, take the appearance of S as a reliable indication that S is necessarily the reality. If x and y extend their relationship, then their love and intimacy develop and deepen as they increasingly feel more relaxed and spontaneous in revealing their other sides, hoping to be loved "as they really are."

Third, if x loves y in virtue of believing falsely that y has S, is it even correct to speak of x's emotion as *love*? Consider another emotion: hate. Suppose that x believes that y has done something especially vicious to x (say, x believes that y has been telling bare-faced lies about x) and that in virtue of this belief x begins to hate y. Simply because x's belief is false—as a matter of fact, y has been saying only nice things about x—do we want to deny that the emotion x experiences is hate? No. Note, too, that we expect that when x corrects his or her belief about y, x's hate will dissipate—the emotion's *absence* is due to a change in x's beliefs about y. For these reasons we should conclude that hate is a fully intentional emotion. (But see D. Hamlyn's claim to the contrary.) Nevertheless, some would say that if x loves y in virtue of believing falsely that y has S, then x's emotion is not love at all. Newton-Smith, for example, claims that if x loves y falsely believing that y has S, then x's emotion is love only if x's emotion would continue after x corrects his beliefs about y; if x would not feel the same after exchanging his false beliefs for true ones, then x "never loved anyone at all." Indeed, if x loves y first believing falsely that y has S and later believing correctly that y does not have S, x's love appears to be *agapic*—not in any way a function of y's having S. This makes sense, given Newton-Smith's other claim that committed concern for the welfare of the beloved is a central element of love. This concern is genuine, in his view, only if it persists through changes in the beloved or, equivalently, through changes in x's beliefs about the beloved. But Newton-Smith's position turns out to be, after all, more Aristotelian than Pauline; it is *erosic* in the sense that in genuine love, x loves y for y's identity properties. Thus, in his view, x's love should persist through all changes in y, except through those dramatic changes that amount to y's acquiring a new identity, becoming a new person z. (How does Newton-Smith handle the problem of distinguishing between the essential and the incidental? See his proposal, p. 207, below.)

D. W. Hamlyn begins his essay by noting that emotions in general are intentional: they are dependent on beliefs about their objects. Further, for each discrete emotion there is a characteristic belief on which the emotion depends, and the various emotions can be distinguished from one another by identifying the characteristic belief of each emotion. For example, if x fears some item A, then x must believe that A is dangerous or a threat to x's well-being. This does not mean that usually a person believes something is dangerous if the emotion she has is fear, but that the emotion logically cannot *be* fear unless the person believes, truly or falsely, that the item is dangerous. Thus, if x believes that A is not dangerous (or does not believe it is dangerous), then x's emotion toward A, whatever it is, cannot be fear. On Hamlyn's account, an occurrence of an emotion is irrational precisely when its characteristic belief is irrational. If x fears A because x believes that A is dangerous, but x's belief is founded on weak, too little, or no evidence, then x's fear is irrational. [3]

Hamlyn proceeds to argue that love is an anomalous emotion: it is not intentional to the same extent as fear and the other emotions. In particular, love does not have a characteristic belief, i.e., a belief such that in its absence x's emotion could not be love. Although usually when x loves y, x does so in virtue of believing that y has property set S, it does not have to happen that way; x need not believe anything specific about the object of x's love. X might not respect y, or might find y "distasteful," or x might clearly recognize that y's glaring faults are not outweighed by y's measly good points, yet x's emotion could still be love. Hamlyn calls such belief-independent (or reason-independent) love "full-stop" love. Indeed, hate in Hamlyn's view also does not have a logically characteristic belief, and x's emotion toward y can vacillate between love and hate without any changes at all in what x believes about y. (If Hamlyn is right that both love and hate have no characteristic belief, then the ordinary way in which the emotions are distinguished fails for love and hate. What, then, is the difference between them? How does Hamlyn distinguish love and hate?)

Because some occurrences of love are belief-dependent while others are "full-stop," some occurrences of love are *erosic* and others *agapic*. Hence, in our terms, Hamlyn's conclusion is that neither the *erosic* view of love nor the *agapic* states a necessary truth about the basis of love. This conclusion should not disturb us, since it is plausible to interpret the debate between proponents of these two traditions as a debate over what love ideally is. Thus we have to invoke other considerations in deciding between the two; say, by evaluating *erosic* love and *agapic* love in terms of their morality and rationality. [4] Hamlyn does say that hate full-stop is objectionable: if x hates y for no reason at all, we tend to judge x's hate (or x) to be irrational and even morally blameworthy. But note that Hamlyn is reluctant to draw that conclusion about love full-stop. It is indeed a challenge to extract from his essay a definitive thesis about the morality and rationality of love full-stop.

Newton-Smith covers much more territory in his essay beyond the intentionality and constancy of love. In addition, he makes some contentious claims about the reciprocity and exclusivity of love. Even though, in his view, x's loving y does not entail that y loves x (i.e., love is not by its nature reciprocal like friendship), [5] Newton-Smith argues that if x loves y, x at least desires that y reciprocate, except in very special circumstances. Newton-Smith also argues that love is not necessarily exclusive. X's love need not be, for conceptual reasons, restricted to only one beloved, and x's carrying on multiple love relationships faces only practical difficulties. Newton-Smith suggests that those who believe that love is for conceptual reasons exclusive probably mean to assert only that for moral reasons x ought not to love anyone else if x already loves y. Notice that the latter claim presupposes that love is under our deliberate control. It makes no sense to say that x ought not to love both y and z unless x could decide whom and how many people to love. These issues—the reciprocity, exclusivity, and constancy of love, as well as to what extent love is voluntary or within our power to dispense—are central issues in the philosophy of love. They are addressed in the remaining essays in this Section by Susan Mendus, Robert Burch, Robert Ehman, and Joseph Diorio.

Susan Mendus prompts us to wonder whether the marriage vow—which contains a promise to love—is conceptually coherent. Does it make any sense to think that we can *promise* to love? Surely, I can promise to be at your house for dinner on Wednesday, since what I am promising to do can be fulfilled by my own efforts. But promising to love might be a different story. If love is a feeling (or in Kantian terms, an inclination), it would be strange to say that I can promise to love you, to the extent that I cannot bring it about by my own efforts to have feelings. If love, however, is more significantly concern for the well-being of the beloved (or, in Kantian terms, beneficence), then I can promise to love insofar as whether I do continue to promote your well-being is under my control. (If love is a mixture of inclination and concern, then in some ways it can, and in others it cannot, be promised.) Hence, if the marriage vow makes sense, it must mean that one promises to show concern even if the feeling aspect of love has dissipated. (What would be left to motivate the concern? A sense of one's duty?)

Note that there is a third lesson to be learned from our lottery ticket story: do not count your ducks until they hatch. You could have—indeed, should have—tempered your emotional response to "recognizing" your ticket's number in the newspaper. You could have quieted your excitement, for good prudential reasons, by telling yourself that you had to check your ticket. In the same way, we might have some control over love: x could temper her response to meeting the attractive person y until she knows him better and ascertains that he really has the properties he seems to have. Not only for prudential reasons, however: declaring love on the basis of incomplete knowledge or false beliefs might be morally faulty, since the declaration creates expectations.[6]

The question, to what extent is love under one's control, is the topic of Robert Burch's essay. He argues that love is paradoxical: x can wish to love y and can even bring it about through her own efforts that she does love y; yet x cannot, for conceptual reasons, actually undertake and successfully complete the project of coming to love y. Note that in reaching this conclusion, an important step in Burch's argument is that if x genuinely loves y, x does not have *any* reasons for loving y. In our terms, Burch assumes that love is necessarily *agapic* or is, by its nature, what Hamlyn calls love "full-stop," since if x has no reasons for loving y, it cannot be the case that x loves y because x believes that y has S. Thus Burch's conclusion can be challenged by arguing that *erosic* love is both possible and genuine love, i.e., that love is not by its nature reason-less.

Mendus draws to our attention a second problem in the marriage vow: even if one can promise to love, can one promise into the future to continue to love? Is the promise to love that x makes to y in 1985 still binding on x in 2025? Mendus argues that the promise to love makes sense only if it is conceived of as a statement of one's intention and not as a prediction about one's future attitudes or behavior. This distinction is important. When I promise to come to your house for dinner, I am not predicting that I will be there. After all, I might get hit by a bus on my way. That event would show that my promise, understood as a prediction, was false; but it would not show that my promise, understood as a statement of intention, was fraudulent. And surely my getting hit by a bus on the way to your house does not mean that I never promised or never intended to come for dinner.

The promise to love of the marriage vow, for Mendus, is therefore a statement that one intends to continue loving. This does not mean that if x loves y, then x will *always* love y. For x can intend to love y always, yet this intention might be frustrated by something unforeseen in their relationship that is analogous to x's getting hit by a bus. Perhaps y becomes sexually promiscuous; in this situation x discovers that he is no longer able to abide by his earlier promise to love. But since x's vow was not a prediction, x's no longer loving y does not show that x's earlier intention was fraudulent. Note, then, two things about love on Mendus' view. First, love is not necessarily constant. It need not last "forever." X's loving y means only, instead, that x intends the love or his commitment to last "forever." Second, when x vows to love y in the future, the vow is not qualified with "as long as you do not become promiscuous" (or with some other condition). If x's vow is a statement of a genuine intention to love, it cannot be hedged when it is made. This does not mean that x must continue to love y if y becomes promiscuous, for x's vow was not a prediction. Mendus makes the point nicely: there is a difference between a commitment that is conditional at the very start and an unconditional commitment that one eventually abandons. The latter, not the former, is part of love.

Mendus derives an interesting conclusion out of her account of the marriage vow. If, when x commits himself to y, x intends to love y in the future *period*, i.e., without any qualifications, then love cannot be *erosic*. Or at least x cannot provide a complete list of the reasons that x loves y or of the properties in virtue of which x loves y. For if x could do that, then x could state in advance what conditions y would have to satisfy such that x would or would not continue to love y in the future. But the nature of the marriage vow prevents x from being able in advance to state what those conditions are—the vow is unconditional.

Consistently, Mendus also asserts that instead of x's loving y because y has valuable S, x finds S in y to be valuable just because x loves y—which is *agapic* rather than *erosic*. But I am not sure that we should be convinced by this argument. Is Mendus correct in claiming that when x declares love for y or makes a commitment to y, x does so or should do so unconditionally? Is it not possible that x knows in advance that if y later becomes abusive or promiscuous, x could no longer love y? We might even be tempted to judge a person who makes a commitment in the absence of *all* beliefs about what would destroy his love to be irrational.

In contrast to Newton-Smith, Robert Ehman argues that love is by its nature both exclusive and reciprocal. In defense of the latter thesis, Ehman asserts that unless x knows y very well, it is incorrect to say that x's emotion toward y is love. Love at first sight, for example, is not really love, because x could not yet know enough about y. The basis of love is the "unique individual style of life" of the beloved, and that takes time for x to discern. But how does this mean that love is necessarily reciprocal? Ehman completes his argument by asserting also that x could not be in a position to know y well enough to love y unless y loved x. (I leave it as an exercise for the reader to work out the convolutions of Ehman's argument.) Regarding the exclusivity of love, Ehman claims that if x loves y, then x puts y first in x's life, above all other persons. If that is right, x could not love both y and z at the same time, since x logically cannot put two people first above all others. What underlies the dispute between Ehman and Newton-Smith, it seems to me, is this: they disagree about the nature of the concern that is involved in love. For Newton-Smith, love does include a certain amount or type of concern for the well-being of the beloved, but the only obstacles to x's being concerned in *this* way for more than one person are the practical limits on x's time, energy and resources. For Ehman, if x loves y then *all* of x's concern must be directed at y. If x tried to parcel out this concern to various people at one time, the amount of concern directed at each person would not be the amount required by love. (See a similar idea in Montaigne's essay "Of Friendship" in the Appendix.) Now we can understand why, for Ehman, there is necessarily a conflict between love, on the one hand, and morality or justice on the other. Singling out one person, the beloved, to be the recipient of this special, preferential concern is to violate a moral principle of equality.

The perennial question "should I marry y or z?" is the cause of innumerable headaches. Since in our culture there is often a connection between love and marriage—if they do not always go together like a horse and carriage, at least love is believed to be necessary for a successful or happy marriage—the question could be rephrased "should I love y or z?" In *Is Sex Necessary?* E. B. White describes the plight of the American male, who seems to be caught within Ehman's conflict between love and justice:

Man faced one very definite problem: . . . [he] had discovered that it was increasingly difficult to make up his mind whether he desired any one woman. . . . [I]n order to contemplate marriage, it was necessary for a man to decide on One Particular Woman. This he found next to impossible [because he had] the suspicion that if he waited twenty-four hours . . . he would likely find a lady even more ideally suited to his taste than his fiancée. Every man entertained such a suspicion. Entertained it royally. . . . To deny the possibility of her existence would be, he felt, to do a grave injustice to her, to himself, and to his fiancée. Man's unflinching desire to give himself and everyone else a square deal was the cause of much of his disturbance.[7]

The tension between the exclusivity of love and the demands of morality is also one topic of Joseph Diorio's essay, which is an extended discussion of a very common belief: indiscriminate or promiscuous sexual behavior is morally wrong *because* sexual activity ought to be confined to a loving relationship.

The view that sexual activity ought to be exclusively confined to one other person, on the grounds that sex is justifiable only in the context of a loving relationship, presupposes that love itself is or ought to be exclusive. Diorio points out a number of tangles in this view. In particular, it is vulnerable to a dilemma: either love is under the control of one's will, or it is not, i.e., it is fundamentally involuntary. In either case, the view under discussion runs into trouble. If love is an involuntary response of the lover to the beloved, there is no guarantee that love will be exclusive. (Surely if hate is involuntary, that does not mean x can hate only y.) If so, tying sex to love will not secure the moral judgment that sexual activity ought not to be promiscuous. We could not even say that love ought to be exclusive, since if love is out of our control we could not follow a command to love exclusively.

On the other hand, if love is within our control it still needs to be explained why love ought to be exclusive. Why, if (as Ehman claims) exclusive love conflicts with the morality of equality? And why, if love is a good thing and therefore ought to be maximized rather than minimized? Further, if love is under our control it must be explained why x chooses just that one person y to love and not someone else. If x has reasons for selecting y rather than z, then persons other than y (even if not z himself) will likely also satisfy these reasons, so we should expect x to love nonexclusively. Is this why invoking the uniqueness of the beloved is frequently a move made within the philosophy of love? If x has *no* reasons for selecting y, the situation is just as bad. For if x has no reason for loving y, x should equally have no reason not to love z. Again the required exclusivity of love, by which the exclusivity of sexual behavior is defended, has not been secured.

NOTES

1. Is the distinction that Mendus draws between love and infatuation the right way to distinguish these phenomena? Here is another proposal: if x loves y, then x primarily has a desire to benefit y; while if x is infatuated with y, x's primary desire is to be in y's presence or to engage in sexual activity with y. If this is correct, then the lack of constancy in infatuation (as opposed to the purported durability of love) is due not to the fact that infatuation is based on false beliefs that will quickly change, but due to the fact that sexual desire or the desire to be in the presence of the other person is more easily satisfied (or otherwise gone) than is the desire to benefit the beloved.

2. See Aristotle on x's having false beliefs about the virtue of y (*Nicomachean Ethics* 1165b ff., in Section II).

3. A more detailed account of the various ways in which love can be irrational is provided by Gabrielle Taylor ("Love," *Proceedings of the Aristotelian Society* 76 [1976], pp. 147–64).

4. John Brentlinger speaks to this issue in his essay in Section III. He concludes that we have little reason to assess one type of love as superior, in general, to the other type.

5. On the reciprocity of friendship-love see Aristotle (*NE* 1155b25 ff., in Section II).

6. William Lyons describes a number of ways in which we have control over our emotions and can be held accountable for them; see his *Emotion* (Cambridge, Eng.: Cambridge University Press, 1980), pp. 195–206.

7. James Thurber and E. B. White, *Is Sex Necessary?* (New York, NY: Perennial Library, 1957), pp. 92, 95, 96, 99.

A CONCEPTUAL
INVESTIGATION
OF LOVE

W. Newton-Smith

CONCEPTS LIKE LOVE, which we use in describing, explaining and ordering the personal relations of ourselves and others, have received scant attention in the recent Anglo-American philosophical tradition. This contrasts decidedly with philosophical interests on the continent. The difference may be explained in part by the fact that here interests have lain in different areas. More interestingly, perhaps, this difference may reflect disagreement about the connection between such an account and more basic issues in epistemology and the philosophy of mind and about the import of a philosophical account of, say, love. For example, Sartre, when discussing relations with others in *Being and Nothingness*, concludes at the end of something bearing at least a family resemblance to an argument, that it follows from his account of the relation between mind and body that an attempt to love is bound to fail. The acceptance of Sartre's argument would have clear import for someone who regulated his or her sex life according to the principle that sex without love was not permissible. A person who accepted the argument and who was unwilling to adopt a chaste life would seem to be compelled either to violate or to revise his or her principles. Clearly, if one accepts that an account of the relation between mind and body might entail conclusions of this force, one would be interested, to say the least, in working out the entailments.

Reprinted from *Philosophy and Personal Relations*, edited by Alan Montefiore (1973; pp. 113–36), by permission of McGill-Queen's University Press. W. Newton-Smith is Senior Tutor at Balliol College, Oxford and the author of *The Structure of Time* (1980) and *The Rationality of Science* (1981).

On a conception of philosophy which has had some currency in the recent Anglo-American tradition such conclusions would not be expected. For, on this view, philosophy is seen as a sort of second-order discipline, which seeks to give a descriptive, and possibly systematic, account of the concepts we employ in dealing with the world. Philosophy presupposes a linguistic practice which it describes and leaves untouched. Within this framework it is highly unlikely that someone would argue that something which we took, at the level of common sense, to be the case was not in fact the case. In the presence of Sartre's strong and counter-intuitive conclusion that love is not possible, it would be argued via paradigm cases that love is indeed possible and that consequently Sartre's account of the relation between mind and body is shown, by *reductio ad absurdum*, to be false. While these few remarks have done justice neither to Sartre nor to the practitioners of this linguistic conception of philosophy, they do suggest an important contrast between these traditions with regard to their expectations of the possible fruits of a philosophical account of concepts such as love.

In this paper I will seek both to provide an account of our concept of love and to explore the possible practical bearing of such an account for our thinking and acting in the context of personal relations. The first part of the paper will involve an attempt to determine some of the concepts analytically presupposed in the employment of the concept of love and to ascertain some of the features which mark the concept off from certain related concepts. Within the confines of this paper, this treatment can only be provided in detail sufficient to suggest the general structure of the concept. A more detailed tracing of the multifarious web of connections will, I hope, come later. In the second part of the paper a number of hypothetical situations in which the protagonists appear to be disagreeing about matters of love will be considered. This will allow us to test the adequacy of the philosophical account of love in terms of its power to account for these disputes. These cases will also be used to determine what relevance the philosophical account might have for us in our personal relations with others. That there may be some practical relevance is suggested by the following considerations.

Any complete account of the state of a relation between persons, as opposed to objects, must take account of what the persons involved take the state of the relationship to be. The state of a personal relationship between business colleagues, Smith and Jones, may be a function more of how Smith sees Jones (i.e. as dishonest) than of how Jones actually is (i.e. honest). Similarly, the practical course of a relationship between Joe and Joel, which they both see as one of love, might be in part a function of what they take love to be or to involve. A philosophical account of love which ruled out one of their ways of thinking of love would then be relevant. Whether this philosophical intervention was for the better is entirely another matter. Rather than defend or amplify this thesis here, it will be left until we consider some hypothetical personal relationships.

Before proceeding further it will be helpful to introduce the following methodological distinctions. As well as speaking of the concept of x, I will talk of someone's conception of x. Someone's conception of x refers to how that person uses the term 'x.' The concept of x refers to those features which anyone's conception of x must possess in order to count as a conception of x at all. This distinction is intended as a device to avoid prejudging the issue concerning the existence of a precise, determinate, public concept of x. That is, different persons might draw the boundaries of their concepts somewhat differently but not so differently that they cannot be said to be speaking of the same thing. For instance, two persons might be said to have the same concept of x in virtue of an agreement about paradigm cases of x but to have slightly different conceptions of x in virtue of making different decisions about borderline cases. I will also speak of someone's picture of x. By this I mean the answer the person would give to the question 'What is x?' Roughly, then, someone's picture of x is the account he would offer of x. This is intended as a distinction between someone's possessing a certain concept where this is displayed through the correct application of the concept and the person's being able to say in virtue of what features he applies the concept. Someone may possess a concept, x, but have no picture of x at all. If we ask him 'What is x?' he draws a blank or can only point to examples. Someone's picture of x might be a full-blown philosophical analysis of x. It might also be incompatible with the actual use he makes of the concept.

Use will also be made of the following distinction between two sorts of noncontingent truth. If, for example, it should be a necessary truth that *all* cases of love must involve sexual desire, I will speak of a necessary connection between love and sexual desire. And if it should be a necessary truth that *generally* cases of love involve sexual desire I will speak of a g-necessary connection. A particular case lacking a g-necessary feature of x-hood, will count as a case of x only in the presence of some special explanation. Obviously this paper is not the place to enter into a discussion of the nature of necessary truth, and I can here offer no defence of this distinction beyond an attempt to display its fruitfulness in application.

I

This study cannot deal with all our uses of 'love.' We speak of loving persons, food, countries, art, hypothetical divine beings, and so on. In this paper I will be interested only in cases where the object of a love is some one or more persons. It would seem fairly clear that this is, as it were, the home territory of the concept of love and that the use of 'love' in conjunction with objects other than persons is best understood as an extension of this use. Having distinguished a kind of love in terms of a kind of object, namely persons, of a love relation, it is necessary to narrow the field of investigation further. And so attention will be confined to cases of love which involve sexuality. For the balance of this paper then, 'love' is to be understood as implying this restriction. 'Sexuality' is used here as a generic term whose species are sexual feelings, desires, acts and so on. Thus the stipulation excludes from present consideration cases of fraternal love, paternal love, and other cases not involving sexuality.

While this restriction is not intended as a substantial point about love, neither is it purely arbitrary. Rather it is intended to reflect a rough distinction that we do make between kinds of love between persons. Cases of love between persons cluster around certain paradigms. On the one hand we have a group of paradigms which includes Romeo and Juliet, Abelard and Helöise, and Caesar and Cleopatra. Jules and Jim provide another set of paradigms; the heroine of Gorky's *Mother* and the father of the prodigal son still another. It would seem that sexuality can serve as a criterial mark for picking out those cases that cluster around our first set of paradigms. Thus for instance, given a parent that loves a child, the occurrence of a prolonged, active and intense desire for sexual relations with the child on the part of the parent would lead us to regard the love, all things being equal, as not purely maternal. Analogously, the absence of sexuality between two persons of the opposite sex whom we think of as loving each other may incline us to describe the love as platonic or aesthetic. Anyone who thinks that this requirement of sexuality does not capture what is the essential delimiting feature of the romantic paradigms, can regard the requirement as simply a device for selecting a more manageable set of cases for this preliminary investigation.

A brief word about the status of these paradigms is in order. One way of displaying in part what someone's conception of, say, Ø is, is by displaying what he would regard as paradigm instances of Ø. While the cases given above would be offered as paradigms by a large number of persons, there is no proper set of paradigms. By this I mean that while the conceptual features of love to be given below rule out certain things as not possibly being paradigms of love, it is possible for different individuals to have different paradigms. In what follows I hope to display what we must think of a relationship in order to think of it as a relationship of love at all. I will suggest that this leaves considerable range for the construction of competing paradigms. This divergence in paradigms leaves room for interesting psychological and sociological investigations in the variations in paradigms from person to person, for instance, or from class to class, or historical era to historical era. And, given the normative aspect of a conception of love, these paradigms take on the character not just of clear examples but of ideals. Some of the consequences of this will be seen in the second half of this paper.

It is not suggested that the sexuality requirement provides any precise distinction. It seems likely that there is not a precise distinction to be marked. For we might wish to allow some feelings of a sexual sort to enter into a case of basically maternal love. And we might allow some aspects of homosexual love in the close relationship between the officer and men of a marine platoon without the relationship ceasing to be basically a fraternal one. However, things are different if the officer is continually wanting to go to bed with one particular soldier. Thus while there may be no precise distinction here, there is nonetheless a distinction. To be any more definite than this would require an exploration of sexuality that cannot be undertaken here. [1]

It might be objected on the basis of certain psychoanalytic theories that all personal relations involve sexuality, and hence sexuality could not be used as the distinguishing feature of a kind of personal relation. The grounds on which such a claim would rest are not uncontroversial. In any event, their acceptance involves the hypothesizing of repressed sexual feelings. This in turn does not invalidate our distinction but rather requires us to draw it in terms of a contrast between repressed and unrepressed sexuality rather than in terms of a contrast between the presence and absence of sexuality. In fact, Freud, in *Civilization and its Discontents*, contrasted aim-inhibited love in which the sexual component is suppressed and sexual love in which it is not suppressed. Freud took this distinction to divide the field roughly as we have done. Thus acceptance of certain psychoanalytic theories would require only the recasting, and not the abandoning, of our sexuality requirement.

The preceding modification would be required if a psychoanalytic theory which claimed that *all* relations involve a form of sexuality was adopted. More plausibly perhaps, it might be argued that in some relationships with no apparent sexuality involved, some form of suppressed sexuality was present. That is, given a psychoanalytic theory of genuine explanatory power, we might want to hypothesize on the basis of, say, some form of aberrant behavior, the presence of repressed sexuality in a relationship apparently devoid of sexuality. In this case we would have a non-analytic counter-factual to the effect that the removal of repression would lead to explicit sexuality. If such a theory is produced our sexuality requirement will have to be extended to include both explicit and repressed sexuality.

It might also be objected to my sexuality requirement that while instances of courtly love belong with our romantic paradigms, not only was sexuality absent in courtly love relations, it was thought to be incompatible with true (courtly) love. Now evidence of the chastity of courtly lovers is decidedly absent. But in any case, courtly lovers must be thought of as possessing sexual feelings which they set aside. This is implicit in their thinking of themselves as noble for not expressing sexual feelings. There would be no trick to it, and hence no nobility involved, if they simply did not have sexual feelings or inclinations at all.

Having defined the field of investigation, we can now sketch the concepts analytically presupposed in our use of 'love.' An idea of these concepts can be gained by sketching a sequence of relations, the members of which we take as relevant in deciding whether or not some given relationship between persons A and B is one of love. These are not relevant in the sense of being evidence for some further relation 'love' but as being, in part at least, the material of which love consists. The sequence would include at least the following:

(1) A knows B (or at least knows something of B)
(2) A cares (is concerned) about B
    A likes B
(3) A respects B
    A is attracted to B
    A feels affection for B
(4) A is committed to B
    A wishes to see B's welfare promoted

The connection between these relations which we will call 'love-comprising relations' or 'LCRs,' is not, except for 'knowing about' and possibly 'feels affection for,' as tight as strict entailment. While perhaps in certain paradigm cases of love these relations would all be satisfied to a high degree, they are not jointly necessary. In a particular case which we are inclined to regard as one of love, some LCRs may be satisfied to only a low degree or not satisfied at all. For there is no contradiction involved in speaking of, say, love without commitment or love without respect. There would of course be a contradiction involved in asserting that some relationship was one of love while denying that any of the LCRs were satisfied. Thus we have a g-necessary truth that love involves the satisfaction of the LCRs to an as yet unspecified degree.

That the LCRs listed are non-contingently involved in love seems fairly obvious and for that reason not particularly interesting. We would not countenance the claims of A to love B if A had neither met B nor knew anything about B. I will argue below when discussing the limitations of the sorts of reasons A can have for loving B in particular that there are certain sorts of things that A must know about B. The items in group 2 embody the fact that love involves having certain pro-attitudes to the object of the love. Group 3 embodies the condition that the lover sees the object of his love as having in his eyes at least meritorious features. In love it is not just the case that the lover holds the relations of groups 2 and 3 to the object of his love; these relations are held to such a degree that the lover is inclined to act on behalf of his beloved in ways that he is not inclined to act for arbitrary strangers or the general run of the mill acquaintances. Suppose that someone has the unhappy choice of saving either his putative beloved or an arbitrary stranger from drowning. If the putative lover elects to save the stranger, then, all things being equal, the relation is not one of love. Acting out of panic or just after a quarrel, among other possibilities, might show that all things were not equal. This feature of love is captured by the items of group 4.

It may seem frivolous to have introduced this thought experiment to prove such an obvious point. However, that the element of commitment is important in marking off love from other related relations can be seen if we vary the parameters in the thought experiment. Suppose the putative lover has to choose between saving his beloved and a group of strangers. In the event of a choice between a single stranger or a large group of strangers, we clearly think that we should opt for the larger number. Does the commitment element entail that the lover place the welfare of his beloved above the welfare of a group of strangers? Or can he call across to her as he saves the strangers, 'I love you, but unfortunately there are more of them'?

A similar dilemma arises if we imagine a putative lover having to choose between his putative beloved and adherence to his ethical or political principles. In fiction anyway, lovers frequently test the devotion of one another by asking if they would steal etc. for their sake. In *Middlemarch*, for example, Rosamund thinks that if Lydgate does in fact love her, he ought to be willing to set aside his moral scruples for her sake. She wants him to withhold large debts owed to the tradesmen in order to sustain her luxurious standard of living. And in Moravia's *Bitter Honeymoon*, Giacome and Simona are portrayed as being in love and as thinking themselves in love. Simona is a committed communist. Giacome describes himself as an 'individualist.' The following interchange takes place:

> *Giacome* 'For instance, if a communist government comes to power and I say something against it, you'll inform on me. . . . '

It was true then, he thought to himself, since she didn't deny it, then she would inform on him. He gripped her arm tighter almost wishing to hurt her. 'The truth is that you don't love me.'

> *Simona* 'I wouldn't have married you except for love.'

These examples are not meant to imply any thesis to the effect that in 'true' love, commitment to the beloved must take preference over all other commitments. The significant conceptual point of the examples is that in the case of love there are these tensions, and this displays the extent to which love involves a commitment. This marks off love from, for example, relations of just 'liking' or 'being attracted to,' where these tensions do not arise. We would not, I think, be tempted to redescribe an apparent relation of liking or being attracted to as not being a relation of liking or being attracted to, just because the protagonists did not tend to place the other party on a par with political or ethical commitments.

It has been suggested that love involves holding the LCRs to the beloved. If someone holds these relations to another, he will hold them to the person under certain descriptions of the person. For a relation to count as one of love these descriptions must be of certain sorts. A's saving his putative beloved, B, from drowning only because she is wearing his watch or has just won the pools, may be incompatible with A's thinking of the relationship as being one of love. Of course motives on a particular isolated occasion are not necessarily conclusive determinants of the kind of relationship one way or the other. But there are general limitations on the sorts of ways in which A thinks of the object of his affections where the ways in question are the grounds of his affection for the person. Very roughly, A must, say, care about B for herself. A must be attracted to B on her own account. That is, not all properties which A sees B as possessing can serve as the grounds for loving B.

Of the descriptions which A sees as applying to B, I will call those which can be the grounds of A's loving B, intrinsic descriptions of B. Descriptions which cannot play this role will be called extrinsic descriptions. Clearly there are some extrinsic and some intrinsic descriptions. Suppose we have an apparent love relation between A and B where B is very wealthy. Suppose B's wealth suddenly evaporates. If A's interest in B should also evaporate, we conclude that, all things being equal, the relation had not been one of love. We might say that A loved not B but B's money. A was interested in B not for her own sake but for the sake of her money. A liked B-the-wealthy-woman and not B *per se*. Of course it is simplistic to speak as I have been doing, as if one isolated incident would lead us to revise our description of a particular personal relation. The complexity of these situations is such that no one incident is likely to be decisive one way or the other. All that is required for the argument is that these incidents give cause to reconsider the descriptions given.

Suppose on the other hand we have an apparent love relation between A and B. A claims to love B largely on account of certain features of her personality and character. But one day, perhaps as the result of some traumatic accident, B undergoes a radical personality transformation. B no longer has those attributes that A loved her for. A, realizing this, can, we suppose, no longer love B. Here we are not so inclined to revise our descriptions of the relation as we were in the case above. We might say that A had indeed loved B but that this was no longer the case as B is no longer the person she once was.

In attempting to draw this distinction I am assuming that it is not a necessary condition of a relationship's being one of love that the lover's attitude to the beloved remain unchanged through all possible changes in the beloved. This question of constancy in love will be taken up later in one of our case studies. The classification of features as extrinsic or intrinsic depends on our attitude to inconstancy, given that the feature in question changed. That is, if A claims to love B in part at least because of her being $\emptyset$, and if A's attitude to B would be negatively affected should B cease to be $\emptyset$, (or, should A cease to see B as being $\emptyset$) then, if we count this inconstancy as evidence against the relationship's having been one of love, $\emptyset$ is an extrinsic property of B; otherwise $\emptyset$ is an intrinsic property. This places no limitations whatsoever on the features which initially attracted A to B. B's money may have been the initial lure. But, if the relationship is to count as one of love, the money cannot be the sustaining feature. In some cases there may be an intimate causal relation between extrinsic and intrinsic factors. In our previous example, B may have been a dynamic capitalist entrepreneur whose personality is intimately bound up with the acquisition of wealth. Financial failure might bring about a personality change. However, only intrinsic factors matter for themselves. The extrinsic factors are relevant only in as much as they are evidence for intrinsic factors.

It was suggested that features of personality and character clearly count as intrinsic and that the state of someone's bank balance was clearly extrinsic. Not all features are so easily classified. Consider the details of the beloved's physical make-up. Traditionally lovers are enraptured with dainty ears, firm thighs and so on. The general acceptance of these sorts of features as grounds for loving suggests that they are to be counted as intrinsic. But, on the other hand, if the moment the ears thicken or the thighs soften the lover falters, we may well have doubts about his alleged love. This suggests that we consider physical features to be extrinsic ones. Perhaps the most that we can say is that someone might love another solely or chiefly because of his or her physical features but that such cases will not be as near to our paradigms of a love relation as cases in which the beloved is loved solely or chiefly for attributes of his or her personality and character. That is, while physical features can be offered as reasons for loving (indeed our sexuality requirement would entail this), we tend to consider relations, which are not also grounded on regard for aspects of the personality and character of the object of the relation, as lacking certain dimensions. A person having as his chief or only reasons for loving another, regard for their physical attributes, would seem to be regarding the object of his love as being less than a person. Persons are not just bodies; they are at least bodies which think and act.

Any attempt to distinguish between physical characteristics as more extrinsic than features of personality and character is complicated by the problematic status of the role of physical features in determining personality and character.

Clearly we identify some personality features via physical features—the look of the eyes, the character of the smile. The possession of some, though certainly not all, personality traits may be tied to the possession of certain physical characteristics. Perhaps some properties, for instance, elegance, while not being entirely physical attributes, can only be possessed by someone with certain physical attributes. I mention this as a question of some interest requiring a detailed consideration which cannot be given here.

That someone might love another for certain of her features suggests a problem. Suppose someone else should appear who also instantiates these properties. If the possession of these properties is someone's reason for loving one, reasons being universalizable, he will have equal reason to love the other as well. Perhaps the second person more perfectly embodies those properties which the lover previously lauded in the first. According to Gellner,[2] if someone in this kind of context should divide his affection between the two persons, neither relationship can be counted as a relationship of love. (We will have reasons to challenge this assumption later.) In most actual cases the universalizability of reasons will not require a person, A, to extend his affection to cover both B and C where C is a second embodiment of those features which A lauded in B. For, often A's reasons for loving B will involve reference to what B has done for him, to what they have done together. If A has been socially interacting with B, he is likely to have reasons of this character and these reasons would not be grounds for loving C as well. However, suppose A falls in love with B from a distance and has no social contact with B. Even here, one of A's reasons for loving B may be that it was B that first excited this passion in him. A might recognize that C would have done the same, if he had first known of C. But, A first met B and B generated the passion. A may now love B for having been the generator of the passion.

Of course it is possible that reasons of this sort are not among A's reasons for loving B and that either A does not love B for the reasons he thought he did, or that A will transfer his affection. I shall argue (part II) that if A extends his affection in this way, he may nonetheless love both B and C. If A does not think of himself as having any reasons for loving B that do not equally apply to C, and if A does not have any inclination to extend his affection to C, this provides us with the grounds for supposing that A is simply mistaken about his reasons for loving. That is, we would, I think, suppose that there is some present feature of B, or some feature of B's history or their history together, that was important to A and was part of A's reasons for loving B whereas the feature in question is not shared by C.

There are two sorts of intriguing and subtle kinds of cases which might seem to suggest that we have been assuming too readily that there is no problem in identifying who the object of a love is. The first relates to the suggestion, to be found in Stendhal, that one never really loves another person but one loves rather some creation of one's imagination based on, but usually bearing little resemblance to, the actual person one appears to love. Following Stendhal, I will refer to this theory as the 'crystallization' theory of love. Stendhal thought of the actual object of a love as an imaginary creation built on and transforming a few true perceptions of the apparent object of the love, in a manner analogous to the growth of crystals on a branch placed in the Salzburg salt mines. Lawrence Durrell, in *Clea*, provides a model of what I take Stendhal to have in mind. Here Darley is presented as suddenly realizing that he never loved Justine. He concludes that he loved some 'illusory creation' of his own based on Justine. The revelation comes to him on Justine's informing him that it was pointless for her to return to him after their separation, for it was not *her* Darley loved. As the case is presented, Darley thinks of himself as loving Justine because of certain intrinsic features. But the features do not apply to Justine.

Darley thinks of himself as loving Justine for a sequence $\emptyset_1, \ldots, \emptyset_n$ of features which he takes to apply to Justine. If the following counter-factual is true, the case is easily dealt with. If Darley would feel as strongly about Justine should he come to see that she does not possess the properties in question, he does in fact, all things being equal, love her. He has simply been radically mistaken about her. Perhaps when he discovers what she is really like his attraction for her will actually increase. Suppose on the other hand, Darley would not think of himself as loving Justine if he came to realize his mistake. In this case he never loved anyone at all and to speak of having loved an 'illusory creation' is, at best, a metaphorical way of saying that he mistakenly thought of himself as loving someone as a result of radically misunderstanding the sort of person she was.

The 'crystallization' theory draws our attention to the notorious fact that we often misapprehend the properties of persons and often act in personal relationships on the basis of our beliefs about persons which are wrong and sometimes radically so. But as a theory to the effect that we never love other persons, it is just wrong. We are not always mistaken about other persons. In many cases the beloved will in fact have some of the properties on the basis of which the lover loves. Even in cases of grave error, the lover may, as I argued above, be said to love in spite of being mistaken.

The other intriguing case concerning the real object of a love arises in psychoanalytic theory. Aberrant behavior on the part of a person A, who appears to love person B, might be thought explicable in some contexts on the hypothesis that A does not in fact love B but really loves, say, a parental figure. B is a sort of stand-in in an elaborate fantasy. This seems like a misleading description of the case. For, it is towards B and not towards, say, his mother, that A performs the action appropriate in a context of love. Perhaps it is therefore best to say that A does love B while admitting the existence of a causal connection between his attitude towards his mother and his attitude towards B.

Perhaps A would not care for B at all if he had not had a certain attitude towards his mother. Or, perhaps A's loving B depends on his thinking of B in ways appropriate to thinking of a mother.

It has been argued that love involves having certain kinds of relations (the LCRs) to some person, and that it also involves thinking of the object of these relations in certain ways. In addition love is essentially reciprocal. Stendhal reports André le Chapelain as writing in his twelfth-century Code of Love 'No one can love unless bidden by the hope of being loved.' It does seem to be a g-necessary truth that if A loves B, A wishes to be loved by B. We can see that this is a conceptual fact and not just a matter of fact about lovers, by seeing what would be involved in imagining a case where A loves B but does not wish to be loved in return. The following situation, drawn with adaptation, from Dickens' *Little Dorrit* seems to provide the sort of case we want. A loves B who is already married to another. A is particularly concerned for the welfare and happiness of B. A knows that B would not be happy loving him. For, if B loved A in return B would suffer extreme guilt feelings at taking on another affection while committed in marriage to another. B has, let us suppose, a loving husband and children. A, being magnanimous, does not reveal his love for B, for fear that the mere revelation would precipitate reciprocated love and subsequent unhappiness for B. In one sense the lover does wish for reciprocated love. He would wish it if all things were equal. But given the circumstances as they are, he does not wish it. No doubt we would countenance the lover's denial of any wish for reciprocated love in the circumstances. But to render this plausible we had to imagine a case where the reciprocated love would be an unhappy love. Other cases can be provided if the lover is imagined to be masochistic or to be involved in some form of self-abasement. In the absence of such a background we would simply fail to understand a denial of a wish for reciprocated love. If someone claims to love another, we understand him as wishing to be loved in return. We do not have to ask, 'And do you wish her to love you?' The inference to a wish for reciprocated love is blocked only if the background is filled out in certain ways. Loving entails, *ceterus paribus*, the desire for reciprocated love.

This essential reciprocity interestingly delimits love from many other concepts used in describing personal relations. A clear case in point is that of worship. A's worshipping B does not, *ceterus paribus*, entail that A wishes to be worshipped by B. Quite the contrary in fact. For, in wishing to be worshipped by B, A would be demeaning B from the elevated position relative to himself, that A accords to B, in thinking of B as an object of worship. Perhaps 'liking' is a more pertinent example for our present purposes. We do not take someone's claim to like another as implying a wish on his part to be liked by the other person. He may or may not. Perhaps we do take him as wishing not to be disliked but this is not the same as wishing to be liked. The reciprocal factor is similarly absent in the case of a commitment outside the context of a love relation (except possibly in the context of a contractual relation). A claim to be committed to my party leader does not imply a wish that he commit himself to me (I may think of myself as a lowly pawn not deserving such a commitment) in the way that a claim to be committed to my beloved does.

It is not suggested that the features of the concept of love which have been given provide anything like a calculus for deciding, objectively, whether or not any given relationship is one of love. The term 'love' has undeniable emotive force. Different individuals may require that the LCRs be satisfied to different degrees before awarding the epithet love to a relationship. It is not uncommon[3] to find the requirements placed so high as to make relationships that count as relationships of love a very rare commodity. The account of love given is intended to display only what one must think of as involved in thinking of a relationship as love. For instance, it is g-necessary that a case of love involves concern. The person who thinks of himself as loving another, and who at some time sees himself as having failed to act as concern requires, must (g-necessarily) think of himself as having failed. He must see himself as being under a *prima facie* obligation to make excuse. If the person does not see the relation as one of love, he may not see his failure to display concern as anything for which excuse need be made. One does not have an obligation to display to just any acquaintance the sort of concern that loving involves. While we can thus display what is involved in thinking of a relationship under the concept of love, we have no criterial test for 'love' simply because there are not public, objective standards as to the degree of concern, respect, etc., that is required to constitute love. In the case studies that follow we will see something of the consequences of this fact.

II

Case one: love and responsibility
This first case will be constructed around conflicting theories or 'pictures' of love. On one picture of love, a picture most prominent in the romantic tradition, love is seen as a feeling or emotion which simply overcomes one with an all-conquering force. The lover is held to be a victim of his passion. And, if the lover can avoid giving in to his passion, it is not genuine. This picture will be called the involuntaristic one.

I have referred to the above as a 'picture' of love. The reason for so doing is to avoid begging the question that the term is used or could consistently be used by those who would offer this picture in a manner consistent with the picture. For instance, someone might claim that 'red' is the name of a kind of purely private mental impression. It might be argued that no one uses the term in this way and that no one could use a term in this way. In my terminology this could be summed up by saying that this person has an erroneous picture of the concept he in fact possesses.

According to another picture, call this one the 'voluntaristic' picture, love is seen as a deliberate, volitional commitment to another. It is this sort of picture that has at times been appealed to in justifying arranged marriage. The partners once selected and brought together will, it is felt, come to love one another if they make a sincere exercise of will.

We can see how subscribing to one of these pictures can have a practical impact on one's personal relationship. For, on the involuntaristic picture, to be in love is to be in a state of diminished responsibility. Once one is in the grip of love, one may act out of passion in ways that one cannot help. The picture is rarely held in this categorical form. Most commonly on this picture, love is taken as a force, difficult to resist, which comes not of the agent's choice and brings not total absence of responsibility but the diminishing of culpability for acts done out of love. This picture is to be found in the writings of George Sand. Interesting illustrations of the effects of adopting it can be found in the far from simple relations of the Herzens to the Herweghs (and others). Under the sway of George Sand, the protagonists, in what can only be described as an eternal polygon, followed courses of action which they themselves regarded as *prima facie* undesirable, involving as they did considerable unpleasantness for other parties. But acting out of love and seeing love in terms of the involuntaristic picture, they saw themselves as not culpable for these consequences. Or, more accurately, they saw themselves as less culpable than they would have seen themselves if the acts had not been done in the throes of love.

One possible impact of the voluntaristic picture is seen in the context of unobtainable love. In the merry-go-round of relationships in Iris Murdoch's *Bruno's Dream*, one of the protagonists, Lisa, is smitten with love for Miles who is unobtainable. Danby, who is presented as seeing love in an involuntaristic manner, loves Lisa. Lisa emphatically does not love him. However, Lisa, presented as subscribing to a voluntaristic picture, simply decides, when it becomes clear that Miles is indeed unobtainable, to cure herself by taking up with Danby and by coming to love Danby. Of course, when she reveals this to Danby, with his rather more romantic picture of things, he is, to say the least, puzzled and skeptical. Danby thinks that either she loves Miles, and if so cannot volitionally pull off what she is attempting, or that she can pull this off and hence does not love Miles. Lisa thinks of herself as both genuinely and passionately loving Miles and as capable of transferring this sort of affection volitionally to another.

Both of these pictures have some basis in the conceptual facts about love as a look at the LCRs will reveal. For instance, among the LCRs are the relations of respect, affection and attraction. The involuntaristic picture calls attention to these. One may identify the presence of affection, attraction and respect in

terms partly of patterns of volitions. A crude example of this would be concluding that someone is attracted to another because he regularly does things with
the intent of being in the presence of this person. But there is a sense in which
these feelings are not subject to volitions. For, I cannot here and now decide to
feel or not to feel attraction for some given person. I can decide to try and see
the girl next door; I cannot decide to be attracted to her. Of course, my deciding
to go and see her may be evidence of a degree of attraction. Being attracted
involves wanting. I do not decide my wants; I have them and decide on the
basis of them to do or not to do various actions. I might decide to give these sorts
of feelings the best chance of developing. I focus my attention on the given
person, I get to know them intimately, I try to dwell on their good points, and so
on. Whether this will lead to attraction, only time will tell. Similarly, I can
attempt to put myself in the worst position for the continuation of current
feelings of attraction. I join the foreign legion, I associate intimately with other
persons, I focus on the given person's worst characteristics and so on. Time and
effort may bring success.

Attention to other of the LCRs will bring out the conceptual basis of the
voluntaristic picture. For instance, consider commitment. A commitment is
something that I can here and now decide to take up. I can promise to commit
myself for ever to another; I can promise to be always concerned. I cannot, in
the same way, promise to be always attracted to another.

On the basis of the account given of love, we can reject any 'picture' which
allows only voluntaristic elements or only involuntaristic elements. But granted
this, different individuals are free to give different stress to the importance of
different LCRs in their conception of love. Someone can give more promi-
nence to the aspects of love involving attraction, than to commitment. This is
likely to reveal itself in the selection of paradigms this person would offer.
Someone else can give more importance to commitment. There is no conceptual resolution of the question as to which features are more important. The
concept is not determinate in this way. We can uncover the features which
anyone's conception of love must have in order to be a conception of love at all.
However, within these confines one is free to stress passion or commitment.

Case two: constancy of love
Suppose that Jude and Jan are two persons of the same or opposite sex who have
been having an intense affair over a period of time. Mutual declarations of love
have been made and all concerned regard the relationship as entirely satisfactory. Until, that is, Jude announces the demise of his love for Jan. The
following dialogue ensues:

Jan   'What do you mean, you don't love me anymore! Have I done
      anything, said anything?'

Jude   'No, it's just that my feelings for you have changed.'

Jan   'Why? I don't understand. Have I changed in your eyes? Have you changed? What is it?'

Jude   'No. It's not anything like that. We're still the same people. It's just that . . . well, the old intensity of feeling just isn't there anymore, that's all.'

Jan   'You flirt! You never really loved me at all. It's just been an adventure. Look, read this, this is what love is: "Love is not a feeling. Love is put to the test, pain not. One does not say: 'That was not true pain or it would not have gone off so quickly.' "[4]

To this Jude replies with a recitation of 'A Woman's Constancy' and 'The Broken Heart' in which Donne describes 'true' love which flourishes and passes in a single day. Jude adds: 'You admit that there was nothing in my former behavior and attitude to suggest a lack of love. What has time got to do with it? Love isn't any less true for having been short-lived.'

It may make a difference to Jan whether she (he) decides that Jude did or did not love her. Deciding that it was love may incline her to view the current situation just with regret for the passing of Jude's love. Deciding that Jude never loved may incline her to think of Jude as having operated under false pretences and to see herself as having been trifled with. As we shall see, the various LCRs differ in their temporal aspects. Thus it may be that Jude and Jan are in a sense disagreeing at cross purposes in that they may be operating with conceptions of love that give different stress to the importance of particular LCRs. Some LCRs, like respect and affection, may be imagined to flourish and pass in a relatively short period of time. Some act or feature of a person might call forth feelings of respect or affection. Some later revelations may reveal that things are not as they appeared, thus ending the respect or affection. If the time span is sufficiently long, I think we would allow that affection can simply fade away without there being any particular occurrence which is seen as ending the affection. Perhaps Jude found some things about Jan intriguing which lose their mystery on constant exposure. However, if the time span during which affection is thought to be involved is short enough, we have to think of some things having happened, some realization having occurred, which can be described as the reason for the withdrawal of affection. If an apparent affection begins in the evening and evaporates in the morning and if the person involved cannot point to something real or imagined which serves as a reason for the withdrawal of affection, we would be inclined to view the affection as merely apparent.

Concern and commitment, on the other hand, seem significantly different in this respect from respect and affection. For it would seem that genuine concern or commitment cannot be terminated simply by some revelation about or change in the object of that concern or commitment. We are inclined to accept: 'I felt affection for her so long as I thought she was pure and innocent' but not, 'I was really concerned for her welfare so long as I thought she was pure and innocent.' Being genuinely concerned or committed seems to involve a willingness on my part to extend that concern or commitment to the person even if I have been mistaken about that person with regard to some feature of her that led to the concern, and even if that person ceases to have those features that led me to be concerned or committed to her. I do not want to suggest that there is a total asymmetry between these pairs of relations. But to some extent, one measure of the degree of concern or commitment at a time, is the time it extends and its constancy in the face of alteration. And the measure of affection at a time is more the way it disposes me to act at that time and not through some period of time.

To return to Jude and Jan. It may be that Jude has a picture of love which construes love as just a feeling which can come and go. In declaring his love he did not think of himself as taking on any commitments. If the account of love provided in this paper is at all near the mark, we see that he has failed to see what the concept involves and has possibly misled Jan in his declarations. Or, it may be the case that while Jude and Jan both see that love involves the satisfaction of the LCRs they have different conceptions, Jude giving less stress to affection than commitment than Jan does. As we saw in case 1, there is no conceptual resolution of this sort of difference. Allowing this freedom to legislate within certain bounds does not mean that each conception is equally appropriate. Concepts are tied to forms of life. Just as our concept of love is tied to the fact that we are sexual beings, it is also tied to general facts about social organization. Thus, someone like Donne in opting for a short-range conception of love would appear to be opting for a form of life in which personal relations are diverse, changing and not closely tied to long-term responsibilities. In a society which institutionalizes personal relations and attempts to tie them to long-term responsibilities in the form of children, it is not surprising that many opt for long-range conceptions of love which lay stress on commitment.

Case three: multiple person love

Much is made of the particularity of love. It seems commonly felt that if A is in intimate relations with both B and C, whatever the state of that relationship is, it is not one of love. We have this on authority as diverse as André le Chapelain and E. A. Gellner.[5] Apparently proposition 3 of le Chapelain's code of love was: no one can give himself to two loves. I want to consider whether anything in the concept of love rules out multiple person love relations. By a multiple person love relation, or MPLR, I mean some social set-up in which a person is in intimate relations with more than one person, each of whom he *claims* to love. According to Fromm, Jaspers and other moralists, MPLRs are ruled out as relations of love by the 'very nature (or essence) of love.' This seems rather strong. What we have here in fact is an attempt for normative purposes to enforce a range of paradigms, i.e. those which do not involve MPLRs. I will suggest that there is nothing in the concept of love which rules out MPLRs as relations of love. Any move to rule out the MPLRs will be a legislative one.

No doubt there are severe practical difficulties involved in staging a MPLR. The protagonist in such a situation is apt to find himself spread a little thin if he attempts to provide the sort of concern, interest, commitment and so on which we take love to involve. In his paper on sexual perversion Nagel has elaborated on some of the complexities involved in staging a multiple person sexual relationship that would approach the paradigms of non-multiple person sexual relations. Such complexities are bound to increase dramatically in any MPLR. But, that it will be difficult to bring off does not show that it is in principle impossible. And there may be those like the carpenter in Agnes Varda's film *Le Bonheur* who find it as easy to do for two persons as for one, what love requires.

Difficulties are most apt to arise if the set-up is not mutual all round. By being mutual all round I mean that each person in the set-up claims to love each other person involved. Suppose Jude thinks of himself as loving both Jan and Joe. Jude, Jan and Joe may be of the same or different sex. Jan and Joe not only loathe each other, they are most unhappy about Jude's divided affection. We may feel that Jude cannot be really concerned for both Jan and Joe if he continues this relationship in a manner which clearly distresses them. But probably all that is required for Jude to be thought of as loving both Jan and Joe is that he be thought of as distressed at their distress. Jude may think, say, that more happiness is to be had all around by this shared affection than by one of them having his whole concern and affection. In any event, to show that love is not so exclusive as to rule out multiple love relationships we need only imagine a set-up that is mutual all round.

For those like Jaspers, who claims in his *Philosophie* that 'He only does love at all who loves one specific person,' we might suggest the following thought experiment. Consider that all factors involved in loving, excepting any reference to numbers, are satisfied to a high degree by the pair of persons, A and B, and by the pair, C and D. What grounds could one have for retracting a description of these cases as cases of love when it is discovered that B and D are the same person? The only grounds for ruling out such a case would seem to be an *ad hoc* rule that love is necessarily a one to one relationship. While Jaspers and Fromm are entitled to make up their own rule here, should they wish, it cannot be presented as a fact about the nature or essence of love. Of course, the desirability of multiple love does not follow from its possibility.

I have tried in this paper to sketch some conceptual features of love and to illustrate the role these features, and pictures of these features, play in judgments about personal relations. And if my account of the case studies is at all plausible, coming to accept a philosophical analysis of the concept of love may bear on how we think about our personal relations and may, in affecting how we think about them, affect the state of the relationship itself, though the affects are unlikely to be of a Sartrian magnitude. The variability in possible conceptions of love has ruled out the sort of precise and determinate conceptual relations that philosophers are prone to seek. Because of this indeterminacy, how one must (conceptually) think about love drifts imperceptibly into how one does generally think about love. Crossing this boundary can give rise to the worst sort of arm-chair psychology. But then to shy away from the boundary for fear of crossing is not entirely satisfactory either.

One final, and perhaps pessimistic, note. To show that an analysis of love is relevant to practical dealings in personal relations, would not in any way demonstrate that beneficial results would accrue for the lover or the beloved from the utilization of such knowledge. Ibsenian life lies may be productive of the greater happiness.[6]

NOTES

An obvious debt of gratitude is owed to all those who participated in the discussions that led to this essay. I would like especially to thank Derek Parfit, Alan Montefiore and my wife for many stimulating discussions.

1. Some beginnings towards such an explication can be found in Thomas Nagel's paper, 'Sexual Perversion,' *Journal of Philosophy*, 66, 1969, pp. 5–17.

2. E. A. Gellner, 'Ethics and Logic,' *Proceedings of the Aristotelian Society*, 55, 1955, pp. 157–78.

3. In this regard see Erich Fromm's *The Art of Loving*, London, Allen & Unwin, 1957 and José Ortega y Gasset's *On Love. . . . Aspects of a Single Theme*, trans. Toby Talbot, London, Jonathan Cape, 1967.

4. L. Wittgenstein, *Zettel*, Berkeley, University of California Press, 1967, p. 89e.

5. Gellner, op. cit., p. 159.

6. Since this paper was written I have come to regard this account of love as in many ways too simplistic.

THE PHENOMENA OF
LOVE AND HATE

D. W. Hamlyn

THERE HAS BEEN a good deal of interest in recent years in what Franz Brentano had to say about the notion of 'intentional objects' and about intentionality as a criterion of the mental. There has been less interest in his classification of mental phenomena. In his *Psychology from an Empirical Standpoint* Brentano asserts and argues for the thesis that mental phenomena can be classified in terms of three kinds of mental act or activity, all of which are directed towards an immanent object. These are, respectively, presentation, judgment and what he calls the phenomena of love and hate. Once again, less interest has been shown in what he has to say about the last of these three than in what he says about the others. I wish to take Brentano's views as the point of departure for a discussion of love and hate, since these notions seem to me to have a good deal of philosophical interest, for at least two main reasons. First, I have recently had some concern with the part that personal relations play in our understanding of others and of ourselves, and love and hate seem to be very important elements in such relations. Second, love and hate have long seemed to me to provide important counter-examples

This essay appeared in *Philosophy* 53 (1978), pp. 5–20. Copyright © The Royal Institute of Philosophy 1978. Reprinted with the permission of Cambridge University Press and D. W. Hamlyn. David Walter Hamlyn was the editor of *Mind*, 1972–84, and Professor of Philosophy, Birkbeck College, The University of London. This paper was presented as the Marett Memorial Lecture (1976) at Exeter College, Oxford. More of Professor Hamlyn's view of love can be found in his book *Perception, Learning and the Self* (1983). (For a brief reply to this essay, see C. H. Whiteley, "Love, Hate and Emotion," *Philosophy* 54 (1979), p. 235.)

to some prevalent philosophical theories about the emotions. I shall take this issue first.

It would not be a plausible move to defend any theory of the emotions to which love and hate seemed exceptions by saying that love and hate are after all not emotions. I have heard this said, but it does seem to me a desperate move to make. If love and hate are not emotions what is? Brentano himself adopts a position which is even further away from that reaction by saying that all emotions involve love and hate. In considering the third of his classifications of mental phenomena he argues that the class includes both feeling and will, but in such a way that they constitute a unity. Feeling, he wants to say, is not merely something passive that happens to us. Even feelings such as those of pleasure and pain involve desires and wants on our part—the willing of the phenomenon to go on in the one case or the willing of it to stop in the other. Hence there are no such things as mere feelings which do not involve some aspect of the will. On the other hand the willing of a phenomenon involves some definite kind of feeling towards it, the sort of feeling that is involved in a desire or an aversion. Brentano concludes, therefore, that feeling and will are united into a single fundamental class, and he argues against other philosopher-psychologists of his time who denied this. He thinks that what unites the phenomena of this class is precisely the role of love and hate in providing the focus for whatever else is involved. Love is in that respect a kind of positive feeling towards an object which is *ipso facto* through the desire that it involves an aspect of the will. The converse is true of hate. If there are other features in any given emotion, one or other of love and hate provides a focus for that emotion. So far, then, from love and hate not being emotions, they are the central core of all emotions; or at least one or the other is.

It might be said that this account stretches our ordinary understanding of the concepts of love and hate, and Brentano faces up to that objection himself (op. cit., London: Routledge and Kegan Paul, 1973, p. 199). I do not wish to approach that issue head on, although considerations that are relevant to it will emerge later. But what of the relation of love and hate to the other classifications of mental phenomena? These classifications are made in terms of 'the different ways in which they refer to their content' (ibid., p. 197). In presentation something is presented to consciousness, and this can be one of a considerable range of things from sensations to thoughts. In judgment, by contrast, there is involved acceptance as true or rejection as false, while in the third category there are the attitudes of love and hate. Brentano believes that in any complete act of consciousness all three of these elements will be included. There is no logical necessity for this to be so, however, and we can conceive of presentation without judgment or feeling, and we can conceive of judgment without any attitude of love or hate. There is nevertheless a logical ordering in the other direction. We cannot conceive, he thinks, of judgment taking place without presentation, nor of love or hate taking place without both presentation and judgment. So he says (ibid., p. 267):

> It is certainly not necessary that someone believe that a thing exists or is even capable of existing, in order for him to love it, but, nonetheless, every act of love is loving the existence of something. And one love would never arouse another, one thing would never be loved for the sake of another, unless there were a belief in certain connections between the one and the other which played some part. An act of love will be one of joy on some occasions, sorrow on others, or hope or fear or any number of other forms, depending upon what judgment is made concerning the existence or non-existence, probability or improbability of the object loved. In fact, then, it seems inconceivable that a being should be endowed with the capacity for love and hate without possessing that of judgment.

Brentano's conclusion is weaker than one might have expected from the earlier part of this passage. For he concludes, not that every case of love and hate involves a belief, but that any being that can love and hate must be capable of judgment. That conclusion is, I think, true, although the considerations that he brings forward in its favor are scarcely compelling; for they seem to suggest only that *some* forms of love and hate and *some* phenomena connected with them presuppose judgment. However, if an argument *can* be brought forward for the thesis that only a creature that can have judgment or beliefs can love and hate, it will have to be a much more complex argument than the one that Brentano actually adduces. Such a thesis is nevertheless very different from the thesis that love and hate themselves necessarily involve belief or judgment. It is a thesis of this latter kind about the emotions in general that has become something of the current orthodoxy, even if there are some exceptions to this. In modern times the thesis goes back at least to Errol Bedford's well-known paper on the 'Emotions' (PAS 1956/57, pp. 281 ff., and reprinted many times), but it is a thesis that was maintained in ancient times by the Stoics, who held, for example, that greed was a false belief in the importance of money.

Let me give a general description of this thesis about the emotions—a description which is, I hope, not a caricature. It is possible to begin with a consideration that is close to something that Brentano has to say, and which is a cardinal feature of most recent philosophical accounts of the emotions—that the emotions take objects and that the range of possible objects of this kind must be restricted in some way. Emotions take objects not just in the sense that there is some actual object on to which the emotion is directed; indeed this need not be so at all since the person concerned may be under a delusion on this point.

There must nevertheless be (with qualifications to be made directly) something which the person takes as such, something that is *for him* an object of his emotion. This is what Brentano was getting at in speaking of the necessity for an immanent object in this case. Thus if we experience pride it must be pride *in* something, in something that is the object of the pride for us whether or not it actually exists. Analogously, we cannot be said to experience envy unless we are envious *of* something (and normally perhaps *for* something). We cannot be said just to be proud or envious except in the sense of those words in which we indicate a character-trait; and the connection of character-traits with emotions in the straightforward sense is a complex matter which need not concern us now.

It is not necessary that the object be explicit to us in that the person concerned must be capable of spelling it out. I can be envious of something without being able to say explicitly what it is that I am envious of. The fact that I cannot do this, however, does not in itself preclude whatever I am in fact envious of being an object of envy for me. There can be other forms of consciousness apart from the explicit consciousness which is involved in the ability to spell things out. But there must be something which is for me the object of my envy, the object of my consciousness in this connection in some way or other. Indeed some philosophers have made this a criterion for distinguishing between emotions and moods; in the latter case we may be in an analogous state of mind, but this need not be directed on to anything explicit, even if it may be caused by something explicit. At the best it may be possible to say of a mood that its object is 'anything or nothing,' or perhaps 'everything.' There are however some emotional states, if I may call them that, which are ambiguous in this respect, e.g. joy, happiness and depression. We may take joy in something, be happy about something, or be depressed at or about something, but it is not necessary that this reference to an object should be there; we can be simply joyous, happy or depressed, in a way that is characteristic of moods.

I have been speaking of the sense in which it is true that emotions must take objects, to the extent that they must. As I suggested earlier, these objects must be restricted in some way. One cannot, for example, take pride in *anything*. There is a sense in which this is true, but one needs to be careful over it. If it were said that one cannot *fear* anything, it might well be replied that there are surely no bounds to human irrationality, or that if there are they are certainly very wide. We might say of some object that no rational person could be afraid of it. If this were true, it would not follow that it was also true that no *human being* could be afraid of it, let alone that there is some logical or conceptual impossibility in being afraid of it. People have irrational fears about many sorts of object that others cannot understand their being afraid of; that however does not amount to its being unintelligible that one should speak of such fears. What is taken as unintelligible is that *they* should feel the fear; it is not that speaking of the fear is logically absurd. If there are things which it is humanly impossible to fear, to speak of someone fearing them involves a *kind* of absurdity, but not a logical absurdity in the strict sense.

However that may be, it remains the case that even in the case of irrational fears the people concerned must find something about the object to be afraid of, even if they cannot say what this is. The position is perhaps even clearer with pride. I cannot take pride in something if it has nothing to do with me. A person can be proud of his achievements, of his children's achievements, or of his country's achievements. It would be odd for him to be proud of his failures or the failures of others who have some connection with him. To justify the intelligibility of that a very special explanation would be required, although one cannot exclude the possibility that one of that kind may be forthcoming; people do sometimes want to fail. What, however, if I have no connection with the object in a way that would make it intelligible for me to have such concerns with it in one way or the other? Can I, to use an example used by others, be proud of the sea? One might at first blush feel like saying 'No,' but that answer would presuppose that the sea has nothing to do with me, not only in the sense that I have in fact nothing to do with *it*, but also in the sense that I do not even *believe* that I have anything to do with it. If someone irrationally believes that he has some responsibility for the sea being as it is, nothing prevents its being said of him that he is proud of it. We should feel that his pride was quite irrational, but that is because the supporting belief is irrational; and without that we might not even understand the attribution of pride at all. This reference to belief brings us back to Brentano.

It brings us back to Brentano because the position arrived at seems to agree with his remarks concerning the extent to which an emotion presupposes some kind of supporting belief. On reflection, however, it may seem that 'belief' is too strong a word to use here. Those who have an irrational fear of mice may in one sense have all the right beliefs about mice. They may know that mice are too small and too harmless in any direct way to be frightening, and whatever view one has about the relation between knowledge and belief it seems right to say that they believe this too—in an intellectual way at least. It may remain true, however, that whatever their intellectual beliefs about mice may be, they cannot help seeing them in practice as frightening little creatures. There is a conflict between their full-blooded rational beliefs about mice and how they see them and cannot help seeing them in concrete circumstances. It might be said that in such a case there is simply a conflict of beliefs, but to insist on this would be misleading. How one sees things may be a function of one's beliefs in a variety of ways; it may, however, be a function of other things, and it is certainly not true that whenever one sees something as such and such one has *ipso facto* a belief to that effect. There are perceptual illusions, e.g. the Müller-Lyer illusion, where one sees things in a certain way whatever one's beliefs about them may be; one's seeing them in that way *may*, in some cases at least, be explicable in terms of beliefs that one has, and it may be that one would not be able to see them in that way if one did not have beliefs, but that does not mean that when one sees them in that way one does have beliefs to the same effect. There is what has been called non-epistemic seeing in that way at least. The same applies to seeing mice as frightening. That may be a function of beliefs, but the seeing need not be believing.

It might be replied that the seeing does in this case have consequences both in action and in feeling. There need be no such consequences when one is subject to the Müller-Lyer illusion, so that there is a difference. That seems true. In view of the consequences of the seeing in this case it may be right to say that whether or not one actually believes that mice are frightening when one is frightened by them one certainly has an inclination to believe this. Yet it remains true that to have a given emotional attitude to an object, or at least an emotional attitude of the kind so far surveyed, one has either to have a certain sort of belief about that object or to see it in the corresponding way, whether or not that belief or way of seeing it is in fact justified. If we cannot say simply that a person cannot feel pride in something that has nothing to do with him, we must say that he cannot feel pride in it if he does not have the corresponding belief or at least see it in that light. If none of this is true, then whatever he feels about the object it is not pride.

The question that now arises—which brings me to my main topic—is about the extent to which this applies also to love and hate. Like Brentano I shall for convenience apply myself mainly to love, although most if not all of what I have to say applies equally to hate. (I shall introduce some qualifications to this later.) Love and hate are to that extent parallel emotions. They are also both positive attitudes, not simply such that one is the negation of the other. Brentano rightly emphasizes that point, and, more arguably, goes on to contrast the phenomena of love and hate with, e.g., judgment, in the case of which he thinks of rejection simply as the negation of affirmation; this is arguable in the light of the possibility of simple withholding of belief. However, no one could plausibly say that hate was simply the withholding of love. Hence if any theory about love carries over to hate it is not because the one is simply the negation or privation of the other, but because the two really do constitute parallel attitudes for these purposes.

The first thing to note about love is that it is, as one might put it, a very 'catholic' emotion; it takes many forms and takes many kinds of object, and it would be a mistake to ignore or underestimate that fact. It may be that reason alone which makes Brentano give love and hate such pre-eminent importance among the emotions. Let us take first the forms that love can take. At one extreme it is almost a mood; I mean by this to refer to the state of being in love. It is of course true that when someone is in love they are normally in love with someone or something. Cynics might say however that in some cases where someone is in love the object is, as it were, found or invented for the state rather than the other way round, and that this is often a precondition for what we call infatuation. Such a view is not just cynicism; there is the state of readiness for an infatuation. Whether one is prepared to dignify it itself with the title of love is a matter for argument. That is why I say that at this extreme love is *almost* a mood; it is simply that in this state *what* the object is may be of less importance than that there should be one to match the state.

At the other extreme love may at least approximate to an attitude which we can adopt pretty much at will. This seems to be implied by the fact that we may sometimes be instructed to love someone or something, and that loving someone or something may be set up as a principle of action, as it is in the command that we should love our neighbor. Such love is near to simple benevolence, to wishing someone well, and if we cannot adopt such an attitude quite at will, we can certainly take measures to get ourselves into the position of doing so. Brentano associates love with willing something as good, and I take it that he has this kind of love in mind. His way of putting it also has one advantage over a reference to benevolence or wishing someone well. This is that these latter terms may be taken, and often *are* taken, as referring to an attitude of mind which need have no implications for action. When we are told to love our neighbor we are not told simply to have nice and perhaps comfortable thoughts about him or her—as might indeed be implied by the reference to *wishing*; the principle is supposed to be a principle for action and conduct (though what action is notoriously difficult to determine in many cases—a principle like that of 'Love thy neighbor' does not, if adopted, obviate the necessity for difficult moral decisions). If the state of being in love is merely *near* to being a mood and not simply identical with one, the positive attitude of love is *near* to willing some course of action and not simply identical with it. It remains true that these two things represent extremes which are separated from each other by a considerable distance, and this fact about love is worthy of note and must not be ignored in any theory about it.

The other point about love that I was going to mention is about the range of possible objects that it can take. I have spoken of loving someone *or something*. I did so quite deliberately. To emphasize that there can be different forms of love between people would be to underline a cliché. It perhaps requires a little more emphasis that there can be love of objects too. It is obvious enough that people can love beautiful objects, particularly works of art; but they can also love quite ordinary things which have no pretensions to aesthetic value, e.g. possessions. Moreover there does not have to be any very close relation between the lover and what is loved, whether that be a person or a thing. Love at a distance is certainly possible, although it is less and less possible to the extent that the person or object is or must be out of mind. It might be objected that all this simply serves to show that the word 'love' is just ambiguous, and that it means something different as applied to people and as applied to things. I am not sure that I know how exactly to reply to such an objection, except to point to the considerations about love that I shall bring forward in the sequel. It can be said now, however, that if the objection held exactly the same thing would have to apply to various forms of love between persons (sexual love as opposed to parental love and so on), since there are differences between these which are as large as those between love of persons and love of things. In the history of thought many distinctions between forms of love have been made (*eros*, *philia* and *agape*; Aphrodite Urania and Aphrodite Pandemos; sacred and profane love, etc.), but these differences have not usually been thought of as constituting an ambiguity in the word 'love.' That there are differences between forms of love and that the nature of the object may affect the possibility of given forms of love in relation to it remains obviously true.

Given all this, the question that I now wish to raise is this: if one does love X, what beliefs must one have about X, and how must one see or regard X if it is really to be love? For, if love is to be parallel to emotions like pride and fear, it follows from what I have said earlier about those emotions that there must be an analogous answer to this question in its case. The lover must value the beloved in some way, but in what way? In particular, must the lover love the beloved *for* anything (for if so it seems to follow that he must have a belief about the object in that respect or at least see the beloved in that way)? There are no doubt some things about which it might be felt that they could be loved *only* for some specific reason. But this would again be a point about human nature and not a point of logic. W. B. Yeats' poem 'For Anne Gregory,' for example, presents the case of someone who, the poet says, could not be loved by human beings except for the color of her hair, even though the woman wants to be loved 'for herself alone.' (In the first of the three stanzas the 'poet' says:

> Never shall a young man,
> Thrown into despair
> By those great honey-coloured
> Ramparts at your ear,
> Love you for yourself alone
> And not your yellow hair.

The woman replies in the second stanza by saying in effect that she can dye her hair and then they may love her for herself alone and not her yellow hair. But the last verse reads:

I heard an old religious man
But yesterday declare
That he had found a text to prove
That only God, my dear,
Could love you for yourself alone
And not your yellow hair.

There seem to me, incidentally, to be certain defects in the argument, which I shall not go into, but I do not hold them against the poem as such!) If it were true that she could not be loved except for the color of her hair, this would have to be, once again, a fact of human nature, not a point of logic. It does not seem logically absurd that she should be loved full-stop. (This may not be what the woman in the poem wants when she speaks of being loved for herself alone, but there is a good deal of difficulty in that idea in any case. What I shall say later may have some bearing on it.)

To be loved full-stop is simply to be loved without there being anything that the love is for. In such a situation there is likely to be some explanation why the love came into being, and it is possible with some objects of love for one to love them for the fact that and because of the circumstances in which the love came into being; but there seems to me no necessity that it should be like that—the circumstances may explain the continuance of the love but they may not be what the love is for. I suggest that love is possible where there is nothing that the love is for—or at any rate that nothing logically prevents that possibility. I confess that I have not yet *shown* that it is a possibility. I wish to move in that direction by a consideration of the range of possible attitudes to the object of love that are compatible with that love. That will at least show what beliefs if any are necessary to love.

What I have to say may seem somewhat dogmatic, but I mean to appeal simply to common convictions on the matter, and if the convictions are not shared further argument will inevitably be called for. It seems to me that loving someone or something is not incompatible with, for example, having no respect for them, finding them in many ways distasteful, or recognizing in them a whole series of bad qualities which are not overridden by good qualities. Love, one might say, is to some extent at least a contingent thing; one cannot always explain why and where it falls. It might be objected that it must at least be true that the lover desires the beloved, wants to be with him/her/it, or something of that kind. I am not sure that even this *has* to be true. Suppose that someone has got to the point of recognizing the absolutely disastrous character of a relationship. It is possible for them to renounce it and any desire for its continuance while still loving the person concerned. Some indeed (including, I suspect, Kierkegaard) have made a virtue of this, although it is no part of the phenomenon that it must have that character.

In the face of all this it is very difficult to think of any particular belief that the lover *must* have about the beloved, or any way in which the lover must see the beloved. It might be objected that even if no single particular belief is necessary one or more of some disjunction of beliefs may be, and that if this were not so love and hate could not be differentiated. I am not sure how to reply to the first part of this objection, except to say that considerations similar to those which rule out the necessity for particular beliefs will in the end rule out the suggestion about a disjunction of beliefs. In any case, it is not necessary to resort to this suggestion because of the need to differentiate love and hate, since they may be differentiated by factors other than beliefs. Moreover, it has often been pointed out that while love and hate are opposed for the most part they may in their extreme forms and in their most primitive manifestations be very close together. Passionate love may turn easily into hate without any beliefs changing at the same time and without the change being due to any newly acquired beliefs, however much different beliefs may follow in due course. If love and hate are not differentiated by beliefs they need not be determined by them either.

I suggest, then, that no particular belief or disjunction of beliefs about the beloved is necessary on the part of the lover, nor any particular ways of seeing the beloved. There is of course what might be looked on as a possible exception to this rule—the trivial fact that he or she must see the beloved as an object for love. Brentano said that 'it is certainly not necessary that someone believe that a thing exists or is even capable of existing, in order for him to love it, but, none the less, every act of love is loving the existence of something.' I take it that what he means by 'loving the existence of something' is what I was trying to get at in speaking of seeing the beloved as an object for love. If this is a belief it is not one that provides any answer to the question what the lover loves the beloved for. It is as a belief a merely formal condition of the possibility of love—that the love must have an object. But this presupposes the other point which I believe to be true in what Brentano says—that love is possible only for a believer, or at least only for one who is capable of seeing something *as* something, i.e. in this case as an object of love. (I shall for the sake of convenience ignore the distinction between belief and seeing-as in what follows, as indeed I may have done already; where the distinction is relevant it can be read into my discussion.) Given all this, it might be argued that if I have shown anything it is that no particular kind of belief *about* the object is necessary for love or hate, but not that belief is unnecessary altogether. That would be fair comment, but the conclusion is enough for my purposes.

It is enough because that conclusion by no means entails that love and hate necessarily have particular beliefs as constituents which determine that they are love or hate, let alone that they must be founded on beliefs. As Brentano points out, one *may* love one thing for the sake of another, and in that case the love is certainly founded on the belief that this thing is connected appropriately with that. But it is not always like that. With pride and envy, on the other hand, belief (or seeing-as) *is* a constituent of the emotion in the sense in question, since to experience them one must not only see the thing in question merely as an object for the emotion, one must see it in a way that is appropriate to the emotion. With love the difficulty is to find anything of this kind which is uniquely appropriate to love. My thesis is that there is nothing of this kind that *must* be so, and that this differentiates it and hate from the other emotions. One might indeed argue, as Brentano does, that the other emotions presuppose love or hate in some way. If this is true (and it may well be so) love and hate would best be characterized as 'feelings towards,' and would be the primary forms of these. As such feelings they are not just passive states that are produced in us, as pains may be, but something that also involves an attitude, a directedness towards an object, as Brentano suggested.

There is a tendency within the philosophy of mind, which may be a residual legacy of Cartesianism and reactions to it, to divide the phenomena of the human mind into two classes—the first being the class of mental states that more or less occur to us and have a certain passivity, the second being the manifestations of our capacity for judgment and other intellectual activity. Thus we have a contrast between feeling and cognition. But in this sense, feeling remains something that just happens to us. Even in Descartes, of course, feelings were thought of as modifications of thought in the sense that the capacity for feeling, which involves the body, is dependent on the existence of the capacity for thinking, which involves the soul. This dependence is a function of the quasi-substantial union between soul and body, of which Descartes thought no account could be given. This general picture has been undermined in all sorts of ways, largely through the writings of Wittgenstein, which has produced for obvious reasons an emphasis on the philosophy of action and its relevance for the philosophy of mind in general. It has thus come to be seen, for example, that the notion of intention does not fit easily into that original position, even if it is intimately connected with the notion of action. In the case of the emotions, however, there is a less obvious connection with forms of action, even if we expect them to find some overt expression in many cases. Thus, given this last recognition together with the recognition that feelings as passive states do not provide a sufficient basis for differentiation between different emotions, recourse has been had to judgment or belief for this purpose, this being the remaining factor in our legacy.

Brentano's 'intentionality' thesis, that mentality involves an intention of the mind, a directedness towards certain objects, constitutes a departure from that legacy to some extent. Even here, however, more attention has been given perhaps to the nature of those objects (their 'inexistence') than to the idea involved in the reference to directedness. Thus one interpretation of or gloss on the Brentano thesis, that all mental phenomena involve a thought (cf. R. A. Wollheim, *PAS*, 1967/68, pp. 1–24), in a way goes back towards the Cartesian position; it certainly leaves out the suggestion that feeling, *qua* feeling, may be directed towards an object. What I have said about love and hate amounts to the suggestion that these be considered as feeling towards objects in just this sense. Moreover it seems to me that it is logically possible at least for these 'feelings towards' to exist without any intimate connections between these feelings and any beliefs on the part of the person concerned of the sort that certainly seem requisite for many emotions. If, however, the objects of these feelings are to be objects in anything more than a purely formal sense, those objects must be identifiable in some way; and that certainly presupposes beliefs on the part of the person concerned. Hence, nothing that could be identified as such a feeling could take place in a creature that did not have beliefs. That, however, does not entail that the feelings necessarily involve beliefs as constituents or as the basis for the feelings.

I said that I had two reasons for being concerned with the subject—one of them being the relation of love and hate to other emotions and the implications that this has generally for philosophical theories in this area. My conclusion on this lies in what I have said about 'feelings towards.' I do not know whether it is right to say, as Brentano did, that the other emotions involve love and hate; a more acceptable thesis would be that they all involve 'feelings towards,' and that love and hate are particularly pure versions of these because of their possible detachment from particular beliefs. One might therefore say that they constitute the paradigm cases of such feelings, and have an importance for that reason, if for no other. The other reason that I gave for being concerned with the subject was the part that love and hate play in personal relations, especially given the part that these in turn play in our understanding of others and of ourselves. I wish now to say something about this second issue, in so far as what I have already said affects it.

My main point can be put as follows: I have paid some attention to the possibility of love being independent of reasons (whether or not there is a reason for it in the sense of a cause). This seems to me a logical possibility and even a human possibility in the sense that it is intelligible in human beings at any rate as an isolated phenomenon. But it would be odd if it were always like that. Personal relations no doubt involve feeling, but they are not just a matter of one person having feelings of some kind towards another, to which that other responds in kind. There is not enough that is human in that, and it may well be true that that description is satisfied by animals or some of them. Where it is a thing that is the object of love, there may have been reasons in the first place why the person concerned had a love for it, reasons that may have ceased to apply and which are now not even up for consideration. Nevertheless, the fondness for it may remain without the person knowing why, let alone being able to say why (at the bottom, so to speak, the love may remain out of habit, but I am not suggesting that this is necessarily the case). Others may feel that there is a certain touching irrationality in this, and it may even be irritating to those with whom he or she lives. But it need have no consequences beyond that. The same could not be said of a similar love for a person, and the person loved would have the right to demand more.

Why is this? In the case of a loved thing, it can remain simply an object of contemplation, something that the person likes to handle, or perhaps use as a tool when other instruments would do the job as well or better. If this were true of the loved person he or she would rightly feel used. The love in this case must have more consequences and implications than that. The reason for this lies in what it is to be a person and in what, *given that*, it is for a person to be an appropriate object of another person's love.

It may be useful at this point to revert to a consideration of hate. A person's hatred of an object may sometimes be set down as a mere quirk, at any rate if that hatred does not impinge on more human concerns. In that case the only place to look for an explanation of the hate, if one is required, is in something about the person himself, not in any general significance that the object may have that makes hate appropriate. An animal's hatred of something or of another animal may be like this more generally; what can only be described as an attitude of hate may be called out quite generally by an object of a certain type, e.g. another animal in its territory. In that case an explanation of the phenomenon must make reference to the nature of the animal, its genetic make-up and the function that the attitude of this kind has for the preservation of the species; it is not a matter of the precise significance that this particular thing has for the animal in question. It would thus be out of place to speak of the animal's reasons for hating whatever it is. When this happens as an isolated phenomenon in human beings we tend, as I have said, to set it down as a mere quirk. When it happens quite generally and in an extreme way in human beings we tend to reach for the category of the psychopath; for it is part of the psychology of such a person that such emotional attitudes as he has are unrelated to any range of appropriate objects. If there is any relationship between object and attitude it is causal only, and to that extent, although to that extent alone, the situation is like that which holds good over the animals that I have mentioned. There are, however, differences in at least two respects; (a) the causal connection is without evolutionary significance, and (b) intellectual functioning remains even if detached from emotion.

In normal human cases neither of these things is true in that way, and if we find the hatred intelligible it is because it is directed to an object which falls within the range of objects appropriate to that attitude. I do not use the word 'appropriate' here in any moral sense. It is not that there are certain things that we ought to hate and others that we ought not. It is rather that we should have no clear understanding of what hatred was in a normal human being if we did not know something of what sort of thing is normally an object of hatred for such a being. In consequence, if we think of some range of objects as appropriate kinds of object for hatred it is because this fits in with our conception of the place that hatred has in a human life. What hatred is is not something that could be learnt simply from the consideration of a set of behavioral manifestations; we have to understand its wider significance for normal human beings, and we attribute hatred to animals to the extent that they approximate to what holds good of human beings (there are clearly some animals in the case of which speaking of hatred makes no sense). Hence while hatred of something without reason or anything that would count as such is possible in a human being, we should have a very different conception of human beings were it always or even generally like that; such beings would not be human beings as we understand them. Our concept here brings with it a set of normal expectations, so that to fall short of the norm is progressively to manifest a case where our concept has no sensible application. Hatred without reason or anything that might count as such is something that can occur in human beings as an isolated phenomenon, but where it manifests itself frequently the word 'inhuman' progressively comes to mind. In that event we tend to look for the explanation of the hatred elsewhere than in the place that the hatred and its object have in the person's life.

Similar things apply to love except that while hatred without reason (and therefore without the beliefs involved in having a reason) may, if persistent, have dire consequences, we may expect love without reason, even if persistent, to be little more than irritating, if that. Even this need not be so; the case of someone being dragged down to some ill fate by someone else's infatuation is not *that* uncommon. Nevertheless, it is reasonable to expect hatred to have, as a rule, more obvious bad consequences than love can have, simply because of the obvious behavioral connections that hatred may have, even if they do not follow of necessity. Correspondingly, it is perhaps more difficult to think of a love as being inhuman than so to think of hatred; even so I do not think that the idea can be ruled out as senseless. Conversely, while we speak of falling in love, there is no similar expression in common usage which signifies falling in hate. It may be that this is because the possibility is not one that we like to think of because of its possible consequences. It is similarly difficult to think of hatred as the basis of a personal relationship, although it would be wrong not to admit the possibility. These asymmetries exist between love and hate. It remains true that, in a way parallel to that which holds good over hatred, where the love is unrelated to any of those objects that we feel to be appropriate in a human being, or where it has no constancy in that regard, we look for the explanation elsewhere than in the sense that the love has within the person's life. In its extreme form we feel perhaps some of this in connection with falling in love, except that, as I said earlier, there is a tendency for people to *find* objects for their love in some such cases. Nevertheless, if a person discovers that he is the object of someone else's love in *that* way he may reasonably feel that he can object—unless of course he has some other reason for accepting the situation. For, he or she may declare, the person in question has not *learnt* to see them with love. It has either come about causally or come about by a chance of fate given a background of such causality. I mean by this that the explanation of the state of being in love will be causal, and that the explanation of their being the object of the love will either be similarly causal or come about by chance.

The idea of learning to love that I have invoked here is important, although it needs careful handling. I was recently involved as a juror in a case in which it was said of the defendant by a medical witness that he had not learnt to love. Yet it was also said of him (and it was clear that it was *truly* said of him) that his whole life was directed towards others; he lived *through* others. At the same time and at the other extreme he had an excessive passion for certain things beyond what most people would probably feel reasonable. 'He had not learnt to love'—but it was clear that his feelings towards certain things and certain people were very strong indeed (the judge said that he was possessive). The point of saying that he had not learnt to love was presumably that he had not learnt to love things and people in such a way that his life had a coherent sense in relation to them. And part of that sense was a matter of what he was to others as well as what they were to him; for the sense of a life is not determined simply by what holds good solely of the person whose life it is. Learning to love is a matter of learning to see objects in appropriate ways, i.e. ways that are appropriate to that love, and when those objects are other people that involves seeing how you are to them as well as how they are to you. It involves seeing them as other persons in the relation and not *just* as objects.

It might be thought that a failure to do this is just what is suggested in speaking of someone as possessive (as the judge did of the defendant); that is to say that it might be thought that in being possessive a person treats another simply as an object which he owns and can therefore treat as he wishes. That may sometimes be the case, but it is by no means always or necessarily so. It may simply be the case that the person concerned sees the other as closer to him than they actually are. This may indeed involve error, but error of a different order from that involved where someone treats another as an object that he owns; and it is not incompatible with a kind of love, while the other case, it might be argued, is. There is a connected point about jealousy, which is often thought to be incompatible with love and to involve possessiveness. I am not here concerned with whether jealousy is ever justified, since I have not been concerned with the justification of attitudes, but rather with the conditions for their intelligibility. I *do* in fact think that jealousy is sometimes justified, but the question whether one is ever justified in being jealous is quite different from the question whether being jealous is compatible with love proper. As far as concerns this second question the answer seems to me that it *can* be so compatible, in so far as love for a person by no means implies seeing that person as someone who can be quite independent of the relationship. But if someone has learnt to love in the full sense he will have learnt what the relationship is.

Hence, it is likely that if someone has not learnt to love he will not be able to form, except by chance, stable relationships. And one, though only one, reason for this may be a failure to see what it is for both himself and others to be appropriate parties to such a relationship. If the love has no connection with anything else, with a way of seeing others and oneself that fits coherently with that love, it is likely to be an inadequate foundation for a relationship. What I am trying to get at here is not possessiveness, but something that may be described as a lack of coherence in attitudes. Perhaps 'coherence' is not the best word to use. What I mean is this: a person who has not learnt to love is not one who has simply not developed 'feelings towards,' but rather one who has not learnt to have feelings towards the sort of objects and in the sort of way that human life involves if it is to have a sense for those living it. This involves the person not seeing himself and others in the kind of relationships that will promote those 'feelings towards' and encourage their persistence in a way that has sense for those concerned.

None of this need apply to love of mere objects (although it has some application on the other hand to hatred of people—one *can* learn to hate some people, and, conceivably, rightly). I do not mean that there is no place for speaking of learning to love certain objects, e.g. works of art. Rather this does not have the same implications for the conduct and course of our lives. Once again, this shows why, while someone might build his life on feelings towards objects of certain kinds without feeling the need to explain to others or to himself why he has those feelings, this would not be *generally* possible with other people as the objects of those feelings.

Finally, let me say again that I have not been concerned in this with the question of the justifiability of the attitudes or emotions of love and hate. What I have said does not rule out the possibility of such justification, but neither does it speak for it. Certainly love and hate can be considered rational when their objects have certain appropriate qualities, and to that extent they can be considered justified; but if such qualities do not exist in their objects love and hate are not necessarily and for that reason to be considered irrational, even if they are, so to speak, non-rational. My concern has been rather with the limits to the intelligibility of speaking of love and hate where beliefs about their objects are missing. My conclusion is that while love and hate need not involve any beliefs—and may thus be non-epistemic—human love and hate could not universally be like that. There is a certain parallel here with the case of perception. As numerous philosophers, e.g. Dretske, have urged, there is such a thing as non-epistemic perception, cases where to perceive something does not entail believing anything about it. But perception could not be uniformly non-epistemic, or it could not conceivably provide any foundation for our beliefs about the knowledge of the world. Our understanding of the concept of perception presupposes for this reason an understanding of the place that perception has in our life in relation to the world in which we live, and thus an understanding of the relation of perception to our general beliefs about the world. There is a similar point about love and hate. I concluded earlier that 'feelings towards' were possible only for believers even if they did not involve beliefs themselves. In the sequel I have tried to say something about the ways in which love and hate relate to beliefs about or ways of seeing their objects if they are to have sense for those involved. It is only against this background that non-epistemic love and hate, as they might be called, can, as with non-epistemic perception, be given intelligibility.

MARITAL FAITHFULNESS

Susan Mendus

> And so the two swore that at every time of their lives, until death took
> them, they would assuredly believe, feel and desire exactly as they
> had believed, felt and desired during the preceding weeks. What was
> as remarkable as the undertaking itself was the fact that nobody
> seemed at all surprised at what they swore. [1]

CYNICISM ABOUT the propriety of
the marriage promise has been widespread amongst philosophers and laymen
alike for many years. Traditionally, the ground for suspicion has been the belief
that the marriage promise is a promise about feelings where these are not
directly under the control of the will. G. E. Moore gives expression to this view
when he remarks that 'to love certain people, or to feel no anger against them,
is a thing which it is quite impossible to attain directly by the will' and
concludes therefore that the commandment to love your neighbor as yourself
cannot possibly be a statement of your duty, 'all that can possibly be true is that
it would be your duty if you were able.' [2] Thus, as Mary Midgley has pointed
out, Moore invests the commandment with 'about as much interest for us as a
keep-fit manual would have for paraplegics.' [3] Moore's sentiments would presumably be endorsed by Russell, who tells of how his love for his wife
'evaporated' during the course of a bicycle ride. He simply 'realized,' he says,
that he no longer loved her and was subsequently unable to show any affection
for her. [4] This, anyway, is the most familiar objection to the marriage promise:
that it is a promise about feelings, where these are not directly under the control
of the will.

A second objection to the marriage promise is that it involves a commitment
which extends over too long a period: promising to do something next Wednes-

---

This essay appeared in *Philosophy* 59 (1984), pp. 243–52. Copyright © The Royal Institute of
Philosophy, 1984. Reprinted with the permission of Cambridge University Press and Susan Mendus.
Susan Mendus is Lecturer in Philosophy, The University of York, and the author of *Toleration and the
Limits of Liberty* (1988).

day is one thing, promising to do something fifty years hence is quite another, and it is thought to be improper either to give or to extract promises extending over such a long period of time. This second objection has found recent philosophical favor in the writings of Derek Parfit. In 'Later Selves and Moral Principles' Parfit refers to those who believe that only short-term promises can carry moral weight and counts it a virtue of his theory of personal identity that it 'supports' or 'helps to explain' that belief. [5]

Here I shall not discuss Parfit's theory of personal identity as such, but only the plausibility of the consequent claim that short-term promises alone carry moral weight: for it is the supposed intuitive plausibility of the latter which Parfit appeals to in defence of his theory of personal identity. If, therefore, the belief that only short-term promises carry moral weight can be undermined, that will serve, indirectly, to undermine any theory of personal identity which supports it.

Claiming that long-term promises do not carry any moral weight seems to be another way of claiming that unconditional promises do not carry any moral weight. Such an unconditional promise is the promise made in marriage, for when I promise to love and to honor I do not mutter under my breath, 'So long as you never become a member of the Conservative Party,' or 'Only if your principles do not change radically.' Parfit's suggestion seems to be that all promises (all promises which carry any moral weight, that is) are, and can be, made only on condition that there is no substantial change in the character either of promisor or promisee: if my husband's character changes radically, then I may think of the man before me not as my husband, but as some other person, some 'later self.' Similarly, it would seem that I cannot now promise to love another 'till death us do part,' since that would be like promising that another person will do something (in circumstances in which my character changes fundamentally over a period of time) and I cannot promise that another person will do something, but only that *I* will do something. Thus all promises must be conditional; all promises must be short-term. For what it is worth, I am not the least tempted to think that only short-term promises carry any moral weight and it is therefore a positive *disadvantage* for me that Parfit's theory has this consequence. But even if it were intuitively plausible that short-term promises alone carry moral weight, there are better arguments than intuitive ones and I hope I can mention some here.

The force of Parfit's argument is brought out by his 'Russian nobleman' example, described in 'Later Selves and Moral Principles':

> Imagine a Russian nobleman who, in several years will inherit vast estates. Because he has socialist ideals, he intends now to give the land to the peasants, but he knows that in time his ideals may fade. To guard against this possibility he does two things. He first signs a legal docu-

ment, which will automatically give away the land and which can only be revoked with his wife's consent. He then says to his wife 'If I ever change my mind and ask you to revoke the document, promise me that you will not consent.' He might add 'I regard my ideals as essential to me. If I lose these ideals I want you to think that I cease to exist. I want you to think of your husband then, not as me, but only as his later self. Promise me that you would not do as he asks.[6]

Parfit now comments:

This plea seems understandable and if his wife made this promise and he later asked her to revoke the document she might well regard herself as in no way released from her commitment. It might seem to her as if she had obligations to two different people. She might think that to do what her husband now asks would be to betray the young man whom she loved and married. And she might regard what her husband now says as unable to acquit her of disloyalty to this young man—to her husband's earlier self. [Suppose] the man's ideals fade and he asks his wife to revoke the document. Though she promised him to refuse, he now says that he releases her from this commitment . . . we can suppose she shares our view of commitment. If so, she will only believe that her husband is unable to release her from the commitment if she thinks that it is in some sense not *he* to whom she is committed . . . she may regard the young man's loss of ideals as involving replacement by a later self.[7]

Now, strictly speaking, and on Parfit's own account, the wife should not make such a promise: to do so would be like promising that another person will do something, since she has no guarantee that *she* will not change in character and ideals between now and the time of the inheritance. Further, there is a real question as to why anyone outside of a philosophical example should first draw up a document which can only be revoked with his wife's consent and then insist that his wife not consent whatever may happen. But we can let these points pass. What is important here, and what I wish to concentrate on, is the suggestion that my love for my husband is conditional upon his not changing in any substantial way: for this is what the example amounts to when stripped of its special story about later selves. (In his less extravagant moods Parfit himself allows that talk of later selves is, in any case, a mere *'façon de parler.'*)[8]

The claim then is that all promises must be conditional upon there being no change in the character of the promisee: that if my husband's character and ideals change it is proper for me to look upon him as someone other than the person I loved and married. This view gains plausibility from reflection on the fact that people can, and often do, give up their commitments. There is, it will be said, such an institution as divorce, and people do sometimes avail themselves of it. But although I might give up my commitment to my husband, and give as my reason a change in his character and principles, this goes no way towards showing that only short-term promises carry any moral weight, for there is a vital distinction here: the distinction between, on the one hand, the person who promises to love and to honor but who finds that, after a time, she has lost her commitment (perhaps on account of change in her husband's character), and, on the other hand, the person who promises to love and to honor only on condition that there be no such change in character. The former person may properly be said, under certain circumstances, to have given up a commitment; the latter person was never committed in the appropriate way at all. The wife of the Russian nobleman, by allowing in advance that she will love her husband only so long as he doesn't change in any of the aforementioned ways, fails properly to commit herself to him: for now her attitude to him seems to be one of respect or admiration, not commitment at all. Now she *does* mutter under her breath 'So long as you don't become a member of the Conservative Party.' But the marriage promise contains no such 'escape clause.' When Mrs. Micawber staunchly declares that she will never desert Mr. Micawber, she means just that. There are no conditions, nor could there be any, for otherwise we would fail to distinguish between respect or admiration *for the principles* of another and the sort of unconditional commitment *to him* which the marriage vow involves. There are many people whose ideals and principles I respect, and that respect would disappear were the ideals and principles to disappear, but my commitment to my husband is distinct from mere respect or admiration in just this sense, that it is not conditional on there being no change in his ideals and principles. I am now prepared to admit that my respect for another person would disappear were he revealed to be a cheat and a liar. I am not now prepared to admit that my love for my husband, my commitment to him, would disappear were he revealed to be a cheat and a liar. Perhaps an analogy will be illuminating here: in his article 'Knowledge and Belief,' Norman Malcolm distinguishes between a strong and a weak sense of 'know' and says:

> In an actual case of my using 'know' in a strong sense I cannot envisage a possibility that what I say should turn out to be not true. If I were speaking of another person's assertion about something I *could* think both that he is using 'know' in a strong sense and that nonetheless what he claims he knows to be so might turn out to be not so. But in my own case I cannot have this conjunction of thoughts, and this is a logical, not a psychological fact. When I say that I know, using 'know' in the strong sense, it is unintelligible to me (although perhaps not to others) to suppose that anything could prove that it is not so and therefore that I do not know it. [9]

Such is the case with commitment of the sort involved in the marriage vow. I promise to love and to honor and in so doing I cannot now envisage anything happening such as would make me give up that commitment. But, it might be asked, how can I be clairvoyant? How can I recognize that there is such a thing as divorce and at the same time declare that nothing will result in my giving up my commitment? The explanation lies in the denial that my claim to know (in the strong sense) or commitment (here) has the status of a prediction. My commitment to another should not be construed as a prediction that I will never desert that other. Malcolm again: 'The assertion describes my present attitude towards the statement . . . it does not prophesy what my attitude would be if various things happened.'[10] But if my statement is not a prediction, then what is it? It is perhaps more like a statement of intention, where my claims about a man's intentions do not relate to his future actions in as simple a way as do my predictions about his future actions.

If I predict that A will do x and A does not do x, then my prediction is simply false. If, on the other hand, I claim that A intends to do x and he does not, it is not necessarily the case that my statement was false: for he may have had that intention and later withdrawn it. Similarly with commitment: if I claim that A is unconditionally committed to B, that is not a prediction that A will never desert B; it is a claim that there is in A a present intention to do something permanently, where that is distinct from A's having a permanent intention. Thus Mrs. Micawber's claim that she will never desert Mr. Micawber, if construed as a commitment to him, is to that extent different from a prediction that she will never desert him, for her commitment need not be thought never to have existed if she does desert him. Thus an unconditional commitment to another person today, a denial today that anything could happen such as would result in desertion of Mr. Micawber, is not incompatible with that commitment being given up at a later date.

In brief, then, what is wrong in Parfit's example is that the wife *now* allows that her commitment will endure only so long as there is no substantial change in character. She should not behave thus, because her doing so indicates that she has only respect for her husband, or admiration for his principles, not a commitment to him: she need not behave thus, as there can be such a thing as unconditional commitment, analogous to intention and distinct from prediction in the way described.

All this points to the inherent oddity of the 'trial marriage.' It is bizarre to respond to 'wilt thou love her, comfort her, honor her and keep her?' with 'Well, I'll try.' Again, the response 'I will' must be seen as the expression of an intention to do something permanently, not a prediction that the speaker will permanently have that intention.

A further problem with the Russian nobleman example and the claim that only short-term promises carry any moral weight is this: when the wife of the

Russian nobleman allows in advance that her commitment to her husband will cease should his principles change in any substantial way, she implies that a list of his present principles and ideals will give an exhaustive explanation of her loving him. But this is not good enough. If I now claim to be committed to my husband I precisely cannot give an exhaustive account of the characteristics he possesses in virtue of which I have that commitment to him: if I could do so, there would be a real question as to why I am not prepared to show the same commitment to another person who shares those characteristics (his twin brother, for example). Does this then mean that nothing fully explains my love for another and that commitment of this sort is irrationally based? I think we need not go so far as to say that: certainly, when asked to justify or explain my love I may point to certain qualities which the other person has, or which I believe him to have, but in the first place such an enumeration of qualities will not provide a complete account of why I love him, rather it will serve to explain, as it were, his 'lovableness.' It will make more intelligible my loving him, but will not itself amount to a complete and exhaustive explanation of my loving him. Further, it may well be that in giving my list of characteristics I cite some which the other person does not, in fact, have. If this is so, then the explanation may proceed in reverse order: the characteristics I cite will not explain or make intelligible my love, rather my love will explain my ascribing these characteristics. A case in point here is Dorothea's love for Casaubon, which is irrationally based in that Casaubon does not have the characteristics and qualities which Dorothea thinks him to have. Similarly, in the case of infatuation the lover's error lies in wrongly evaluating the qualities of the beloved. In this way Titania 'madly dotes' on the unfortunate Bottom who is trapped in an ass's head, and addresses him thus:

> Come sit thee down upon this flowery bed
> While I thy amiable cheeks do coy
> And stick musk roses in thy sleek, smooth head
> And kiss thy fair, large ears my gentle joy.

and again

> I pray thee, gentle mortal, sing again.
> Mine ear is much enamoured of thy note;
> So is mine eye enthralled to thy shape,
> And thy fair virtue's force perforce doth move me
> On the first view, to say, to swear, I love thee. [11]

Both cases involve some error on the part of the lover: in one case the error is false belief about the qualities the beloved possesses; in the other it is an error about the evaluation of the qualities the beloved possesses. These two combine to show that there can be such a thing as a 'proper object' of love. This will be the case where there is neither false belief nor faulty evaluation. They do not, however, show that in ascribing qualities and characteristics to the beloved the lover exhaustively explains and accounts for his love. The distinction between 'proper' love and irrationally based love, or between 'proper' love and infatuation, is to be drawn in terms of the correctness of beliefs and belief-based evaluations. By contrast, the distinction between love and respect or admiration is to be drawn in terms of the explanatory power of the beliefs involved. In the case of respect or admiration the explanatory power of belief will be much greater than it is in the case of love. For this reason my respect for John's command of modal logic will disappear, and I am now prepared to admit that it will disappear, should I discover that my belief that he has a command of modal logic is false. Whereas I am not now prepared to admit that my commitment to and love for my husband will disappear if I discover that my beliefs about his qualities and characteristics are, to some extent, false.

W. Newton-Smith makes something like this point in his article 'A Conceptual Investigation of Love':

> Concern and commitment cannot be terminated by some change in a revelation about the object of that concern or commitment. We are inclined to accept 'I felt affection for her so long as I thought she was pure and innocent' but not 'I was really concerned for her welfare as long as I thought she was pure and innocent.' Being genuinely concerned or committed seems to involve a willingness on my part to extend that concern or commitment even if I have been mistaken about the person with regard to some feature of her that led to the concern, and even if that person ceases to have those features which led me to be concerned or committed in the first place.[12]

This, though initially plausible, cannot be quite right, for on Newton-Smith's analysis it is difficult to see how I could ever give up a commitment without it being the case that I never was committed in the first place. But we can and do distinguish between those who had a commitment and have now given it up and those who never had a commitment at all. We need not, I think, go so far as to say that 'love is not love which alters when it alteration finds,' but only that love is not love which allows in advance that it will so alter. The love which shows that it will alter when it alteration finds is at best sentimentality, at worst opportunism. (Of course, the reasons which one cites for giving up a commitment will cast light on whether one was committed at all. Thus 'I was committed to her as long as I thought she was an heiress' is highly dubious. 'I was committed to her as long as I thought she was pure and innocent' is, I think, not so dubious.) What is at least necessary is that one should not be prepared to say *now* 'I will love her as long as she is pure and innocent, but no longer.'

I turn now to a somewhat bizarre element in Parfit's talk of ideals. Parfit portrays the Russian nobleman as one who 'finds' that his ideals have faded, as one who 'loses' his ideals when circumstances and fortune change. What is bizarre in this talk is emphasized by the following extract from Alison Lurie's novel *Love and Friendship*:

> 'But, Will, promise me something.'
> 'Sure.'
> 'Promise me you'll never be unfaithful to me.'
> Silence.
> Emily raised her head, 'You won't promise?' she said incredulously.
> 'I can't, Emily. How can I promise how I'll feel for the next ten years? You want me to lie to you? You could change. I could change. I could meet somebody.'
> Emily pulled away. 'Don't you have any principles?' she asked. [13]

The trouble with the inappropriately named Will and the Russian nobleman in Parfit's example is that it is doubtful whether either man has any genuine principles at all. Each is portrayed as almost infinitely malleable, as one whose principles will alter in accordance with changing circumstances. The point about a moral principle however is that it must serve in some sense to rule out certain options as options at all. In his article 'Actions and Consequences,' John Casey refers us to the example of Addison's Cato who, when offered life, liberty and the friendship of Caesar if he will surrender, and is asked to name his terms, replies:

> Bid him disband his legions,
> Restore the Commonwealth to liberty,
> Submit his actions to the public censure
> And stand the judgement of a Roman Senate.
> Bid him do this and Cato is his friend. [14]

The genuine principles which Cato has determine that certain options will not ultimately be options at all for him. To say this, of course, is not to deny that life and liberty are attractive and desirable to him. Obviously he is, in large part, admirable precisely because they are attractive to him and yet he manages to resist their allure. The point is rather that not *any* sort of life is desirable. The sort of life he would, of necessity, lead after surrender—a life without honor— is not ultimately attractive to him and that it is not attractive is something which springs from his having the principles he does have. What Cato values above all else is honor and his refusal to surrender to Caesar is a refusal to lead a life without honor. By contrast, when the Russian nobleman draws up a legal document giving away his inheritance, we may suspect that he is concerned not with an honorable life or with a life which he now conceives of as honorable, but rather with his present principle. Where Cato values a certain sort of life, the Russian nobleman values a certain principle. It is this which is problematic and which generates, I believe, the bizarre talk of ideals fading. For Cato's adherence to his principles is strengthened, if not guaranteed, by the fact that he treats a certain sort of life as an end in itself and adopts the principles he does adopt because they lead to that end. The Russian nobleman, however, is portrayed more as a man who finds the principle important than as a man who finds the life to which the principle leads important. Obviously, in either case there may be temptation and inner struggle, but the temptation is less likely to be resisted by the Russian nobleman than by Cato, for the nobleman will find his principle undermined and threatened by the prospect of affluence, which is attractive to him. His ideals will fade. For Cato, on the other hand, things are not so simple. He is not faced by a choice between two things, each of which he finds attractive. The fact that he treats a life of honor as an end in itself precludes his finding life attractive under *any* circumstances. For him, life will ultimately be attractive and desirable only where it can be conducted honorably. Nevertheless, he finds life attractive and desirable, but this means only that if he surrenders he will have *sacrificed* his ideals, not that his ideals will have faded. Thus, the nobleman is a victim, waiting for and guarding against attack upon his principles; Cato is an agent who may sacrifice his principles after a struggle, but not one who would find that they had altered.

In conclusion, then, the claim that the marriage vow is either impossible or improper is false. It is possible to commit oneself unconditionally because commitment is analogous to a statement of intention, not to a prediction or a piece of clairvoyance. It is proper, since if we refuse to allow such unconditional commitment, we run the risk, of failing to distinguish between, on the one hand, sentimentality and commitment and, on the other hand, respect or admiration and commitment. Further, it is simply not true that I am helpless in circumstances in which I find my commitment wavering: this is because my principles will initially serve to modify my view of the opportunities which present themselves, so that I simply will not see certain things as constituting success because my principles are such as to exclude such things being constitutive of success. In this way, my principles determine what is to count as a benefit and what is to count as an opportunity. As Shakespeare has it:

> Some glory in their birth, some in their skill,
> Some in their wealth, some in their body's force,

Some in their garments though new fangled ill:
Some in their hawks and hounds, some in their horse.
And every humour has his adjunct pleasure,
Wherein it finds a joy above the rest,
But these particulars are not my measure,
All these I better in one general best.
Thy love is better than high birth to me,
Richer than wealth, prouder than garments cost,
Of more delight than hawks and horses be:
And having these of all men's pride I boast.
Wretched in this alone, that thou may'st take
All this away, and me most wretched make. [15,16]

NOTES

1.   Thomas Hardy, *Jude the Obscure.*

2.   G. E. Moore, 'The Nature of Moral Philosophy,' in *Philosophical Studies* (London: Routledge and Kegan Paul, 1922), 316.

3.   Mary Midgley, 'The Objection to Systematic Humbug,' *Philosophy* 53 (1978), 147.

4.   Bertrand Russell, *Autobiography* (London: George Allen and Unwin, 1967–69).

5.   Derek Parfit, 'Later Selves and Moral Principles' in *Philosophy and Personal Relations*, A. Montefiore (ed.) (London: Routledge and Kegan Paul, 1973), 144.

6.   P. 145.

7.   Pp. 145–146.

8.   Pp. 14, 161–162.

9.   Norman Malcolm, 'Knowledge and Belief,' in *Knowledge and Belief,* A. Phillips Griffiths (ed.) (Oxford University Press, 1967), 81.

10. P. 78.

11. W. Shakespeare, *A Midsummer Night's Dream,* Acts III and I.

12. W. Newton-Smith, 'A Conceptual Investigation of Love,' in *Philosophy and Personal Relations*, A. Montefiore (ed.), 132–133. [See above, pp. 214–15.]

13. Alison Lurie, *Love and Friendship* (Harmondsworth: Penguin, 1962) 329–330.

14. As quoted in J. Casey, 'Actions and Consequences,' from *Morality and Moral Reasoning*, J. Casey (ed.) (London: Methuen, 1971), 201.

15. W. Shakespeare, Sonnet 91.

16. I wish to thank my colleague, Dr. Roger Woolhouse, for many helpful discussions on the topic of this paper.

THE COMMANDABILITY
OF PATHOLOGICAL
LOVE

Robert W. Burch

THE MEANING OF Kant's claim in the First Section of *Foundations of the Metaphysics of Morals* that "pathological love" cannot be "commanded" is clearly that the emotion love cannot be the content of a moral injunction or rule. But what is the rationale for such a claim? Kant gives none, and apparently thinks that the rationale is too obvious to need mentioning. I shall first argue that the rationale is not at all obvious. But then I shall try to give a justification of the Kantian claim.

One might first think that only actions can be the content of moral rules and injunctions, and that, since love is a state and not an act, it follows that love cannot be "commanded." But do we have any clear idea of what it is to be "an action," and is it clear that love is not one? "To love" is, after all, a verb in good standing; one not only *falls* in love, and *is* in love; he also *loves*, and he may "do" this weakly, strongly, waveringly, passionately, and so forth. Furthermore, is it so very clear that states cannot be commanded? Compare the situation with love to that with attention. Attention looks on the surface of it as little like "an action," and as much like a state, as love does. Yet, "to attend" and "to pay attention" are verbs, and one can attend carefully, completely, weakly, waveringly, and so forth. Moreover, attending, or attention clearly can be "commanded." You could make this point another way by saying that "being

Reprinted from *The Southwestern Journal of Philosophy* (now *Philosophical Topics*) 3, No. 3 (1972), pp. 131–40, with the permission of that journal and Robert Burch. Professor Burch teaches philosophy at Texas A & M University, College Station, Texas.

attentive" can be "commanded," and so make less tempting the idea that states cannot be "commanded."

So, since the difference between love and "things" commandable does not after all appear to be that between states and actions, perhaps it is the difference between one sort of action and another? One might think that Kant means to contrast love to actions like lifting one's arm or smiling, these latter sorts of acts being thought of as in some way "basic"[1] in that they can usually be *just simply done*, and not done only *by means of* some procedure or *via* doing anything else. Kant's point would then rest on facts like these: if someone commanded us "Lift your arm," most of us without further ado could simply lift our arm; but if someone commanded us, "Love Mary," or "Love God," we would not without further ado be able simply to start loving. But whatever the thought that love is not a "basic action" is worth, it can hardly support the thesis that love cannot be "commanded." For surely there are many "commandable" actions which we cannot just simply do in the way that we can just simply lift our arm. Poisoning or not poisoning people, waging or preventing war, collecting rent, and cleaning up the slums are surely "commandable" acts: they are intelligible contents of injunctions and rules, and they do not come close to being "basic" in any familiar sense.

Perhaps, then, the sort of claim Kant is making about "pathological love" is to be supported by arguing that in some important way we *cannot* love? That is, we may want to rely, as perhaps Kant himself might have been relying, on some form of the thesis that "ought" implies "can." Following this general line, one might argue in several ways.

It might be said, for example, that we have no control over our emotions, so that it is pointless, and therefore somehow out of place, to command anyone to have or not to have certain emotions. But regardless of the quality of this argument's logic, the premise here—that we have no control over our emotions—is plainly false. People commonly alter their own emotions, as for example when they calm themselves from an angry rage by "counting to ten," put themselves in a happy frame of mind by listening to lively music, or vanquish their fear by whistling. If we try to protect the premise from these counter-examples by slightly weakening it, we only render it useless as the basis of a defense of the Kantian thesis. That is, suppose we weakened the premise to the thesis that love is so extremely difficult to get into that, no matter how much one tries to love, he is not very likely to succeed. Then it could not provide a rationale for Kant's point that love cannot be "commanded." Difficulty is no logical bar to commandability.

Doing what is moral should not even be expected to be easy: the virtuous life is often extremely difficult and sometimes even agonizing. Surely, it is a sensible command of morality, and many people even hold it to be an actual injunction of morality, that one alter his destructive emotions and promote in himself benevolent ones. The difficulty of doing these things does not negatively affect their commandability. It does affect the character and/or degree of one's guilt for not having done something. We condemn failures to do what is difficult, other things being equal, with less severity than we condemn failures to do what is easy. The difficulty of doing something can be presented as an excuse, over and above whatever other excuses there may be, for not having done it. But acts that are difficult to do, even in the extreme, may still be commanded, if the notion "commanded" is to have any useful moral function.

Still another way to argue that love *cannot* be "done" is to maintain that, as things now stand, there is no *way* to fall, or *method* of falling, in love. Contrast falling in love with doing a major overhaul on a car or with building a house. All three are difficult to do; but falling in love, as things now stand, is of a different order of things from the other two. For in the case of doing the overhaul or building the house there is a set of steps, each one of which could be taken very easily, and the totality of which simply *amounts to* the doing of them. But there is no such set of steps in the case of love. In response to this, it ought first to be pointed out that the absence of such steps does not show that there is no way to fall in love, nor even that there is no method of falling in love. For, of course, with respect to many deeds there are methods of doing them and ways of doing them which do not consist of a set of steps the doing of which simply amounts to the doing of the deed. For example, there are certainly methods of *fixing* (a notion which imports success) the car which are not of this sort, and indeed cannot be, for many ways and methods of doing things consist of steps which do not amount to the doing of the deed, but which if done make the deed causally necessary or imminent in some other way, or at least extremely likely.

For example, there are ways (perhaps there are not methods) of hitting home runs or shooting baskets, and these are not like the methods envisaged above. And furthermore, these are sorts of things which surely can be commanded. Cleaning up the ghettos is such a deed: there are no methods of the simple car-overhauling sort for doing it; yet it can be commanded. Perhaps it will be said that it can be commanded only because there is a *way*, albeit in the second sense of "way," of doing it. And to this I respond that it seems that the same thing could be said of love. It may be true that there is no set of steps the taking of which simply amounts conceptually to loving. But I see no reason to assume that there could not be a set of steps one could take which would ensure, or more or less ensure, that one falls in love. For example, it seems to be possible for members of some societies who view themselves—rightly or wrongly—as having duties to love their spouses (who perhaps have been arranged for them as spouses by their parents), to engage in activities which normally result in their loving their spouses. They, out of a sense of duty, spend lots of time with the spouse, try to understand her, work for her, confide in her, raise children by and with her, and so forth. And in such societies, such activities do nearly always result in real love. Engaging in these activities, then, seems to be, for them, a way of falling in love.

Furthermore, it does not seem conceptually impossible to have some sort of love potion, like one finds in A Midsummer Night's Dream, which makes anyone who takes it first fall asleep and then fall in love with the first person he sees after waking up. A way to fall in love, even a method for falling in love, would be to take this drug and ensure that the person with whom you want to fall in love is the first person you see upon waking up. So, if we take the suggested tack for making sense of Kant's claim that pathological love cannot be commanded, then it seems that Kant's point so interpreted is either false, or at best only contingently true pending the invention of such a drug as the love potion.

But Kant's point seems not to be contingent in this way. He seems to want to say that love is not the sort of thing which is logically a candidate for the content of a moral rule. And thus, to interpret him in the suggested way trivializes his intended point even if it does not make it downright false. [2] There is, however, a way of interpreting Kant that does not trivialize him and is faithful to his intentions. We can show, I think, that love is not the sort of thing which is logically fit to be the content of a command. Why not? Because a genuine command, as opposed to what merely has the grammatical form of a typical command, must be such that it is logically possible that it be obeyed. To obey a command is not merely to do what is commanded, but is to do this *for the sake of*, or *because of*, the command which commands it. This means that it must be logically possible to undertake to do what a genuine command commands. But love cannot be undertaken; hence it cannot be commanded. Let me explain this.

When I say that love cannot be undertaken I do not mean that it can never be enlightening, perhaps even true, to say nonironically of someone that he tried to, and even undertook to, love. It might be said about virtually anything which has the grammatical form of an action, even about what is paradoxical or mathematically impossible, that it has been undertaken. For example, it is true to say of certain mathematicians that they were undertaking to square the circle, even when what they were undertaking to do was mathematically impossible. [3] So it seems to be possible to say nonironically and truly that someone is undertaking to love. Why then do I want to deny that love can be undertaken?

I claim that anything we properly call undertaking to love is an undertaking only in a truncated or restricted sense. This is because the 'undertaking' in this case, one's 'project,' is logically debarred from being successfully accomplished. In a certain sense undertaking to love is paradoxical,[4] for the person 'undertaking' to love would not really be loving even if he carried through with all his endeavors. I shall argue for my claim below, but first let me make clearer the meaning of the claim itself.

In claiming that love cannot be undertaken in a non-truncated sense I am not saying that one cannot undertake in a non-truncated sense to *show love*, or to do all the things that someone in love typically does, or to act *like* someone in love. What I am saying is that this sort of non-truncated undertaking to *show love* can never amount to a non-truncated undertaking to *love*. It need not, of course, amount to what it often does—namely an attempt to deceive a person about loving him, or to pretend to love him. It might be the case that one does honestly and sincerely want to love the person to whom one is undertaking to show love and also the case that one is undertaking to show him love precisely so that the result will be actual love.[5] Nevertheless, the attempt to show love can never amount to a non-truncated attempt to love; for such an 'attempt,' I claim, is logically debarred from success, i.e., logically necessitated to be futile.

Obviously, I must say more about the notion of "success," since it will be immediately objected that undertaking to love certainly can be successful. For it can happen that one does actually fall in love as a *result* of his "endeavor to love," i.e., as a result of his endeavors (the ones he calls endeavors "to love"). In some societies this may even be the usual and expected case, for in them it may be the case that the usual endeavors are nearly certain to result in actual love. And in our own society it may be only the lack of a love potion that prevents our endeavors from being capable of being equally likely, or even more likely, to result in actual love.

My reply is that the conception of "success" employed in this objection is over-simple. The notion of "success" is more complex than we usually assume. Everyone would admit that carrying out a project successfully does not just mean that at one time your intention was to do or get X and that at some later time you did in fact do or get X. These are necessary conditions for the success of an undertaking, but hardly sufficient. For, if the doing or the getting of X is not the result of your endeavors, then you are not successful but rather lucky. But the notion of "success" is still more complex than this. X may come to you as a result of your endeavors, but you have not succeeded if X did not come in the way you planned or expected. You have not successfully shot a basket if you carefully shoot the ball, but instead of going right in, it bounces off the rim into the street, where a passing car then happens to knock it through the very basket you were shooting at.

There is still more to the complexity of "success." X might be done or gotten, as a direct result of your endeavors and in the way you plan them to get X or get

X done; but if you change your mind about intending to do or get X in the meantime, you will not be successful in your project. Planning to commit suicide, you lock yourself in a room, throw away the key, and turn on the gas. But at this point you decide that all this drama is foolish and that you want to live after all. In trying to turn off the gas, however, the handle breaks and you cannot stop the gas. Your death is hardly the successful carrying out of your original project for you dropped or gave up your project.

Most importantly for my purpose in this paper, there is still another dimension to "success." Suppose that you keep your intention to do or get X, and that you do or get X as the direct result of your endeavors, and in the way you planned; but suppose that, nevertheless, the reasons why you intend to do or get X completely change. Then your original project will not be carried out successfully. You start to go downtown to buy a pair of red shoes for Aunt Sally. Halfway to town you recall that Sally has recently disowned you and also remember that Aunt Maud, who still has you in her will, loves red shoes. So you buy that pair of red shoes that you were going to get for Sally, for Maud instead. Have you carried out your *original* project successfully? No.

The last two considerations show that it is wrong to say that you have successfully carried out your original intention or undertaking when the intention you originally had—including the intention to do or get X and also your reasons for doing or getting X—get altered[6] in the process of doing or getting X, or at least when they get altered in certain ways. I want to apply this point to the case of undertaking pathologically to love. But since so far my examples have been about acts, whereas love is perhaps more like a state which one gets into and remains in than an act, it might be thought that the point about "success" would not extend to states.

So consider the following case which is in this regard more like love: A woman wants to be married (to *be* married, not just to go through the ceremony of getting married) because the state is respectable. If she actually does get married, we might in appropriate circumstances say that her being married is what makes her original undertaking successful, or that her being married constitutes the successful carrying out of her original intentions. But we can say this of her only if she did not somewhere along the line change her mind about her reasons for wanting to be married. If, for example, she said to herself, "Well, it's not the respectability of it I'm interested in now, but rather the money (but rather him and him alone)," then her being married after that does not constitute the success of her original project. If she did not change her mind about her reasons for wanting to be married, then the original reason(s) must still be "functioning" for her. That is, if she is asked why she is (staying) married, she would have to say, if she is truthful and not self-deceived, "Because of the respectability of the thing." If she could truly respond otherwise, e.g., "Because I really do love him (now)," then the state of being married which she is in now is *not* going to make her original project successful: for she has given that project up.

I want now to argue that pathological love is always and necessarily like the above case of marriage when the motives have changed, and when therefore the undertaking is not successful. For first the project of loving someone in particular cannot be motiveless. You must have reasons for loving someone in particular, else the desire to love just that someone is not intelligible. Second, if the project of loving a particular person is to be successfully carried out, then, as we have seen, these reasons, which you must necessarily have, for loving that person cannot have altered or changed anywhere along the line or in the process. If this is so, then you must still be able sincerely to avow them as your reasons for being (or remaining) in love. You must still see the love you are in as the very thing you wanted (and want) and were undertaking to achieve, and you must see the love as what you wanted (and want) for the reasons that it furnishes the very things you wanted the love *for* in the first place. The original reasons you had for loving must, then, in a certain sense still 'survive.' You would have to be able still to say, "I love her because . . . ," referring to the state of love you are now in as, for example, satisfying the "desires" you had and still have. However, this is paradoxical, because if you love someone, you cannot say, "I love her because . . . ," referring to *anything*. Genuine love has got to be without any motives at all. If you can correctly give any reason for that tender attitude you have toward her, then that attitude you have is not love but something else, be it admiration, respect, pity, selfish interest, or whatnot. So, since love has to be completely motiveless, then your original motives, regardless of what they were, for wanting to love cannot have 'survived' if the state you are now in is really love.

It follows that even if you do end up really loving as the result of your endeavors, your project has still not been successful, because your original motives must have dropped out somewhere along the line; thus, like the buyer of the red shoes, your original project has not been successfully completed, but has rather been abrogated. You have now dropped it, even though as a result of having started it you may have fallen in love, and may now be in love.[7]

It might be objected to the argument I have given that if the original intention was really to love (genuinely), then the original intentions the person had must have *included* the intention that his intentions with regard to the "beloved" *should* change. So that when they do change, then the change does not, as I maintained, constitute the dropping of the original project to love—or of the original intentions—but rather constitutes its—or their—successful completion, or their successful carrying out. However, there is a confusion in this objection. In willing (i.e., wanting, desiring) something that you can only will intelligibly if you have reasons for it, you cannot include in what you will that those reasons which give the willing intelligibility should themselves disappear. For that would render the original willing unintelligible after all. It is unintelligible to say that you want A, and to make this intelligible by saying that you want A for the sake of B, but, then to add that you want not to get B. If you "negate" the reasons which alone give intelligibility to the want, then the want is no longer intelligible. [8]

So, in this way the very will to love is itself paradoxical. One could will to "love" nonparadoxically only if he failed in a certain way to understand what love is. But if he does understand that love requires to be motiveless, then he cannot really will to love. [9]

The "undertaking" to love, then, is *necessarily* unsuccessful; and so it is not an undertaking in the full sense at all. But an undertaking in the full sense, with the logical possibility of success, is a necessary condition for the logical possibility of a command's being obeyed. For, as we said, a command is not obeyed unless the doing of what was commanded is done *because* it was commanded. This requirement makes it necessary that it be logically possible to undertake successfully to do what the command commands. But in the case of pathological love this is not logically possible. Therefore, a "command" to love is logically debarred from obedience. Consequently, such a "command" is only one in a truncated sense: it merely has the grammatical form of a typical command. Kant therefore seems correct in saying that pathological love cannot be commanded.

NOTES

1. After the manner, let us say, of Arthur C. Danto's "Basic Actions," *American Philosophical Quarterly*, II (1965).

2. Compare the claim that jumping to the moon cannot be commanded. To be sure there is, as things now stand, no way of jumping to the moon. So this deed is not just difficult, like fixing one's car is. But it is not impossible that scientists so alter our capacities that jumping to the moon becomes a possibility. Thus, the claim that jumping to the moon cannot be commanded is contingent and rather trivial. It is still the *kind of thing* which might well, in other circumstances, actually get commanded.

3. It would be unintelligible, though, for a mathematician who knew the impossibility of squaring the circle to keep on trying to do it. A person who says he is trying to square the circle betrays that he does not understand this notion fully. Similarly, I will say, a person who declares love as his goal shows a certain failure to understand the notion.

4. I hope no one takes me to be suggesting that falling in love is itself paradoxical as is squaring the circle.

5. One might show his honesty and sincerity by doing things that show that he really does want to love, and not for reasons incompatible with love, such as in order to get the 'beloved's' money, or his salvation. One works to understand the woman's feelings, tries

to imagine her in tender or intimate situations, reminds himself of her faithfulness and devotion, keeps mementos of her ready to hand, and so on. Or he prays daily, reflects on God's mercy and goodness, considers his own hard-heartedness.

6. Now sometimes the reason you have for undertaking something is a desire, like hunger, for example. This desire may, when you successfully complete the project, *be satisfied*; indeed it seems that it usually must be. And so the desire, in a certain sense disappears. But even though your hunger disappears, your motives for the deed do not alter. Your motives for eating or your reasons for eating have never ceased to be hunger even though your hunger eventually ceases in eating. On the other hand, if you keep on eating after your hunger is satisfied, then *that* stretch of eating no longer has the motive of hunger. But neither is it the successful completion of your original project: you are no longer satisfying your hunger.

7. Someone might object that the project was not to *be* in love but rather to *fall* in love (just like one's undertaking might be to *get* married, i.e., to go through the ceremony, and not to *be* married, i.e., to stay married), so that the falling in love sees the satisfaction and hence the disappearance of the original desires (motives), which then "allow" one to stay in love and to have successfully completed his project. To this objection it might be replied that it contains a confusion. For falling in love is not itself an identifiable act separate from what one does when he gets in the state of being in love. You do not fall in love and then contingently sink (or rise) into the state of being in love. You *are* in love, and *then, simply* for the reason that you are in love, you can be said to have fallen in love. (This is often the relation between being and becoming.)

8. Compare this case. It is indeed possible to want that (some, at least, of) one's intentions, motives, and wants change, and to do things with the intention of changing them. And it is possible to be successful at this. It is for this reason that such things as changing one's wants, and even one's character, *are* capable of being commanded (even though, as we have said, they are not "basic" in any clear sense, and even though they may be extremely difficult). But notice that you can only wish to change a *certain subset* of your wishes, wants, intentions. This subset may be a large one as well as a small one, but it is logically impossible that it be *all* of your intentions. Why? In willing to change all your wants you must have reasons: it is no more intelligible to want to change your wants for no reason at all than it is intelligible to want to love someone in particular for no reason at all. But, if you want something that you must have reasons for wanting, then it will be unintelligible for that something you wish either to be or to include that your very reasons for that wish change or disappear. For it would in effect be cancelling out the intelligibility of your wanting if you simultaneously rejected as your reasons the reasons that give intelligibility to it by also wanting not to have those reasons. (We can see that suicide is always an unintelligible desire, if there is not some confusion about what it means.)

9. At this point I want to head off possible objections by emphasizing that I am not claiming that the desire to love is necessarily *insincere*. Having a motive to love a woman *might* make the desire insincere in itself, as for example when my motive is to "really love her" so that she will be given enough emotional security by my behavior so that she will reward me with a weekly allowance of fifty thousand dollars. But if I desire to love her "because she is so sweet and gentle" or "in order to reciprocate her love," or if I desire to love God, not so that He will save me from the torments of hell, but rather "because He is so merciful and good to us," then these desires are not insincere or "phony" in the same way as is the desire to love a woman to get her money or God to get His salvation. Nevertheless, these desires too are paradoxical in the same way as that one.

PERSONAL LOVE

Robert R. Ehman

IN THE MEASURE that we detach ourselves from our roles in immediate social life and develop our own subjectivity and our sensitivity to the subjectivity of others, we become aware of ourselves and others as unique personalities and thereby become touched by the possibility and appeal of personal love. Personal love is the most radical attempt to transcend the solitude of our separate self and to participate in an intimate common life with another self. For this reason, it presupposes an awareness of the separate self both in our own case and in the case of another. The mere child is incapable of personal love in the full sense even though the full and wondrous unity of parent and child recollected from our earliest days serves as a model of love; and in one respect love can be seen as an attempt to recover the closeness of childhood familial life. While there are many who never realize personal love in their own life, they nevertheless feel its absence as a peculiar lack and are in this sense involved with it. Those who anxiously turn away from love and protect themselves against it witness to its peculiar power in their very evasion of it. In its inescapable relevance to the human self, it is as fundamental as morality, work, play, and death. The understanding of personal love is on this account essential to an understanding of the self.

Reprinted from *The Personalist* (now *Pacific Philosophical Quarterly*) 49, No. 1 (1968), pp. 116–41, with the permission of that journal and Professor Ehman. Robert Ehman is in the philosophy department at Vanderbilt University. He has written another essay on love, "Personal Love and Individual Value," *The Journal of Value Inquiry* 10, No. 2 (1976), pp. 91–105.

However, although personal love fulfills an otherwise unavoidable lack in our life, it opens us to radical pain and suffering and never fulfills the whole of its promise. Hence, while it promises the highest personal happiness and for many persons is an essential ingredient in genuine happiness, it often delivers us over to sorrow and disappointment for which it has no defense or comfort. Moreover, although the lover hopes to achieve an untroubled security in his relation to another on the model of his idealized recollection of childhood, he in fact finds himself confronted with and at the mercy of the independent attitude of the other. Further, the lover might fail to recognize the intrinsic limits of love since there is nothing in love itself to announce them. He might in the blindness of his love shatter himself against the ultimate limits of union with another and be thrown back upon himself with a more acute sense of loneliness and isolation than anyone else. He will find that however close he comes to his beloved, he still feels distant and alone and can never bridge the gap between himself and the other. The lover attempts to put his love above the usual scale of values and to free it from the relativity of being merely one value commensurable with others. However, he can never escape from the demands of the other dimensions of his social life or from the appeal of other values; and he cannot fully carry out his aim of putting the relation to his beloved above all else. Finally, the lover seeks a relationship with his beloved that cuts beneath the roles and functions in terms of which he ordinarily comports himself toward others and seeks to relate to his beloved as she is in her uniqueness behind roles and masks. However, in the same manner as others, the beloved tends to vanish behind roles and masks; and the lover can never be sure that he relates to her as she really is. Even when they attempt to strip off their masks for one another and disclose their naked selves, both the lover and beloved tend to fall into simply another role and to present a facade rather than their unique self. From the point of view of love, other modes of social life appear superficial and constraining; from the point of view of these other modes, personal love appears as a threat since it puts itself outside of them and fails to respect the limits of their forms and rules.

The main philosophical interpretations of love view it as an instance of a more general project with a basis and aim which are species of the basis and aim of more generic modes of existence. Thus classical and Christian philosophers regard love as essentially an ethical relationship and interpret the basis and aim as falling under those of ethical relationships in general. For thinkers in both of these traditions, love reduces to lust in the measure that it forgets or conflicts with valid ethical principles. They deny that love is autonomous. Hence, while they admit that the original choice of a beloved is not based solely on ethical considerations, they hold that love is fulfilled only in marriage or some other institution that is regulated by the valid rules of society and objectively based on the respect for the other as an ethical person. Freud and

Sartre in recent times have sought for more fundamental categories in which to interpret the distinctive nature of love. However, they too deny the autonomy and irreducibility of the erotic. For Freud, love is a form of sexual desire to be understood primarily from the perspective of biological sexual drives in their interaction with social reality. In the measure that love appears to transcend mere sexual desire, it is simply a "sublimated" and modified version of sexual desire. The basis of love on the Freudian view is the sexual attractiveness of the object; and the aim is the sexual act. For Sartre, on the other side, love is one of several alternative projects by which we attempt to come to terms with our being for others. The basis is the other's threat to our freedom; and the aim is the recovery and mastery of our being for the other. [1]

In this paper, I shall put radically into question the claim that personal love is a mere species of either ethical relationships, sexual desire, or the dialectical struggle to dominate the other. In the first part of my discussion, I shall describe the distinctive basis and aim of personal love and show that these are irreducibly other than those of the other forms of relationship to which love is subordinated in the traditional discussions. I shall argue that the basis is the unique individual style of life and feeling of the beloved and that the aim is a sharing of the private and intimate dimension of life. The distinctive basis and aim of love bestow central importance on precisely the dimensions of the self which are incidental from other perspectives. In the second part of my discussion, I shall turn to the dilemmas that arise in the realization of love. The full phenomenon of love is not found in its mere meaning but includes in addition the tensional relation between the meaning and the concrete fulfillment. The description of the dilemmas that arise in the concrete realization provide further evidence for our interpretation of the meaning and at the same time point up the ultimate limits of love. Only by attending to the relation between the aim and the concrete realization is it possible to understand the anxiety, frustration, and disillusionment that arise from the radical attempts to fulfill the erotic ideal.

In asserting our love for a person, we single out the person and raise her above the field of the social relations and obligations in terms of which we comport ourselves toward others. The assertion of love implies that the beloved has a value for the lover above that of others and that the lover regards his relation to his beloved as more important than his other relationships. In the measure that the lover fulfills the ideal demands of love, he is forced to concentrate his love on a single person. For although he might put two or more persons ahead of all others, he cannot put two persons absolutely first in his life; and this is what love demands. The beloved ought to have a *unique* place in his life. When a person finds that she shares love with others, she feels jealous and deceived, not because she is selfish or possessive, but because this goes against the ideal of love itself. The distinctive joy of being loved is that of finding oneself singled out as a unique individual for special evaluation. When the lover admits that his beloved is merely one of several whom he counts as equal, he takes back his claim to love her.

In the presence of our beloved, we feel in the presence of a supreme and wondrous value. The emotional affection for the beloved is not a mere blind force but a disclosure of the person as is evidenced by the fact that we feel as though we know the person we love more intimately than we know others. The love appears to be an experience of the most concrete personal reality of the beloved. The idea that love is a gratituous or arbitrary commitment or a blind passion fail to do justice to the feeling of value in the presence of the beloved. If love were simply an arbitrary commitment, faithfulness to the beloved would reduce to faithfulness to our own commitments and the beloved would be a mere occasion for us to prove our own consistency. On the other hand, if love were blind passion, it would not even make sense to demand faithfulness since in this case it would be a mere aberration without valuational basis which would come and go as an illness or hypnotic spell. The ideal faithfulness of love is based on the permanence of the value at the root of our love. In the measure that a person's love develops and focuses on a single person to the exclusion of others, he will feel that the basis is something unique to his beloved and goes beyond all repeatable qualities that the person shares with others. For this reason, he will not be satisfied with attempts to provide reasons for his love or to describe the valuational basis. He will tend to claim that his love is based on nothing less than the unique personality and style of the beloved. However, even though this be the case, repeatable traits will be relevant and will be the grounds of the initial attraction. Moreover, even the lover cannot fully reveal the unique concrete personality of his beloved; and although this might be the ideal basis of his love, it will always transcend his grasp, and his actual attitude toward his beloved will be rooted in more general and less concrete values. He might *mean* to love the person only for what she is in her peculiar individual reality but he will always in fact love her for qualities that are in some degree general.

In raising the issue of the role of repeatable qualities, it is important to distinguish the grounds of initial attraction from the grounds of deeper love, even though we never escape from repeatable qualities even in deeper love. The repeatable intellectual, moral, social, aesthetic, and sexual traits of a person are fundamental to our initial attraction even though we do not necessarily choose the person who is most desirable from the perspective of any of them. Hence, we might single out a person because of his moral goodness, his high station, his intelligence, or his good looks or again because of his daring immorality, his low station, his slowness, or his ugliness. The role of sexual attractiveness is in every case central; and in the initial stages, there is no clear distinction between love and sexual desire. The traits that erotically attract us to the person are traits that make him sexually attractive, even though sexual attractiveness is not reducible to the possession of any given traits. The person is perceived as having certain sexual potentialities and has a distinct value as a sexual object which is not wholly dependent on other traits, even though there might be important correlations. When we select a brilliant handsome person as an erotic object, envy and esteem and aesthetic sensitivity play an important role; when, on the other side, we choose someone without these qualities, sympathy, benevolence, and desire to dominate play important roles. The notorious difficulty that we have in the effort to persuade someone to love (or not to love) a certain person by pointing to his personal qualities does not imply that these are irrelevant and that the lover has insight into something more fundamental; it is rather a result of the fact that given qualities do not play a constant or predictable role. The same qualities that attract one person to another repel a third.

However, although the general qualities are relevant to our initial attraction, they are too changeable and too general to serve as the basis for love in the full sense; and the lover attempts to penetrate beneath them to the unique personality of the beloved. The fact that love is ideally independent of fundamental changes in the repeatable qualities of a person has led to the claim that our love is altogether unconditioned by any empirical considerations and is addressed to the person in his ideal personal value. However, to regard love in this manner is abstract. The promise to love a person *no matter what* would be a blind and fanatical commitment to a person in his abstract identity rather than in his full concreteness. If no change in or action of the person were relevant to our love for him, our love would be directed toward an abstract idea and not a real concrete person. While in the deepest forms of love, we continue to love a person in spite of fundamental changes in his age, appearance, health, social position, and even talents and moral character, we would feel that our love is baseless if we were no longer able to communicate our intimate feelings with her, no longer felt that we were "close" to her and "attuned" to her, and no longer shared the same "sensitivity" to things or the same "tastes." In order to love a person, we must delight in her presence and in the peculiar manner that she responds to us and to other things. There is a serious question as to whether we can continue to love a person for whom we no longer feel sexual desire. The sexual desire follows from our love; and the very features of her personal style that lead us to love a person will lead us to desire her even though in some cases we might no longer be able to fulfill our desire. In illness, age, or other disability, it might no longer be possible to become sexually united with the person we love. However, a genuine lover will feel this as a lack; and he will still desire union even when it is impossible. The lover indeed will still desire the beloved after her death. The sexual is a fundamental mode in which we participate in the personal being of the beloved and share our life with her.

The basis of our love for a person therefore shows itself to be the distinctive manner in which the person responds to us and to the world that we share. The style of the person is realized in ever-changing circumstances and occasions and is made up of countless individual responses and gestures that we can never fully describe. The general descriptions that we give of the person always fall short of the concrete actions and manner of life which we feel in her presence and which ever again arouses our love for her and leads us to desire to be with her. The very fact that it takes time to reveal the individual style of life of a person means that we can never in the strict sense love a person at first sight. The basis of genuine love takes time to be revealed. At first sight, we might indeed be sexually attracted to the person and impressed with her in numerous other ways; we might even catch a glimpse of her whole manner of life and find that we enjoy being with her. However, in order to raise this initial attraction to genuine love, we must put it to the test of time and see whether the attraction lasts and is based on something more fundamental than some quality that is easily seen and which is liable soon to vanish. The deeper and purer our love for a person the more deeply it is based on the qualities of the person that are at once most unique and most permanent. The personal identity of the beloved as beloved is the identity of her personal style of responding to the feelings and actions of her lover and to the things that they share with one another.

In the same way that there is in the strict sense no love at first sight, there is no purely unrequited love. If a lover has never had the opportunity to share his life with his beloved, has never been able to establish an emotional and valuational attunement with her, he cannot in the full sense love her. He might, to be sure, desire to know her and feel assured that if only she would open herself up to him, he could love her. However, in this case, he is in fact in love with an idealized version of the person, not the actual person herself. For he does not and cannot love her as she actually is but only as he imagines she might be. The sorrow in this case is not in the strict sense sorrow over non-reciprocity but sorrow over the failure of the other to be a person we can love. While we might long for a person who turns away from us and feel that life is worthless without her, we are in fact longing only for an ideal and not for an actual reality. In the same manner as an insane person, we give the imaginary an even higher emotional value than the real. Thus while reciprocity is not a condition of our desiring a person and even wishing to love her, it is nevertheless a condition of genuine love and even of the experience of the person which can put our original desire for her to the test and distinguish illusion from reality in respect to it.

While our love for a person is certainly a factor in determining our concrete obligations to her, it is already evident that the basis of love is irreducibly other than that of moral obligation. For the basis of love is the unique concrete personality of the beloved and the basis of moral obligation is our respect for the person as a person. The fundamental requirement of love is to raise the beloved above others and to give her a privileged status in our life so long as she retains the personal style of life which serves as the ground of our love for her. The fundamental requirement of morality in contrast is to treat all persons as having equal worth and to justify all special treatment of a person by reference to universally valid principles. In putting the beloved ahead of others, the lover might at any time find himself in conflict with acknowledged obligations to others; and there is always something immoral in the privilege and attention that the lover gives to the beloved at the expense of others who might have an even higher moral claim on the beloved. The lover finds himself torn between the demands of his love and the demands of his moral obligations to others which count for nothing from the point of view of his love. The lover might indeed demonstrate his love by violating moral demands in his treatment of others in order to give his beloved a special place in his life. There are even some cases, as we shall have occasion to discuss, in which the lover remains with the beloved even though he morally ought to renounce the relationship and the relationship is morally degrading. A person might find that he is closer to another than to anyone else and finds more delight in her company than in the company of others even though the other degrades him and causes him pain and suffering. The pain and suffering of the lover at the hands of his beloved might be the manner in which he shares in her life and realizes his love for her. The personal style that he adores might be one that causes him pain.

Moral deliberations ideally take into account *all* of the empirical factors relevant to a given decision, action, or relationship to another; love takes into account only the factors that constitute the personal style of life of the beloved and motivate our love for her. Morality must take into account a wide range of factors precisely because it forbids our treating one person in the same empirical situation and status in a more favorable manner than others. In order to assure that we treat each person according to principles valid for all, we must take into account all relevant factors. Love neglects factors that play a part in morality because it cares nothing for general principles and fairness; it singles out an individual for special concern simply on the basis of her personality and of the delight that we take in being close to her. For love, all persons are not equal and the beloved simply as an individual is more important than others. For morality, on the other hand, the individual in his mere individuality is incidental. Hence, even when the lover acts in a manner compatible with moral demands, his actions are as such independent of them. In the measure that he takes love seriously, he cannot be counted on to act on moral principles even when he is a man of sound moral character. When a man "falls in love," his character is deeply altered and together with his beloved he retreats to a world that stands apart from the universal ethical reality.

In its very respect for the person as a person, morality is in a peculiar sense impersonal since it fails to acknowledge the uniqueness of the individual and to place the importance on his feeling and moods that he himself or his lover does. When a person is treated merely in accordance with morality, he feels that he is treated impersonally and abstractly without full consideration for his individual reality. Fairness, justice, and respect come to him simply as a person; and he is aware that insofar as they are genuinely moral, they apply to him in the same way as to others. The special delight that comes from being loved arises from the recognition that the lover singles us out and affirms us in our unique personality and not simply as a human person in general. Friendship might seem to be an exception to the principle that moral relationships fail to focus on our individual personality. However, friendship is not supreme and incommensurate with our other public relationships in the manner of personal love and is in principle open to all those with whom we share the same values and interests. The ideal of friendship does not permit us to take the personal style of life of the other and our delight in sharing his personal life as the sole basis of friendship. Friendship is based on respect for the other as a person specified by a sharing of common interests and ends. The personal style of the friend is merely one factor; and the choice of a friend is properly a moral choice: anyone with a certain character and under certain conditions ought to be accepted as a friend. The moment that a person takes the sharing of the personal side of the life of his friend as his ultimate motive in his relationship and puts his relation to his friend simply as the individual he is beyond the sphere of his other relationships, he moves beyond friendship to genuine personal love; and he dramatically reveals the distinction between friendship and love.

While friendship rules out personal love, marriage does not, and, for this reason, the relation between love and marriage is more complex than that between love and friendship. However, although we might fulfill love in marriage and in this manner bring love into conformity with ethical reality, marriage is nevertheless independent of love and love is independent of marriage. For as an ethical relationship, marriage is based on the commitment and obligation to care for, remain faithful to, and to live with a person who reciprocally fulfills the same obligation with respect to us. Marriage is essentially an ethical agreement; and although love might be a relevant condition, it is never the sole basis of the obligation to maintain the agreement and persons might be obligated to remain married even when they no longer or never did love one another and even when they love someone else. The absence of love would in every case invalidate marriage if marriage were *simply* an institutional fulfillment of love. In a given society, it might be hard to realize love apart from marriage. However, this does not in the least imply that the *valuational* basis of the two is the same or that marriage enters essentially into the ideal of love. The independence of love and marriage is dramatically brought to the fore in homosexual love. There is nothing in the pure ideal of love itself to rule out love between those of the same sex. The sexuality of the person is simply one factor; and it is possible to take an equal delight in sharing the personal life of a person of the same sex as in sharing the life of a person of the opposite sex. The sexual attraction for a person of the same sex might be even more intense than for a person of the opposite sex. If sexuality itself transcends the natural law that opposites attract, it is certainly possible for love to do so. There is nothing erotically wrong with homosexual love even though it might be morally or socially wrong. The erotic and moral evaluations are independent. The denial of homosexual love and the attempt to restrict love to courtship and marriage is an effort on the part of the ethical reality to subordinate love to ethics and to deny its autonomy. The result in many cases is radical conflict. The very concern of morality to subordinate love to itself betrays an implicit awareness that love is an independent reality.

There is a wondrous and inseparable connection between love and sexual desire, as we have already had occasion to remark. However, there is nothing in sexual desire alone or in its interaction with social reality to explain the ideal of love for a single person. The sexual drive is originally highly indiscriminate and admits of a wide range of objects. The restriction to a narrow range comes as a result of a long process of repression. However, the repression might not go so far as to repress desire for all but a single person; and in any case, the *ideal* of exclusive love cannot be accounted for as simply a product of repression. The repression might lead us to limit our sexual desires in accordance with it but it cannot generate the ideal. Moreover, the ideal exists even when there is no social pressure to conform to it and might itself be a factor in the repression and restriction of sexual desire; it is certainly not in every case a mere consequence of repression. The lover might have to inhibit and restrict his sexual impulses in order to fulfill the ideal demands of his love.

While love might take the sexual up into itself, there remains a clear distinction between the basis of sexual desire by itself and the basis of genuine love. The basis of the one is found in momentary qualities that might at any time be shared by a plurality of diverse persons. The most important of these qualities are physical appearance and style of sexual conduct. The basis of love, on the other side, is found only in the concrete style of the personal life of the person which can only be revealed over time and is distinctive of the single person. From the perspective of sexual desire, the other person is of value only as a sexual object; and the person motivated by sexual desire alone has no further interest in the other person. There is nothing in sexuality to lead to permanence in the relationship; and indeed from a purely sexual point of view, a series of new and even more exciting sexual partners is more desirable than faithfulness to one. When we attempt to interpret love as a mere form of sexual desire, we find ourselves unable to do justice to the exclusiveness, permanence, and concern for the other in his full concreteness that are essential to genuine love.

When we put to Sartre the question of the basis of love, the answer might at first sight appear to be the freedom of the other. The freedom of the other is the power to make us an object, to transcend and outstrip us, and to put our own being into question. The disclosure of his freedom motivates our attempt to recover the dimension of our being that he holds under his control by making ourselves a supreme value in his world and a limit and final end of his freedom. However, although the freedom of the other is a necessary condition of the project of love, it is not the valuational basis. The freedom of the other is not a value but a *threat* that we seek to master. The valuational basis of love for Sartre is not located in the other at all but is a value of our own being: it is the value of being affirmed as a supreme value and of recovering our alienated being for the other. The lover therefore seeks the supreme valuation for himself that he ought to give to the beloved and is concerned with the value of his own self, not with that of the other. The beloved becomes incidental. Thus Sartre fails to account for the feeling of adoration and even worship that the lover has for his beloved and therefore fails to account for the value that the lover attributes to his beloved. Moreover, although Sartre has no difficulty accounting for the desire of the lover to be the sole object of the love of the beloved, he cannot account for the demand on the lover to give his love to a single person. There is nothing in Sartre's view to prohibit a person's projecting love in relation to numerous persons; indeed for Sartre love appears to be simply a basic mode in which we relate to the other in general. The beloved might be anyone for whom we exist.

When we raise the issue of the aim of love, we must take as our clue what we have already discovered as the basis of love. If the basis is the personal intimate style of action and feeling of the beloved, the aim must be to participate in and share in the personal life of the beloved. In the same manner as a friend will seek to pass his time with and be in the presence of his friends, the lover will seek to pass his time with and be in the presence of his beloved; and he will fulfill his love by being with the beloved. However, while the lover will comport himself toward the person he loves in much the same manner that he does toward a friend, there will be something distinctive about his relationship. Unless there is a special aim and content to their relationship, the claim of lovers to be something more for one another than they are for anyone else would be empty and vacuous, a mere claim without reality and truth. The demand that we reserve our love for a single person alone would be meaningless since we could not relate to him in any other manner than we relate to a plurality of persons.

The requirement that the relationship to the person we love be reserved for her alone means that the essential aim of their behavior toward one another must be set apart from aims that can be fulfilled with a plurality of persons.

There is no necessary limit in the number of persons with whom we might co-operate in the fulfillment of such universal ends as civic projects, business, art, or knowledge and for this reason, these cannot be the distinctive aims of lovers, even though the lovers might also incidentally pursue them together. Their aim will be to share those aspects of their life which they share with no one else and to constitute a "world" together which is their own alone and in and through which they can share each other's moods and feelings, hopes, and dreams in a manner more intimate than they do with others. In order to fulfill this aim, they will seek to be alone and will cover their relationship in secrecy. They will reveal to each other the side of their self that they reveal to no one else. They will always attempt to express more to each other than they do to others; and for this reason, in the measure that they successfully achieve their aim, a third person will feel left out. He will find that the lovers live in a private world of their own which he cannot fully decipher and in which gestures, words, and things have meanings for them that they do not have for him. From his point of view, the lovers see "too much" in things and make "much ado" about nothing.

In sharing their privacy, lovers give a significance to whims, desires, and moods that receive no recognition in the larger social world. The lover caters to and makes an issue of the purely personal tastes of his beloved and tries to please her simply to please her and not for any further motive. He gives her things, treats her attentively, and is sensitive to her moods and feelings and shows her in countless ways that she counts more for him than others do. There is playfulness in the relation of lovers in that their whole comportment is simply for its own sake and has no further end, is free of fixed universal rules, and is spontaneous, light, and full of delight and transforms the world in which it occurs into a magic world where the beloved is the center. While others might attend to the personal moods and wishes of a person, they do so for some ulterior motive; and a criterion of love is the lack of any further motive in the attention that we pay to the person. For the lover, there is not even a moral ground for making his beloved the center of attention and indeed his action might even go against his moral obligations to others. In many cases, one acts as though one were in love with a person with whom one is not in love in order to manipulate him, seduce him, or to win his favor. The pretense of love in this case is successful in its aim precisely because it is a semblance of the real thing and the real thing is a delight to the person who receives it. There is no one who is totally untouched by the charm of being loved since it fulfills a lack and neglect that is present in other domains of life. Part of the satisfaction of being important and rich is that one receives a semblance of that concern for one's personal whims and feelings that is found in personal love. While the important and rich might in fact be hated, they are treated as though they were loved.

The aim of love is achieved when the lovers retreat by themselves to a personal world apart from the world of everyday social and moral life. They constitute their world by their language, moods, gestures, and actions that have a meaning for them beyond what they have in the everyday world. There is no lover so prosaic and unimaginative that he cannot in some degree transcend the world of the everyday and give a new nuance and tone to the common words with which he expresses his love. When lovers retreat into their own world of meaning, they attain the security and mutual affirmation they fail to find in the public world. However, in this very retreat into a personal world, they show that the aim of love is independent of and even opposed to the moral aim. There are, of course, a wide variety of interpretations of the moral aim but most would agree that one component is the attempt to constitute a common social world in which each person is recognized as being of intrinsically equal worth and treated in a manner valid for anyone in the same circumstances. Morality is in principle opposed to a retreat into a private world in which personal whims, feelings, and moods take precedence over universal obligations. Morality finds a place for love only within the institution of marriage and family life. From the perspective of morality, the aim of love is marriage and children; and both of these are extrinsic from the purely erotic point of view. The aims of morality and love might come into sharp and irreconcilable conflict in cases where the aims of marriage and family life conflict with the pure erotic aim. The conflict might arise when a person loves someone else than the person to whom he is married or loves someone already married to another. In other cases, it arises within marriage when the partners fail to fulfill the ethical duties toward their children or other members of the family because of their retreat into an erotic world that they share alone. They might show their love to one another by putting each other above their children and devaluing their children in favor of their own aims. The presence of children in any case poses a problem for love since it threatens to turn the parents away from each other toward children and to reduce their relationship to a purely ethical project that pursues the common goal of rearing children. From the perspective of love, children are outsiders in the same manner as others. The distinctive aim and fulfillment of love is found in the mutual relation of the lovers themselves and has no room for a third.

While it is impossible to interpret the aim of love in terms of sexuality alone, the fulfillment of the sexual aim is a central act by which lovers achieve their aim of participating in the personal life of each other. The gestures and words of lovers as well as all forms of their bodily contact have a sexual significance in that they point towards the sexual union as the most complete form of the very same personal unity toward which these words, gestures, and actions are themselves directed. In the sexual union itself persons do not come together merely at the "ideal" level of language and meaning but come together in their concrete bodily reality. They become as far as possible one body, and in the measure that the person is his body, they become one person. The significance of sexual union depends on the significance of a person's body; and in the measure that one regards his body as himself, sexual union will be the highest form of personal union. Unless one detaches himself altogether from his body, he will regard sexual union as a vital form of personal union. The sexual union, to be sure, in some cases reduces to a mere means of pleasure or even a means of livelihood as in prostitution. For this reason, we cannot identify the sexual aim with the aims of love; the sexual aim is in any case simply a moment of the full erotic aim. However, the sexual union is never altogether without the significance of a personal union and is always a semblance of love. The peculiar satisfaction that it brings and its peculiar attraction arise in part from the fact that it is never merely a physical union or merely a physiological process but always a sharing in the intimate life of another. The prostitute or other person who must engage in sexual acts without having any attraction for the partner must for this reason detach herself from her body and her sexual life and regard them as alien. However, even she will find in the sexual union an image of genuine participation. The *merely* sexual is a limiting case.

For Sartre, the sexual act and other modes of action by which the lover participates in the life of the person he loves are not a fulfillment of the aim of love. They are merely strategies by which he pursues his proper aim of making himself a supreme value for the beloved and a limit on her freedom. The sexual is taken up as a mere phase of the struggle to dominate the other who threatens our own freedom. In regarding the aim of love as a state of being affirmed and being made a supreme end, Sartre takes it as a state rather than as a manner of life and action and fails to see that the very actions by which we are with our beloved are in fact the fulfillment of our love for him. The lover on Sartre's view never really transcends the circle of his own selfhood and is never genuinely concerned about sharing his loneliness and private selfhood with the person he loves. He is so concerned about himself and so involved in a struggle for domination that he is oblivious to the joy of being together. The lover is in fact concerned about the attitude of the beloved toward him; but not, as Sartre thinks, primarily because he is threatened by her and feels himself alienated by virtue of his existence for her, but rather because he already seeks to be with her and to share his life with her. From the perspective of the aim of love, we find the same failure to recognize the genuinely transcending and ecstatic character of love that we saw in Sartre's account of the object and basis of love.

Given his premises, there is nothing surprising in Sartre's conclusion that the aim of love is unattainable. The aim is selfish and has no place for the reciprocity that is essential to love. For Sartre, love reduces wholly to the desire to be loved; and therefore in the strict sense there is neither a lover nor a beloved. Nevertheless, Sartre's whole account operates with a conception of love as the supreme valuation of the person; and the fact that on Sartre's view, we seek this only for ourselves and never bestow it on another does not in the least mean that he does not conceive of love as supreme valuation. The basic mistake of Sartre is not in his interpretation of the ideal meaning of love but in the attempt to fit love into the general struggle for domination. The very fact that love cannot be realized within the sphere of this struggle ought to lead Sartre to re-examine the framework of his discussion. From the point of view of the struggle for domination, love reduces to pure self-love and leads to the futility that Sartre describes. However, this simply goes to show that love transcends this struggle. In the act by which we perceive the unique value of a person and take delight in her presence and receive back from her our invitation to share the intimate dimension of our life, we leave behind the struggle to dominate and enter into a world of playful freedom. The lovers do not feel alienated by the look of the beloved but rather feel affirmed. They find themselves in each other and abandon all aims in respect to one another but the playful sharing of their inmost life.

When we turn from the pure ideal to the actual reality, we find the inevitable shadow that falls between the ideal and the real. In the pursuit of the aim of his love, the lover comes up against the independence and freedom of his beloved and up against the inescapable demands of the other irreducible dimensions of his social life. The person he loves might fail to reciprocate his initial gestures of love, might turn away after initial acceptance or might use his love as a means of degrading him in favor of herself. Moreover, the beloved might at any time die and leave her beloved alone. The public dimension of our life demands our attention and prevents us from giving ourselves wholly to our relation to the person whom we love. From the perspective of love, there is no answer to the problems posed by the failure of reciprocity and no means to adjudicate the conflict between the claims of love and of the other sides of life. For love, there are no limits of love; and it always experiences limits as an alien necessity against which it thrusts itself in futile pain and suffering. The impulse of love is to persist in its aim in the face of reality even at the cost of a distortion of personality. This naiveté of love is the ultimate ground of the perversions to which it is open and the threat it poses to the dignity and integrity of the person. In its relation to a wider reality, love is fanatical.

While love in its initial immediacy goes out to the beloved without an explicit demand of reciprocity, reciprocity need only be called into question in order for the love itself to be put into question. In the absence of reciprocity, it is not only impossible to fulfill the erotic aim but also impossible to test the truth of the erotic claim. The truth of a claim to love a person can only be shown in the process by which the lover participates over time in the life of his beloved. The unrequited lover may make a show of loving, but in fact he loves a mere unrealized ideal; and to remain faithful to that is not the same as remaining faithful to a concrete person. The mournful longing for another might indeed be easier than actually living with the other since the ideal is without the flaws of reality. The ideal picture of the beloved we can never attain is more perfect than any person we can ever concretely love; and the higher our ideal, the more difficult to love an actual person.

When a person turns away from us, we can at least hope that she will turn back to us and make it possible to put our professed love to the test of actual reality. However, when the beloved dies, we can no longer share in her life. The dead are inaccessible, remote, and unresponsive in a manner more radical than the coldest and most distant living person. There is no hope of ever again communicating with the dead within the horizon of the present life. However, the distance of the dead is not self-imposed. The separation of death is in most cases not deliberate, as another's rejection of our love. The deceased person might have loved us with all her heart and soul right up to the end. From the point of view of love, she is therefore no less worthy of our love after her death than she was during her life. The death of a person does not make her less worthy of our respect and affection since death is in most cases simply something that overtakes a person and therefore does not affect her inner worth. However, from the moment of death, our love for a person reduces to a mere longing and can only be expressed in gestures of respect, in mourning and sorrow, and in turning away from others to the solitude of our being with the dead. There is now loneliness and silence instead of communion and animate speech. In a way, love makes the dead present but the presence is in the form of a heartfelt absence. Love is no comfort for the loss of the dead and holds no answer for it; on the contrary, love makes it the harder to bear. If the lover turns away from his beloved, he will feel that he has betrayed her and allowed her to die a second time; on the other side, when he remains faithful to her, he finds that his love becomes increasingly empty and abstract and finally reduces to a futile gesture. In death, love experiences the absurd negation of its own reality.

There are cases between the full non-reciprocity of absolute rejection or death and the full reciprocity of ideal love. These perverse forms illustrate in a dramatic manner the independence of love and morality. From the point of view of love, they in part fulfill its aim even though from a moral point of view they might be degrading and reprehensible. These are cases in which the beloved uses the love of the beloved in order to dominate and exercise her power over her lover and to receive affirmation at his hands. Her motives belong to the domain of the struggle for power; and they might be understood along the lines that Sartre proposes. The motives of the degraded lover are on the other side quite different. He shares in the personal life of his beloved and therefore in part attains the erotic aim. He has no alternative to degradation but to give up the project of love altogether. The conduct of the sadist toward her lover in this perverted relationship is the precise reverse of that by which she would reciprocate his love and in this respect belongs to the same sphere of life. The sadist does not degrade and humiliate her partner on the level of his public self but on the level of his most intimate personal self. Instead of doing and saying the things that she knows will please him, she does and says those that she knows will hurt him; instead of tenderness and reverence, she shows him cruelty and disdain. She attempts to make him act in an obscene manner; and she abuses him sexually. However, in this very behavior, she shares with him an aspect of her own intimate selfhood and shares in personal life with him. The very pain that she causes him is a source of pleasure to him insofar as it is a mode in which he participates in her life. To give up his pain in this case would be to give up being with his beloved.

The active partner in this cruel game might at first sight appear to be the independent essential reality. For in every act by which her lover humiliates himself in front of her and accepts her abuse, she finds a proof of her own supremacy in the eyes of the lover. However, there is a dialectic in the relationship which makes it less one-sided than it initially appears to be. The beloved appears to maintain her independence and superiority over the lover in the behavior by which she devalues and degrades him. However, she is dependent on her lover for the position that she enjoys. She can put herself above him and subordinate him only so long as he allows it. He might at any time declare his independence and turn her abuse into a futile gesture that no longer strikes home. Moreover, he is himself in some measure aware of his power over his beloved, and this makes the relationship tolerable to him. In the very act by which he submits to her abuse, he plays something of an active role; and in the very interest that she shows in subordinating him, she is dependent on his love for her.

In some cases the sadist loves her victim as much as he loves her; and in these cases she degrades and subordinates him not merely in order to test the love of her beloved but also to try to escape from putting herself in the position he is in. She attempts to prove both to herself and to the other that she is superior to the power of love and is not open to the pain and degradation of being rejected. This futile defensive move arises from the painful realization that a lover is at the mercy of his beloved and is open to being hurt by him. The lover in this case is driven by anxiety in the fact of the possibility of her own humiliation and pain to humiliate and hurt the very person who has the power to humiliate and hurt her. Sadistic love is troubled and reflective and is torn between the ecstatic attraction for the other and anxious self-concern. First love is never sadistic; sadistic love is never naive.

In the same manner that moral and communal domains attempt to subjugate personal love to their own values and ends, personal love endeavors to subordinate these to its own distinctive value and end. In its purity, the ideal of love demands of lovers that they put their relationship to each other first in their lives and devalue other persons, values, and projects in favor of their own personal union. From the perspective of love, personal union with the beloved is the supreme value of life; and in the measure that one is serious about love, one will find oneself in a conflict with the demands of other persons and the demands of other values and tasks. From the perspective of these other realms, love has only a limited validity and is merely *one* relationship on the scale with others. The lover is in fact never *merely* a lover, even though he might desire to be; nor, on the other side, is the person in love fully a moral agent or a member of the larger community. He is torn between both and is inescapably involved with both; and in practice, he is forced to compromise with regard to the demands of both and in this manner falls short of all ideals. In the measure that he attempts to do full justice to the ideal requirements of love, he will turn away from communal life and give up the attempt to make a substantial recognized achievement in the public world; on the other side, in the measure that he attempts to fulfill his moral requirements and contribute to larger goals, he will fail to give his beloved the attention that his love for her demands. If he goes too far toward the pole of the private world of the erotic, he volatilizes his life by cutting himself off from the serious work of the community and morality in favor of the play of mood and sexuality that constitutes the main content of the pure erotic life. If, on the other side, he goes too far toward the pole of the public world of civic and professional life, he neglects his beloved and allows his love to reduce to a mere claim. The very demand that lovers make the purely personal side of their lives the center of focus prevents them from resolving the conflict between substantial achievement and moral responsibility, on the one side, and their love for one another, on the other side, by co-operating on common ventures and projects that have a significance beyond their personal relationship. In the measure that they make something beyond themselves their fundamental aim, they pass beyond the pure erotic. Their love dissolves into the general ethical reality.

From the present perspective, we may conclude with a brief remark regarding the role of personal love in disclosing our own self and the self of the other. In a more radical manner than other forms of experience, personal love reveals the value and uniqueness of the individual person. When a person loves another, he penetrates beneath the public self defined by interchangeable tasks, roles, and functions to the unique style of feeling and action by which the individual fulfills them and the inward life into which he withdraws from them. In aiming at the concrete individual personality of the beloved, the lover at the same time reveals her personality to the beloved herself and thereby helps to constitute and realize her personality. The beloved first becomes radically aware of her own uniqueness through the eyes of her lover. In this respect, love gives us an affirmation and recognition beyond that which we receive in other forms of relationship. When she reciprocates love, the beloved does the same for her lover in this regard that her lover does for her and thus leads him to a fuller awareness of his own individual being. The lovers teach each other who they are and serve as a conscience for each other. The individuality of a person is covered over and hidden in the general conduct of everyday public life where one tends to become anonymous and to conceive of oneself and be conceived in terms of one's function and status alone. The individual, of course, is not denied in the public life but is rather passed over as insignificant. The individual first becomes central and fully present in personal love.

However, the very individuality of the beloved puts her at a distance, since any individual stands apart from everyone else with a center of personal freedom and a perspective all her own. In the measure that the lover becomes aware of the radical uniqueness of his beloved, he will feel separation from her. The separation arises both from his own freedom and from the freedom of the other. They both discover that the dimension of their selves which they share with the other and which constitutes the substance of their relationship is merely an aspect. They are always both something more for themselves and for others than they are for each other even though they might both aim to be the whole world for each other and to put themselves wholly into their personal relationship. They both open to a wider world which relativizes the personal world that they constitute together and both retreat even from that personal world into personal worlds of their own. They never fully succeed in moving wholly out of the public world to the world that they share with each other nor wholly out of the private world of their own unexpressed feelings, desires, and emotions. Hence, while the lovers come together on the level of their concrete individual being and share in the personal side of their lives, opening themselves to each other and treating the other as being as important as their own self, they fall short of full union and in fact reveal their irreducible otherness. The sexual act, where they come closest to full union, is momentary and ephemeral. The magic spell of their union is over at the very point where it appears to have taken the lovers fully outside of themselves and made them really one. The sexual union provides an ecstatic release from the privacy of our own self; and yet its fulfillment throws us back again into the recesses of that very privacy. Not surprisingly, the apartness of persons reveals itself most dramatically in the most radical attempt to transcend it. In revealing the apartness, love reveals the loneliness of our own self and the uniqueness and distinct value of the other which serve as the subjective and objective grounds of its own reality.

NOTE

1. For Sartre's account of love, see *Being and Nothingness* (translated by Hazel Barnes), Philosophical Library, New York, 1956, pp. 364–79.

SEX, LOVE, AND JUSTICE: A PROBLEM IN MORAL EDUCATION

Joseph A. Diorio

THE PAST DECADE has seen the appearance of a number of philosophical discussions dealing with issues of sexuality, rectifying in part philosophers' earlier avoidance of such topics. [1] In particular, sexual desire, sexual "perversions," promiscuity and other concepts and practices important to sexual ethics have become the subjects of philosophical study. Unlike their disciplinary cousins, however, philosophers of education have not reflected this interest in sex, and the literature of sex education remains largely innocent of philosophical analysis. [2]

This lack of interest by philosophers in sex education is both surprising and disturbing. It is surprising because sex education commonly is assumed to be linked closely to moral education, which long has been of interest to educational philosophers. It is disturbing because the lack of philosophical attention only can facilitate the maintenance of doctrinaire, conventional assumptions about sex as foundations for sex education programs. Problematical attitudes about sex more easily can be injected into sex education under the guise of certain truth when philosophers, however minimal their influence, turn away.

There undeniably are pressures militating against the open discussion in

Reprinted from *Educational Theory* 31, Nos. 3 & 4 (Summer-Fall, 1981), pp. 225–35, by permission of the Office of Patents and Copyrights of the University of Illinois and by the editorial office of *Educational Theory*. Joseph A. Diorio is Senior Lecturer in Philosophy of Education, University of Otago, Dunedin, New Zealand. He has made a few changes in this reprint.

273

schools of many of the complex aspects of sexuality. Sex continues to be viewed in many quarters in ways which make it difficult to gain a hearing for the very arguments intended to increase awareness of the issues surrounding it. Merely raising some of these issues in a classroom is likely to be taken as evidence of moral depravity. As John Passmore has noted:

> No one is going to protest at an examination question which asks what changes take place in the heart as it expands and contracts and instructs the examinee to illustrate his answers with line drawings. A parallel question about the expansion and contraction of the sexual organs will be accused of corrupting youth. [3]

The effect of such pressures is to force educators either to ignore sex entirely or, where its discussion is permitted in schools, to conduct this discussion so that orthodox notions of conventional sexual morality often are left unexamined. As one source in New Zealand bluntly puts it, the child "needs to learn to control and direct his sex drives in socially acceptable ways."[4]

ANTI-PROMISCUITY AND HUMAN RELATIONS EDUCATION

Given this context, advocacy of sex education of any kind in schools often is taken to be a "liberal" position. Such advocacy can mask an uncritical commitment to orthodox sexual attitudes, however. Historically, this can be seen in certain contexts where movements for the introduction of sex education into schools became widespread. Writing of the sex education movement among American Progressives early in the present century, Steven Schlossman and Stephanie Wallach have noted that:

> The main goals of sex education were to purify discourse on sex, particularly in the popular press and among children, and to instill moral inhibitions against sexual gratification now that effective birth control and cures for venereal disease were becoming widely available. The sex educators were moral crusaders marching under the banner of medical and pedagogical science. They sought to develop instructional techniques for innocently conveying new medical knowledge about sex to children and, at the same time, imbuing sex with older spiritual meanings. Sex education was a means of pedagogical warfare against the purveyors of sexual titillation. Far from encouraging freer discussion of sex, the sex educators wanted to discipline lust and channel it to conventional moral ends. [5]

Today, many advocates of sex education argue that any instruction in sexuality will be too restricted unless sex is considered within the context of human relationships. Use of the umbrella notion of "human relations education" in part represents an attempt to avoid viewing sex as an exclusively physiological matter. It can involve the definition of sex as acceptable only within the context of personal relationships of a certain sort, however, thereby providing a contemporary example parallel to earlier Progressive attempts to "discipline lust" by channeling it unreflectively toward conventional marriage. In the following discussion, reports published by the New Zealand Department of Education and other official bodies in that country will be used to illustrate the connection which can prevail between advocacy of human relations education and the failure to consider critically many of the ethical issues of sexuality.

It has been claimed, for example, that attention to sexuality should not be limited

> solely to the traditional form of sex education usually concerned with a limited and specific body of factual knowledge and dealing with reproduction and pubertal changes. In this form sex education has not necessarily helped students to understand themselves and their relationships with others. . . . sex education in its truest and deepest sense is based on education in human relationships and personal responsibility.[6]

Placing sex within the context of personal relationships here provides a means of introducing morals into sexual relations under the aegis of "responsibility." But what constitutes responsibility in sex? One answer which often is given— the answer which many people in many countries want from sex education programs but fear will not be forthcoming, prompting them to reject sex education *in toto*—is that sexual promiscuity is irresponsible. The same source states that:

> it is difficult to establish the nature of the differences in attitudes and behavior from one generation to the next but research findings both overseas and in New Zealand suggest that the majority of teenagers are responsible in personal relationships and are not sexually promiscuous.[7]

Responsible sexuality, therefore, links sexual intimacy with personal relationships and excludes promiscuity.

Mere proclamation of a link between sex and personal relationships is not sufficient to establish the condemnation of promiscuity, however. No implication is drawn that an individual should have personal relationships only with one other individual. If a person is not culpable for having a plurality of personal relationships, and if sex is to be linked with such relationships, why is sexual promiscuity declared to be irresponsible? Once this question is asked, it becomes clear that advocates of human relations education usually have more in mind than a simple connection between such relationships and sex. Rather, a theory of personal relations is required which will demonstrate the place of sexuality within some, but not all, such relations. Such a theory has to be supported by more than just the fact that it condemns promiscuity.[8]

Love often is appealed to as the proper criterion for distinguishing human relationships in which sexuality has a place from those in which it does not. According to the New Zealand Committee on Health and Social Education:

> we want students to realize that sexuality involves self-discipline and involves loving and caring for another person—not the mere seeking of self-release. It is the basis of a lasting relationship; it is a most powerful emotional drive and has great capacity for bringing happiness and giving meaning to life.[9]

This passage advances a view of sexuality which begs a series of complex questions. What, for example, is meant by the claim that sexuality involves "self-discipline"? Why must sex be the *basis* of lasting relationships? What are the implications of identifying sex as an "emotional drive," and are those implications compatible with the links which are declared to hold between sex, love and happiness? While this Committee does not attempt to answer any of these questions, its basic point is clear: sex is not to be associated with just any relationships, but only with those of a lasting and caring sort which are taken to involve love. Love is to be the moral legitimator of sexual intimacy.

The sex-love linkage is no more sufficient as a basis for a code of sexual ethics in which opposition to promiscuity is a central tenet than the connection between sex and personal relationships generally. Basing the morality of sexual intimacy unqualifiedly upon the presence of love could legitimate sexual intimacies within homosexual couples, between adults and children, between households and among the members of all sorts of communal groupings. That these are not the sort of relations that the point of view represented in the documents quoted above would endorse can be seen from the great emphasis placed by that viewpoint upon the family as the proper venue for sex. Hence it is not just love, which if left to itself conceivably could be promiscuous and thus could legitimate sexual promiscuity, but rather love within the confines of monogamous, heterosexual marriages which is to serve as the legitimator of sexually intimate behavior. Sex is to be a family affair, and sex education is to aim at socializing children into conventional family living.

The family has been identified explicitly as the focal point of sex education by the New Zealand Department of Education, which stated that one of the "objectives in providing sex education . . . [is] the preservation and enrichment of family life."[10] Legitimate sex, then, is sex within the family, and acceptance of this view is supposed to provide for "stability" in the community.[11] The purpose of sex education thus becomes the preservation of social stability, and failures of sex education to curb sexual promiscuity are seen to threaten the onset of social chaos. Since the family is the proper place for sexual intimacy, indulging promiscuously in such intimacy outside the family is irresponsible behavior because it blurs the boundaries between discrete households.

Is the restriction of love and sex to within the family on the grounds of social stability justifiable? The viewpoint represented by the documents we have been discussing presumes a positive answer to this question without addressing it directly. The presumption would seem to be based on the popular conception of the family as a natural form of human organization and as an institution in which love naturally prevails. The family is seen as the natural and hence the proper sort of organization into which persons who love each other should place themselves. As Carole Pateman has noted:

> The family is seemingly the most natural of all human associations. . . .
> [it] is also grounded in the natural ties of love and affection . . . and it has
> its origin in the biological process of procreation, in the natural differ-
> ence between the sexes. . . . The family is widely regarded as the natural
> basis of civil life. Familial or domestic relations, are based on the natural
> ties of biology and sentiment, and the family is constituted by the
> particularistic bonds of organic unity.[12]

The family thus is seen as the natural product of that particularistic attachment between persons known as love. The family is what should result from love, and what does result unless something intervenes to derail the natural course of events. Since love is natural, and since the family is nature's organizational response to love, the worth of the family and its link with love thereby is established. Promiscuity then can be condemned as unnatural, because it violates the particularistic bonds of love and the natural and proper forms of stable social organization which result from those bonds.

By directing sex toward love, and by reinforcing nature by helping to keep love within the family, sex education often is expected to result in young people restricting their sexual activities to a single heterosexual individual with whom they are involved in a loving relationship in a marriage or its equivalent. One question which often stands out in the minds of young people is "Whom should I love?" Given the vast range of possible partners, and faced with the demand that only one individual be selected out of this range, a person might reasonably expect some guidance as to how to go about this selection. Sometimes, however, all that is offered are statements such as the following:

> school programs should be designed and implemented in ways that ensure pupils who leave school early are adequately prepared for life in the community and the roles they will play as adults. The programs should include . . . [the] immediate and long-term implications of dating, *choice of partner*, marriage and family relationships. [13]

Here choosing a partner is assumed to be something to be carried out after a certain amount of dating but before marriage and the establishment of a family. Nothing is said about what criteria are to be used in making this choice. Indeed, that it *is* a choice is an assumption that is neither clarified nor defended. Clearly, it is intended that love in some way should be involved in this choice, but in what way is not indicated. The remainder of this paper will discuss the difficulties which arise for the anti-promiscuity position from clarification of the ways in which love could be relied on in choosing one's partner for enduring, familial sexual relations.

LOVE AND THE "CHOICE" OF A SEXUAL PARTNER

Love generally is taken to be something of inherent value. If love is to provide a bulwark against promiscuity, however, its distribution by any person must be restricted to a single recipient. To carry out this restriction one of two assumptions could be made. The first is the moral claim that love in fact is not an unqualified good, and that there are times when bestowing or receiving love can be evil. The second is the conceptual assumption that "love" excludes anything which could be extended to more than one person at a time. The first assumption threatens to engulf those who make it in circularity. If love is not good some of the time, then some criteria must be advanced for distinguishing the times when it is good from those when it is not. These criteria must involve more than just the claim that love is bad when it is offered to more than one person at a time, because whether this is so is precisely what is in doubt. The second assumption flies in the face of much human experience, for one of the most commonly reported and written about of human situations is that of persons who love or are loved by more than one person at a time. To deny the term "love" to these cases would be both question begging and an affront to common language.

If love is to be relied on as a legitimator of sexual intimacy, it must appear prior in time to the intimacy which it legitimates. This means that the question of how one's love should be distributed is among the most basic of those involved in the anti-promiscuity argument. One approach to this question conceives of love as providing criteria for its own distribution. This is essentially a romantic view, which holds that we *should* love those whom we *do* love. This approach, however, takes love out of the realm of choice and places it within the domain of occurrences which happen to individuals. Hence we might "fall" in love with someone, who thereby becomes the proper object of our love. The trouble here from the point of view of the anti-promiscuity argument is that unless love is defined as something which cannot occur between more than two persons at once, the occurrence of romantic love leaves open the possibility of a simultaneous plurality of loves and hence of sexual promiscuity.

It is doubtful that love could provide criteria for its own distribution, any more than could any other distributable good. Determining the proper distribution of goods is the subject of justice, though the relationship between love and justice has been relatively unexplored.[14] Justice has been proclaimed to be both "The first virtue of social institutions,"[15] and the "central principle of morality."[16] Love, on the other hand, readily is identified as the foundation of sexual morality and the basis of the particularistic attachments to specific individuals that supposedly are found naturally within the family. As Pateman has observed:

> Justice is not the virtue of *all* social institutions. . . . it is love, not justice, that is the first virtue of the family. The family is a natural social not a conventionally social institution, but justice is a public or conventional virtue. In the family, individuals appear as unique and unequal personalities and as members of a differentiated unity grounded in sentiment. In civil life individuals transcend, or leave behind, the particular ascribed characteristics which distinguish them in the private sphere and appear as unrelated equals. . . . In a civil association, individuals are bound together and their actions are regulated solely by general or universal rules and laws that apply impartially to all. . . . Particular or private interests of individuals must be subordinated to the public interest, or to the virtue of justice. . . . Love and justice are antagonistic virtues; the demands of love and of family bonds are particularistic and so in direct conflict with justice which demands that private interest is subordinated to the public (universal) good.[17]

If love and justice really are antagonistic it would be impossible to subject the distribution of love to the demands of justice. It is far from unlikely, however, that this antagonism, rather than inhering necessarily within these two principles, rests instead on contingent views that the family is constituted by particularistic attachments which ought to fence it off from the demands of justice. That is, a view of the family is used to determine the nature and the applicability of justice, rather than commitments to justice being given precedence in determining the proper nature of the family and its relationships. Defining the family so as necessarily to exclude from it the demands of justice is to beg the question of whether those demands should apply to it.

The effect of separating the institutional domains of love and justice in this way is to separate moral education, oriented toward the pursuit of justice, from sex education concerned with promulgating conventional family living. If the family is outside the domain of justice, if justice is the primary virtue of morality, and if the family is the primary focus of sex education, then sex education itself ceases to be a part of moral education. Hence the price of separating love from justice is the separation of sex from morality, a price which most persons holding orthodox views on sex education would find unacceptable. On the other hand, if sex is acknowledged to be a legitimate concern of morality, and if justice is accepted as an overriding moral virtue, then the applicability of the demands of justice to the distribution of love and the enjoyment of sexual intimacies also must be acknowledged.

There is a further reason for subjecting the distribution of love to the rules of justice. Even if we accept that involvement in loving relationships conveys upon individuals responsibilities and privileges antagonistic to justice, this says nothing about determining who to love in the first place. Certain actions might come under the governance of love rather than justice after love has been established, but the establishment of love in itself cannot be governed in this way. If love can be thought of as a distributable good, then the rules for its distribution cannot themselves depend upon love. Hence however much the demands of love might supersede those of justice once love exists in a relationship, love cannot supersede justice in the determination of whom to love unless love is an occurrence.

Any assertion that the identification of one's partner in love is a *choice* involves a commitment to a certain conception of the nature of love. If we are to choose the person whom we will love, then love must be something under our volitional control, and the conveying of love must be subsequent to the choosing of a recipient. We cannot choose our partner *because* we love him or her—which is to say that love cannot be prior to the choice of a loved one—for then love would be something beyond our control which happens to us or into which we fall. This, however, would place the occurrence of love outside moral regulation, and multiple loves, if they occurred, could not be condemned nor could the sexual promiscuity which they could legitimate.

Condemning persons for promiscuity in cases where promiscuity was based upon multiple loves implies that love can be controlled; that love is a decision and not an occurrence. Since rational decisions demand criteria, this would require us to open cases of love to justification on the grounds of whether choices of loved ones were made on the basis of good or poor reasons. This would subject the distribution of love to the demands of justice.

The nature of these demands cannot be ascertained unproblematically, however, for "justice" itself is subject to competing conceptualizations. Without attempting either to review the literature on this subject or to provide a comprehensive list of alternative views of justice, we can note three significantly different concepts of justice which prevail in current discussions. Two of these, namely, justice as equality which demands equal treatment of all individuals by virtue of their personhood or other universal characteristic, and justice as desert which calls for a differential distribution of goods to individuals on the basis of their abilities, efforts or contributions, are supported by extensive traditions in the literatures of several disciplines. The third, justice as entitlement, takes as its principle "From each as they choose, to each as they are chosen," and holds that individuals can distribute anything over which they have legitimate control in any fashion they wish, provided only that nothing is forced upon unwilling recipients.[18]

If we attempt to subject the distribution of love to the demands of justice, serious problems are posed to the view connecting love with the deterrence of promiscuity regardless of which of these conceptions of justice is employed. If justice as equality is accepted and if every person as such is seen as an appropriate recipient of love, then every person would have at least a *prima facie* claim on the love of every other. Insofar as love legitimates sexual intimacy, unless that claim can be deflected in some way in the vast majority of cases, general promiscuity would be authorized thereby. If justice as desert is accepted, we then face the problem of determining who is deserving of being loved, on what grounds, and by whom. Unless it were the case that every individual possessed a unique set of characteristics which made them deserving of receiving the love of one and only one other unique individual—the situation envisaged by some forms of romanticism—the qualities which merit love probably would be general at least to several individuals. On the principle that equally deserving individuals deserve to receive equal goods, love toward and hence sexual intimacy with a plurality of persons would be justified. And if justice as entitlement is accepted, then an individual could distribute his love in whatever way he chose, including to a number of persons at once.

In order to restrict sexual activity to a single partner, many opponents of promiscuity rely on two claims: that sex is a matter of morality, and that sexual intimacy should be connected with love in the exclusive context of the family. Including sex under the regulation of morality implies making its distribution, through love, subject to the demands of justice. Regardless of the conception of justice which is followed, however, these demands arguably justify at least a degree of promiscuity. Hence those who oppose promiscuity find that asserting the moral quality of sex threatens this very opposition. Alternatively, if they adhere to their opposition they risk acknowledging sex as extra-moral, thereby depriving their viewpoint of its moral footing.

The orthodox position must hold that an individual always can decide *not* to love any given person. That is, once a person has chosen—in whatever manner—to love someone, they must be capable of choosing not to love anyone else. There is a criterion of choice built into this view, which tells the individual whom not to love—namely, anyone not loved already—once someone is loved. It provides no criteria for determining who to love in the first place, however, thereby placing the individual in the position of having to make a criterionless or non-rational choice of partner in love.

If there *are* no criteria to be employed in determining whom to love, then in effect whether love is under the volitional control of the individual makes no difference. Anyone can be loved, provided only that at the moment of decision no one else is loved already and that the person chosen does not love another. [19] Within these limits, whomever is chosen apparently is selected on arbitrary grounds. Before the choice is made the person to be chosen cannot be said to have a greater claim on the as yet undirected love of the would-be lover. Since the initial choice of a loved one is non-rational, and since many possible objects of love would be equally lovable, a person often would be unable to justify choosing to love A but not B or C.

The result of this would be that the entire edifice of sexual morality, including the condemnation of sexual promiscuity, would rest upon the foundation of a non-rational choice. Choices which are made extra to reason, and against which reasons cannot be adduced, have the same moral status as occurrences. The determination of who to love through a choice of this sort thus is identical in moral impact to the non-volitional occurrence of love. If X "falls" in love with A, through no rational choice of his own, then the only reply he can make to the entreaties of B and C as to why he does not love them instead is that he "cannot help the way he feels." There is neither appeal nor defense against such occurrences of love, and no justification can be demanded for them. The same is true of non-rational choices, and it is not difficult to think of such choices as a species of occurrence. "Choosing" to love A by flipping a coin, drawing a name out of a hat, or relying in some obscure way upon one's tastes—all of which would be possible on the entitlement view of justice—are ways of having the love of A happen to one that parallel "falling" in love with A. Loving A, B or C is equally possible for X, and which of these persons X actually will love in these ways is determined by an arbitrary event separate from X's rational deliberation.

Those who believe that love is one of the foundations of a happy and meaningful life, however, on this account would have to contend with the complaints of those who miss out undeservedly on this good life because by chance they do not become the object of another's love. There does not appear to be any way in which such complaints could be dealt with effectively, apart from assuming—no doubt wishfully—that some romantic hidden hand operates to ensure that there is "someone for everyone," and that all a person needs to do is wait. Those whose anti-promiscuity outlook leads them to adopt the view that love is an arbitrary occurrence or an irrational choice, therefore, really ought to include in the sex education programs which they base upon this view, the warning to young people that they quite possibly might be left out of the good things which are taken to depend upon love.

JUSTIFYING LOVE

We have not as yet considered the nature of love directly. Unfortunately, love promises to be no more simple a concept than justice, for it is, as D. W. Hamlyn has noted, "a very 'catholic' emotion . . . [which] takes many forms and . . . many kinds of object."[20] This being so, educators who wish to base sex education programs embodying a pro-family, anti-promiscuity position upon a foundation of love properly should identify first the type of love which is intended to serve as a legitimator of sexual intimacy. The ways in which that form of love arises then could be examined, and a solution to the problem of arbitrary or irrational distribution of love thereby might be found.

One of the most famous typologies of love is Kant's distinction between practical and pathological love. Discussing the difference between inclination and duty, Kant stated that:

> It is in this way, undoubtedly, that we should understand those passages of Scriptures which command us to love our neighbor, and even our enemy, for love as an inclination cannot be commanded. But beneficence from duty, when no inclination impels it and even when it is opposed by a natural and unconquerable aversion, is practical love, not pathological love; it resides in the will and not in the propensities of feeling, in principles of action and not in tender sympathy.[21]

Practical love, which is universal brotherly love demanded by—and perhaps equivalent to—justice, depends upon universal qualities of all persons, and hence demands that all human beings be made its object. Such universal love would be useless in limiting the legitimation of sexual activity; hence when sex educators speak of linking sexual intimacy with loving relationships it cannot be anything like Kant's practical love which they have in mind.

The sentimental or passionate inclination toward a specific person which is pathological love, on the other hand, is a discriminating emotion. This would appear to be the kind of love to which advocates of the anti-promiscuity position would have to appeal to support the family-based limitation of sexual intimacy. Since pathological love is not felt toward every person, it must be asked what distinguishes cases where it is felt from cases where it is not. If criteria for determining whom to love with the kind of love that leads legitimately to sexual intimacy can be identified, then sometimes we would be able to praise love as well founded and other times to condemn it as unjustified. In searching for such criteria, we encounter yet another philosophical dispute: does love depend upon the qualities and characteristics of the person loved?

The orthodox position sees the achievement of a special loving attachment to a specific individual as the foundation of the family and as one of the objectives of sex education. The type of love involved in such an attachment is supposed to be *personal*, but is not supposed to be directed toward the specific personal qualities of the recipient.[22] Furthermore, in order to serve as the foundation of the family, love must endure. One of the major objections to tying love to manifestly transient personal qualities is that doing so would deprive love of its durability.[23]

If love is not to be tied to the qualities of the beloved, however, in what way are we to distinguish the person we love from the many whom we do not? John McTaggart attempted to provide a solution to this problem a half century ago. In his view, love could be *because* of personal qualities of the beloved but never could be *in respect of* those qualities.[24] That is, love could arise because of our perception of certain characteristics of another, but if it really is love then it could not be *of* those characteristics, but must be directed toward the person who possesses them. In McTaggart's words:

> To love one person above all the world for all one's life because her eyes are beautiful when she is young, is to be determined to a very great thing by a very small cause. But if what is caused is really love—and this is sometimes the case—it is not condemned on that ground. It is there, and that is enough. This would seem to indicate that the emotion is directed to the person, independently of his qualities, and that the determining qualities are not the justification of that emotion, but only the means by which it arises.[25]

McTaggart argues that in this respect love is different from other emotions, which are condemnable if based on trivial or irrelevant causes. Hence great hatred of a person for a trivial reason results in us declaring such hatred unjustified, and similarly we condemn a great fear of something harmless. Love, on the other hand, however great it may be, is not to be condemned on account of arising from a trivial cause, nor indeed because we can find no cause for it at all. "We do not condemn love," McTaggart says, "because it is not known why it is C and not D whom B loves. No cause can be inadequate, if it produces such a result."[26]

This view has been reformulated recently by Hamlyn, who states that:

> To be loved full-stop is simply to be loved without there being anything that the love is for. In such a situation there is likely to be some explanation why the love came into being, and it is possible with some objects of love for one to love them for the fact that and because of the circumstances in which the love came into being; but there seems to me to be no necessity that it should be like that. . . .[27]

Hamlyn believes that love is an inherently good thing which should not be subjected to justification, and which is not to be condemned because no justification for it can be given. Where would this view leave the orthodox position with its concern to counter promiscuity by tying sex to love? If it is true that love never can be condemned through reference to the qualities which gave rise to it or the characteristics of the person loved, presumably this would be true in any case in which a person felt love for several persons. Since none of these loves would require justification, and since none of them could be condemned, then if love authorizes sexual intimacy, sexual promiscuity likewise would be legitimated.

Furthermore, since *no* cause of love could be inadequate, *any* cause would be adequate, thereby making the provision of criteria for the distribution of love unnecessary and, indeed, impossible. Since any quality could be loved, all qualities could be loved. Love either would have to be distributed equally to everyone, since every quality of every person would be equally capable of provoking it, or else it would have to be distributed only to one or a number of persons on arbitrary grounds. The former alternative admits widespread promiscuity, and the latter raises the problem of justice and of rectifying the situation of those who "miss out" on love through no fault of their own.

We could, of course, reject the views of McTaggart and Hamlyn and argue instead that love does require justification in terms of the specific characteristics of its recipients. Whether such an argument would be correct is not our concern here, but merely whether such a view would provide comfort to the anti-promiscuity argument of the orthodox position. The answer to this appears to be "no."

The justification of love directed toward a beloved might be made in terms of the lover's own tastes for the other person's qualities,[28] or upon an arguable conviction that those qualities deserve to be loved. Insofar as the qualities in question can be found in more than one person then either one's tastes or one's sense of justice would lead to directing love to all who bore these characteristics. Thus unless love first is defined as singular and exclusive, there is nothing to prevent an individual from loving at least several persons on the basis of their possession of common characteristics.

Furthermore, since there is no obvious reason why only one type of qualities will be deserving of love or will appeal to a person's tastes, it seems to be possible for an individual to love a number of different people possessing different qualities. In the words of John Donne,

> I can love both fair and brown;
> Her whom abundance melts, and her whom want betrays:
> Her who loves loneness best, and her who masks and plays;
> Her whom the country formed, and whom the town;
> Her who believes, and her who tries;
> Her who still weeps with spongy eyes,
> And her who is dry as cork and never cries. [29]

As long as tastes are not mutually exclusive, or as long as there is no single collection of characteristics which can be identified as exclusively deserving of love, then if love is to be justified in this fashion the door to promiscuity cannot be shut.

CONCLUSION

If love requires justification, therefore, then whether justification is to be through appeal to the tastes of the lover or through the deserving nature of the qualities of the beloved, a plurality of loves is not ruled out. If love does not require justification, then regardless of what love is or how it comes about, if a person loves more than one other individual, there is no obvious way to condemn any of his loves.

The foregoing argument is not intended as a comprehensive defense of promiscuity. It has not taken account of many possible objections to promiscuous sexual behavior, including those based upon prudence, nor has it considered moral arguments supporting restriction of love to a single partner. It does show, however, that an effective anti-promiscuity argument cannot be derived from the kinds of conventional ideas about love which New Zealand sources have been used to illustrate. Furthermore, it illustrates the complexity of the issues surrounding sexuality and the distribution of love—issues arising in part from the application of justice to personal relationships. In attempting to cut through these issues by tying sexual intimacy to love, sex education programs can mislead students by presenting as simple and straight-forward something which actually is complex and contentious.

If sex education programs based upon notions of "education in human relationships" are to misrepresent human life in this way to students, we would be better off with the "traditional form of sex education . . . concerned with a limited and specific body of factual knowledge" which was condemned as unhelpful in New Zealand. This is a case where a position which has been identified by many as "liberal," namely, the broadening of sex education to include the study of human relationships, in practice can involve the indoctrination of students. Sex education of this kind shares with the sex education of the American Progressives, as noted by Schlossman and Wallach, the concern to channel students' "lusts" to conventionally defined moral ends.

NOTES

1. See, for example, W. M. Alexander, "Philosophers Have Avoided Sex," *Diogenes* 72 (Winter 1970): 56–74; also Alan H. Goldman, "Plain Sex," *Philosophy and Public Affairs* 6 (1976–77): 267.

2. One exception is John Wilson, *Logic and Sexual Morality* (Harmondsworth: Penguin Books, 1965).

3. John Passmore, *The Philosophy of Teaching* (London: Duckworth, 1980), p. 240.

4. New Zealand Department of Education, *Health—Suggestions for Health Education in Primary Schools* (Wellington: Government Printer, 1970), p. 177.

5. "The Crime of Precocious Sexuality: Female Juvenile Delinquency in the Progressive Era," *Harvard Educational Review* 48, 1 (February 1978): 90.

6. *Human Development and Relationships in the School Curriculum* (Wellington: New Zealand Department of Education, 1973), p. 7. The final clause quoted here was itself quoted by the authors of this document from Birmingham Education Committee, *Sex Education in Schools; Report of the Working Party on Sex Education* (Birmingham: L.E.A., 1967).

7. Ibid., p. 10. This report is careful to identify its position with that of the "majority," not only within New Zealand but in the larger world outside as well. By basing its identification of this majority view on "research," the authors deflect any charge that they are advocating a special morality for the limited scope of New Zealand conditions.

8. Discussions of the ethics of promiscuity can be found in Robert Baker and Frederick Elliston, eds., *Philosophy and Sex*, 1st. ed. (Buffalo, NY: Prometheus, 1975), pp. 166–243.

9. *Growing, Sharing, Learning: The Report of the Committee on Health and Social Education* (Wellington: New Zealand Department of Education, 1977), p. 38. This booklet generated a great deal of discussion in New Zealand. Because it advocated introducing sex education into primary schools under the aegis of human relations education programs, it received the support of many liberal educators, though for the same reason it was the subject of considerable negative popular reaction. A sample of critical comments on the report can be found in *Delta* 22 (June 1978).

10. New Zealand Department of Education, *Health*, p. 176. See also *Growing, Sharing, Learning*, p. 37.

11. *Growing, Sharing, Learning* identifies the family as a "basic value" possessing "universal appeal" and serving as a "cornerstone" and an "essential feature of a stable community"; pp. 28, 32. See also *Contraception, Sterilization and Abortion in New Zealand: Report of the Royal Commission on Contraception, Sterilization and Abortion in New Zealand* (Wellington: Government Printer, 1977), which states on p. 88 that "The Commission sets great store by stability in society and sees the family as the essential feature of such a society."

12. Carole Pateman, " 'The Disorder of Women': Women, Love, and the Sense of Justice," *Ethics* 91 (October 1980): 22, 23. See also Francis Schrag, "Justice and the Family," *Inquiry* 19 (1976): 193–208.

13. *Human Development and Relationships in the School Curriculum*, pp. 25–26. Emphasis added.

14. See J. Betz, "The Relation Between Love and Justice: A Survey of Five Possible Positions," *Journal of Value Inquiry* 4 (Fall 1970): 191–203.

15. John Rawls, *A Theory of Justice* (Cambridge: Harvard University Press, 1971), p. 3.

16. Lawrence Kohlberg, "From is to Ought: How to Commit the Naturalistic Fallacy and Get Away with it in the Study of Moral Development," in Theodore Mischel, ed., *Cognitive Development and Epistemology* (New York and London: Academic Press, 1971), p. 221.

17. Pateman, " 'The Disorder of Women' . . . ," p. 24.

18. The "principle" quoted is Robert Nozick's in *Anarchy, State and Utopia* (Oxford: Basil Blackwell, 1974), p. 160.

19. How far this argument should be pursued is not clear. Should the restriction be added that no one who is loved by another should be chosen? What of "secret" loves? This route takes us into the swampy ground of trying to base the ethics of love on the dubious notion of "eligibility."

20. D. W. Hamlyn, "The Phenomena of Love and Hate," *Philosophy* 53 (1978): 10–11.

21. Immanuel Kant, *Foundations of the Metaphysics of Morals*, transl. by L. W. Beck (Indianapolis: Bobbs-Merrill, 1959), pp. 15–16. For discussions of this passage see Edward Sankowski, "Love and Moral Obligation," *Journal of Value Inquiry* 12 (1978): 100–110; and Robert W. Burch, "The Commandability of Pathological Love," *Southwestern Journal of Philosophy* 3 (1972): 131–140.

22. "In Christian and post-Christian cultures the most important forms of love are seen as essentially personal . . . [though] a love which is of the qualities a person has rather than of the person himself may be seen as a poor form of love." Martin Warner, "Love, Self, and Plato's *Symposium*," *Philosophical Quarterly* 29 (1979): 333–334.

23. See Shakespeare's *Sonnet* 116: "Love is not love which alters when it alteration finds."

24. J. McT. E. McTaggart, *The Nature of Existence* (Cambridge: Cambridge University Press, 1927), Vol. II, pp. 151–152.

25. Ibid., p. 153.

26. Ibid., p. 158.

27. Hamlyn, "The Phenomena of Love and Hate," p. 12. [See above, p. 226.]

28. While it might seem illegitimate to employ tastes as a basis for justification in this manner, this kind of situation would be covered by Nozick's entitlement theory of justice. It can be noted that Nozick hereby provides a means whereby choices made on the basis of non-rational criteria can be seen as part of justice rather than as external to it.

29. "The Indifferent," in W. S. Scott, *Poetry and Prose of John Donne* (London: John Westhouse, 1946), pp. 32–33.

SUGGESTED READINGS, SECTION IV

Bernstein, Mark. "Love, Particularity, and Selfhood," *Southern Journal of Philosophy* 23 (1986), pp. 287–93.

Brown, Robert. *Analyzing Love* (Cambridge, Eng.: Cambridge University Press, 1987).

Caraway, Carol. "Romantic Love: A Patchwork," *Philosophy and Theology* 2 (1987), pp. 76–96.

Caraway, Carol. "Romantic Love: Neither Sexist nor Heterosexist," *Philosophy and Theology* 1 (1987), pp. 361–68.

De Sousa, Ronald. "Self-Deceptive Emotions," *Journal of Philosophy* 75 (1978), pp. 684–97.

Fisher, Mark. "Reason, Emotion, and Love," *Inquiry* 11 (1977), pp. 189–203.

Gilbert, Paul. "Friendship and the Will," *Philosophy* 61 (1986), pp. 61–70.

Hunter, J. F. M. *Thinking About Sex and Love* (New York, NY: St. Martin's Press, 1980).

Kalin, Jesse. "Lies, Secrets, and Love: The Inadequacy of Contemporary Moral Philosophy," *Journal of Value Inquiry* 10 (1976), pp. 253–65.

Kraut, Robert. "Love *De Re*," *Midwest Studies in Philosophy* 10 (1986), pp. 413–30.

Lesser, A. H. "Love and Lust," *Journal of Value Inquiry* 14 (1980), pp. 51–54.

Nakhnikian, George. "Love in Human Reason," *Midwest Studies in Philosophy* 3 (1978), pp. 286–317.

Pitcher, George. "Emotion," *Mind* 74 (1965), pp. 326–46.

Robinson, Jenefer. "Emotion, Judgment, and Desire," *Journal of Philosophy* 80 (1983), pp. 731–41.

Rorty, Amelie. "The Historicity of Psychological Attitudes: Love is Not Love Which Alters Not When It Alteration Finds," *Midwest Studies in Philosophy* 10 (1986), pp. 399–412.

Sankowski, Edward. "Love and Moral Obligation," *Journal of Value Inquiry* 12 (1978), pp. 100–110.

Soble, Alan. "The Unity of Romantic Love," *Philosophy and Theology* 1 (1987), pp. 374–97.

Soble, Alan. *The Structure of Love* (New Haven, CT: Yale University Press, 1990).

Solomon, Robert. *Love: Emotion, Myth and Metaphor* (Garden City, NY: Anchor Press, 1981).

Stafford, J. Martin. "On Distinguishing Between Love and Lust," *Journal of Value Inquiry* 11 (1977), pp. 292–303.

Taylor, Gabrielle. "Love," *Proceedings of the Aristotelian Society* 76 (1976), pp. 147–64.

Telfer, Elizabeth. "Friendship," *Proceedings of the Aristotelian Society* 71 (1970–71), pp. 223–41.

Vannoy, Russell. *Sex Without Love: A Philosophical Exploration* (Buffalo, NY: Prometheus, 1980).

Wojtyla, Karol (Pope John Paul II). *Love and Responsibility* (New York, NY: Farrar, Straus and Giroux, 1981).

APPENDIX:
DISCUSSION
MATERIAL

I HAVE appended a number of footnotes to these selections rather than writing an introductory essay about them. I want the student to read and then think about these passages without any editorial intervention, in order to be able to develop his or her own perspective on the issues that arise in each of them. Having spent some time doing so, the student might then read the footnotes to supplement or complement his or her own analysis.

FOR ANNE GREGORY

William Butler Yeats

'Never shall a young man,
Thrown into despair
By those great honey-coloured
Ramparts at your ear,
Love you for yourself alone
And not your yellow hair.'

'But I can get a hair-dye
And set such colour there,
Brown, or black, or carrot,
That young men in despair
May love me for myself alone
And not my yellow hair.'

'I heard an old religious man
But yesternight declare
That he had found a text to prove
That only God, my dear,
Could love you for yourself alone
And not your yellow hair.'[1]

Reprinted with permission of Macmillan Publishing Company from *The Poems of W. B. Yeats: A New Edition*, edited by Richard J. Finneran. Copyright © 1933 by Macmillan Publishing Company, renewed 1961 by Bertha Georgie Yeats. Also reprinted from *The Collected Poems of W. B. Yeats* by permission of A. P. Watt Limited, on behalf of Michael B. Yeats and Macmillan, London Ltd. W. B. Yeats (1865–1939) was an Irish poet and dramatist; he won the Nobel prize for literature in 1923. (Footnote added by A. S.)

NOTE

1. The interesting question is whether Yeats' thesis (here I paraphrase) that "a human being loves another human being only in virtue of the latter's attractive properties" (1) purports to state a logical truth about love or about the ontology of the human being, (2) states a psychological truth about human nature, or (3) merely reports the typical pattern of love—contingently true, but usual.

WHAT IS THE SELF?

Blaise Pascal

WHAT IS THE self, the *me?*

A man who puts himself at the window to see the passers-by: if I pass by there, can I say that he has put himself there to see me? No; for he doesn't think of me in particular. But that person who loves someone on account of her beauty, does he love her? No; for smallpox, which will kill the beauty without killing the person, will make him not love her any more.

And if one loves me for my judgment, for my memory, does one love me, *me?* No; for I can lose these qualities without losing myself. Where then is the *me,* if it isn't in the body nor in the soul? And how to love the body or the soul, if not for these qualities, which are not at all what makes the *me,* because they are perishable?[1] For would one love the substance of the soul of a person, abstractly, and whatever qualities were there? That is not possible,[2] and would be unjust.[3] One does not then love any person, but only certain qualities.

One does not then mock those who make themselves honored for commissions and offices, for one loves no person except for certain borrowed qualities.

The Brunschvicg number of this passage from Pascal's *Pensées* is 323. The passage is No. 688 in A. J. Krailsheimer's popular edition (New York, NY: Penguin Books, 1966; p. 245). This translation was prepared for this volume by Edward Johnson from the French: *Oeuvres Complètes* (Paris: Editions Gallimard, 1954), p. 1165, No. 306. (Notes added by A. S.) Blaise Pascal (1623–62) was a French philosopher, mathematician and scientist, perhaps known best for his "wager," an argument designed to convince people to believe in God.

NOTES

1. Does Pascal commit a non sequitur here? From the fact that if y loses P yet y remains, and that if y loses Q yet y remains, it does not follow that if y loses both P and Q, y remains.

2. A Christian might draw the conclusion (and why not Pascal, too, who was a Christian) that y, not being any of y's properties, is instead a soul, and this soul *is* the object of x's love, not something that it would be impossible to love.

3. Why both impossible and unjust?

TWO LOVE SONNETS

William Shakespeare

116

Let me not to the marriage of true minds
Admit impediments; love is not love
Which alters when it alteration finds,
4   Or bends with the remover to remove.
O, no, it is an ever-fixèd mark
That looks on tempests and is never shaken;
It is the star to every wand'ring bark,
8   Whose worth's unknown, although his height be taken.
Love's not Time's fool, though rosy lips and cheeks
Within his bending sickle's compass come;
Love alters not with his brief hours and weeks,
12   But bears it out even to the edge of doom. [1]
    If this be error and upon me proved,
    I never writ, nor no man ever loved.

---

2 *impediments* (an echo of the marriage service in the Book of Common Prayer: "If any of you know cause or just impediment . . .")   5 *mark* seamark   7 *the star* the North Star   8 *Whose worth's* . . . *taken* whose value (e.g. to mariners) is inestimable although the star's altitude has been determined   9 *fool* plaything   10 *compass* range, circle   11 *his* Time's   12 *bears it out* survives   12 *edge of doom* Judgment Day   13 *upon* against

130

My mistress' eyes are nothing like the sun;
Coral is far more red than her lips' red;
If snow be white, why then her breasts are dun;
4   If hairs be wires, black wires grow on her head.
I have seen roses damasked, red and white,
But no such roses see I in her cheeks,
And in some perfumes is there more delight
8   Than in the breath that from my mistress reeks.
I love to hear her speak, yet well I know
That music hath a far more pleasing sound.
I grant I never saw a goddess go;
12   My mistress when she walks treads on the ground. [2]
And yet, by heaven, I think my love as rare
As any she belied with false compare.

NOTES

1. Shakespeare seems to be saying throughout the sonnet that love is perfectly constant ("it is an ever-fixèd mark"). Yet maybe he does not mean this literally. First, in line 12 he writes that love bears it out (only) to the edge of doom, not to doom itself. Second, lines 2–3 allow that love alters (ends) for reasons other than changes in the beloved. (Are we compelled to read "edge of doom" as the Day of Judgment?)

2. Compare this sonnet, which bucks the trend of flowery love poetry, with, for example, the 1595 poem by Edmund Spencer, "Epithalamion." ("Her lips like cherries charming to men to bite.")

---

5 *damasked* mingled red and white   8 *reeks* emanates   11 *go* walk   14 *she* woman   14 *compare* comparison

---

From Sonnet No. 116 and Sonnet No. 130 in *Sonnets* by William Shakespeare. Copyright © 1964 by William Burto and W. H. Auden. Reprinted by arrangement with New American Library, a division of Penguin Books, USA, Inc., New York, NY. William Shakespeare was an English poet and dramatist (e.g., *Romeo and Juliet, Othello, King Lear*), born 1564, died 1616. (These two sonnets appear on pages 156 and 170, respectively, of the Penguin edition. Footnotes in small type are Burto's; those above it are by A. S.)

OF FRIENDSHIP

Michel de Montaigne

... FOR THE REST, what we ordinarily call friends and friendships are nothing but acquaintanceships and familiarities formed by some chance or convenience, by means of which our souls are bound to each other. In the friendship I speak of, our souls mingle and blend with each other so completely that they efface the seam that joined them, and cannot find it again. If you press me to tell why I loved him, I feel that this cannot be expressed, except by answering: Because it was he, because it was I. [1]

Beyond all my understanding, beyond what I can say about this in particular, there was I know not what inexplicable and fateful force that was the mediator of this union. We sought each other before we met because of the reports we heard of each other, which had more effect on our affection than such reports would reasonably have; I think it was by some ordinance from heaven. We embraced each other by our names. And at our first meeting, which by chance came at a great feast and gathering in the city, we found ourselves so taken with each other, so well acquainted, so bound together, that from that time on nothing was so close to us as each other. He wrote an excellent Latin satire, which is published, in which he excuses and explains the precipitancy of our mutual understanding, so promptly grown to its perfection.

This excerpt from Montaigne's essay "Of Friendship" is reprinted from *The Complete Essays of Montaigne*, translated by Donald M. Frame, with the permission of the publishers, Stanford University Press. Copyright © 1958 by the Board of Trustees of the Leland Stanford Junior University. (Footnotes added by A. S.) Montaigne (1533–92) was an essayist and philosopher, the author of the treatise on skepticism *Apologie de Raimond Sebond*.

Having so little time to last, and having begun so late, for we were both grown men, and he a few years older than I, it could not lose time and conform to the pattern of mild and regular friendships, which need so many precautions in the form of long preliminary association. Our friendship has no other model than itself, and can be compared only with itself. It is not one special consideration, nor two, nor three, nor four, nor a thousand; it is I know not what quintessence of all this mixture, which, having seized my whole will, led it to plunge and lose itself in his; which, having seized his whole will, led it to plunge and lose itself in mine, with equal hunger, equal rivalry. I say lose, in truth, for neither of us reserved anything for himself, nor was anything either his or mine.

* * *

If, in the friendship I speak of, one could give to the other, it would be the one who received the benefit who would oblige his friend. For, each of them seeking above all things to benefit the other, the one who provides the matter and the occasion is the liberal one, giving his friend the satisfaction of doing for him what he most wants to do. When the philosopher Diogenes was short of money, he used to say that he asked it back of his friends, not that he asked for it. And to show how this works in practice, I will tell you an ancient example that is singular.

Eudamidas of Corinth had two friends, Charixenus, a Sicyonian, and Aretheus, a Corinthian. When he came to die, he being poor and his two friends rich, he made his will thus: "I leave this to Aretheus, to feed my mother and support her in her old age; this to Charixenus, to see my daughter married and give her the biggest dowry he can; and in case one of them should chance to die, I substitute the survivor in his place." Those who first saw this will laughed at it, but his heirs, having been informed of it, accepted it with singular satisfaction. And when one of them, Charixenus, died five days later, and the place of substitute was opened to Aretheus, he supported the mother with great care, and of five talents he had in his estate, he gave two and a half to his only daughter for her marriage, and two and a half for the marriage of the daughter of Eudamidas, holding their weddings on the same day.

This example is quite complete except for one circumstance, which is the plurality of friends. For this perfect friendship I speak of is indivisible:[2] each one gives himself so wholly to his friend that he has nothing left to distribute elsewhere; on the contrary, he is sorry that he is not double, triple, or quadruple, and that he has not several souls and several wills, to confer them all on this one object. Common friendships can be divided up: one may love in one man his beauty, in another his easygoing ways, in another liberality, in one paternal love, in another brotherly love, and so forth; but this friendship that possesses the soul and rules it with absolute sovereignty cannot possibly be double. If two called for help at the same time, which one would you run to? If they demanded conflicting services of you, how would you arrange it? If one confided to your silence a thing that would be useful for the other to know, how would you extricate yourself? A single dominant friendship dissolves all other obligations. The secret I have sworn to reveal to no other man, I can impart without perjury to the one who is not another man: he is myself. It is a great enough miracle to be doubled, and those who talk of tripling themselves do not realize the loftiness of the thing: nothing is extreme that can be matched. And he who supposes that of two men I love one just as much as the other, and that they love each other and me just as much as I love them, multiplies into a fraternity the most singular and unified of all things, of which even a single one is the rarest thing in the world to find. . . .[3]

NOTES

1.   Montaigne is speaking about his friendship with Étienne de La Boëtie.
2.   Compare with, for example, W. Newton-Smith's claim that there is nothing about love that makes multiple loves conceptually impossible ("A Conceptual Investigation of Love," p. 216, above).
3.   I wonder if Montaigne had specifically Aristotle in mind here, for even though Aristotle agrees that perfect friendships are rare (see *Nicomachean Ethics* 1156b25, 1171a19–20), on the grounds that virtuous men are few and far between, Aristotle also claims that multiple perfect friendships are possible (1171a4–9). All the friends live together, on the model of a tiny city-state (Montaigne's fraternity?).

LETTER TO CHANUT

René Descartes

. . . I NOW PASS to your question about the reasons which often impel us to love one person rather than another before we know their worth. I can discover two, one belonging to the mind and one to the body. The one in the mind presupposes too many things concerning the nature of our souls which I would not dare to try to explain in a letter, so I will speak only of the one in the body. It consists in the disposition of the parts of our brain, produced by sense objects or by some other cause. The objects which strike our senses by means of the nerves move certain parts of our brain, and make there certain folds. These folds undo themselves when the object ceases to operate, but the place where they were made afterwards has a tendency to be folded again in the same manner by another object resembling even incompletely the original object. For instance, when I was a child, I loved a little girl of my own age, who had a slight squint. The impression made by sight in my brain when I looked at her cross eyes became so closely connected to the simultaneous impression arousing in me the passion of love, that for a long time afterwards when I saw cross-eyed persons I felt a special inclination to love them simply because they had that defect. At that time I did not know that was the reason for my love; and as soon as I reflected on it and recognized that it

---

This letter, dated June 6, 1647, is reprinted by the kind permission of Professor Anthony Kenny, from his *Descartes. Philosophical Letters* (Oxford University Press, 1970; pp. 224–25). Descartes, often called the father of modern philosophy, was born in France in 1596 and died in Sweden in 1650. He was the author of *Meditations on First Philosophy*, which contains the famous "*cogito.*" (Footnote added by A. S.)

was a defect, I was no longer affected by it. So, when we are inclined to love someone without knowing the reason, we may believe that this is because he has some similarity to something in an earlier object of our love, though we may not be able to identify it. Though it is more commonly a perfection than a defect which thus attracts our love, yet, since it can sometimes be a defect as in the example I quoted, a wise man will not altogether yield to such a passion without having considered the worth of the person to whom he thus feels drawn.[1] But because we cannot love equally all those in whom we observe equal worth, I think that our only obligation is to esteem them equally; and since the chief good of life is the possession of friends, we are right to prefer those to whom we are drawn by secret inclinations, provided that we also see worth in them. Moreover, when these secret inclinations are caused by something in the mind and not by something in the body, I think they should always be followed. The principal criterion by which they can be detected is that those which come from the mind are reciprocated, which is not often the case in the others. . . .

NOTE

1.   What Descartes says about our ability—indeed, almost our duty—to make sure we are not moved to love by defects, leaves it open whether he also believes that we should discover the causes of our loves in order to eliminate all of them, thereby loving *agapically* and independently of the worth of the beloved. But this sentence reaffirms that we should love in virtue of the perfections of the object; we should perhaps discover these causes but not eliminate their power. (Someone once quipped to me: when Descartes discovered that he had a tendency to fall in love with women who squinted, he had a difficult and terrible choice to make, between giving up that sweet preference and allowing his emotions to be swayed by that property for his whole life. He finally abandoned his taste for squinters, and wrote the *Meditations* instead.)

A LOVE SONNET

John Berryman

Still it pleads and rankles: 'Why do you love *me?*'
Replies then jammed me dumb; but now I speak,
Singing why each should *not* the other seek—
The octet will be weaker—in the fishful sea.
Your friends I don't like all, and poetry
You less than music stir to, the blue streak
Troubles me you drink: if all these are weak
Objections, they are all, and all I foresee. [1]

Your choice, though! . . . Who no Goliath has slung low.
When one day rushing about your lawn you saw
Him whom I might not name without some awe
If curious Johnson should enquire below,
'Who lifts this voice harsh, fresh, and beautiful?'
—'As thy soul liveth, O king, I cannot tell.'

This is *Sonnet* No. 24 from *Berryman's Sonnets* by John Berryman. Copyright © 1952, 1967 by John Berryman. Reprinted by permission of Farrar, Straus and Giroux, Inc. (Footnote added by A. S.) John Berryman (1914–72) was an American poet. He won the Pulitzer Prize in 1964 for 77 *Dream Songs*.

NOTE

1. Why is it that reasons for *not* loving (whether they are, as in Berryman, on balance indecisive, or powerful enough to prevent love) are easier to come by than are reasons *to* love? Or is Berryman wrong about this?